What the reviewers said...

"He has a journalist's flair for the dramatic, the comic and even the tragic. But he's at his best when he paints himself as a Chaplin-like character forever fumbling goodheartedly but naïvely from one bizarre episode to another, never winning but never completely losing.... Gray is Everyman."

— George Melnyk, *Alberta Motorist*

"A remarkably fine and honest reporter."

— Frank Walker, Montreal *Star*

"Outspoken ... literally writing himself out of jobs. His irreverence and candor ... make this book especially enjoyable.

— Montreal *Gazette*

"Entertaining reading ... vividly portrays a span of Western Canadian history ...

Brings back memories — not all fond, but many made rosy with the passsage of time, while younger readers will find in it a personal viewpoint of some of the toughest and yet greatest times in Western Canada's history."

— Saskatoon *Star-Phoenix*

"*Troublemaker!*'s blend of personal, social and national history makes unusually enjoyable, sometimes demanding, often riveting, reading."

— Pat Barclay, *The Edmonton Sun*

TROUBLEMAKER!

Books by James H. Gray

The Winter Years
Men Against the Desert
The Boy from Winnipeg
Red Lights on the Prairies
Booze
The Roar of the Twenties

TROUBLEMAKER!

A Personal History

James H. Gray

Goodread Biographies

Canadian Cataloguing in Publication Data

    Gray, James H., 1906–
      Troublemaker!

    Includes index.
    ISBN 0-88780-111-0

    1. Gray, James H., 1906-   2. Journalists —
    Canada — Biography.   3. Prairie Provinces — History
    — 1945-   * I. Title.

FC3243.G73 1983   971.2'03   C83-098339-2
F1060.92.G73 1983

First published in 1978 by Macmillan of Canada

Published in paperback 1983 by Goodread Biographies

Canadian Lives series publisher: James Lorimer

Goodread Biographies is the paperback imprint of

Formac Publishing Company Limited
333-1657 Barrington Street
Halifax, Nova Scotia
B3J 2A1

Printed and bound in Canada

Contents

List of Illustrations

Preface

Choosing a title for this book, I was faced with the ticklish problem that seems to have become endemic for Canadian writers and editors in recent years. Should I go for realism and quote verbatim any one of several highly deletable expletives with which various politicians, policemen, bureaucrats, mandarins, oil executives, and educators have qualified the word troublemaker? Or should I let the noun speak for itself, with only an exclamation mark or two for emphasis? I chose the latter solution, because I have never felt comfortable with the men's room lexicon.

For my sub-title I have appropriated the words used by Vincent Sheean for his superb autobiography of forty years ago. In doing so, I confess a certain empathetic identification with Sheean. He went to the Soviet Union to report the development of post-revolutionary Russia for American newspaper readers. From a sympathetic reporter, he evolved into an inflamed zealot, a partisan polemicist in the intellectual controversies that soon enveloped his subject. I, too, began my career in journalism as a reporter and a commentator on mankind's foibles and faults. And I, too, became caught up in the currents that were changing the face of western Canada and became a partisan shouter against the tide.

The era that began in 1935 and ended with the mid-fifties was the golden age of western Canada—the most exciting, most elevating, most critical, and most illuminating two decades in prairie history, and perhaps in all Canadian history. It saw our prairie wheatland emerge triumphantly from the grip of combined economic depression and natural disaster. It saw prairie Canadians reclaim their savaged land and help to revolutionize the food production of the world. Mercifully spared the physical convulsions exerted by the horrors of war, we Canadians nevertheless mounted a war effort that was second to none. In the process, we conscripted material and human resources in such a way that Canada emerged from the Second World War with the world's least inflated economy. We entered it with one of the world's poorest social-welfare systems and emerged with one of the best. We developed the potential to become one of the world's foremost industrial powers. It was an era when Canadians came to feel, thanks in particular to the Second World War, that being a Canadian was about the best thing there was in all the world to be.

Then, of our own volition, we just stood around and frittered away the Canadian dream.

That is what this book is all about, an attempt to recall for Canadians some of the trials, triumphs, and tragedies of that period of prairie history. I say "some of," because I have returned here to the formula I used in *The Winter Years*, wherein I described the impact of the Great Depression on the people of the prairies in terms of my own experiences. The result was a highly personalized account, a personal history in which autobiography mixed with objective reportage.

Such a mixing must inevitably result in a historical memoir that some may regard as flawed by fatal omissions. In putting this book together, I found it inappropriate to include one of the best of all prairie stories: the British Commonwealth Air Training Plan, which so deeply affected the lives of thousands of people in scores of prairie communities. To do that story justice would require a book of its own, for it is a poignant, romantic saga of human nature at its best. Nor have I attempted to include the impact of the prisoner-of-war camps or the tragedy of the forced resettlement of the Japanese Canadians during the post-Pearl Harbor panic, or the Winnipeg flood. My attention was elsewhere and I was otherwise engaged, so that I had no personal contact with these events.

This, additionally, is very much a non-political book in the party-politics sense. I have deliberately left the re-threshing of the party politics of the period to the learned professors of political science. As a political correspondent, my experience led me to the conclusion that George Jean Nathan's comment about religions was really more fittingly applied to political parties. Nathan wrote: "I am in favour of all religions equally, because I believe them all equally ridiculous."

In a way, this book is almost a sequel to *The Winter Years*, because it begins where that book left off—in the newsroom of the *Winnipeg Free Press*. I have always counted myself one of fortune's favourites in having launched myself on a career in journalism at the very peak of the glory years of Canadian newspapers. In 1935, Canadians still relied on their newspapers for both their news of the world and whatever intellectual stimulation their tastes required. The newsroom rivalries in those days centred on getting to the subscribers first with the best stories of the day, not on the frantic daily amassing of out-of-date material to fit, willy-nilly, around seemingly limitless volumes of retail advertising. Ours was the era in which the names of editors of newspapers were names to conjure with, for journalists and subscribers alike. There was Dafoe of the *Winnipeg Free Press*, O'Leary of the *Ottawa Journal*, Ford of the *London Free Press*, MacRae of the *Leader-Post*, Galbraith of the *Calgary Herald*, Nicholas of the *Victoria Daily Times*.

The trend that would lead to the submergence of editors and the domination by publishers of Canadian newspapers may not have begun with the *Winnipeg Free Press*. But after the "war of the Dafoe succession," the direction was inescapable. That, too, is part of the story, for the diminution of the newspaper editorial as an influence upon the public mind was a notable feature of the era, and I was there when it was happening. I was there, too, in Alberta, at the onset of the invasion of American multinational oil companies, which would expropriate our vast petroleum resources with their ten-cent tax dollars. Not only was I there, I was caught up in the middle of it, and ground to a pulp by it.

From all this, it follows that I am mainly my own authority for most of what this book contains. There is, therefore, little need for footnotes to direct readers to other sources of corroboration. However, I have benefited from conversations with Mrs. Gloria Queen-Hughes and Mrs. Mary Dover to enhance my own recollection of the evolution of the Canadian Women's Army Corps. And I am indebted to Grant Spratt, Ralph Will, and Matt Newell for assistance in clarifying specific aspects of the Turner Valley story.

I am long overdue in expressing my appreciation to two people who have worked with me for so long on the manuscripts of my books. Lois Gregor has brought her superb typing skills to bear on my rough drafts and made the job of Ken McVey ever so much easier. He, in turn, has been a superlative editor, who has frequently been called upon to pummel my sometimes convoluted sentences into readable English. This, for both, is the fourth occasion on which they have worked their magic.

A word of explanation is in order for the use of direct quotations to reconstruct conversations of thirty and forty years ago. I have no notes of any of these conversations. So I have trusted to my memory, and a deeply etched memory it is in many cases, to report what various people said. In doing so, I have used quotation marks simply as a means of advancing the narrative and not to indicate verbatim reporting of conversation. I felt that, if I was conveying an accurate sense of what was being said, the violation was justifi-

able. To the shades of the departed who may protest against mis-
quotation, I can only say: "You may be right about the words I
have used, but the sense of what was said is perfectly conveyed."

Calgary   JAMES H. GRAY
June 1978

1
The Way We Were

For almost a minute and a half, in mid-December 1934, I found myself standing apart as a one-of-a-kind Canadian. At a time when three hundred thousand pauperized Canadian families were being kept alive by government relief, I was faced with the choice of three jobs. One offered $50 a week, the second offered $20 a week, and the third was already paying me $15 a week.

My family had been members of that army of unemployed from January of 1930 until April 1933. Then Roosevelt came to power in the United States, the grain futures market showed signs of recovering from its three-year torpor, and I got a job marking a brokerage-office quotation board at the Winnipeg firm of Bingham and McKay for $10 a week. That was a full $5 a month less than the unemployment-relief allowances Kay and I and our daughter Patty were receiving, but I grabbed the job without a second thought.

Some weeks later the Roosevelt New Deal was launched and, with the revaluation of the price of gold from $20.67 to $35 an ounce, an unparalleled gold-mining boom broke out in Toronto. A small army of high-pressure, get-rich-quick, bait-and-switch mining-stock promoters swarmed into Toronto from the United States and were soon using long-distance telephones to persuade Canadian investors to trade their sound investments for worthless mining shares. It was not long before the Bingham and McKay boardroom was overflowing with gullible penny-stock speculators seeking confirmation of the fairy tales they had been hearing from Toronto. The office manager, recalling that I had been a margin clerk during the 1928–29 boom, appointed me the company security analyst in charge of mining-stock inquiries, at $15 a week. My instructions were to dig out what facts I could about the mines being promoted and set them out for our customers, but never to recommend or disapprove purchase or sale.

When it had become clear in 1931 that our stay on unemployment relief was likely to be prolonged, I decided to continue my education by reading my way through the public library. Somewhere along the way I concluded that what I would most like to do for a living was to become a writer. So, over the next couple of years, I put some two hundred thousand words to paper without ever selling anything, until I managed to sell a piece to the *Winnipeg Free Press* magazine, just about the time I got the board-marking job. As the mining-stock boom got completely out of hand, I wrote a critical analysis of what was happening and sent it in to George Ferguson, the managing editor of the *Free Press*. He not only bought it; he called me in for an interview and asked me to let him see anything else I wrote along the same lines. As an afterthought, he suggested that I send some of my unsold articles to Steven Cartwright at the *Canadian Forum*. It didn't pay for articles, he warned, but the *Forum* was widely read by influential people: it would get my name known and maybe get me a job.

I bombarded Cartwright with articles and he used most of them. One, a history of the monkeyshines that preceded the erection of the Winnipeg cenotaph, elicited a fan letter from H. L. Mencken. Two of my pieces on the mining-stock racketeers brought a complimentary letter from John M. Godfrey, the newly appointed Ontario Securities commissioner. Out of the correspondence that followed, Godfrey, of his own volition, persuaded C. George McCullagh, who would later become the publisher of the *Globe and Mail*, to offer me a $50-a-week job in his Toronto brokerage office. He not only sold me to McCullagh sight unseen; he wrote to J. W. Dafoe, the editor of the *Free Press*, to make another deal. If Dafoe would pay my expenses to get to Toronto, Godfrey would open his files so I could write a series of articles for the *Free Press* in repayment.

Dafoe, of course, had never heard of me, so he sent the letter out to Ferguson, who convinced Dafoe the *Free Press* ought to hire me. Ferguson then called me in to offer me a job as a news reporter on the *Free Press* staff. However, he warned that the salary, about which he would have to talk to Victor Sifton, would be quite a bit less than $50 a week. When I agreed to take the undefined salary, he took me in to introduce me to Dafoe. It so happened that Sifton was in Dafoe's office when we got there. So I met him, too, and after introductions all around, Sifton and Ferguson went off into a corner to settle my salary. We then took our leave and went back to Ferguson's office, where he broke the news to me how much below $50 a week my salary would be. It would be $20 a week!

The sugar plums that had been dancing before my eyes since the offer of the $50 a week had come to us exploded into sand particles dipped in vinegar. For a minute and a half I was sorely tempted to renege on my acceptance and take the Toronto brokerage job. But

I had been trying so hard to break out of the brokerage business and into a writing career that the sugar plums returned quickly and the Toronto job disappeared over the horizon. I went off with a couple of borrowed textbooks on newspaper writing to give my notice to Bingham and McKay.

The timing of my entry into journalism was most propitious. After several months on the night side of the paper, I was shifted to the day side just as the On-to-Ottawa march of the relief-camp strikers was getting underway in British Columbia. I was assigned to cover the local arrangements, an assignment that quickly mushroomed beyond all expectation. I was thus on hand to report the storming of the Winnipeg soup kitchens by five hundred unemployed on the night of June 30, 1935, and covered the attempt of the local strikers to get to Ottawa after the mass of the strikers were halted in Regina on July 1.

Between the relief-camp strike and the general election of 1935, there was a never-to-be-solved lovers'-triangle murder in St. Boniface, and I got to work night and day on all three stories. But in the six weeks preceding the election on October 14, the *Free Press* lost interest in almost everything else. On the editorial page, the thunder switched from the Conservatives to the CCF to the Stevens Reconstruction party and back, but the strongest bolts were always reserved for Prime Minister R. B. Bennett. In addition, a full page was opened in the news section to document the errors of all who opposed the election of W. L. Mackenzie King and his Liberal party. On the reporting staff, however, there was not a reporter who did not lean over backwards to report fairly the statements and speeches of all the politicians involved. And we covered everything from the major rallies of the leaders with audiences of thousands to the handful-sized audiences that turned out to hear individual candidates. Yet, despite the monopolization of the news columns, the federal election of 1935 must rank very close to the top of any list of the historical non-events of the Canadian prairies.

The result of the election on a national scale was, of course, spectacular enough. The Conservative government of R. B. Bennett lost almost 100 seats, while Mackenzie King's Liberals gained 80 and returned to office with the greatest majority ever given a political party in Canada to that point. For the Conservatives, the disaster on the prairies even exceeded the national average, for they had gone into the election with 22 of the 55 seats and emerged with but three. The Liberals, who started with 21 supporters, increased their numbers to 30.

The raw numbers would seem to indicate that there had been a massive outpouring of support for the Liberal party. In truth, 65 per cent of the electors on the prairies voted against the Liberals—24 per cent for the Conservatives, 20 per cent for the Social Crediters, 18 per cent for the CCF, and 3 per cent for the Reconstruction party. They won their 57 per cent of the seats with 35 per cent of the vote. On the basis of arithmetic alone, the election certainly had the appearance of an event. Intrinsically, it was far from being so. For the people of the prairies the election changed nothing except the name-plates on the desks of the House of Commons.

Donald Creighton has described Liberal politicians, in opposition and in power, as practitioners of the "politics of evasion." That is a most felicitously descriptive phrase for the Liberal campaign of 1935. No one ever accused Creighton of objectivity where the Liberal party was concerned, yet few Liberals could quarrel with this pithy Creighton summary of the 1935 election:

> The meaning of the general election of 1935 was purely negative. Two plans for the reform of Canadian capitalism, one offered by Bennett in the solid measures of the New Deal, and the other vaguely indicated in windy generalizations by H. H. Stevens, had both gone down to defeat. The socialist solution, presented for the first time in a Canadian general election, was even more decisively rejected. The CCF, which for three years had been instructing the electorate in the virtues of state socialism and centralized planning, got only a few thousand more votes than the hastily improvised, ramshackle party that Stevens put together in the summer of 1935, barely three months before the election. Political victory came to the party that had the least to offer—the party that, so far as the central issue of the welfare state was concerned, had no proposals at all.*

In a real sense the election was not so much "won" by the Liberals as it was lost in the destruction of Prime Minister R. B. Bennett's credibility by the impact on Canada of the worst depression the world had known. Bennett came to power as the post-war era was ending and the pre-war era was beginning. During Bennett's term of office, Hitler came to power in Germany, Mussolini reached his manic peak in Italy, Japan launched its bloody conquest of China, and the governments of Europe were hell-bent on becoming self-sufficient in food production against the inevitable day on which a new world war would break out.

Rampant protectionism in Europe speeded the collapse of world wheat prices and the disastrous contraction of world trade. The

---

* *Canada's First Century* (Toronto: Macmillan, 1970), p. 220.

Canadian economy, beset by mass unemployment, was shattered by the double shock of ruinous wheat prices and the worst series of crop failures in prairie history. The Bennett government poured millions of federal dollars into the West in loans and grants to sustain the urban unemployed and destitute farmers, but nothing seemed to work. Across the country, thousands of individual enterprisers were being driven into bankruptcy by the sophisticated merchandising techniques employed by the chain and department stores. Corner grocers went down like tenpins under the assault of the invading American chain stores, with their mass-buying, self-service, cash-and-carry, loss-leader gimmickry. The chain stores attracted customers to their shelves of high-profit merchandise by selling bread and milk below cost, a practice that forced the price to the milk producers to ruinous levels. The competition among manufacturers for department-store and chain-store business forced the wages of the workers to starvation levels.

All this was documented, ad nauseam and ad infinitum, through the spring and summer of 1934, in the testimony of the high and the mighty of Canadian business before the Royal Commission on Price Spreads and Mass Buying—the Stevens Commission. The top executives of retail merchandising, meat packing, and the food-distributing, electrical, clothing, and footwear manufacturers paraded before the commission with audited reports of their operations. Theirs was a litany of watered-stock financing and ruthless exploitation of their workers and suppliers, unleavened by even a spark of social consciousness.

So outraged did Bennett's minister of Trade and Commerce, the Honourable Harry Stevens, become at the conditions he had discovered that he jumped the gun on his commission's report. That precipitated such a quarrel between Bennett and Stevens that the latter resigned and formed his new party to crusade for the adoption of the commission's report. It called for federal regulation of business ethics, profits, employment practices, and, most of all, price spreads between producers and consumers. Across the country, Stevens attracted a motley assortment of disgruntled small-businessmen to his party. The most naïve of political neophytes, utterly devoid of organizational skills, they succeeded only in siphoning off enough votes from Conservative candidates to cost Bennett 15 or 20 seats across the country.

The baffling feature of the Stevens Commission was the lack of any noticeable public response to its disclosures. In the United States, thirty years before, the "muckraking" writing of Ida Tarbell, Lincoln Steffens, Edward Markham, Upton Sinclair, and Frank Norris had aroused tremendous public reaction, which in turn led to the restructuring of U.S. government agencies. In Canada, the disclosures of starvation wages, sweated labour, and the exploitation of women and children in factories caused nary a ripple on the public consciousness. Despite the fact that their sins were exposed on the front pages of the newspapers for days on end, none of the department stores, chain stores, or manufacturers seemed to suffer in the least from any public reaction.

The same all-encompassing apathy also characterized the public response to the Bennett New Deal program when he unveiled it in the spring of 1935 in a series of five radio addresses. The New Deal called for the establishment of a National Unemployment Insurance Plan; a Trades and Industry Commission which would have the power to enforce a code of business ethics; a Federal Minimum Wage Act; an act to protect women and children in factories and compel employers to give workers one day off in seven; an act to enable primary producers to set up boards to establish minimum prices for their products; a Limitation of Hours of Work Act; and an act to set up boards to enable farmers to reduce their debt obligations without going through bankruptcy.

The Bennett New Deal was attacked by Canadian newspapers, and by Liberals everywhere. Most of its provisions were ultimately held by the Privy Council to be unconstitutional. Yet, on any rational basis, the Bennett New Deal ought to have carried the West for the Conservatives. It re-established the Wheat Board, for which the farmers had been agitating for many years. It established farmer-operated marketing boards to enable producers to combat the chain-store pricing policies. The Farmers' Creditors Arrangements Act was landmark legislative assistance to debt-burdened farmers.

The very least that could be said for Bennett was that somebody was at last trying to do something to break the grip of the Depression. And he was doing it in face of the most vigorous opposition of the Liberals who, from the onset of the Depression, had been unable to come up with a single constructive suggestion for alleviating the distress of the people of the West. And they had none to offer the electors of 1935.

As for this star-crossed millionaire Tory from Calgary, the times were simply hopelessly out of joint, doubly so after the On-to-Ottawa trek of the single unemployed from the relief camps ended in the fatal riot in Regina's Market Square on Dominion Day, 1935. Whatever public kudos Bennett gained from his New Deal, and it was minimal, was lost along with the last traces of his credibility in the barrage of flying rocks on that holiday weekend. And yet—and here was the cream of the jest—it was Richard Bedford

Bennett, the arch-conservative of the Conservatives, who was the real father of the Canadian welfare state, who set the country on a course from which it could never retreat. And he did it, not with his New Deal package, but with the fiscal and legislative precedents he set during his half-decade in power.

That the abandonment of root-hog-or-die capitalism was by no means deliberately contrived by Bennett does not make it any the less a historic first. In plain fact, his most enduring reform was conceived as nothing more than the most temporary of stop-gaps. The name of the transient measure was "unemployment relief."

One of the factors that led to the victory of the Conservatives in the 1930 election was Bennett's promise to blast his way into the export markets of Europe, and thereby cure unemployment in Canada, or perish in the attempt. When he took office in the late summer of 1930, unemployment was a growing problem in the cities of western Canada and prospects were that the problem would get worse before it got better. Because the Conservatives in the 1930 election campaign had insisted that unemployment was a national problem, it followed, when they took office, that they were under some obligation to take it on as the responsibility of a national government.

Until that moment in Canadian history, responsibility for doing anything about unemployed workers had been shunted from federal to provincial to municipal governments. In the West, the cities and towns tended to ignore the problem in the hope that it would go away—and frequently it did. After fifty years, the construction workers, for example, had learned that if they did not save something from their spring and summer wages, they would have to survive the winter on a snowball diet. Seasonal unemployment was a universal fact of life, and people learned to live with it most of the time. Under unusual circumstances the cities did provide minimal, always niggardly, assistance to permanent residents. But it was settled policy never to provide any assistance until well into the winter, until well after all battalions of Ontario harvesters, who had come west to assist with the threshing, had returned home.

Hived away in the nether recesses of the city halls were the welfare offices, which were empowered, almost surreptitiously, to assist the totally destitute to avoid starvation, temporarily. Those eligible for assistance in the form of food hampers were mostly families whose condition was doubly debased by serious illness as well as unemployment, who had to prove that they had exhausted all sources of succour from relatives, friends, and specializing charities. For the ne'er-do-wells and other flotsam and jetsam of the system, there was the Salvation Army, and nothing much else.

When emergency work was provided to the unemployed, it invariably took the form of heavy manual labour that otherwise would have gone unperformed—cutting cordwood, cleaning up the accumulated debris in exhibition grounds, sorting and piling used streetcar rails. All this ended with the election of the Bennett Conservatives in 1930. The acceptance by that government of federal responsibility for unemployment, and, as a consequence, the setting up of a system to provide unemployment relief, marked the beginning of the end of the Protestant work ethic as a dominant force in the socio-economic system of the country. The end came slowly, of course, but it was inevitable, once the Bennett government accepted the notion that, if the system was unable to provide ready and willing workers with life-sustaining employment, the workers had a claim upon the state for sustenance. From the evolving system of unemployment relief which came in with the Tories emerged the principle that the unemployed were entitled to obtain relief from the state, not as a privilege but as a right.

The evolution of privilege into right came rather quickly. As the winter of 1931–32 approached, it found many of us on relief in Winnipeg lacking winter clothing. There was no provision anywhere in the regulations for supplying clothing of any kind. After prolonged agitation among the unemployed, there was a mass meeting followed by a small riot at the city hall. Arrangements were then made to supply us with emergency clothing. Those temporary arrangements resulted in the grafting of a clothing-allowance schedule on to the food and rent schedules. Similarly, an emergency shoe-repairing depot, established to handle only the most desperate cases, led to the issuing of vouchers for footwear along with clothing.

In the urban areas of Alberta, relief was distributed only in return for the performance of certain routine civic chores by the unemployed. These included work on public roads, street cleaning, and garbage collection. Each week, out of a couple of thousand relief recipients, two or three hundred would be drafted to put in a week working for their grocery vouchers. For a family of four the grocery allowance was $5.78 a week. By 1937, retail prices had moved upward somewhat from 1933 levels and the unemployed were agitating for an increase in their allowances. When the cities refused, the unemployed refused to accept the orders to go to work. In short, they went on strike all over Alberta, and after several weeks the cities yielded to their demands.

The notion that there was something sinful about both giving and accepting relief without work died hard. Demands that the unemployed be put to work echoed through service clubs, chambers of commerce, city councils, and school boards. And the unemployed themselves agitated endlessly for work for wages instead of handouts from relief offices. The trouble was that any work projects devised for the unemployed took wage-paying jobs away from the employed. About all that happened was token response to the more strident demands for putting the unemployed to work. Winnipeg officialdom came up with such boondoggles as raking leaves, digging dandelions, cleaning the trash out of back lanes, picking up rocks, and weeding vacant lots. In the end, even these half-bows of obeisance to the work ethic collapsed under the weight of their own absurdity.

For the farmers on the land, Bennett went even further than for the unemployed in the cities. As the toll taken by drought, grasshoppers, and rust increased through the 1930s, the future of western agriculture itself was being brought more and more into question. So was the ability of Saskatchewan and Alberta to carry their shares of the cost of unemployment and agricultural relief. The farmers drew much less in the way of sustenance relief than the city unemployed because many farmers were still able to produce some of the food they consumed. But in the worst of the dustbowl, even the gardens failed, and more than 80 per cent of the residents of several large municipalities were forced to apply for relief.

Not only relief for people was needed, but food for livestock, feed for chickens, and seed with which to plant and replant crops destroyed by the drought and the grasshoppers. In 1931 it cost the federal government over seven million dollars to supply emergency feed to livestock. The government bought and shipped in 141,000 tons of hay that year, and over 100,000 tons in 1934–35. These and other measures for non-human relief established a principle that would become a permanent feature of farm life during the Depression: it was better to keep livestock alive than to allow it to die of starvation in the fields, even though the cost of the feed exceeded the price the animals would bring at the abattoirs. When the municipalities could no longer finance their share of relief, the provinces had to lend them the money. When the provinces in turn could not finance the provincial share, the federal government had to lend the money to both provinces and municipalities.

Even more important than the relief assistance provided by Ottawa was its enactment in the spring of 1935 of the Prairie Farm Rehabilitation Act. At a time when the people themselves were deserting the prairies by the thousands every month, when other thousands of farm families were loading their household effects on to their farm wagons in southern Saskatchewan and heading into the God-forsaken bush country to the north to escape the awful drought and wind, the passage of the PFRA was the proclamation of an act of faith in the future of western Canada.

The PFRA established an emergency conservation corps of earth scientists and engineers to go out into the most severely affected areas of the eighteen million acres of impaired crop land within the Palliser Triangle. There they would take what measures they could to tie down the blowing topsoil, establish stock-watering dams, and assist the farmers to dig out holes on their farms to catch and hold spring run-off water to sustain their households and water their gardens and livestock. It was a magnificently conceived and structured organization that would, in the following twenty-five years, write one of the greatest of western success stories.

Among the flower-children cultists of the 1960s, when interest was burgeoning in the "global village" and brotherhood was "in," a phrase from John Donne enjoyed a brief revival: "No man is an island, entire of it self; every man is a piece of the continent, a part of the main." If Donne's concept is simply reversed, if the thought is stood on its head, as it were, it is aptly descriptive of the prairie West after the Liberal victory of 1935, when all men became islands and ceased to be "a part of the main."

People became hived away in regional islands, provincial islands, economic islands, social islands. It was almost as if the telegraph had never been invented, for one could live in Calgary, Edmonton, Regina, and Winnipeg without ever getting to know anything much about what was happening in Winnipeg, Calgary, Edmonton, and Regina. Winnipeggers and Edmontonians, for example, could have known about the monumental disaster in Saskatchewan in 1937 only if they were financial-page readers and noticed that the price of wheat on the Winnipeg Grain Exchange had soared to $1.44 a bushel from 91 cents the year before. A year later they would discover that the rains had come back, the drought was over, and a good crop was being harvested, because the price had dropped to 59 cents a bushel, the lowest in five years. Between times, there were only occasional, juiceless Canadian Press dispatches quoting pronouncements by worrying politicians, and overblown reports of local thunderstorms.

Ultimately, of course, the magnitude of the crop disasters forced the story on to the front pages of the newspapers. But at no time did it ever command the space devoted to city-provincial financial wrangles, the search for Amelia Earhart, the aviatrix who was lost over the Pacific Ocean, the New York antics of Father Divine, the Orangemen's parades, or the widespread search for George Roediger, the West's champion bigamist of the 1930s.

The isolated way of prairie life is well illustrated by a happening in Alberta in 1936. On June 16, the most spectacular single development in the economic history of Alberta occurred in Turner Valley, thirty miles southwest of Calgary. On that day the Turner Valley Royalties No. 1 oil well discovered crude oil in the Mississippian limestone. That discovery led to the development of a home-grown oil industry, which ultimately supplied the petroleum requirements of the West during the Second World War and made possible the establishment of the Commonwealth Air Training Plan. But weeks passed before the *Edmonton Journal* got around to reporting the Turner Valley discovery. Winnipeg only got to hear about it a year later when the stock promoters ran amuck.

During most of Bennett's regime, the plight of unemployed people had been on the top of everybody's worry list. After the Liberals came to power, there was a gradual shift of emphasis from people to money. The unemployed people became a fogged-in island in the political-economic stream. The currents that burbled around the island emphasized not people but the financial crises engulfing provincial and municipal governments. The banks shut off the credit of urban councils and school boards. The provinces pleaded with Ottawa for loans of money they could lend to municipalities. When loans were not forthcoming, the province of Alberta defaulted on its bond interest and impaired the solvency of every municipality and charitable institution that had invested in Alberta securities.

The unemployed people, as the focus of anybody's attention, dropped from sight in the endless wrangling over money. The economy, though the fact went unnoticed at the time, had become fully functional without the unemployed. Life went on without them pretty much as it had gone on before they had become a fixture in the economy. They were akin to the barnacles that attach themselves to the hulls of tramp steamers; though they might slow the progress of a ship through the waters, they did not fatally impair its seaworthiness.

It was easy for the employed citizens of Winnipeg, Brandon, Edmonton, and Calgary to go about their varying ways of life, oblivious to the existence of thousands of families in their communities living on unemployment relief. The radios, to which our ears were glued at night, provided no hint of the existence of the unemployed island. The attention of the news columns of the newspapers was elsewhere. Inherent in everything that appeared in the advertising columns was the assumption that there were armies of consumers out there with the wherewithal and desire to buy new cars, radios, gramophones, fur coats, new clothes, and trips to Europe.

In fact, there were. In the form of other islands. There were islands of middle-class people who were untouched by the Depression, and smaller islands of the upper crust to whom the Depression was an unmixed boon. The *Calgary Herald* and the *Edmonton Journal* kept very close track of the partying, the comings and goings, of these islanders. There were more of the elite circulating in Winnipeg, and the competition between the *Free Press* and *Tribune* women's-page editors had a Hatfield–McCoy quality to it. Each paper allotted a couple of pages daily to social butterflying, and on Saturdays, up to five pages to society news. Two photographers on each paper spent most of their waking hours pursuing the socialites through receptions, teas, and soirées. Nothing so triggered a collective tantrum around the *Free Press* city desk as having a big news story, like a bank hold-up or a three-alarm fire, break in mid-afternoon while all the photographers were out on social-page assignments. In the month before the coronation of King George and Queen Elizabeth in May 1937, the departures of the society leaders for London to ogle the event came to look like a migration of lemmings. That most definitely was the "in" thing for everybody to be doing that summer.

The ghost of the cynical Juvenal, contemplating the social scene of the prairies in the post-Bennett era, might well have amended his famous dictum to read: "The people of the Canadian prairies are interested only in bread and circuses."

On July 1, 1937, when civic Winnipeg was up to its armpits in financial crises from which there seemed no escape, the horse races at Whittier Park attracted one of the greatest crowds ever. More than fourteen thousand spent the day in a park that normally was considered crowded with half that many horse players. During the same week in Edmonton, the summer fair broke attendance records as well as records for the volume of cash poured through the pari-mutuel machines.

That was the climactic week of the worst crop failure in prairie history. While that disaster was happening, the people of Saskatchewan were embarked on a massive nose-thumbing at the fates in a veritable orgy of baseball watching. The town of Fillmore, Saskatchewan, in the heart of the dustbowl, staged its first sports day in seven years and managed a tournament of eight girls' softball teams competing before fifteen hundred spectators. At Rouleau they had twenty-nine baseball teams in a tournament, and a sports day attracted seven thousand at Moosomin. More than four thousand turned up in Estevan for its Dominion Day celebrations. What anybody was celebrating would have been difficult to define, but lack of definition did not dampen enthusiasm.

The extent of the crop disaster was, of course, front-page news in the Regina and Saskatoon newspapers throughout July. All-time temperature records were broken daily. Chickens suffocated in their pens in the backyards of Regina when the temperature reached 110° in the shade and there was no shade. But when the "Hell Drivers" from Detroit staged an automobile steeplechase around the Regina fairgrounds they had fifteen thousand in the stands. That was in a city of fifty-three thousand that had three thousand families on relief. Later in July, when the annual summer fairs were staged in Saskatoon and Regina, the horse races had the best crowds in several years, and in Regina, only a cloudburst and windstorm kept the crowd from breaking attendance records.

Inside the prairie newspapers, the sports pages were enlivened with the exploits of such gladiators as Joe McCarthy's Yankees, Jimmy McLarnin, Barney Ross, Max Schmeling, Jack Sharkey, and Joe Louis. Migrant football players from adjacent American states were making their appearance in Calgary, Edmonton, Regina, and Winnipeg to enliven the onset of autumn, as cricketers, baseballers, and soccer footballers enlivened the summer, and hockey players of varying ages and skills enlivened the winter.

For the culture-prone, Fred Gee was importing the gaudiest ornaments of the world's opera and concert stages for one-night stands in Winnipeg, Edmonton, and Calgary, and such people as John Charles Thomas, Lawrence Tibbett, Roland Hayes, Helen Jepson, and Muriel Kerr attracted capacity crowds. For the lovers of popular music, the Depression years were vintage years. The big-band era was dawning, the technical reproduction of recorded music had improved immensely, and an army of American composers was producing a veritable cornucopia of singable, danceable, and playable tunes. Arlen, Romberg, Gershwin, Porter, Kern, Youmans, Carmichael, Weill, Rodgers, and Berlin literally filled the airways with their music, for the technical advances of radio matched those of the recording industry.

The late 1930s were vintage years for radio, too, for Canadians; they could escape from the sombre reality of the day into the fantasy world of night-time radio—to the Lux Radio Theatre, Jack Benny, Fibber McGee and Molly, Eddie Cantor, Edgar Bergen and Charlie McCarthy, Wayne King, Paul Whiteman, Glenn Miller, Bing Crosby, the Kraft Music Hall, Mart Kenney and His Western Gentlemen. For those seeking only to improve their minds, there was a galaxy of book writers that ranged from H. G. Wells, Galsworthy, Hilton, and Shaw to Wolfe, Sinclair, Steinbeck, Lewis, and Mazo de la Roche. And for those seeking only escape from the realities of life there were the movies of that glittering era of glamour queens and kings—Garbo, Grable, Hepburn, Colbert, Davis, and Astor; Gable, Chaplin, Stewart, Tracy, Cagney, and Taylor.

With such imported abundance, the process of transforming the prairies into a cultural hinterland of the United States was completed before anyone was aware it was even beginning. In a real sense, it was a conquest by default, of a diversity of forces moving in to fill a vacuum of leadership and spirit. The post-Bennett era was a period of drift, of ennui, of pervasive helplessness on the prairies. To this there were but two exceptions, James Gardiner and William Aberhart. Both moved to attack the "nothing-can-be-done" attitude of everybody else.

While his federal Cabinet colleagues were navel-gazing, awaiting the recovery of world trade to solve Canada's problems, Gardiner was in and out of the dustbowl like a whirling dervish. By some miracle of persuasion he had pried enough millions out of the Cabinet to mount a vigorous campaign to save the West and restore its topsoil to productivity. The soils scientists at the experimental farms were nudged from their laboratories into the fields to lead task forces of instructors who would teach the farmers how to nail down their topsoil and tame the forces of wind and sun. Millions of acres of drifting soil were reclaimed and turned into productive community pastures.

The message Gardiner and his army of indoctrinators carried across the Palliser Triangle was that, even after ten years of drought, there was hope for the West. Scientists like Asael Palmer at Lethbridge and L. B. Thomson at Swift Current had solved the riddle of soil productivity. All that was needed was to revolutionize farm practices, to stand the science of agronomy on its head and do the reverse of everything the farmers had been doing. To wit: stop manicuring the summer-fallow with cultivators, discard the mouldboard ploughs, leave the stubble and trash on the top of the soil to retard the wind velocity.

William Aberhart knew nothing about agriculture and cared less. His attention, instead, came sharply to focus on the shortage of money in the hands of the people, on the high cost of borrowing money, and on the capriciousness of the banking system. Already a mildly renowned radio lay preacher of fundamentalist Christianity, Aberhart was converted to Social Credit in 1932. Thereafter, his broadcasts veered sharply from biblical prophecy to attacks on the Canadian banking system and its monetary policy.

Social Credit theory held that vagaries within the system prevented sufficient money ever being in circulation to buy back all the goods being produced and services offered. Too much was extracted in excess profits and squirrelled away into savings and unproductive investments. What was needed, among other things, was a "just-prices" system of profits control, and the insertion by the state of sufficient added purchasing power to enable the people to buy all the goods and services they produced. This state intervention in the economy was called Social Credit, and in Alberta, Social Credit was translated into a promised dividend of twenty-five dollars a month for everybody. So enchanted did Albertans become with the prospect of that dividend that they voted Aberhart into power over the scandal-ridden farmers' party that had governed the province for fifteen years.

But it was not Aberhart's dividend promise alone that carried him to power. In a predominantly religious community, his widespread credibility as a man of God enabled him to get the attention of the people for his message. And his message was a message of hope at a time when despair gripped the land, when the banks were giving up and closing their branches, when the mortgage companies had closed up and gone home. His promise to the people was that prosperity could be restored, not by abolishing capitalism but by reforming the banking system, so that capitalism could work to its full potential. Except for Charles Bowman, the editor of the Ottawa *Citizen*, nobody outside Alberta would give Aberhart and his theories the time of day. Scorn was heaped on his dividend, and on his catch-phrase that whatever was physically possible was financially possible.

The full weight of the Canadian establishment—the banks, trust companies, and mortgage companies, the newspapers and the learned economists of academe—rained down on Aberhart as he tried vainly to put his theories into practice. Between his election and the outbreak of the Second World War, his struggles with Ottawa, the banks, the newspapers, and the courts were seldom off the front pages for long. There was no disposition anywhere to give his ideas an objective examination. Nobody noted that there seemed to be similarities between Social Credit and the revolutionary new doctrine enunciated by John Maynard Keynes in *The General Theory of Employment, Interest and Money* (1936). Ten years later, nobody noticed publicly that the Canadian baby-bonus system resembled an illegitimate offspring of Aberhart's ridiculed twenty-five-dollar-a-month dividend.

Aberhart's importance, however, was not in his role as a monetary reformer or as ogre of the banking system; it was the leadership he provided in an era of drift, of faithlessness, of loss of conviction and any sense of purpose. Nothing so typified that era as the response of the people of the prairies to the rise of Hitler in Germany and the drift of the world into the Second World War.

From the burning of the Reichstag in 1933 to the march into Poland in 1939, Adolf Hitler all but monopolized world attention. He had detailed his plans for world conquest by a master race in his book, *Mein Kampf*. It was all there. Yet the world watched in mute bafflement as he repudiated treaties he had signed with great solemnity and fanfare. Propaganda, he had written, was in part the art of telling the big lie. He had mastered the art. He demonstrated, in the process of militarizing the Rhine and conquering Austria, that the League of Nations was an empty façade and that there was an impotency of will in the world when it came to resisting his aggression.

The Canadian prairies were the world in microcosm. Here the Canadian Germans organized their German-Canadian leagues to sponsor pro-Nazi rallies and persuade already naturalized German Canadians to return to their fatherland and the service of Hitler. The reports in the prairie newspapers of persecution of the German Jews and the violent destruction and confiscation of Jewish property were denounced in regular letters to the editors as malicious anti-German propaganda. Here and there across the prairies, where the Communists had managed to infiltrate and take over the Ukrainian Labour-Farmer Temple Associations, and in the north end of Winnipeg, anti-Nazi organizations sprang up amongst the Jews and Ukrainians. But for all the interest they took, and for anything they had to say, the Anglo-Saxon majority could not have cared less what was happening in Europe. When the *Winnipeg Free Press*, in particular, and the other prairie papers generally, deplored the decline of the League of Nations and urged re-dedication to the principle of collective security, accusations of war-mongering flew thick and fast.

The day after Neville Chamberlain returned to London from Munich on September 30, 1938, clutching his agreement with Hitler which "guaranteed peace in our time," the *Free Press* did a survey of the reaction of the people of Winnipeg. I was by then the city-hall reporter and was instructed to poll the mayor, aldermen, civic employees, and wayfaring taxpayers encountered in the city hall corridors.

On that day, Chamberlain could have been unanimously elected as the saviour of mankind! There was no dissent. Not in the dominion government, not in any of the provincial governments, not in the local governments, nor among any of the labour leaders, preachers, or freelance thinkers who frequently rushed their opinions into print. There was one exception. That was the *Winni-*

peg Free Press. J. W. Dafoe was then holed up in Ottawa writing the final draft of the report of the Rowell-Sirois Commission, on which he had been sitting for the past fifteen months. He played hooky from that chore long enough to write a scathing leading editorial on the sell-out to Hitler and wire it to the paper. It appeared under the heading "What is the cheering for?"

Like many of Dafoe's editorials, it ran to unseemly length. It was too long, in fact, to fit into the usual leading editorial space if set in the large-type, two-column format. So it was set in single-column small type. It documented the history of Nazi perfidy and ended with a warning that the Munich pact would be but the prelude to further aggressions. In tone the general body of the editorial was restrained and objective, remarkably so. But to use one of Dafoe's own favourite expressions, there was "a stinger in the tail." It concluded:

> The doctrine that Germany can intervene for racial reasons for the "protection" of Germans on such grounds as she thinks proper in any country in the world which she is in a position to coerce, and without regard to any engagements she has made or guarantees she has given, has now not only been asserted but made good; and it has been approved, sanctioned, certified and validated by the governments of Britain and France, who have undertaken in this respect to speak for the democracies of the world.
>
> This is the situation. Those who think it is all right will cheer for it.

Nothing the newspaper had published ever triggered so explosive a response by the *Free Press* readership as that editorial. The switchboard was flooded with calls from irate readers eager to denounce the editor as a war-monger who would not be content until the flower of Canadian manhood was again being slaughtered on the battlefields of Europe. The reception I got in the city hall that morning rocked me back on my heels. The mildest-mannered of the assistant city clerks, a veteran of the First World War, was reduced to sputtering incoherence by the editorial. At last he gathered his breath sufficiently to shout: "And I hope you and that bastard Dafoe are first in line when they start conscripting the cannon fodder for the war you're trying to start!"

I left city hall early that day; when I got back to the office, I was assigned to one of the newsroom phones to which protesting calls were being directed. "And look," I was told, "try to play it cool. Be polite and listen and don't argue. Just let them blow off steam."

Most of the callers I got seemed intent upon getting to Dafoe himself to blast him with abusive speeches they had been rehearsing. They greeted the information that he was in Ottawa with snorts of disbelief, sometimes charging he was not man enough to listen to the caller's rebuttal. The burden of the complaints, the one we heard over and over, was that what was happening in Europe was none of Canada's business, that a thousand years of national and racial hatred had so poisoned relationships in Europe that wars were inevitable. What did Canada get to justify the hundred thousand Canadian lives lost in the last war? Interspersed with the pacifist calls were a few from the pro-Germans, who recited by rote the Nazi catalogue of the "injustices of Versailles" and protested against the anti-German bigotry of the *Free Press*.

Within a matter of months, Chamberlain would be gone and the word "appeasement" would achieve its pejorative maximum as a term of contempt. But in the autumn of 1938, the word for Canadians was isolationist, carried to about the tenth power. In no area was this isolationism more pronounced than in the case of Hitler's persecution of German Jews. The idea that humanitarian considerations should generate a mass movement to rescue the Jews from the clutches of the Nazis never surfaced in Canada until the tail end of the war. Instead, there was an all-too-prevalent attitude that what was happening to the Jews served them right.

Some time after Munich, probably the following spring, there was a small demonstration at the corner of Main Street and William Avenue where the German consulate was located in the Royal Bank Building, a stone's throw from the city hall. I got a call from the city desk to wander over and cover the story. By the time I arrived, the demonstration was pretty well over and there were just a few dozen picketers milling about, talking to the uniformed policemen. I searched out the detective who was in charge of the police department's "Red Squad" to fill in some details. He was supposed to keep track of the Communist leadership in the trades unions and put dossiers together on the local subversives. He was a loutish fellow who took himself and his job very seriously.

"I can't understand what these people are always raising hell about Hitler for," he said. "What's Hitler ever done to anybody? All he's done is butcher a few thousand . . . Jews."

That detective sergeant was far from alone in holding that opinion. It permeated the police force, and one heard it on streetcars, around service-club tables, at baseball and football games, around department-store bargain tables. That, of course, was only to be expected, for anti-Semitism in particular and racism generally were pervasive forces in prairie society in the inter-war years.

It took Hitler less than six months to repudiate his guarantees to Czechoslovakia and complete his conquest of that country. The streams of refugees fleeing Nazi terror in Germany, Austria, and Spain were joined by more thousands fleeing from Czechoslovakia into Britain, France, and the Low Countries. But not to Canada. Efforts of organized Jewry in Canada to obtain permission to provide a haven for German Jews foundered on the rocks of Canada's restrictive immigration policy of 1930, which Mackenzie King refused to amend or liberalize. When Canada was asked to allow the entry of eight hundred Czech farm families, it did consent, provided each family had at least fifteen hundred dollars in cash and undertook to settle on a farm. As for the Jews, Canada condescended to allow some Jews into the country, on a selective individual basis, by Cabinet decision.

In the summer of 1938, as the refugee problem intensified, the *Free Press* launched an editorial campaign to arouse public interest in the plight of this bloc of suffering humanity, to the end that Canada would open its doors to a fair share of people being persecuted because of their race and religion. The "stinger" in the tail of its leading editorial on August 2 read:

> Any nation which can watch with indifference the agonies of these victims of persecution has lost its soul; has proved itself no better than the tyrannies.

Harsh words indeed! And yet that editorial evoked not a spark of response anywhere, in Winnipeg, across the prairies, least of all within the Liberal party in power in Ottawa.

For all anybody seemed to care about the plight of refugees, the unemployed, the farmers, each other, or the onrushing war, the prairies might well have been peopled by a nation of sleepwalkers. The awakening came with an almighty bang of bombs exploding halfway round the world, with the invasion of Poland by Germany on Friday morning, September 1, 1939. The declaration of war by Britain was still two days off. Canada would not officially declare war for another nine days. But by some magical osmosis, the people of the prairies, with but a few dissenters, knew that the Second World War had arrived and that we were in it.

Across the West, the commanders of three dozen militia units received orders to mobilize and recruit their units up to strength. The next day, in Calgary, while two hundred young men marched to the recruiting offices, the *Herald* reported that housewives were marching to the stores to lay in supplies of sugar and flour. On the first weekend of the as-yet-undeclared war, a dozen Winnipeg units reported that they had signed on one thousand recruits. And in Ottawa, a government that had been hibernating for four years exploded into a frenzy of activity, most of it *sub rosa.*

It did not, to the chagrin of Canada's sizable Britain-right-or-wrong minority, declare war by Order-in-Council the moment the British went to war. Instead, it sent out a call for Parliament to assemble and presented its resolution declaring war to that body in almost leisurely manner. The War Measures Act gave the government authority to turn Canada into as complete a dictatorship as any the world had yet produced. It proceeded to do so. In less than a week it enacted six measures of unprecedented sweep:

1. The provinces were reduced to impotency in their ability to take any action inimical to the needs of the federal government in its prosecution of the war.
2. A Censorship Board was established to control everything printed, telephoned, telegraphed, or cabled in, into, or out of the country.
3. A Wartime Prices and Trade Board was established to control all manufacturing, wholesaling, and retailing, and to set the prices for goods and services throughout the country.
4. A Foreign Exchange Control Board was established to take complete power over imports and exports and to make all the banks agents of its control mechanism.
5. A Department of Munitions and Supply was established to control every industry and every product useful in the prosecution of the war.
6. The Agricultural Board was armed with powers to control production, distribution, and the price of everything the farmers grew.

In between times, the government found the energy to rush through a one-hundred-million-dollar war budget and to "modernize" the army's pay and allowance system. As a Winnipeg recruiter pointed out, the army's primary interest was in young single men, but young married men might also find joining up attractive. A private's pay was $1.45 a day or roughly $45 a month. The allowance from the government for a soldier's wife was $35 a month, provided the soldier signed over $20 a month from his pay to his wife. That would give the wife $55 a month, which was more than many single women, stenographers, and store clerks earned. The recruiter's story provided an enlightening footnote to the mores of the times. It suggested that some enlisting soldiers were getting married but keeping their marriages secret, so the wives could keep working after the soldiers departed for the war. This would enable a couple to put the $55 assigned pay and allowance aside for post-war use in purchasing furniture or a house.

During the Depression, there had been universal opposition to married women working because they were, supposedly, taking the bread out of the mouths of people who needed jobs. For the over-whelming majority of the distaff population, marriage meant the dead-end finish of a business career. Those who did not voluntarily separate from their jobs were pushed out by company policy against employment of married women. The restrictions on mar-ried women continued until well into the war, when the problem of unemployment was solved by recruitment and war production, and married women were encouraged to take jobs in industry and commerce.

2
In and Out of the Communist Spy Network

During the free-speech demonstrations and anti-war riots on the campuses of United States colleges in the 1960s, questions were raised about the influence of television cameras on the escalation of violence. Situations that had been only tense tended to erupt into physical violence whenever representatives of the television medium came on to the scene. The street riots at the Chicago Democratic convention of 1968 were cited as examples. And of this there cannot be the slightest doubt—all reporters, whether television, radio, newspaper, or magazine, prefer to be where things are happening rather than where they are not happening. After a long siege of nothing happening, television cameramen, from sheer boredom, may unwrap their cameras and start focusing around, attracting the attention of equally bored demonstrators who, like the cameramen, are seized with an irresistible urge to do something, anything, to break the boredom.

Among newspaper reporters, the gambit is known as searching for a new angle. As a tyro reporter on my first important assignment in Kenora, Ontario, in 1935, my desperate search for new angles in what had degenerated into a non-story led to a Communist conspiracy to blackmail me into becoming a Communist spy. Or so I became convinced, anyway.

The only people in Canada in 1935 evincing any interest in the thousands of single unemployed who were denizens of the twenty-cents-a-day work camps were the Communists. The Communists led the struggles within these rigidly disciplined camps for improvements in conditions and led the struggle outside the camps to have them abolished. After several large strikes, they organized the famous On-to-Ottawa trek of the relief-camp strikers in 1935. On June 4 and 5, almost one thousand young relief-camp strikers boarded CPR freight trains in Vancouver and headed for Ottawa. By the time they reached Regina, the trekkers' army had swelled to two thousand. That was the end of the march. The federal government moved in the RCMP in force and forbade the railways to allow the trekkers to continue use of their freight trains. Meanwhile, as the trek had moved eastward from Vancouver, the Winnipeg Communists moved into the leadership of the single unemployed who had left the Manitoba camps and were congregated in Winnipeg. After the original trek ended in a bloody riot at Regina on July 1, the Winnipeg group was still determined to proceed east. Mass public rallies were held on the legislature grounds, followed by parades and tag days to raise money to charter buses to take the men east. In mid-July, 250 strikers boarded nine chartered buses in Winnipeg and headed for Ottawa. At the Ontario boundary, the Ontario Provincial Police blocked the road and the buses could go no farther. Faced with the choice of returning to Winnipeg or walking thirty miles into Kenora, the bulk of the strikers chose to walk.

I had taken the train to Kenora to cover the arrival of the strikers. They marched in the following morning and a local church arranged to turn its basement into a dormitory for the duration of their stay. The strikers held a tag day and raised enough money to provide food for a couple of days. As elsewhere in the West, public sympathy was very much with the single unemployed. In Kenora, however, it was the height of the tourist season, and in a town that lived off tourists, sympathy quickly cooled when it was rumoured that the strikers might be holed up in the church basement for weeks instead of leaving immediately.

Back in Winnipeg, the news desk was expecting me to file at least five to six hundred words a day on developments in Kenora. There were no developments in Kenora. The provincials patrolled the highway. The Mounties and CPR police patrolled the CPR property. The rank and file of the strikers loafed on the grass in the parks or slept. The leaders, Bill Ross, Harry Binder, and Mitchi Sago, all recent graduates of the Young Communist League, held interminable discussions among themselves and with their followers.

With me on this assignment were Frank Bowness of the *Winnipeg Tribune* and Ross Munro on his first assignment for the Canadian Press. We went our separate ways, of course, but Munro and I compared notes occasionally and once or twice sat with our ears glued to a connecting door in my hotel room, trying to hear what the provincial police were discussing in the next room. We could not decipher any of the muffled conversation that filtered through the door.

With deadlines approaching and nothing to write, the temptation mounted to try to make something happen. I went from the city police to the mayor's office to the OPP with conjectural questions. What will you do if the strikers walk out of town in small groups with the idea of catching a freight? Suppose they board a passenger train without tickets, counting on the train being in motion by the time the conductor comes around to collect tickets? The authorities shrugged off the questions with noncommittal answers. Similar conjectural questions were directed to Sago and Binder and Ross, who probably assumed that the questions arose after we had been talking to the OPP or the Mounties.

After a couple of days of frustration and lack of copy to write, we all became more and more desperate for new angles. We'd talk to the police having coffee and the strikers having breakfast. In neither case did the leaders approve of our talking to the rank and file. The strike leaders had a front to maintain—they would get to Ottawa come what may. But the individual followers were far from enthusiastic one way or another—they had nothing better to do and no place to go. I was in and out of the strike headquarters so often the strikers might have assumed I was one of them, or at least a messenger between the strike leaders and the authorities.

Despite my efforts to get something to write, Kenora was a nothing assignment and little that I wrote in desperation was considered worth using. Despite the endless pep talks from the leaders and persistent affirmations that nothing would stop their going to Ottawa, the strikers eventually gave up and returned to Winnipeg in a couple of colonist cars provided by the CPR. A year later, the "nothing" Kenora episode led to one of the most traumatic experiences of my life.

The *Free Press* Saturday magazine section differed from other weekend supplements of the prairie newspapers in the open attitude its editor maintained toward local contributions. While other newspapers depended heavily on syndicated features, the *Free Press* encouraged local people to write for it. The writing took the form of short stories, feature articles, and occasional bits of poetry. All newspaper editors developed a wariness toward poets because of the ease with which they could be conned by plagiarists. But article writers, essayists, and nostalgia buffs all got a friendly reception from Frank Williams, the magazine's editor, who was totally devoid of the hard-shell cynicism of his news-side colleagues. He was sufficiently patient to work with a writer on a piece to bring it into publishable form. As he once said, he liked to try to make up with encouragement what he lacked in money, for the rates paid for submissions were, in a word, outrageous—between a tenth and a fifth of a cent a word. But in the summer of 1937, Williams was stumped. A reader had wandered in with a manuscript and an idea Williams could not resist, but the form in which it was presented was impossible. Eventually he came to me with a proposition I could not resist.

"How," he asked, "would you like to make fifty bucks?"

Whatever his proposition was, I accepted, sight unseen. It was this: some weeks previously a reader had brought in a hand-written manuscript that filled three school scribblers. It was an exposé of the Communist conspiracy against the commonweal by a former Communist who had broken with the movement.

The efforts of the Communists to bring on a revolution in Canada had been exposed time and again. The RCMP had a specialist named Sergeant Leopold who infiltrated Communist cells and then surfaced in uniform to testify against the comrades in court. At the 1931 trial of Tim Buck and seven other Communists under Section 98 of the Criminal Code, massive documentation was produced from Communist party files to link Canadian Communists with the Comintern in Moscow. So exposés were not all that newsworthy. But this case had both a lot that was new and a great deal of material that would be bound to appeal to Ukrainian readers in Winnipeg's North End. So how would I like to take over the material this guy had written and rewrite it into some good articles for the magazine section? For fifty dollars?

I took the scribblers home with me and got out my typewriter. Two hours later, the mound of discarded copy paper on the floor was a measure of my frustration. Clearly our author had a great story to tell, but piecing it together out of this disjointed manuscript was impossible, by reason of both omission and commission. Vital details were omitted on every other page and the writer was probably thinking in Ukrainian and translating into English, a process complicated by the intrusion of Marxist jargon. In the end, I concluded that the assignment was hopeless and returned the scribblers to Williams. He, however, was not prepared to give up.

"Instead of trying to rewrite the manuscript, I think I have a better idea," he said. "Suppose you and this guy get together and you use what he has written as a sort of guide. Then you interview him and you write the story." The fifty dollars still beckoned, so I agreed. The next evening I met John Hladun.

He turned out to be a very difficult guy. A well-built native of the Ukraine, he had come to Canada prior to the First World War as a babe-in-arms and had grown up in a Ukrainian settlement in Saskatchewan. A man in his late twenties, he was now married, the father of two, and was working as a labourer in a packing plant.

Instead of having our meeting at Williams' desk, we moved into George Ferguson's office because Hladun was nervous about the stream of traffic in and out of the newsroom. His was the most conspiratorial mien I had yet encountered. He seemed tormented by suspicion of everything around him. He was persuaded that he and I should collaborate on his memoir, but insisted it must be done anonymously, for fear of reprisal from his former comrades.

"Mr. Gray, Mr. Williams, until only recently I am one of them. I know what they will do, not only to me but my family. They will beat up on my wife and kids, even they would kill me!"

Neither of us was impressed by his fear, and I said, "Look, John, the Ukrainians have been fighting the Russian Revolution in the north end of Winnipeg for almost twenty years. They refight it at every civic election and every provincial election when the Whites and Reds are at each other. But in between elections and strikes they live together and sometimes they even play together on the same teams at the CUAC [the Canadian Ukrainian Athletic Club which sponsored softball and gymnastic teams]."

"Ah, but this is different," he insisted. "This is treason. Already I have lost two jobs. The last one they put a wrench in my lunch box and tip off the boss and I get fired for stealing. So now I must go through my coat pockets and lunchbox a couple of times a day and once a car just misses me on the street. Believe me, already they are trying to get back at me for quitting. If they find out I write this article it will be worse. Believe me!"

Taking him seriously was difficult. This was Winnipeg, not Russia, and what did his former comrades have to gain by harassing one of their drop-outs? Nevertheless, we agreed that we would include enough inaccuracies in the story to direct suspicions elsewhere and we would take steps to keep his visits to the *Free Press* as well hidden as possible. We would meet each evening in Ferguson's office, which was handy to the elevator. Not that he used the elevator. Mike, the elevator man, was also a Ukrainian, and after making that discovery, Hladun took the stairs to and from our fourth floor.

To me it was inconceivable that he would write his memoir without the Communist party brass being able to identify him quickly. His was the story of a young Canadian Ukrainian who had been recruited into the Communist party through his activities in a local branch of the Ukrainian Labour-Farmer Temple Association, a co-operative which owned a couple of hundred community halls in the Ukrainian settlements of western Canada. He had so impressed the Communist leaders that they had enrolled him in their agit-prop training school at Lockport, Manitoba. There the ULFTA had acquired at tax sale two mansions erected by Jerry Robinson, Winnipeg's millionaire merchant prince of the gay nineties, who went broke in the 1920s. In a tutorial, round-table system, Hladun and several other potential party leaders had spent all one winter in daily study of the works of Marx and Engels, with special emphasis on mastering the theory of dialectical material-ism. Clearly one of the brightest pupils, Hladun was selected for further training at the Comintern's superschool in Moscow, the Lenin Institute.

One of Hladun's cherished goals on his visit to Russia was to visit the village in the Ukraine from which his parents had migrated. It was full of relatives on both sides of his family. In Moscow, authorization to make the trip turned out to be very difficult to obtain. In the end, permission and transportation came through, and he embarked on the journey that would take him clear out of the Communist movement. He arrived at the home village during Stalin's long campaign to "liquidate the Kulaks as a class" and the central administration's campaign to stamp out all vestiges of Ukrainian nationalism. Hladun encountered tales of savage suppression of Ukrainian aspirations. Local leadership cadres were being decimated by arrests and deportations. Whole villages were conscripted for resettlement in Siberia. There was famine everywhere. The Ukrainian language was being eliminated from the schools of many districts. A completely disillusioned Hladun returned to Canada to break all ties with the Communists and throw in his lot with the anti-Communist Ukrainians whose leaders helped him to get a job in Winnipeg.

How could such a person write this exposé in any detail and not be immediately identifiable to the local Communist bosses? Surely there were not so many Ukrainians going back to Russia for post-graduate instruction in making revolution as to make identifica-tion of any one of them difficult. As it turned out, the numbers were apparently quite large, for the Communists did in fact have difficulty.

The project proceeded slowly, for I was fitting it in around my regular work. Using Hladun's scribblers as a guide, I would rough out the items I wanted to gather together. Then I would question Hladun, make notes, write the material out, and submit it back to him for checking. When the pile of material in Frank Williams' drawer reached about 2,500 words, he came up with a different idea.

"Instead of running this as a page or two in the magazine section, why don't we break it down for a series of one-column pieces for the daily?" The news department liked the idea, so I recast the article into one-column articles and went on with the interviews. Then Williams had another idea. Why not syndicate the series to other newspapers across the country and split the proceeds with Hladun? He got that idea approved as well.

It took us two or three weeks to polish off the job. Then we edited the copy, wrote two-column heads for each piece, and turned everything over to the composing room for typesetting and assembly into a dummy four-page newspaper which could be sent out to prospective publishers. Frank and I shook Hladun warmly by the hand, Williams paid him off, and that was the last we ever saw of him. Or heard of him. Almost.

A few days later I got a call from Howard Wolfe, our city editor, at the city hall where I had been assigned to cover a committee meeting.

"Jim Litterick just called for you from the Communist party office and said he had a story for you if you'd call around and pick it up. I told him you'd drop in this afternoon."

Jim Litterick was a Clydeside Communist from Toronto who had been parachuted into Winnipeg some months before to be the Communist candidate in Winnipeg in the provincial election. In taking that step, Toronto had passed over Alderman Jacob Penner, Andy Bilecki, John Navis, and other veteran wheelhorses of the western Communist movement. The rationale for doing so was never publicized, and there was a lot of grumbling among the comrades.

After years of tooth-and-nail warfare against all milder socialists and reformers, Canadian Communists were ordered by Moscow in 1934 to do a complete about-turn and co-operate with everybody in sight to whom the label "progressive" could be applied. The militantly doctrinaire Marxist stance was abandoned in favour of promoting a raft of "front" organizations devoted to social reform, to which Anglo-Saxon non-Communists could be attracted. The end purpose, of course, was to mobilize world opinion to support Russia in the coming war against fascism. In the back of the mind of the Canadian Communist hierarchy was probably the thought that the predominantly Ukrainian-Jewish leadership of the Winnipeg Communists was too closely identified with the hard-line, head-cracking, meeting-disruption tactics of the "down-with-everybody" pre-Hitler Communists. A new image was needed to go with the new party line, and Litterick provided it as a clean-cut Scottish Canadian in a business suit and white shirt and tie who could appeal to Anglo-Saxon "progressives." In the provincial election of 1936, Litterick appealed very well and eased into the legislature behind Lewis St. George Stubbs, the recently unbenched crusading judge who polled more votes than the next-closest five candidates combined. I got to know Litterick during the campaign when I covered many of his meetings.

As befitting its new image, the Communist party had taken office space on the second floor in the old Chamber of Commerce Building on Princess Street, just across from the Market Square and the civic offices building. That ancient edifice was half empty, and the Communists occupied rather spacious premises on the second floor. It consisted of a large outer office with five or six unoccupied desks and an eight-by-ten-foot glass-partitioned private office off in one corner.

From the outer-office entry door I could see Litterick sitting at his private office desk, and was about to walk in on him when I noticed he had a couple of people with him and stepped back.

"Come on in, Jim," he called and waved me to a seat in the corner. Litterick was sitting with his back towards a large plate-glass window. A man in his twenties sat leaning back on a chair against the wall on the left of the doorway and, as I entered, I saw another man on the right, sitting backwards with his arms resting on the back of his chair. I looked from one to the other, nodded, and when Litterick made no move to introduce us, opened the conversation.

"Howard Wolfe said you had a story for us, Jim. What are you up to now?"

"Well, it's not really a story for you," he replied. "In fact it is what we might say was the reverse. We thought you'd be able to help us with a story." My face must have screwed up in puzzlement because, instead of continuing, Litterick opened the centre drawer of his desk and slowly took out a folded newspaper. As he unfolded it I stretched my neck to see what it was, and as he held it up I was flabbergasted to see that it was a copy of our dummy of the Hladun series of articles with the promotional blurb I had written in bold-face prominence! I had not yet seen the copy myself and here was Litterick with one in the Communist party office!

My head whirled with questions. How the hell did he get a copy of that dummy when I had only turned in the final copy two days before? Obviously, from a Communist fifth-columnist in the *Free Press.* But who? Somebody in the composing room, a janitor, maybe a delivery-room employee? Somebody in the newsroom itself? It was inconceivable. Litterick held the dummy up, full-sized.

"Who is this guy, Jim?" he asked in a low voice.

I did not have any trouble looking surprised at the production of the newspaper. But trying to look baffled at the question was something else. With all the skill of a little-theatre understudy, I reached for the dummy, firing questions like: "What the hell is this? What is this all about? Who wrote this? How did you get hold of it?"

"Oh, come off it! Who do you think you're trying to kid?" Litterick broke in. "Who is this guy who wrote this crap?"

I feigned concentration on the articles in the dummy, stealing a glance at the two strangers as I did so. I thought of simply bolting through the door and out of the office, when I noticed that the door was now closed; from my place on the opposite side of the room, the two strangers suddenly loomed as guards of the door. I became very nervous as some of Hladun's tales of physical brutality by Communist bully-boys clattered back into my mind.

"How, how the hell do I know who wrote it," I stammered. "And anyway, what gave you the idea I'd tell you even if I knew?" I asked.

"You'll tell," he replied. "So let's quit all this kidding around. We know who rewrote it. You did. We know you used to meet this guy in the managing editor's office at night. Your name was on the top of all the copy. You were working with this guy for three or four weeks until the day before yesterday."

My mind whirled. At least, I thought, the Communist spy in the *Free Press* was narrowed down. It had to be somebody in the composing room, to have seen the copy. But not necessarily so. The janitors were in and out all the time. And so were the stereotypers. And so were all the people from the newsroom. I made a movement towards the door and the stranger on my right stood up. I stopped and began to shiver in panic. Then I grabbed a glass inkwell from Litterick's desk and took a step backward.

"All right," I blurted. "If you guys don't open that door and let me out of here, I'm going to fire this goddam inkwell through that window glass and start yelling my head off."

Suddenly Litterick's mood changed and his voice dropped.

"What's the matter with you, Jim? I know, you've taken to believing all this crap. You're acting like a child. You want to go?" He spoke to the man by the door. "Open the door, let him go." He turned to me and said, "But don't go running off with my inkwell." He smiled. Then, as I stepped towards the door, he held up his hand. "But before you go I want you to read something." He reached into the drawer again and took out a piece of notepaper and placed it face upwards on his desk in front of me.

"Read this. And then walk through that door if you like . . . and when you do, let me tell you that a copy of this is going to the Mounties and a copy to the publisher of the *Free Press*."

On the notepaper, dated July 1935, were a half-dozen lines of typescript which read something like this:

MEMO FOR THE CENTRAL COMMITTEE

Special mention should be made of the work of Comrade Jim Gray, who is now employed as a reporter by the *Winnipeg Free Press*. He was able to obtain much valuable information about the plans of the Ontario Provincial Police and the Kenora police to attack us if our work went on. As a result of this information we were able to change our strategy to prevent these attacks. Comrade Gray is to be highly commended for his initiative in this regard.

I recall babbling some sort of denunciation of the memo as a pack of lies as I fled from the room and out on to the street. The fast pace with which I took off for the *Free Press* slowed to a foot-dragging halt as some of the implications of what had happened came home to me. What, for example, would happen to my job when that memo reached Victor Sifton's desk? How could I combat the implication that I was a member of the Communist party? Worse, how would I repudiate the statement that I had spied on the police and carried information to the Communists? How could I prevent the accusations from blighting my career forever, even if I did not get fired on the spot?

Clearly, Litterick had expected me to cave in and identify the source of the articles. If I had, they would still have had the memo to hold over my head in the future. But to what purpose? What kind of a favour could they demand of me that the threat of exposure could force me to grant? It was unreal. Could it have been that there was a Jim Gray who was a member of the party and they had got him confused with me? Why should Litterick have gone to the trouble of staging this elaborate charade, to say nothing of the spurious memorandum, just to ferret out Hladun's identity? That, I was still certain, could be easily done by a process of elimination. And what difference did it make who was behind the articles? Of all the teapot tempests! The articles would appear in due course, create a modicum of interest across the country, and be completely forgotten, just as the other political exposés had flared momentarily and died. The only conclusion I could come to was that there would be hell to pay in the party hierarchy over Hladun's defection and exposé, and that quick detection of the culprit was necessary to enable those who had brought him into the party and advanced his career to prepare their defences and perhaps avoid chastisement or expulsion.

By the time I got back to the office, Howard Wolfe had gone for the day and there was no one else around for me to talk to. After a sleepless night I got to him first thing in the morning with the whole story. His reaction was one which did much to dispel my gloom and foreboding.

"Son of a bitch," he said. "Who the hell in our staff could have gotten hold of that dummy and given it to those bastards?"

Howard Wolfe was clearly taking me on trust and would listen to no disclaimer from me of the statements in the memo. Instead, his mind turned at once to the question of the snitch on the staff who had purloined the dummy for the Communists. "You can be damn sure of one thing," he said, "it was nobody on this floor." He thought maybe he should talk to George Garbutt, the composing-room foreman. Then he called over Cy Louth, the police reporter.

"Cy, make a note of this name, will you. It is John Hladun, H-l-a-d-u-n. He provided the stuff for a series of articles Jimmy wrote on the Communist party. He is fearful that the Communists will find out about it and waylay him. For the next month, keep close check on the assault cases and if anything does happen to Hladun, we'd better get to Chief Smith with the information that this is a reprisal thing. I'm sure he'll make a special effort to get the guys who do it."

So far as I can recall, nothing happened to Hladun. He eventually moved to Toronto and a job with a Ukrainian-language anti-Communist magazine. As for the threat that the memo would go to the publisher and the Mounties, I never raised the question with Sifton and he never mentioned it to me. But I am certain it did go to the Mounted Police.

During the Second World War, the Mounted Police were in close contact with all newspapers in connection with a number of war-related activities. When they thought it wise, they regularly took the editors into their confidence about investigations they were undertaking so that information might not be published pre-maturely and short-circuit their efforts.

The Mounted Police contact man for the Winnipeg newspapers was Sergeant George Renton. I met him a couple of times when he was in to see George Ferguson, the executive editor. After one such visit, Ferguson came into my office smiling broadly.

"What the hell have you been up to to get the Mounties' backs up at you?" he asked. "Renton was just in to see me and I told him I was going to be away for a couple of weeks and if anything came up in my absence he could talk to you. He said no, he didn't want to talk to you; he'd just wait. And by God, I got to thinking he always clams up when you come into my office. What are you,

Gray," he asked with a grin, "some kind of Communist stool-pigeon boring from within these sacred portals?"

Obviously, if my report on the Litterick episode had reached him at the time, he had forgotten all about it. Or maybe he had remembered it and was having a joke about it. I was about to pursue the matter when the phone rang, the opportunity passed, and the question was lost in the shuffle.

Ferguson's comment certainly seemed to clear up one point. Litterick had been serious about sending a copy of the phoney memo to the RCMP. Did the Mounties attempt to check the memo and determine for themselves whether there was a Comrade Jim Gray on the *Free Press* staff? Probably not. It was easier simply to open a file on James Gray and add his name to the subversive list, for how, in the world of international espionage, does any security force go about proving that anyone is *not* an espionage agent?

Ten years after the Litterick episode, the Taschereau–Kellock Royal Commission added some massive footnotes to the part played by Canadian Communist leaders in recruiting unwary Canadians into Russian spy rings. Igor Gouzenko was the Russian-embassy cipher clerk who defected with an armload of files which broke the famous Canadian espionage cases in 1946. The royal commission probing the espionage ring which Gouzenko identified concluded that several Soviet spy networks were operating in Canada during the war. The commission also provided elaborate documentation of the way in which Canadian Communist functionaries acted as recruiting agents for spy rings. Were such recruiting chores entrusted to lower-level hinterlanders like Litterick? Probably not, but as the royal commission was able to determine, blackmail was a tool used by the Communists to keep their dupes in line whenever they began to develop a distaste for what they were doing. If I had yielded to the threat of the memo, what else would have been asked of me? But what information would a newspaper reporter have been privy to that would have been useful to the Communists, here or abroad? Such questions have come to mind periodically with such memory stimulators as the Profumo, Munsinger, and Watergate cases. None of this pondering has ever produced answers that made any sense. What made the least sense of all was sending the phoney memo to the RCMP after I had refused to be trapped. It always seemed to me a bit incongruous that conspirators who could devise a successful scheme to steal the secrets of the atomic bomb could be capable of such an act of petty meanness.

3
Turner Valley, Where They Killed the Goose That Laid the Golden Eggs

In the summer of 1937, I fell headlong into a wisenheimer trap, and as a result stumbled upon what might well have become one of the most important milestones in Canadian economic development. The lost economic opportunity was the way in which Turner Valley Royalties, Ltd., was set up corporatively to guarantee its investors that they would profit directly from its discovery of crude oil in the limestone of Turner Valley. That the royalties system failed to revolutionize the financing of Canadian natural-resources exploration can be attributed about equally to the inbred avarice of all promoters and to the myopic stupidity that has been the trademark of the Ottawa mandarins responsible for making tax policy for more than fifty years.

First, the wisenheimer trap. The expression is old-fashioned journalese to describe what happens to a reporter who fancies himself to be an expert on a subject and writes off the top of his head instead of re-checking his facts for further developments. It was easy, in the pre-war era of thoroughness in reporting, for reporters to acquire a high level of expertise in highly technical subjects. A reporter covering a royal commission hearing, for example, had to acquire as clear an understanding of what was happening as any of the learned counsel who were earning five times his salary at the commission hearings. A reporter had to be able to summarize the proceedings accurately into prose newspaper readers would understand. Moreover, reporters had so to report proceedings that their editors could compose sense-making editorials to guide public opinion. A reporter who got carried away with his own expertise and fell into error was said to have fallen into the wisenheimer trap.

Early in the spring of 1937, I was a wisenheimer waiting for the trap to spring. I probably would have confessed, if pressed, that I knew more about stock-market frauds than any journalist working in Canada. My interest in the subject was triggered first when I was a margin clerk in a brokerage office in 1928 during the big mining boom. My desk was a calling point for a stream of gullible mining-stock buyers eager to take fliers in the latest moose-pasture promotions being touted by *Hush* and other Toronto and Montreal tipster sheets. Self-protection led to a crash course in the fundamentals of mining-stock promotion, which led eventually to a morbid curiosity about all manner of fraudulent corporate financing. When Franklin D. Roosevelt kicked off the big Canadian gold-mining boom in 1933 by revaluing gold, it was 1928 all over again in Toronto, as the promoters launched their blitzkriegs against the solvency of Canadian investors. For me, this was where I had come in in 1928, and in 1934 I wrote several series of articles exposing the frauds.

I returned to the subject in the spring of 1937, with a series of *Free Press* exposures of the newest wrinkles in frauds that were being used by Toronto "boiler-room" telephone solicitors to separate widows and orphans from their savings. Hard upon this series, I was asked by Frank Avery, the *Free Press* financial editor, to take a look at the latest Turner Valley oil boom. The Winnipeg brokers, he said, were getting excited about a new gimmick being used by the Alberta oil promoters. It was called royalty financing, and our financial desk was getting a lot of calls from subscribers wanting explanations and advice.

I was working on another assignment at the time and put Avery's job aside. When I did get around to it, I barely scratched the surface of the subject before doing a piece that turned into a short editorial warning investors against the machinations of the wily Alberta stock peddlers. I reminded readers that Turner Valley had boomed in 1914–15; it boomed again in 1924 and in 1929, but in the end the investors lost their money, even when the companies in which they had invested found great gobs of natural gas and small amounts of oil. It was inevitable that this would happen, I wrote, because the promoters took far too great a chunk of each company's shares for the leases they sold the companies at inflated prices. The watchword for Alberta oil stocks was still *caveat emptor*!

Two or three days after the editorial appeared, I got a telephone call from a Winnipeg stock broker named Alex Freeman. He gave me a verbal chastising for writing about something I did not understand, and worse, for getting my facts all wrong. He invited me to call on him and get straightened out because there was now no way any Turner Valley investor could lose money if the company discovered oil. I called on Freeman not once but several times before I became convinced that I had libelled the industry.

By 1937, most of the stock brokers who had managed to survive the Depression in Winnipeg were a conservative and colourless crowd who lived mainly on the small commission they earned from placing government bonds with insurance companies and sinking funds. Alex Freeman was a promoter of the old school, an epitome of unabashed enthusiasm, a super-salesman who exuded optimism from every pore. It turned out that he suffered from a slightly asthmatic condition that accentuated the breathless quality of his sales pitch. Alex Freeman never spoke except with a sales pitch, even when he was ordering a lunch-counter sandwich.

"I get from your article," he challenged, "that you don't know what's going on in Alberta. So let me bring you up to date, because what's going on in Alberta is the biggest thing that ever happened in Canada! First off, they discovered crude oil in the limestone at Turner Valley! I don't mean wet gas or naphtha or that stuff they burn off to get gasoline. I mean crude oil! Last year they discovered crude oil and now they are drilling wells all over and finding oil in every well they drill! Not a dry hole yet! And these wells come in at two thousand barrels a day!

"That, my friend is what you're knocking in that lousy article in the *Free Press*. And that ain't all. In Alberta they've invented a whole new way of financing oil wells so an investor is absolutely guaranteed to get a run for his money!" He did a stage pause and reached for a cigar to let what he had said sink in.

"Look, Jimmy" (we were on a first-name basis almost at once), "I know from these articles you have been writing about the Toronto boiler rooms and the bait-and-switchers that you know what you know about mining-stock rackets. I simply say: into these Turner Valley royalties you haven't looked deeply enough. This isn't the old common-stock thing any more. They don't sell stock. They sell a percentage in the oil that comes out of the ground. Look, let me show you."

Freeman dug into his filing cabinet and came out with a file on Turner Valley Royalties, Ltd., the company that started it all. He half opened the file and then changed his mind and dropped it on his desk. "No," he said, "before I show you what Turner Valley Royalties are all about, I've got to put you in the picture."

The picture he put me into was one with which I was as familiar as he was. The curse of the previous Turner Valley oil booms had been under-capitalization of the companies doing the drilling. The promoters were too greedy, as I had written; they did take too large a bite of the companies' shares for their leases; they did give too large a commission to the brokers; and they sold shares at too low a price. Time and again they ran out of money before they could complete the wells they were drilling. So it was small wonder that, after 1929, everyone not totally stupid came to regard shares in oil companies as something akin to shares in mining companies, the Brooklyn Bridge, and gold bricks—as downright swindles. In 1936 and 1937, nobody would have bought an oil share from Diogenes himself if it were printed on solid gold plate.

"So that's it," said Freeman. "You know the picture like I know the picture. Nobody in his right mind would buy oil stock. Well, out in Calgary there is this guy Brown and nobody has got the picture better than him. The difference is he is just one hell of a smart guy. He runs the Calgary streetcar system. But he is so hepped on oil he can't sleep. He's got this twenty-acre lease out at the south end of Turner Valley and he's convinced that if he drills on this lease he'll find oil instead of gas. Gas they got coming out of their ears, but crude oil is what they need most and can't find.

"Like I say," Freeman continued, "this Brown can't raise a dime to get his well started. Two, three years ago nobody in Calgary had a dime, never mind a dime to invest in oil stock. So then this Brown comes up with the royalty idea. Maybe Brown was not the original inventor. In fact I'm sure he wasn't because I know this general idea has been used in the States under different names. But Brown puts the idea to work in Calgary and it's revolutionary! It's so simple you can't believe it! Instead of a million shares and all that crap, you set up a company with one hundred royalty units. If the well strikes oil, every holder of a one-per-cent royalty unit gets one per cent of the net production from the well. But you live in Winnipeg and the oil is in Alberta, so what the hell good is barrels of oil to you? Easy. The lawyers work it out this way:

"Instead of a company you create a trust. With a trust company yet. The manager of Turner Valley Royalties is required to sell the oil and turn the proceeds over to the trust company. The trust company then pays out the money to each of the individual royalty owners. Suppose you have put up fifteen hundred dollars for a one-per-cent net royalty in this well. Every month or two months or maybe three months you get a cheque for one per cent of the oil that was produced in thirty, sixty, or ninety days.

"And you know what that means? Look here." Freeman reached into the Turner Valley Royalties file and produced a table of figures. "This well came into production on June 16 last year. So far it has produced two hundred thousand barrels of oil and has repaid to each one-per-cent royalty owner three thousand dollars. And if you happened to be an original investor in Turner Valley Royalties, you can sell that royalty today for five thousand. Not too bad for a fifteen-hundred-dollar investment!"

It all sounded too good to be true. And I said so, in a rejoinder that went something like this: "The missing link in this explanation of yours is, what the hell does Brown get out of all this? Look, Alex, to rephrase Gertrude Stein, a promoter is a promoter is a promoter. If you don't have a heart full of larceny, you'll never make a promoter. The essence of being a promoter is to have your cake and eat it too. You do a deal that enables you to get a promotion going and the objective of all promoters is to wind up owning the deal, or most of it, without risking any of their own money."

Freeman searched his file for an answer to the question of what Brown got. He failed, but promised to find out. We spent the rest of the afternoon arguing about promoters. Freeman conceded that a larcenous soul was essential for a promoter. Greed made the game go. But there was more to it than greed and larceny. Even a guy promoting a shady deal had to half-believe in it or he could not generate the energy and conviction essential to putting it over. A gold-brick salesman had to mesmerize himself into believing that the worthless fake he was selling was a gold brick when he was reaching the peak of his sales pitch. And anyway, he argued, who was to say that some fraudulent promotions did not serve the best interests of the community?

"Look, my friend, nothing happens without promotion, never has since the Garden of Eden. Promoters get things moving. Give a promoter a chance to make a dollar and he'd get the most unlikely project you ever heard of off the ground. My God, look at the Canadian railways, the CPR, the Grand Trunk, and the Canadian Northern. Who wound up with all the profits? The promoters of course, not the poor bloody British investors, that's for sure. But none of these projects would have got off the ground if it had not been for the promoters, and where would Canada be today, or the United States, without the railroads? So what if a lot of promoters get rich and a lot of suckers get screwed? Doesn't the existence of Sudbury and Timmins and Kirkland Lake and Flin Flon and Trail all say something good about promoters? Where the hell were all you hair-shirted critics when Bill Wright and Harry Oakes were out freezing their asses in northern Ontario looking for gold?

"Look at it this way. In Minneapolis there is a big office building called the Foshay Tower. You can see it from all over Minnesota, almost. Well, a guy named Foshay promoted it. He eventually went to jail, as I recall it. A lot of people lost money in his promotions. But so what? People lose money when they buy cars sometimes, or when they buy houses. But Minneapolis has the Foshay Tower; a lot of people got jobs building it, and it will be there long after we are all dead and gone. And it is a very good thing for Minneapolis to have. Same thing with the CPR and the Grand Trunk.

"And it's the same thing with everything else. The best idea mankind ever produced wouldn't be worth a damn unless somebody got hold of it and went out and promoted it. You guys write as if promoters were some kind of scum, for God's sake. Well, I'm a promoter and proud of it because I build industries and make jobs for people. And I hope I get as rich as Rockefeller. And you think it's easy? Look, my friend, for every winning promotion there can be a hundred losers. You work yourself into a frenzy and push and push and in the end you strike out. You lose twenty times but you keep at it because the twenty-first will be the winner and make up for all the losses. And it has to make up the losses or what the hell are we in business for?

"Take me. I've got a couple of prospectors out in northern Manitoba looking for anything they can find in the way of gold prospects. But if they find the mother lode, it won't be worth a damn unless I get busy and promote it. So why should I put out my money to grubstake prospectors and then spend a lot more promoting development of my mining property, unless I can cash in on it? Look, if there was one thing my old economics profs at Columbia agreed on, it was that people who take risks are entitled to rewards commensurate with the risks they take. That's almost textbook verbatim. But what about the physical efforts that people put into things as well as money? If you take some hopeless proposition and bust your gut trying to make it work, aren't you entitled to a big score if you do make it work?"

There was, of course, a difference between a promoter busting his gut trying to make something work and the Toronto and Calgary share-pushers whose stock-in-trade was the near-worthless mining and oil stocks they pushed by high-pressure telephone solicitation, or through manipulation of the stock-exchange quotations. And there was a world of difference between prudent investors, who weighed yields and the prospects of modest appreciation, and the gamblers who were addicted to the high risk, high returns of the penny mining and oil stocks. Freeman and I argued endlessly about where one began and the other left off and where the vast grey areas became one or the other. Where we never came close to a meeting of minds was in defining the function of newspapers or regulatory agencies in the financial world. Freeman was simplistically against all control, all interference, and all newspaper crusading.

"The hell with them all. Enforce the law to the hilt, put the crooks in jail, and if the laws aren't tough enough, stiffen the criminal code! Then get the hell out of the way and let the developers develop the country!" He had even less use for newspaper critics than he had for securities commissions. "What right have you got to come butting into our business? Do you tell Eaton's how to buy clothes and what they should pay their help? What gives you the right to tell people how to invest their money, or not invest it? Have you ever invested your own money, or your own time, trying to make a success of a business? You newspapers got some special licence from God that gives you the privilege of ordering other people's lives?"

Both of us were tiring of the argument about the time Freeman came up with the figures of the promoter's cut in the first Turner Valley Royalties promotion. They revealed that R. A. Brown had been almost a model of forbearance in the promotional bite he took of the TVR well.

The upshot of my talks with Freeman and the new information he provided was a *mea culpa* piece I wrote and turned over to Frank Avery. In it I found little wrong with the royalties system and a great deal right with it. Most important, it would remove the stigma of dishonesty that had become so firmly attached to the financing of oil and gas exploration. And it could become a mechanism for a self-financing system, because people who got a quick return on their royalties would be likely to plough their winnings back into additional speculations. If the royalty system worked in getting oil wells financed, it should work in financing mining development, and the development of mineral resources was what the prairie provinces hoped would free them from the hazards of a one-crop wheat economy.

Avery was not convinced. He could not see how the royalty system could have a practical application to mining development, and here his knowledge was extensive. For every McIntyre, Hudson Bay, or Noranda, he said, there were bound to be a dozen marginal mines which could never find the lodes that would turn them into bonanzas. But they provided an immense amount of employment even if they never paid a dividend to the people who financed them. Besides, he did not think people who invested in mining stocks cared about dividends, or even about merely doubling their money. They were addicted to the drill-hole markets in which reports of strikes on raw prospects pushed share prices from ten to seventy-five cents in a matter of days. He put my article aside while he pondered its arguments, and eventually it was filed and forgotten.

A year or so later I ran into Alex Freeman on the street and, ebullient as ever, he chided me loudly for not having got aboard the royalties gravy train. "So far old TVR has paid back over $5,000 for every $1,500 invested. It's paying back at the rate of $2,000 a year and is selling for $7,000 for a one-per-cent royalty. Where in the world can you find an investment with returns like that? And that guy Brown we talked about last year, he's now got half a dozen more wells on production."

That guy Brown—Robert Arthur Brown—had clearly moved in with C. W. Dingman and Stewart Herron as a legend-maker of the Alberta oil industry, and the most unlikely of legend-makers he was, for legends are seldom made by such prosaic people as super-intendents of street railways. That had been Brown's job in Calgary for twenty years, and by 1930 he had become the city's highest-paid employee. Thereafter everything had gone downhill. From a peak of $466.67 a month, a succession of civic wage cuts had whittled his salary to $326.67 a month—hardly a stipend that left much of a margin for financing wildcat oil wells, even in the 1930s. On the other hand, superintending a streetcar system left Brown with a lot of time for pondering the promotion of wildcat oil wells, and pondering the promotion of oil wells was the one thing of which he never tired.

Bob Brown was bitten by the oil bug at the blowing in of the famous Dingham-Herron discovery well in Turner Valley in July of 1914. When the newspaper photographers arrived to get their pictures of the first Dingman oil being piped into drums, Brown was front and centre when the shutters clicked. Thereafter, his job as superintendent of the streetcar system was very much a some-time thing. During the 1920s, Brown played a minor role in the promotion of several small companies and a major part in a deal which saw Home Oil pay one million dollars for a Turner Valley quarter-section on which no well was ever drilled.

The Wall Street crash and the ensuing brokerage-house failures in Canada put the kibosh on Calgary's frenzied oil-stock market. The oil companies that intrigued the gamblers of the 1920s became the dogs and cats of a dead market of the 1930s. Some of them, like Home Oil, sold off their oil properties and became completely dormant. Others provided their promoters with modest incomes from royalties on Turner Valley gas production. That production dropped off sharply in the first half of the Depression decade as new drilling failed to make up for dwindling reserves. Strangely enough, the more the industry declined, the greater Brown's interest seemed to become.

During the great drilling boom in Turner Valley in the 1920s, Grant Spratt, the Canadian government geologist in Calgary, began keeping track of the drilling wells with a series of up-ended glass tubes spotted on well locations on a large-scale table map of Turner Valley. The depth at which production was achieved was marked on each tube, along with the various formations through which the bit had travelled to reach the pay zone. The tube assembly provided an accurate mapping of the substructure of Turner Valley. Spratt's tube display ultimately gave birth to new theories about the nature of the Turner Valley limestone from which the natural gas was being produced.

The limestone formation ran in a southeast-to-northwest direction. Most of the prolific gas wells were drilled along the eastern side of the north-south axis. The theory was that wells drilled to the west would strike water rather than gas. However, as time passed, it became apparent that the gas wells closest to the centre of the reservoir tended to produce brownish-coloured naphtha or condensate, while those farther east produced clear naphtha. That led to the theory that the colour in the naphtha was coming from crude oil which existed in a pool under the gas cap on the reservoir. Brown became particularly hepped on the theory, and wore a path between his city-hall office and Grant Spratt's, keeping track of the changing patterns of naphtha production.

By 1933, theorizing over the geology of Turner Valley was evoking lively discussions over luncheon tables at the Club Café, over drinks in the Ranchmen's Club, and over putts at the Golf and Country Club. Ironically, the soundness of the crude-oil-under-the-gas-cap theory had already been demonstrated beyond cavil. The trouble was, nobody had bothered analysing the evidence that was being produced every day.

Back before the 1929 crash, W. S. Fisher had promoted the Model Oil Company and drilled a well on the north end of Turner Valley. Like many other wells of the era, it found pockets of oil in sand formations above the Mississippian limestone that contained the vast reservoir of wet gas. After recovering some oil, the well drilled through the sand into the limestone and the wet-gas reservoir. The well had been on production for some months when the naphtha in the wet gas turned a dark brown colour and continued discoloured for as long as the well was on production. The accepted theory of the time was that the discolouration was caused by oil from the sands higher up leaking into the limestone through a break in the well casing. That was the conventional explanation for all the discoloured naphtha being produced in the valley. It was not until 1937 that Jim Lowery, with a push from Charles Dingman, drilled his Home-Millarville well, and demonstrated spectacularly that the Model well's naphtha discolouration came from the huge pool of crude oil under the gas cap.

However, oil-patch conversations were more concerned with how to raise money than with geological theory, and, as time passed, the royalties idea became the conversational coin of the realm.

"Okay, we need $100,000 to drill a well. No point organizing a 3,000,000-share company because nobody is going to buy any more two-bit oil stock. And even if they were, it'd take forever to raise $100,000 at $50 and $100 a crack. We all know that. But if we could convince people they would get their money back in oil, I bet a lot of people would be more willing to take a chance. I would myself, I think. . . ." Pencils came out and the arithmetic devoured receptacles full of Club Café paper napkins.

In 1933, Calgary was sinking steadily deeper into the maw of the Depression: unemployment was rampant, construction was at a standstill, business was stagnant, and agriculture was in the grip of the worst price collapse in three hundred years, as drought and grasshoppers were turning the surrounding countryside into a desert wasteland. In such an economic climate, anybody who suggested that a wildcat oil well could be promoted would have risked being certified as a dangerous lunatic-at-large. There is, however, an ancient dictum that says that the potential for mischief by small boys doubles with each addition to a group. The same is true with promoters. A scheme which one promoter could never get off the ground can soar triumphantly when two or three promoters combine to exercise their wiles upon it. And that is what happened, after a fashion, with the Turner Valley royalties idea.

The more Brown heard of the royalty idea, the more he liked it, and the more he liked it the more enthusiastic he became for doing something about it, for marrying the royalty idea to the theory that there was oil under the gas cap on the west side of Turner Valley. On one of his drum-beating rounds, his path crossed that of George Bell, the financially harassed publisher of the near-bankrupt Calgary *Albertan*, and John Moyer, a practising lawyer with a paucity of clients. Bell was an enthusiast both for the royalties system and for the west-flank theory. Moreover, he knew of a baker named Brown in Gleichen, seventy miles east of Calgary, who had a 160-acre mineral lease on the southwest side of the field. He had already leased sixty acres to Fay Becker, who had started to drill a couple of wells and had run out of money. Because it was nearing the end of its twenty-one-year life, Bell suggested that the lease could probably be obtained from the baker very reasonably.

While Moyer was preparing the incorporation papers for their new company, Turner Valley Royalties, Ltd., Brown chauffeured Bell out to Gleichen to dicker with the baker. They returned with a sub-lease of sixty acres that adjoined the Becker lease to the northwest. They congratulated themselves for having talked the baker out of the lease without a cash payment and with only a five-per-cent overriding royalty. Brown and Bell remembered that they had some well casing, drill bits, and wire line, and a lot of miscellaneous junk stored in Turner Valley from previous ill-starred drilling ventures. Along with this equipment, they turned W. R. Brown's lease into Turner Valley Royalties, Ltd., in return for its entire capital stock of 20,000 shares. They then gave Moyer 1,000 shares for his legal contribution to the cause.

With a lease and a company, Brown, Bell, and Moyer next worked out a royalty set-up they would use to raise money to erect a derrick and drill the well. Somebody else's money, of course, for as they worked out the royalty plan, their promotional instincts bubbled quickly to the surface. Instead of putting the entire sixty acres into the royalty deal, they decided to hold forty acres back for themselves in Turner Valley Royalties, Ltd., and have a subsidiary called Turner Valley Royalties No. 1 do the drilling. In addition to holding back the forty acres, Bell and Brown siphoned off 12½ per cent as gross royalty for themselves on the twenty-acre sub-lease. That, coupled with the 5-per-cent gross royalty to the baker and the 5-per-cent gross royalty due the government, meant only 77½ per cent of the well's production would be left for division among the purchasers of the net royalties Brown and Bell proposed to sell. They split the royalties into one-per-cent certificates which would sell for $1,500 each and they were prepared to split the one-per-cent units into minor fractions if any prospective purchasers for such fractions appeared. None did.

Despite the enthusiastic efforts of Bell and Brown, most of their neighbours, friends, and relatives avoided their importuning as they would have spurned the blandishments of gold-brick salesmen. Only mildly discouraged, Bell and Brown abandoned the public and focused their attention on where the money was—in the tills of a dozen small oil companies which were in receipt of regular royalty incomes from Turner Valley natural-gas and natural-gas-liquids production developed in the 1920s.

The first name on their list of prospects was McDougal-Segur Exploration, the oldest extant oil company in Alberta. It went back to the days of the 1914 Dingman discovery and over the years had enjoyed a modest income from wells drilled on its land. Even in the 1930s it had a net income of a few thousand a year and had two hundred thousand dollars salted away in Royalite Oil stock. John I. McFarland, A. G. Graves, and T. M. Carlyle, who directed the company, were not only old friends and lodge brothers of Brown and Bell; they liked the oil-royalty idea and agreed to put up $15,000 of the company's money for a 10-per-cent net royalty. Brown then was able to tap the treasury of Spooner Oils, of which he was a director, for $7,500 for a 5-per-cent royalty. Calmont and Vulcan oils were persuaded to come in for a like amount.

In a matter of weeks, the promoters raised $37,500 from the sale of 25 per cent in net royalties, and on April 17, 1934, a cable tool began pounding into the earth on the TVR No. 1 lease. It kept pounding only until July 18, when the money ran out and the drillers were laid off. Almost a year passed before the promoters managed to sell another 3-per-cent royalty, which gave them money enough for another couple of weeks of drilling; then activities ceased, apparently for good.

On to the scene in November 1935 rode an unexpected apparition with an armload of manna from heaven. It was the British American Oil Company, which had built a small refinery on the American border at Coutts and was looking for a supply of crude oil. The company agreed to lend the promoters $30,000 with which to replace the cable-tool outfit with a rotary rig and resume drilling. In return, BA would receive a 12½-per-cent gross royalty till the loan was repaid and then a net of 5 per cent. After the BA loan, Brown and Bell were able to pry $22,500 worth of needed equipment from Imperial Oil, in return for a gross royalty of 7.5 per cent.

The well-drilling went on through the winter of 1935–36 and into the spring of 1936, when George Bell died. His interest in Turner Valley Royalties, Ltd., was divided by Brown and Max Bell, the publisher's son, with the bulk of the shares in TVR going to Brown.

On June 6, 1936, TVR No. 1 blew in with a roar that almost drove Bennett's New Deal, Calgary's threatened default on its bonds, and Aberhart's Social Credit dividend off the front pages of the Calgary papers. The oil well got the banner headlines while the Supreme Court's rejection of the New Deal got secondary play and Britain's abandonment of sanctions against Italy, which might otherwise have rated a banner, got only a one-column heading.

At the first word of the success of the biggest crude-oil well ever drilled in Canada—it blew in at better than one thousand barrels of oil a day—every oil-stained wretch of the Calgary promotional fraternity got high-tailing it back into business. Before the week was out, a dozen of the most prominent were rushing for leases and new incorporation. Phil Byrne, Maynard Davies, Fred Reeves, Bob Wilkinson, Stewart Herron, Herb Greenfield, D. J. Young, W. C. Fisher, and A. H. Mayland were all either on the hunt for potential drill sites or beating back those who had leases and were intent upon prying royalties subscriptions out of them.

The Calgary oil promoters of the 1930s were a different breed from the Toronto share-pushers who were then fleecing the public. The Ontario and Quebec mining prospects which the latter were promoting were essentially vehicles for the promoters' stock-market manipulations. If some of them eventually became producing mines, it was more by accident than by intent. Indeed, most of the eastern mining promotions, even the successful mines, frequently went through three and four capital reorganizations before they reached profitable production. The Calgarians, on the other hand, were oilmen first and promoters second—in the sense that the real pay-off for them all was in the thrill that came when a successful well blew in with a roar that could be heard a mile away. Without exception, they knew the geography of Turner Valley like they knew the path to the bathroom. For every full-time promoter like Phil Byrne and Maynard Davies, there were four or five part-timers like Bob Brown. There was Bill Fisher, who, like half the lawyers in town, was happier swapping lies with oil-rig roughnecks than worrying about the problems of his large legal clientele; there was A. H. Mayland, who ran his big cattle operation with one hand while promoting oil wells and refineries and service stations with the other. There was Bob Wilkinson, the electrical-appliance dealer and oil-company director. There was George Harris, the herbalist bottler of Harris's Wonder Health Restorer. The most prominent of the oil-stained dentists was Dr. L. A. Maxwell, while his opposite number among the medicos was Dr. A. B. Singleton.

Throughout the decade, it would have been easy to make up a baseball team from the oil-company directors who regularly lunched at Kolb and McCaw's Club Café, which many of them regarded as their private club. Of all the promoters who enlivened the premises, none was more popular than Bob Brown, who in another age might well have got rich as a stand-up comic. He was a masterful storyteller and past master of the dialect joke. He was equally at home in an oilfield cook shack and at a formal banquet. As Grant Spratt said, "He was fun to be with. He was the kind of guy for whom, when he came into the Club Café, people would automatically move over to make room at their table. Then they'd sit back and wait for his latest story." To his Club Café cronies, the success of his Turner Valley Royalties well was akin to their all-star centre scoring the winning Stanley Cup goal.

During the week that followed the Turner Valley Royalties' blowing in, the near-moribund Calgary Stock Exchange returned slowly to life. The shares of companies holding royalties on the discovery well crept upward. McDougal-Segur rose from 6 to 12 cents a share; Spooner got from 21 to 25, Calmont from 7 cents a share to 15, and A.P. Con. from 11 cents to 19.

At another time under different circumstances the prices of all the shares on the exchange would have doubled and redoubled. But the economy of Alberta was deeper in the glue in 1936 than it had been in 1934 when TVR was put together. The Aberhart government had defaulted on its bond interest; the city of Calgary was contemplating doing the same; the province was about to launch its funny-money "prosperity certificates" on a passively resistant sea of public opinion. Only the mildly affluent of the city tiptoed into the stock market, and they were so few in number that their impact was minimal. In plain fact, the excitement generated by the gushing wildcat was confined almost exclusively to the Calgary–Turner Valley corridor, for it made not a ripple in any of the outside newspapers on the prairies.

In the Brown family, however, the excitement was beyond containment. Brown's son, Robert, Jr., then a student at the University of Alberta, caught the first train back to Calgary to begin a life-long immersion in the oil business. As soon as the well passed its production testing, and oil was flowing into the storage tanks at the rate of one thousand barrels a day, the elder Brown began laying plans to abandon his city-hall job in favour of becoming a full-time oil promoter. So many things piled up on him, however, that weeks would pass before he could find time to tender his resignation. Of immediate concern was the financing for the drilling of two or more wells on the off-setting acreage he had cannily retained for himself in TVR Ltd. Then he would have to get out to Gleichen to pick up the rest of Baker Brown's quarter-section.

Brown, however, was beaten to Gleichen by the news of his Turner Valley success, and the baker was in no mood to make any more cheap deals. For his remaining twenty acres a quarter of a mile south of TVR No. 1, the baker now wanted ten thousand dollars in cash and a ten-per-cent gross royalty. Promoter Brown gulped, thrashed around, counter-offered, but in the end raised the ten thousand and made the deal. It turned out to be one of the best deals Brown ever made. It might have been one of the worst, because the other wells drilled on the baker's 160 acres within two hundred yards of the Brown wells were both dry holes.

While Brown was commuting between Calgary and Gleichen, negotiating with the baker, John Moyer was rushing through the incorporation of another company—B. and B. Royalties, Ltd., which like TVR had a share capital of twenty thousand shares. Brown transferred the baker's lease into B. and B. Royalties and issued all the company's shares to himself, along with a ten-per-cent net royalty on its production. He then went back to all the backers of his successful wildcat and persuaded them to invest in B. and B. Royalties at only a modest increase in price, as befitted a well located only a quarter-mile from the successful wildcat. This time, A.P. Con. came in for eight one-per-cent units at $2,000 a unit, Calmont increased its participation to ten per cent, McDougal-Segur dropped back to five per cent because it was by now into several other royalty deals, and Vulcan took five per cent, as did two newcomers, Commonwealth and United Oils. Another 18½ units were sold to the public and other companies so that just over one hundred thousand dollars were raised. That left 13½ units in the treasury of the company. As Brown owned all the shares of the company, the result, in effect, was that he emerged with 23½ per cent of the net production from B. and B. Royalties No. 1 in compensation for his efforts to promote the drilling of the well. All this was done without the investment of one dollar of his own money. And it was done in a way that Alex Freeman would have said showed the genius of a super-promoter whose driving energy entitled him to a rich pay-off for his efforts.

B. and B. Royalties blew into production on February 2, 1937, at better than one thousand barrels a day. A year later, the *Western Oil Examiner* reported that the well had returned three thousand dollars on each per-cent unit, and the units were now selling in Calgary brokerage offices for five thousand dollars apiece.

While B. and B. Royalties was drilling, Brown was out busily promoting the development of other leases. The Browns voted themselves farm-outs of the two twenty-acre leases remaining in Turner Valley Royalties, Ltd., and promoted joint-stock companies to develop each. Several others followed in quick order, so that by the end of 1937, the Browns had seven successful wells producing at the rate of seven hundred thousand barrels of oil a year. Yet Brown was hard put to keep ahead of his rival promoters. Phil Byrne had five wells on production and another five drilling. He was also in the process of organizing Anglo-Canadian Oils, which would develop into a thriving Canadian company. Maynard Davies and D. J. Young each had three producers on stream, and there was hardly a surviving company from the 1920s that was not back in business.

The Turner Valley boom was a classic example of money begetting money. Within weeks of the wells coming into production, royalty payments were flowing out to the investing companies and individual royalty owners. And as quickly as it came in, they pushed it back out into more royalty investments. And success followed success as night followed day.

Thus tersely stated, it might be assumed that bringing in successful oil producers was simply a matter of raising money, hiring a driller, and sitting back and waiting for the oil flow to start. And it was almost that good, because the field was struck by two lightning bolts of good fortune, in the shape of a couple of American engineers who arrived in Turner Valley with the onset of the 1937 drilling boom. Their names were Ralph Will and Matt Newell, and before they arrived there had been no guarantee that any well would reach its target depth in less than a year, if it ever did.

During the 1920s boom, Turner Valley rightfully earned the reputation as the crooked-hole capital of the continent. The deeply sloped Turner Valley formations sent drilling bits veering fifteen and twenty degrees off perpendicular. Cable-tool rigs were replaced by rotary rigs to overcome the crooked-hole problem and things got worse instead of better. Weeks stretched into months and, on two occasions, into years, while drilling crews struggled to retrieve bits and pipe from holes. Nothing cooled the enthusiasm of investors like months of no news from their wildcats.

Matt Newell was a Texas engineer who first came to Turner Valley in 1930 as a salesman for the Hughes Tool Company. Turner Valley drilling died in the Depression, and Newell went back to the States and into the contract-drilling business for himself. When word of the Brown discovery reached him in Wyoming in 1936, he loaded up his rigs and headed back for Alberta. Ralph Will had a master's degree in geology from his native Oklahoma and earned a doctorate in drilling-rig problems as a roughneck and tool-pusher in the oilfields of Texas.

On the strength of his completion of his second well in Turner Valley in December of 1936, Phil Byrne persuaded the Oilwell Supply Company to sell him $450,000 worth of drilling rigs on credit so that he could drill his own wells instead of hiring contractors to do the work. For a superintendent for his new venture, Oilwell put him in touch with Ralph Will. When Byrne overcame the language difficulty of trying to communicate with an Oakie from Texas in his own broad Anglo-Irish accent, he persuaded Will to migrate to Turner Valley to run his drilling rigs.

Newell and Will brought with them a world of experience with the crooked-hole formations of the Rocky Mountains. They combined to stand the drilling business on its head. Newell introduced fixed-price bidding on drilling contracts instead of the cost-plus system then in use. Will introduced newly developed techniques to keep holes straight and cut the time needed to complete wells in half. Ralph Will became the Ann Landers of the drilling colony, as the drillers of wells for other companies brought him their problems and took back his solutions. By cutting the cost of drilling in half, Newell and Will dramatically improved the economics of the fledgling industry.

The sharp reduction achieved in the time it took to complete an oil well naturally increased the tempo of the drilling boom in Turner Valley, as it increased the level of activity in the brokerage offices. For all the small investors who had preserved their oil shares from before the crash, things were infinitely better at the end of 1937. Shares in McDougal-Segur rose from 5 cents to 78 cents, in Mercury from 10 to 85, in Okalta from 3 cents to $4.60, in C. and E. from 25 cents to $6.55, and in Vulcan from 10 cents to $3.25. The fact that thousands of dollars were flowing back into the hands of investors in oil royalties was helping to restore confidence in the oil industry as an investment. Many of the newer promotions in Turner Valley sold royalty units for as little as a fiftieth of one per cent, so that persons with fifty dollars invested were getting regular five-dollar-a-month cheques. Several wells were financed by promoters combining royalties with ordinary shares on which regular dividends were paid, based on net production. All these factors combined to send the oil-stock market soaring at the very nadir of the Depression. Business may have been terrible for Calgary's Eighth Avenue merchants, but the hatters, druggists, and haberdashers joined the doctors, lawyers, and dentists in finding ways of diverting what income they had into the oil market.

Within a matter of months after Turner Valley Royalties blew in, there were twenty wells being drilled in Turner Valley, to make it the only boom town in western Canada in 1937. Not only were there two hundred new jobs on the drilling rigs, but the place was overrun with pipe salesmen, truckers, timber jobbers, and equipment suppliers. For Calgary itself, the Depression was over. The long-vacant space in the Eighth Avenue office buildings between the Lancaster Building and the Burns Block quickly filled with oil-company promoters and royalty brokers. The anterooms of the doctors' and dentists' offices in the Southam Building frequently contained more royalty salesmen than patients, and the hinterlands were overrun by bird-dogging lease brokers seeking to locate mineral-lease owners who could be persuaded to part with their leases.

In the vortex of this storm of activity was a whirling dynamo of royalty promotion who, more than any other, was responsible for putting oil royalties into nation-wide orbit. He was a pint-sized insurance broker from Regina, Clifton C. Cross. In late January 1936, he had travelled to Calgary from Regina in an effort to collect some long-overdue accounts from his sub-agents. The excursion had been only partly successful when, just as he was checking out of the Palliser Hotel, he was embraced by George Bell. Though in failing health, Bell was none the less bubbling with enthusiasm about his Turner Valley Royalties well, which was then approaching the limestone. He was even more enthusiastic about the royalty system of well financing, and, before Cross escaped from Bell's clutches, he had parted with a cheque for five hundred dollars as a down-payment on a one-per-cent royalty. Six months later Cross was back in Calgary en route to Turner Valley, where he became permanently infected with the oil bug. He converted his Regina insurance agency into an oil-royalty agency, and moved to Calgary to open a permanent headquarters. Within months he had opened offices in Winnipeg, Saskatoon, and Vancouver, and was leasing space in Toronto, Ottawa, Montreal, and London, Ontario. In his spare time he had set up his own oil company and was preparing to drill on a forty-acre lease in Turner Valley.

Thanks to the efforts of Cliff Cross and Phil Byrne, the master salesman-promoter-developer, and the unbroken string of successful wells, the demand for oil royalties soon began to exceed the supply. As a market, the trade in oil royalties was complete anarchy. The price at which they traded depended mainly on the whim or the forbearance of the brokers. The brokers did not act as go-betweens for sellers and buyers. They bought and sold on their own account. Thus, in Winnipeg or Vancouver on a given day, a prospective purchaser conceivably could have been offered a one-per-cent interest in a producing well at three different prices. Or he might have been offered three or four separate kinds of royalties. There were gross royalties, which entitled the holder to a percentage of all production; preferred royalties, which entitled the holder to a percentage of all the royalties until the original purchase price was repaid; deferred royalties, which entitled the holder to start collecting after the preferred royalties had been paid out. There were simple net royalties, which paid what was left after gross royalties and expenses were deducted.

It was along about here that two clouds spelling disaster began their ascent above the horizon. The first was success. The second was the arbitrary decision of the Ottawa bureaucracy to tax oil royalties in the hands of the producing companies as if they were corporate profits.

The success rate of the Turner Valley drillers was phenomenal. In the two years after TVR, sixty-nine wells were drilled and only two were dry and abandoned. Of the thirty-five wells drilled in 1937, only one was a dry hole. By the middle of 1938, production had so far outstripped demand that most of the wells were able to produce at only forty per cent of their rated capacities. At the same time, the government of Alberta brought in its first Oil and Gas Conservation Board, which was charged with ending the wastage of gas in Turner Valley.

For fourteen years, the practice had been to extract the natural-gas liquids from the wet natural gas and burn the dry gas in flare pits. As a result, billions of cubic feet of natural gas were wasted, and the wastage drained the reservoir of the pressure that would be needed to produce the oil that was in place. The board ended drilling on twenty-acre leases by establishing forty acres as the minimum spacing unit. It established a system of pro-rating production of all wells to what the market could absorb. In effect, the board brought some scientific regulation into an area where anarchy had reigned. But it could do little to increase the demand for petroleum products. Nor could it do anything to prevent the completion of forty-odd wells that had been spudded in 1938 before the glut developed and would increase the surplus.

However, a better crop in 1938 and the closure of the BA refinery at Coutts with the opening of its larger facility in Calgary did help. Freight-rate reductions enabled Alberta crude to be shipped to Saskatchewan refineries, which developed product markets in Manitoba.

Just as a slight improvement became apparent, however, the government in Ottawa dropped the other shoe. It ordered that the income from oil production had to be taxed as profits in the hands of the producing company before being passed on to the royalty owners. Coming as it did at a time of reduced production coupled with lower crude prices, the government action severely shook public confidence in royalties. Confidence was restored briefly, however, when B. and B. Royalties challenged the order in the Exchequer Court and won. By then the war was on, and the country needed all the oil Turner Valley could produce, to meet civilian requirements and to fuel the rapidly expanding British Commonwealth Air Training Plan.

By this time, too, something new had been added to Turner Valley. Jim Lowery, the president of Home Oil Company, had come scurrying back to the valley with the discovery of Turner Valley Royalties, only to discover that most of the best acreage in the south end of the field had been taken up. And anyway, the way things were being done did not appeal to Lowery. Too many wells were being drilled by promoters whose land holdings were limited to the forty-acre lease on which they were drilling. Their successful wells proved up all the surrounding acreage owned by other people. Lowery was the first Canadian with an international-oil-company outlook. The name of their oil-exploration game has always been extensive land holdings: if oil is discovered, the discoverer already owns all the surrounding drill sites.

Lowery got together with Charles Dingman, the professional geologist who had drilled the first well in Turner Valley. Dingman pointed to the Model well as an indication of oil in the limestone at the north end of Turner Valley and pointed to a site he would select for a wildcat. Lowery went on a leasing spree and wound up with more than seven thousand acres before he took Dingman's advice and drilled the Home-Millarville No. 2 wildcat. That well came into production at two thousand barrels a day in January 1939, stayed on production for twenty-five years, and produced two million barrels of oil and four billion feet of gas. Home went on to drill over forty successful wells in the north end of Turner Valley and became Canada's most important independent oil producer. Charlie Dingman, who neglected to get an overriding royalty in writing on the discovery well, ended with nothing.

The increased demand for oil caused by the war, combined with the Home Oil discovery, restored public confidence. Oil royalties again sold readily above their issuing prices. They were particularly attractive to the unsophisticated investors. Royalties which had sold originally for $1,500 to $2,500 per one per cent sold readily at $5,000 once the wells were on production. At $5,000 and paying $150 a month, it was by far the best return available anywhere in the country, if one assumed it could go on paying $150 a month forever. Unhappily, production tended to drop off rather sharply with the aging of the wells, so royalty income declined over the years. The income reaching royalty owners also diminished as the promoters became more exacting about the management and administration of the field operations.

To sweeten the deal for new issues, Cliff Cross in 1941 came up with the preferred-royalties idea, which allocated all production to the investors until the investment was recovered. Preferred royalties sold for four or five times the price charged for net royalties on the same well. Cross financed nine wells by this method. In the majority of the later wells, the preferred-royalty holders got their money back, but the net-royalty owners seldom earned bank interest on their investments and many actually lost most of what they had put in.

Oil royalties unquestionably served a useful purpose in restoring public confidence in oil development, but they ran counter to everything oil-company promoters held sacred. The fundamental concept of the promoters was that the purpose of an oil well was to provide money with which to drill more oil wells to provide more money to drill more oil wells, ad infinitum. It was not for the purpose of returning the income from production to the people who had financed the drilling of the wells. Only the joint-stock company lent itself to the use of the cash flow from a successful well for drilling more wells.

But would it not have been possible, given the success of the royalty system, when nothing else would work at the depth of the Depression, to modify both systems to achieve both ends? To provide the investing public with the confidence-creating kind of returns they got from royalties, and to finance on-going development at the same time? Was there not a clue to an ideal system—from the investors' point of view (though hardly from the promoters')—in Turner Valley Royalties, Ltd.? There were three drill sites on its original sixty-acre lease. Could not part of the income from its first well have been used to drill the second well? and part of the income from the second to drill the third? and thus reduce the promotional bite extracted from the very top of the income?

Nobody had time to pursue such questions for long, because in 1952 the Ottawa bureaucracy, stung by the reversal of their attempts to tax oil royalties before distribution, persuaded the government to amend the Income Tax Act. Thereafter, oil income of the royalty trusts became fully taxable at confiscatory wartime rates. And that was the end of the oil-royalty system, as it was a discouragement to investment in the oil industry. The value of the shares in the companies that had pioneered royalties dropped back to where they had been before royalties were invented. Calmont, which sold for $1.84 in 1938, was back to 10 cents in 1942; Vulcan dropped from $3.05 to 8½ cents; A.P. Con. was down from $1.69 to 10 cents; McDougal-Segur was back to 7 cents and Spooner to 3 cents. Even Royalite, the blue-chip of Turner Valley and an Imperial Oil subsidiary, was down from sixty dollars to sixteen.

Eventually the government tacitly admitted its error and in 1950 repealed the pre-distribution tax on royalties. But by then the harm was done. And by then the map of Alberta was plastered with international-oil-company reservations of drilling rights. Canadian small-fry companies trying to elbow their way into the oil business had to be satisfied with scraps from the international companies' tables. The promoters of all the lesser companies were back in business at the old stands with joint-stock companies.

4
Noblesse Oblige –
What the Hell Is That?

Two more unlikely salary negotiators for the *Free Press* newsroom
than John Sweeney and James Gray would have been difficult to
imagine. In asking for a pay raise, we were presuming to speak for
the entire staff, dayside and nightside, but in plain truth we were
authorized to speak only for ourselves and three or four other
reporters. That we were leading from weakness would have become instantly apparent to Victor Sifton had he chosen to cross-
examine us at the conclusion of our presentation on that day in the
early summer of 1937. Compared with us, Oliver Twist, in his
celebrated porridge confrontation, was akin to the leader of a
Roman legion exacting tribute. Instead of questioning our bona
fides, however, Sifton took our word that we were speaking on
behalf of the staff. In fact we were, though five-sixths of the staff
were unaware we were doing it.

John Sweeney was the son of the former business manager of
the *Free Press*. The elder Sweeney had lately been shipped off to
Regina to run the *Leader-Post*, the first of a number of personnel
shuffles which came after Victor Sifton arrived in Winnipeg from
Regina to take charge of the Sifton newspaper and radio empire.
That empire included three daily newspapers, three radio stations,
and that money-printer to end all profit-makers, the *Free Press
Prairie Farmer*. The younger Sweeney was the ablest reporter on
the *Free Press* staff, perhaps one of the ablest in the country. He
could cover any story assigned to him with accuracy and dispatch.

Then in his twenties, Sweeney had been the resident *Free Press*
correspondent in the Chicago bureau of the United Press, where
his job had been to scan the massive flow of news into that bureau
in search for anything with a western-Canadian angle, and to
summarize and refile it to Winnipeg. In 1931 he returned to Winnipeg to get married, and expected to return to Chicago to take a
full-time job with United Press at almost double what the *Free
Press* had been paying him. It was his bad luck to have chosen an
English-born bride who had come to Canada as a babe in arms.

Because of his bride's English birth, the couple was barred from the United States at the border by the minions of the United States Immigration Service, who, in 1931, were interpreting their restrictive-entry regulations with utmost severity. The experience later placed uncommon strains upon Sweeney's marriage and opened a suppurating wound on the surface of his pride. By 1937, his friends in the United Press bureau were covering wars in Spain and China, coronations in England, and the goings-on in American prize rings and baseball stadia. And Sweeney was stuck in Winnipeg.

The malcontented Sweeney would have been a logical member of any negotiating committee. Logic played no part in my being a member, for I was one of the most junior members of the staff in point of service. From a fifteen-dollar-a-week job as a board-marker *cum* security analyst for a local stock broker, I had achieved a twenty-dollar-a-week reporter's berth on the *Free Press* in 1935. In the summer of 1937 I was still so thankful to have a job of any kind, and particularly a writing job, that I was reluctant to jeopardize it by becoming involved. Besides, I had received a raise to twenty-five dollars a week the year before and hence stood apart from most of the rest of the staff, who had been without raises of any kind since the onset of the Depression. Like everybody else in western Canada, the staff of the *Free Press* had been afflicted with a ten-per-cent wage cut in 1931, and six years later the cut was still in force. The pitch Sweeney and I decided to make was that economic conditions had improved enough to justify rescinding the cut; that the profitability of the *Free Press* operation had improved sufficiently for it to be able to afford the increase. And for ourselves, we proposed to argue that the *Free Press* pay scale for reporters, when compared with that of the printers, was submarginal impoverished.

The economic climate in Winnipeg in the summer of 1937, as it was perceived by those of us who had jobs, was much improved over anything we had seen in recent years. A bumper crop was ripening on the Portage Plains and the price of wheat was twenty-five cents a bushel higher than it had been the year before. As everyone in Winnipeg knew, a good wheat crop and a profitable price spelled Prosperity with a capital P for Winnipeg. Of the worst crop disaster in Canadian history, being fashioned at that moment by the weather in the Palliser Triangle, we had only the vaguest awareness. Now and then a dispatch from Regina found its way into our inside pages, but the Winnipeg newspapers were far more interested in news from Europe, the United States, and Ottawa than in grasshoppers and drought in Saskatchewan.

For us, the searing heat that was destroying Saskatchewan and setting temperature records across the West evoked only an urge to try to fry eggs on the sidewalk, as an ingredient for a photo-feature story. It also sent the business and professional classes of Calgary, Edmonton, and Winnipeg hurtling out to golf courses and lakeside cabins when temperatures nudged the hundred-degree mark.

Elsewhere in Canada, 1937 promised to be the best year since 1929. Thanks to the higher tariffs and British preferences of the Bennett government, which the Grits had done nothing to dismantle, the Depression was clearly over in Ontario and Quebec. The auto assembly lines, electrical branchplants, and textile sweat-shops of both provinces were back in full operation. Roosevelt's revaluation of gold to thirty-five dollars an ounce from twenty not only created a king-sized mining boom in the hinterlands, it set off an out-of-control orgy in mining-stock promotion in Toronto and Montreal, reminiscent of 1929.

In the United States, the massive expenditures of the Roosevelt New Deal and the action taken to get rid of surplus farm production were being reflected in improvements in both employment and farm prices. Wages were still hovering around Depression lows but, under the shelter of Roosevelt's federal labour legislation, a new militancy was developing within the moribund, boss-ridden American labour movement.

John L. Lewis's Committee for Industrial Organization had broken away from the American Federation of Labor and was out organizing the millions of unorganized mass-production workers into militant unions. That was the year indeed in which the militancy of the United States labour movement reached its all-time peak, thanks to the spreading epidemic of "sit-down" strikes. The strikes drew their title from a spontaneous action in the huge Akron, Ohio, plant of the Goodyear Rubber Company in November 1935. Angered by the refusal of the company to deal with their union, a thousand production workers simply downed their tools, shut off their machines, stopped work, sat down at their machines, and refused to leave the plant. This spontaneous gesture, which quickly captured the imagination of mass-production workers all over the States, became the most effective of all strike tactics. The following year its use spread to hundreds of production centres across the country and in 1937, Lewis, Walter Reuther, and Dick Frankinstein used the sit-down strike to attack that giant of American industrial giants, General Motors itself. CIO sit-downers took over General Motors' plants throughout Michigan and, after a two-months struggle, General Motors capitulated. After General Motors came Chrysler, Hudson, Studebaker, and Packard, and the gigantic United States Steel Corporation caved in almost without a struggle.

But struggles there were aplenty in other plants across the United States. The police in Chicago charged into the Republic Steel picket lines with guns blazing, killing ten strikers and wounding more than a score. So violent did things become across the U.S. in 1937 that President Roosevelt, whose National Labor Relations Act tilted the scales well over in labour's favour, felt constrained to chastise both the unions and the bosses with his "plague on both your houses" criticism of the serious threats their strikes and lockouts posed to American economic recovery.

Fresh from their victories in the American auto, rubber, textile, and steel industries, CIO organizers quickly filtered across the border into Canada to mastermind the unionizing activities of Canadian mass-production workers. Textile plants in Quebec and Ontario, along with automobile assembly plants in Oshawa and Windsor, went out on strike. The invasion of American organizers and a modicum of picket-line violence set off a long-distance shouting match between Toronto and Ottawa. Ontario Premier Mitch Hepburn demanded that Ottawa arrest and deport the foreign agitators. When Ottawa refused to act, Hepburn launched his own war of words against the CIO. First he went stumping through the Ontario onion patches. Then he turfed out a couple of his most senior cabinet ministers, Arthur Roebuck, the attorney general, and David Croll, the Minister of Labour. Finally, he called a fall election against the bemused and baffled Tories, who found themselves bloodied by Hepburn's anti-labour blitzkrieg. But the CIO organized the automobile, electrical, and steel industries, and added insult to injury for Hepburn by daring to take on his particular sacred cow, the northern mining industry.

All these changes in the economic climate filtered through to us on the *Free Press*, but the filtering process meant that we got the news in snippets instead of the columns they rated elsewhere. However, the strike stories from afar were augmented occasionally by developments closer to home. The garment workers in Winnipeg were being organized and obtaining contracts. Employees of the huge Hudson Bay Mining and Smelting operation at Flin Flon went on strike. What was happening in 1937 was simply that the delayed-action militancy of desperation was becoming a factor of North American life which kept elbowing its way on to the front pages. An economic system that had ground its workers into an intolerable environment was in the grips of an intolerable reaction. Ironically, it was a reaction that came not at the bottom of the Depression, but at a time when substantial progress had been made on the road to recovery.

In Winnipeg, as in every other western community, the signs that the Depression was easing locally were hen's-teeth scarce, but an assiduous search by a patient explorer would turn them up none the less, even as prairie cities bounced from financial crisis to financial crisis like marbles in a pinball machine. The National Housing Act, which offered twenty-year, four-per-cent mortgages to new home builders, was beginning to nibble at the edge of the pall that had engulfed the house-building industry. Winnipeg that summer could proudly record that eighty new houses had gone under construction, though a grand total of thirty thousand building lots had gone back to the city for taxes and more lots were being taken for taxes than were being sold. The city was still wrestling with the problem of the influx of destitute rural families seeking to get on to the city's unemployment-relief rolls. In 1937, however, the number of families on relief was down to 4,000, a decline of 1,000 from 1936 and 2,500 from the peak of 1933. At the very least, the cloud of utter resignation was beginning to lift.

Civic employees and provincial civil servants had stopped quaking in fear of losing their jobs and had begun to agitate with increased vigour for the restoration of their pay cuts. Both had suffered two cuts which brought their pay levels to eighty-three to eighty-five per cent of the pre-Depression levels. Both governments were sympathetic, but pleaded empty treasuries and did nothing. The railway workers had better luck. A conciliation board gave them back their 1931 cuts of ten per cent, at one per cent every other month over the next year and a half.

The movement to appeal to Sifton for the restoration of the *Free Press* pay cut began as casual conversation as we sat around the newsroom after the paper had gone to press. Somebody would glance up from reading to note that somebody had got a wage increase or a cut restored. That led to the inevitable, "Hey, I wonder when we're going to get our cut back." Ultimately, the talk got around to forming a committee to ask the publisher point blank to restore the cut. That ·was followed by a lot of futile talk and scurrying around trying to lasso a couple of people willing to be members of the committee. John Sweeney ultimately yielded to the arm-twisting, provided Burt Gresham or I would go with him. Gresham and I both begged off. I was on unemployment relief when the 1931 cut was made and would be there for another two years. So how could I argue for restoration of a pay cut I had never suffered?

Such objections were waved aside by my persuasive colleagues. "Look, Jimmy," they said, "what you get paid has to be related to what the rest of us get paid. But what the hell. What's important is this—you can talk to Mr. Sifton on a first-name basis. You're one of his boys because he hired you in the first place. Nothing's going to happen to you. All that can happen to you is he'll say no. But who knows what his reaction may be to the rest of us?"

Victor Sifton had come down from Regina, the year before I was hired, to take over as publisher of the *Free Press* on the death of his brother, John. In fact, John Sifton had never been more than a free-loading supernumerary on the *Free Press* payroll. The presiding genius in all matters commercial was Edward H. Macklin, a boozing, goateed penny-pincher who had built the paper from near-bankruptcy to impregnable affluence. By 1934, however, Macklin was rapidly descending into old age, and a lifetime addiction to Scotch whiskey was taking its inevitable toll. When a chance to retire him presented itself, the Sifton brothers seized it with alacrity. To replace Macklin and his key people, and he replaced them all, Sifton brought in the top personnel who had run the *Leader-Post* for him in Regina. He transplanted William Lord, his business manager, Percy Keffer, his chief accountant, and Jack Owen, his stable manager, horse trainer, and mechanical superintendent.

In some curious way I was thought by several of my fellow reporters to be a member of what in later years would probably have been called the Regina Mafia. The new brooms Sifton was bringing in from Regina were beginning to move the dust of generations around. The building superintendent was fired after forty years' service. The aged head janitor was handed a broom and told to start sweeping. Winds of change blew with such force through the garage, the business office, and the composing room that the newsroom became understandably jittery. It was not until much later that we learned that it had taken the combined efforts of Dafoe and Ferguson to dissuade Sifton from moving in on the newsroom staff as well.

After a short stint on the night staff, I had been transferred to the dayside, where I quickly drew assignments covering a royal commission and a couple of murder trials, and did part-time coverage of the city hall, the police beat, and the legislature. At the end of six months I was an experienced reporter capable of handling any assignment, at least in my own eyes.

But in the eyes of my fellow workers, I was a big question mark. Was I what I claimed to be, or was I a Victor Sifton stool-pigeon? As time passed, the impact of Sifton's new brooms became heavier, and closer to home, when a couple of copy editors were brought down from Regina. Despite my protestations that I had never worked in Regina, had never met Victor Sifton until I was hired by Dafoe, the impression would not die down that I was an old Sifton hand. A couple of the newsroom drunks, suffering the Monday-morning miseries, would sidle up to me with a whispered question. "Look Jimmy, give me the straight dope, will you? Straight dope, now. What does Victor Sifton think of my work?"

It did no good to plead ignorance, and my denials were hardly reinforced by Victor himself. Like most one-eyed people, he walked with his head tilted slightly to the side so that his good eye took in a wider field of vision directly in front of him. The effect, of course, was to reduce his lateral field of vision on one side; as a result, he would frequently pass people without seeing them.

If he did see them, all they got from him was an unrecognizing nod, for he had a sort of intake impediment where names were concerned. Then, too, he was a stern-visaged six-footer who strode through the newsroom rather than sauntered. Understandably, the staff oldsters came to regard him as a stuck-up martinet, particularly when echoes of the horror stories from the other departments kept reverberating through the newsroom.

The fact that I had accepted his twenty dollars a week in preference to George McCullagh's fifty certainly made a permanent impression on Victor. So when he encountered me, he remembered me and he'd stop and exchange a pleasantry or two. He'd ask what I was doing and was I enjoying it. And at some time I had taken to calling him by his first name, a fact that impressed my colleagues beyond anything else because nobody except George Ferguson ever called him Victor.

My image as a Sifton crony was capped by the appearance in Winnipeg of Victor's brother, Clifford, on one of his whirlwind visits. Clifford spent his time in the Siftons' Armadale Corporation counting house in Toronto. Out of it he would explode periodically with ideas for editorial campaigns. He had heard of me and my interest in exposing mining-stock frauds, and on one of his early visits to Winnipeg, Victor brought him out to my desk and introduced us. He was loaded with inside dope about stock frauds that had been supplied by his bosom pal, George Drew, who would later become leader of the Conservative party. Drew had been the Securities Commissioner for Ontario, and he was one of the first Tory bureaucrats fired when Mitchell Hepburn defeated the Conservative government of George Henry in 1934.

While biding his time until the Tories returned to power, Drew was running an undermining campaign against my friend John

Godfrey, who succeeded him. He was collecting dossiers on the frauds Godfrey was allegedly neglecting to suppress, and Uncle Clifford was eager to apprise me of the situation in Toronto so that I could write some articles attacking Godfrey. I listened and tried to take notes. The listening, by itself, was an experience unique in forty years of journalism.

Clifford Sifton had emerged from the First World War with a tic, the wildest tic I have seen or could discover in a day's search. As the encyclopedias notice, the word comes from the French *tique*, meaning twitching. Clifford's tic compared to twitching the way a lightning bolt compares to a fire-cracker. Ordinary tics affect only one part of the body and cause involuntary movements which the sufferer cannot resist. Clifford's tic affected his arms, neck, head, nostrils, throat, and occasionally a leg. He could not sit still and his body went through a whole series of repetitive contortions. He would half explode out of his chair, fling his right arm in the air like a boxer countering a feint, twist his head up and down, snort loudly, click his throat, grimace, and all the while talk a blue streak. No man alive could concentrate on what he was saying while his body was wracked by these violent tics. But I tried, and as I tried I became aware that the entire newsroom had stopped work and was staring at Clifford. As I stole a glance around, I caught a look of baffled wonderment on everyone's face. Suddenly I realized that I was blushing in embarrassment over Sifton's tic while he seemed completely unaware of his bodily movements. After an hour of unbroken listening, I blurted out an excuse about another assignment and made my escape. But only temporarily. He was back again that day, and the next, for repeat performances.

To my suspicious colleagues, the evidence that I was a Sifton protégé must have seemed incontestable. And it mounted steadily with developments that had nothing to do with my seeming cosiness with the owners. The assignments prized most highly by newspaper reporters are those which take the reporters out of town on expense accounts, even though *Free Press* expense allowances seldom permitted more than a *soupçon* of high living. In short order I drew more outside assignments than the rest of the news staff combined. I was sent on a tour of American cities to explore the traffic-safety programs of various police departments, and to write a series of articles on slum-clearance programs and housing developments. After several minor junkets, I had ten days in Toronto researching a series of articles on stock frauds. Ordinary expectations were that these assignments would have gone to the police reporter, the city-hall reporter, and the financial editor. That they all went to one of the newest members of the staff was indicative of something pretty suspicious. On the evidence, I would have been pretty suspicious myself.

The misgivings, fortunately and just as fortuitously, were counter-balanced in part by a snarling match I got into one morning with Albert Edward Hector Coo, the iron-fisted news editor. It followed a deflating discovery, and I made it slowly, that the life of a newspaper reporter in Winnipeg most of the time was about as exciting as the life of an elevator man or a men's-room attendant. Between the covering of murder trials or bank hold-ups, there were long periods of puttering around on trivia. After days of boredom, a reporter would jump at a chance to cover a Masonic convention, a caterers' picnic, or the annual meeting of the Young Men's Section of the Board of Trade.

It had always been my ambition to write my way on to the editorial-page staff of the *Free Press*, to function in the realm of ideas instead of straight news-reporting. To combat the boredom of the newsroom, I took to writing "think pieces" for the editorial page and several of them were published. One day one of these pieces was published over my initials, and when Abbie Coo saw it he exploded. Ordinarily, Coo's favourite spot for chastising a delinquent reporter, copy reader, or sub-editor was the midway point on the circular iron staircase that connected the fourth-floor newsroom with the fifth-floor composing room. It always seemed to the news staff that Coo's basis for assessing the worth of a story was the way the *Tribune* handled it. If the *Tribune* gave front-page play to something the *Free Press* had buried on page twelve, he would come storming down the iron stairway clutching the *Tribune*. Halfway down he would stop, lean over the railing, and let fly with a storm of criticism of everybody involved, by name, and in drill-sergeants' invective.

My chastisement, however, came full throttle, with Coo standing at his desk with his foot planted on the seat of his chair. I had committed the unforgivable sin of bypassing his desk with the editorial-page article. His invective raised such blisters on my psyche that I must have looked like a cornered rabbit. On one point, however, I was being unjustly accused, and when he paused for breath I broke in:

"God damn it, Abbie," I interjected, "I did hand that piece in to your desk! It was lying around on your desk for a week. I just assumed you weren't interested in it so I turned it over to George Ferguson." That made him even angrier.

"Who the hell are you to decide what I am interested in and not interested in? And who gave you the right to go pawing around on my desk?" I slumped into my seat in a mild panic for fear that the finish of the episode would be an order to get the hell out of the newsroom and off his staff.

It never came. What did happen was that the Sifton-protégé image started to fade, for it was highly unlikely that Abbie Coo would have subjected one of the publisher's favourites to any such verbal chastisement. In any event, when the notion of actually going after the paper for restoration of the pay cuts began to harden, so did the pressure on me to be part of the delegation. It is likely, however, that nothing but talk would have come from these agitations, had it not been for two other developments.

The first was the birth and squalling growth of the American Newspaper Guild, which was founded in 1933 by Heywood Broun and was becoming a power in the editorial rooms of American newspapers by 1937. We followed its progress in the columns of *Editor and Publisher*, and occasionally somebody would come up with a copy of the union paper, the *Guildsman*. We talked about the guild frequently, but the talk was strictly academic. There was no way in which a guild chapter could be organized on the Winnipeg papers, which were so overloaded with greying holdovers from the Great War era. Whenever we counted noses, we seldom reached the dozen mark before we were out of prospective companions for a tiger hunt against the publishers of the *Free Press* and the *Tribune*. But whenever the guild won new contracts at double our wage rates, we glowed vicariously with the guildsmen.

As important as the guild's existence, perhaps more so, was the announcement that the composing rooms of both papers had signed a new five-year contract that called for an eighty-seven-cent-per-hour wage for a forty-six-hour week. That agreement, though it gave no raise to the printers, signalled the definite end of the wage-cut era. Why else would the publishers have tied themselves to a fixed wage rate over five years? But that wasn't the main significance of the agreement to us. It was the arithmetic. When we did the arithmetic, it came out to forty dollars a week, and forty dollars a week was more than either paper paid reporters or deskmen. Nothing burred a reporter's ego more than the fact that the printers traditionally were paid higher wages than reporters or copy editors. There wasn't a reporter alive who was not convinced he was twice as smart as the smartest printer, that his contribution to the success of a newspaper was equal to that of a dozen printers. Somehow or other it was the printers' wage agreement that nudged us into action, though the nudge was not strong enough to head us in the direction of Victor Sifton's door. Instead, we decided to take our request to George Ferguson, in the hope that he would carry the ball for us to Sifton. We watched until we saw Ferguson in a cheerful mood and moved in with our presentation. As a presentation it lacked everything—cohesion, organization, and well-marshalled argument. And we never got halfway through what we wanted to say.

"Hold on, boys," Ferguson interrupted, "because you're in the wrong church. This baby of yours belongs smack on Victor's doorstep. If you want to take aim at the owners, let me know and I'll set up a date for you. I'll even come in and listen to your pitch. But a general raise is out of my ballpark completely." As we were leaving after agreeing to take the case to Sifton, Ferguson called us back.

"Two things," he said. "First, Jimmy, I don't think you should be involved in this at all. You weren't here when the pay cut was called for and it seems to me for you to be involved in the argument weakens your case. Still, I guess your pay is affected by the pay cut. Anyway, you fellows decide. But before you go to talk to Victor, go off in a corner and practise your speeches. For Christ's sake, get your arguments down pat because you are all over the yard like a deconstipated cow. The hell with generalities about the economy. Get the case down to nuts and bolts. It probably won't drag any money out of Victor but you'll sound a hell of a lot better doing it."

Ordinarily there was an Olympian aloofness to Ferguson as managing editor that discouraged familiarity on the part of the news staff. When he had reason to communicate with a reporter, he "went through channels" and did it through Abbie Coo. In my two years in the newsroom I hadn't exchanged half a dozen sentences with him. What impressed us, and completely surprised Sweeney and me, was his down-to-earth approachability and the goodwill he evinced towards our project. As we went off to a quiet corner of the library to take his advice, we were buoyed up with the conviction that his friendly attitude was indeed a happy augury.

Sweeney and I eventually came up with a three-pronged argument. Our first was based on a highly optimistic survey that the *Free Press* advertising department had recently concocted to impress national advertisers with the wisdom of increasing their budget allocation for the *Free Press* and the *Prairie Farmer*. The second point was that *Free Press* advertising was running far ahead of what it had been in 1931 when the pay cut had been made. Instead of the 20- and 22-page papers of 1931 and 1932, we were publishing 28 and 30 pages most days and up to 44 pages on Saturdays. After working for an hour getting both of these cases down letter-perfect, we turned to what Ferguson called nuts and bolts. Our basic argument was quite simply that we all needed more money; we were worth more money if the printers were worth forty dollars a week, and it was in Victor's interest to pay us more money.

Excluding senior editors, we compiled a list of the reporters and deskmen on both night and day shifts of the paper. There were four night reporters, ten day reporters, four sports writers, seven copy editors, a couple of photographers, and half a dozen peripheral personnel. We did an audit on these thirty people and came up with these figures: The paper paid for the phones for three reporters and shared the cost for three others. Out of all the rest, only four had telephones in their homes. Of the reporters, sports writers, and deskmen, only one of the twenty-seven owned a car. That was Burt Gresham, a reporter-photographer who had a special deal that enabled him to claim the cost of the gas he used on assignment.

We did a survey of the wearing apparel of the reporters and sports writers, and found that only a third of us had a change of suits to wear to work. Some had second suits, but they were "good" suits kept for special occasions. When our everyday suits wore out, we switched to the good suits and started saving up for a replacement. Most of us kept ourselves reasonably presentable by always buying two-pants suits. When it came to shelter, only the very oldest employees lived in homes they owned or were buying, even though houses were going begging on the market for a few hundred dollars down and rent-sized monthly payments.

Whatever the impact this survey would have on Victor, it had a shattering effect on John and me. What the hell kind of a trade was this that could not provide us with a living that included a telephone or a change of working clothes, much less a decent house or a car? Christ! We'd be better off as—and we rattled off words like city-hall clerks, stenographers, firemen, policemen, streetcar conductors. We, of course, would not have been much better off. But that did not stop us from feeling both sorry for ourselves and convinced that our case for a raise was even stronger than we had imagined it to be.

Victor Sifton in 1937 was ensconced in a makeshift office near the one occupied by J. W. Dafoe. It was everything a modern executive suite was not—linoleumed rather than carpeted, austere to a point well beyond plainness, nondescriptly furnished. An office, in short, that one might have expected of a briefless lawyer or a down-on-his-luck auctioneer rather than the multi-millionaire owner of a million-a-year profit-making enterprise. He greeted us warmly when we entered, waved us to a couple of chairs at his desk front, pushed an ashtray towards us, and offered cigarettes from his package of Millbanks, which we declined in favour of our own brands. Mine was Philip Morris and John's was Buckingham. So we laughed about smoking idiosyncrasies.

"Well," Sifton said at length, "George tells me you want to talk about a raise in pay. That's something we are all concerned with these days so let's get on with it." His manner was friendly and he seemed in a receptive-enough mood. At least we had not been fired on the spot for bringing up the subject. So we got on with it. I led off with a re-hash of the advertising department's promotion figures. Sweeney came on with his recollection of the rationale for the pay cuts and how times for the paper had improved. Then we both went to work on the borderline of poverty at which we lived, and I concluded with a strong pitch that we represented the *Free Press* wherever we went. We had no identity of our own in many cases; we were "the *Free Press* reporter" to the citizens, politicians, businessmen, and community leaders with whom we came in daily contact. At the very least we should be paid enough to be able to meet the public on common ground.

Sifton clasped his fingers behind his neck, and stretched as he leaned far back in his chair. After gazing at the ceiling for what seemed like minutes, he suddenly relaxed, dropped his hands to the desk top, and cleared his throat.

"Jimmy and John, I think you should be congratulated on the way you have made your case. It's a very good case, even though I would disagree quite strongly with you on a couple of matters of principle. One of you said that the time was ripe for a change in public attitude toward wages, and that the *Free Press*, which was recognized as the leader of our community, should give leadership in this regard to the business community. Well, I completely reject that advice. The decisions that businessmen make in regard to wages and salaries, and indeed in all other things, must be based upon their own self-interest. We must become involved only when the serving of self-interest comes into conflict with the public interest. We must be vigilant to guard the public interest and to speak out strongly when we see the public interest being abused." He was soon wandering so far afield that we began to fidget.

"But enough of this," he said at last. "Look, give me a couple of days because this is not at all as simple as it may look to you. I'll get out our editorial budget and see how it relates to the mechanical and business departments. I've got a couple of ideas I'd like to test out. Let me do that and we'll talk some more and see what we can work out."

It was an infinitely more favourable reception than we had expected. We began to take our leave with rising expectations, which were heightened still further when he stopped us at the door. "Oh, by the way, we usually have tea about this time. Would you join me in a cup of tea?" We would indeed, and spent the next thirty minutes in pleasurable small-talk as remote as the moon from the subject at hand.

A couple of days later, when Sweeney and I returned from afternoon coffee, Abbie Coo called us over. "Victor Sifton sent word out just now that he wants to see you two. What the hell is going on? What's he want to see you about, anyway?" Coo was angrier than he was curious about why two of his minions were consorting with the owner. Sweeney improved his mood not at all when he replied, "Don't worry about it, Abbie, we're just trying to get you a raise in pay!"

Again our reception from Sifton was as friendly as it could have been, and as he ploughed his way through his long wind-up, we began to be convinced that we were going to get something when he got down to the final offering.

"Let me start by saying that I was quite happy when you raised the question of newsroom salaries at this time because it is a subject that has given me some cause for concern. It seemed to me that our best people, those of you who are carrying the main load, have been inadequately rewarded in comparison to those who contribute much less. But before I go into that, I must deal with your over-all request that the pay cut of 1931 should be restored. I am afraid that is impossible for a number of reasons which may not concern you. That pay cut, I believe, only brought *Free Press* wages into line with those paid for similar work in Winnipeg. So far as I can learn, our wages are still in line or even somewhat higher than the city average. Our wages for our unskilled workers are certainly well above the minimum-wage level. Our business office and circulation wages are equal to what other firms are paying for similar jobs.

"You must agree that we cannot raise the fourth-floor wages without doing the same for our business office. And if we do it for the pressmen we will have to raise the wages of the printers, and that's a problem because we've just signed a long-term contract with them.

"Now let me get back to the newsroom. Even though our wage rates over the years might not have been as high as those paid elsewhere, the *Free Press* is proud indeed of the way in which we have otherwise taken care of our employees. Perhaps we have been too paternalistic. Sometimes I think we have. Perhaps it would have been better for all concerned if we had laid off people incapable of satisfactory service. But we never have. We kept them on and tried to find something they could do to earn their pay. Some did and some didn't. Then, when the Depression came and there was so much unemployment, we kind of drifted into a policy of keeping people at work long after they had passed the usual age of retirement. So what has happened is that we now have a news-room payroll that is overloaded with deadwood, with people who in ordinary circumstances would have retired years ago."

Sifton reached to his desk, picked up a note on which were listed the names of five or six newsroom employees whose service went back to the First World War and beyond, who were now hived away in jobs of no particular consequence. He read off the list of the employees and their salaries. I was struck by the way he chose the words for what came next. He did not say, these people have an average of thirty years of service with the *Free Press*. He said: "These people have had steady jobs with us for the last thirty years. They have suffered no lay-offs like the railway employees or Eaton's employees. When they have been sick, their wages have gone on. In particular they have had jobs at better-than-average pay throughout the Depression. I am sure, Jimmy, I don't have to tell you how fortunate they have been in that regard. One can assume, I hope, that they have had the prudence to have accumulated some savings for their old age during this long, unbroken span of em-ployment. In any event, all but two of them will soon be eligible for the old-age pension." (It was then twenty dollars per month to persons reaching seventy years of age and was conditional on passing a means test.)

He paused, took a very long breath, and went on. "So here's what I am going to propose as an alternative to your proposal that the 1931 wage cut be restored. We are prepared to grasp the nettle and retire these non-productive employees and use the two hundred dollars per week now going to them in salaries to increase the salaries of the editorial employees like yourselves who are ob-viously worth more to our paper than we are paying you. But we'll do it on an individual basis, because we do not believe in the principle of general wage increases for everybody regardless of their worth and productivity."

Sweeney rather limply raised the question of what was to be done financially for the aged retirees. I was too shattered to speak.

"With those who are eligible for the old-age pension, there is no problem. They will simply apply for the pension. The others are a problem and I think it would be only fair if we undertook to provide an amount equal to the old-age pension until they reach seventy."

He had put the responsibility for firing the paper's longest-serving employees, with little more than the clothes on their backs to show for more than thirty years' service, right on the ends of our noses.

Neither Sweeney nor Gray had the guts to respond to Sifton in the way his offer invited us to respond. Instead, we took our leave, and mumbled something about talking it over with our fellow workers and getting back to him. We rounded up Burt Gresham, Harry Steel, and several others and adjourned to a back booth in the Okum Inn to spread the word of Sifton's offer. Burt Gresham, who was fated to die with the Winnipeg Grenadiers in the defence of Hong Kong, was seldom heard to swear. He did that day.

"Jesus Cheeerist, do you know what we've done? We've opened the way for him to fire Leyden and Conk and Bill and Frank and we'll get the blame for suggesting it!"

Nobody replied and no one spoke for the longest time. We just nursed our coffee and Burt filled the ashtray with match stubs as he lit and relit his pipe. Then somebody said: "You know, George Leyden was right! And none of us thought much about it at the time, did we?" And that brought the sour memories of the Christmas bonus and the pension scheme fluttering down on our reveries about the Sifton interview.

Until the Christmas of 1936, the *Free Press* had followed the practice of distributing a Christmas bonus equal to a week's pay to its salaried employees. That Christmas we opened our Christmas-bonus envelopes to the rudest of shocks. A letter from Victor Sifton told us that there would be no more Christmas bonuses. Instead, the *Free Press* was going to pay the equivalent of the Christmas bonus into the employees' contributions to the new pension scheme he had recently established. The company would also make an additional substantial contribution. This would enable the insurance company that was administering the scheme to carry back the date at which their length of service, for pension-scheme purposes, would begin. Employees under the scheme would become eligible to retire at sixty on pension and the size of the pension would be based on the number of years they had contributed to the scheme after its inception in 1936.

The cancellation of the Christmas bonus triggered an explosion of outrage that rattled every window in the building. By mid-December there was hardly an employee of the company who had not committed his Christmas bonus to Christmas shopping. To have cancelled it so close to Christmas, without warning, was the dirtiest of dirty pool.

To try to dampen down the uproar, George Ferguson and Bill Lord suggested a compromise to Victor—reinstate half the bonus and pay the other half into the fund. At the time of the Christmas-bonus unpleasantness, we had all forgotten the mild stir that the unveiling of the pension plan itself had caused. Several meetings had been held to explain it to us and those of us in our thirties regarded it more or less as a proposition whose main virtue would be the obligation it laid on us to save money. Besides, if it lasted ten years, we would acquire a vested interest in the company's contribution. So we joined. But for the over-fifty employees, it loomed as a disaster bearing rapidly down on them. They might look back on twenty-five or thirty years' service with the company, but under the scheme they would be forced to retire at sixty with a pension of ten or twelve dollars a week. And for those who were already nudging or were beyond the retirement age, it was infinitely less attractive.

George Leyden, the aged editor of country correspondence, who was ordinarily the quintessential Caspar Milquetoast, typified the almost terrified reaction of the oldsters on the staff. He lurched out of the staff meeting back into the newsroom, muttering, "It's a dirty Sifton trick to get rid of all the oldtimers on the staff. It's just a damn conspiracy—just a scheme to fire all the oldtimers. I won't join. I won't join."

None of us paid much attention to Leyden and his conspiracy theory at the time. But when we recalled it at the post-mortem, it bathed the Sifton performance in a garish new light. Of course; that *was* what Victor had been about from the beginning, scheming to get rid of everyone on the staff over sixty! What a bastard! What a miserable sonofabitch!

Despite Leyden's gloomy forebodings, nothing happened to the over-aged staffers as a result either of the pension scheme or of our negotiation with Victor Sifton. Most of them remained in their jobs until the infirmities of age forced their retirement. We left it to Ferguson to carry our response back to Sifton and write "30" to our labour-negotiating careers.

What none of us realized at the time was that nothing could have more sharply etched our ignorance of our history, our society, and our economic system than our reaction to Victor Sifton and his proposed firing of his aged servitors. Far from being the unique kind of sonofabitch we believed him to be, Victor Sifton was only doing what came naturally to the overwhelming majority of Canadian employers. *Noblesse oblige* imposed but a single responsibility upon them: to safeguard the solvency of their enterprise by maintaining its profitability. The evidence of the truth of that statement was everywhere available for all who cared to read it. In the *Free Press* library were three fat volumes of testimony before the Royal

Commission on Price Spreads, into which none of us had ever dipped. In a year of probing into the inner workings of Canadian business, the commission had exposed working conditions and wages that recalled the reports of the factory inspectors of England during the Industrial Revolution of the 1830s. In the process, the commission heard an unbroken litany of unabashed testimony from the business leaders of Canada which demonstrated a total unawareness of the existence of the idea of social responsibility.

When governments enacted minimum-wage laws to protect workers from starvation-wage levels, the manufacturing branches of the great retail empires switched to piece-work payment and continued to pay most of their workers less than the law allowed. While one family-owned retail chain was enforcing the most rigid wage sacrifices on its employees, it was paying its forty top executives an average of more than thirty-five thousand dollars a year. Not one of the hundreds of employers who appeared before the commission had a pension scheme that entitled their long-service employees to retirement allowances. One company, which paid out two hundred thousand dollars a year in pensions for its twelve directors, did have a scheme of sorts for its employees. At age sixty-five they could be retired, at the pleasure of the company, on a minimum of five dollars a week and ten per cent of their weekly salaries. That was for employees with twenty-five years' service. Those with lesser service got less. Neither class of workers had any rights to anything. One other company had established a fund from which it was able, on compassionate grounds, to pay gratuities to long-service employees. For the overwhelming majority of Canadian business, the superannuation of employees was unheard of.

As a general rule, the only pension schemes in operation in 1937 in Canada were those of the railways and the civil services, and all were employer-administered. One administrative decision made unilaterally by the CPR created serious hardship for hundreds of CPR employees in western Canada. Those who returned to the CPR after the 1919 general strike lost all the seniority they had built up prior to the strike. They were rehired as new employees. The CPR pension was paid to all employees with twenty-five years' continuous service upon compulsory retirement at sixty-five. Those who were in their forties at the time of the strike were unable to meet the length-of-service qualification before reaching sixty-five. Even if they had worked for the company for forty years, they got no pension.

That Victor Sifton was far from unique in his attitude towards his aged employees was emphasized by a coincidence a year later.

One of the arch-conservatives on the Winnipeg city council, Alderman Fred C. Thompson, was seized with an inspiration to create job opportunities on the civic payroll. He introduced a motion to instruct all civic departments to dispense with the services of all employees over the age of seventy. Most civic employees were covered by a pension scheme that required them to retire at sixty-five. But the city also employed several hundred so-called casual employees, mainly seasonal labourers. Regular employees had to retire at sixty-five, but nobody asked the casuals for their birth certificates when they turned up each spring, again to become "regular-temporary" employees. So many went on working well into their seventies. Thompson argued that they should be dropped because they could go on the old-age pension and open jobs for men on relief, thus reducing the drain on the city budget. When the motion was sent to a committee for study and report, problems were discovered. The old-age pension of twenty dollars a month went only to people who could pass a means test. Delays were inevitable between the time of application and ultimate receipt of the pension. The committee approved the proposal, provided the city would pay each employee the twenty dollars a month pending qualification for the pension. The full city council balked at committing itself to the payment of the twenty dollars a month and sent the proposal back to the committee for further study. It died there.

The lack of social consciousness that flowed from Marie Antoinette through Sir Charles Trevelyan to Sir Rodmond Roblin epitomized the attitude of the business leaders of Canada until the onset of the Second World War. Trevelyan was the British under-secretary whose solution to the Irish potato famine was to let the people starve. Roblin refused to enact a School Attendance Act or a Factory Act to protect women and children, on the grounds that such acts would adversely affect Winnipeg businesses. By comparison, if one picked one's examples carefully, Victor Sifton could be made to appear almost philanthropic in his attitude. *Free Press* employees at least got two weeks' vacation with pay each year. That was more than the thousands of employees whose plight was described before the Price Spreads Commission. We also drew full pay when we were away sick, a benefit enjoyed by few other employees in Winnipeg.

The adherence of the Sifton brothers to the fundamental precepts of laissez-faire, laissez-aller, was Jesuitical in its intensity. Their belief that the law of supply and demand was the perfect solution to every economic and social problem of mankind was unshakable. Anything that reduced prices to consumers was good, and anything that raised prices to consumers was bad. Clifford, despite his tic, was a forceful advocate of cut-throat competition. A lawyer, he was one of the few of that profession who argued that all professions should be free to advertise their services and the prices at which they were prepared to provide them. He waged a lifelong and ultimately losing battle against the slick campaign of the optical trust to convert spectacles-retailing into a "profession" barred from advertising the price of its wares. As an earnest advocate he came prepared with great dossiers of horror stories about the cost to consumers of all such conspiracies to raise prices.

The problem that faced the people of the West in the 1930s, however, was not high prices for anything, but ruinously low prices for everything. And for this the Siftons had no solution, except that they seemed to be against anything and everything anyone else suggested. They were against artificial floors under farm prices and minimum wages. The cure for crop surpluses and mass unemployment was to let prices and wages find their own levels, and the result would be the increased demand for both goods and services that low prices would generate, presumably by spontaneous combustion of some kind. That grain prices fell to three-hundred-year lows after the 1929 crash and crop surpluses piled higher the lower prices went, that mass unemployment became even more massive as wages dropped below the starvation level, in no way impaired their confidence in the divine inspiration of the law of demand and supply. If that law was not working, it was because intervention by governments was preventing it from working.

In defence of the market as the only measure of value, Victor Sifton had an example of his own which he never tired of quoting. When he was in Regina he was aware that the *Leader-Post* building was in need of some extensive renovation and repair. The cost of these improvements prevented their being undertaken. When both wages and prices collapsed with the onset of the Depression, the projects became attractive. So work was undertaken that provided unemployed tradesmen in Regina with several thousand man-days of employment. If wages had not dropped, the expenditures would not have been made and these thousands of man-days of labour would have been lost to the unemployed tradesmen. Similarly, low prices and low wages made extensive alterations to the *Winnipeg Free Press* building possible after Sifton came to Winnipeg. Ergo, the cure for unemployment was lower wages and lower prices.

This, moreover, was an article of faith to J. W. Dafoe and Grant Dexter, no less than to the Sifton brothers. Thus, when the provincial governments took steps to rescue the milk producers from the bankrupting impact of the chain stores' loss-leader selling of milk, the *Free Press* editorial page reacted angrily, as it did to most efforts of governments to ameliorate the effects of cut-throat competition. The difference was that, for the Siftons and Dexter, commitment to the law of supply and demand was for life. For John Dafoe, the trans-Canada tour of the Rowell-Sirois Commission, of which he was a member, was his road to Damascus. So compelling was the evidence presented to the commission in the West and in the Maritimes that he became a subscriber to the doctrine that Canadians, wherever they lived, were entitled by citizenship to a reasonable standard of social and educational services, regardless of the ability of their governments to pay for them. It was a revolutionary rejection of laissez-faire, laissez-aller, though it is doubtful whether either of the Siftons or Dexter ever understood the significance of the Rowell-Sirois Report, calling as it did for massive intervention in the economy by the federal government.

Given the rigid cast of the Sifton mind, it is almost inconceivable that Victor Sifton could have assumed the role of a corporate-pension pioneer. There was in the Siftons, however, a deep sense of dynasty. As the sons of Sir Clifford Sifton died off, the surviving sons moved to buy out the heirs so that the fortune amassed by Sir Clifford during his tenure as federal minister of the Interior would be perpetuated intact in Sifton hands. The concern was by no means with the Sifton name alone. It meant that the various Sifton enterprises would always have to be under the control of able and enterprising managers. In the Sifton lexicon, that meant young men in their prime, not doddering oldsters. Unhappily for that concept, the *Free Press* seemed to have become an escalator that would continue through eternity overloading its higher echelons with senior citizens. It had become a horrible example of the inevitable result of excessive paternalism. And it would go on being such an example, even if the current clutter of deadwood were removed. What was needed was a long-term solution that would prevent any deadwood from accumulating. A pension scheme with compulsory retirement at sixty would serve that purpose. Even though it would be a modest drain on current income, it would serve the long-term dynastic goals of the owners of the enterprise.

Then, too, a pension plan would enable the Siftons to reaffirm their faith in another tenet of their economic religion. It was a tenet widely held through the realm of business: no man is indispensable or worth more to the company than his capacity at the moment justifies. This concept was well stated by Harold Ross, the editor of *The New Yorker*. In a letter to one of his writers who was paid on a piece-work basis, Ross wrote:

You say that you have been here eighteen years and are not treated better than a good writer a couple of years out of college would be, so far as pay for individual articles is concerned, and ask me to correct you if you are wrong. You are not wrong, I guess. My firm viewpoint is that we ought to pay what a piece is worth, regardless of age, race, color, creed, financial status or any other consideration. I don't know how, in an enterprise of this sort, one in my position can take into consideration anything beyond the actual value of the things he buys. . . . I [*sic*] be damned if I want to inject into that the long-and-faithful element or any other element than sheer value. How in the hell could I do that?*

If we were to define value in this context as whatever the employer decided it was, then Ross in 1945 was defining the Draconian code of business management that permeated the Canadian economy of the 1930s. If an employer decided that employees who had been paid by the week should be paid at piece-work rates, piece-work it was. If they decided that weekly employees should work only part-time during slack periods, they worked only part-time during slack periods. If the employer decided that work that had been worth forty cents an hour was only worth twenty cents an hour, the workers were paid twenty cents an hour.

Our difficulty at the *Free Press* arose simply because, before the anguish John Sweeney and I had triggered, none of us had ever thought of the place as a business enterprise. The *Free Press* was us. We were the *Free Press*, even to the point where, when covering assignments, we introduced ourselves simply, "*Free Press*," and got around to our own names later if it seemed necessary. Our loyalty to the paper was so deep as to be almost pathological, for when we were covering an assignment we lost all sense of time. If covering a story meant working ten to fifteen hours a day for days on end, we worked those hours and regarded it as an affront to our ability to be spelled off by another reporter. The idea of asking for compensatory time off was as foreign to our make-up as was the concept of our working a forty-hour week. There was, moreover, a magnet in the fourth-floor newsroom that drew us to it whenever we got within a dozen blocks of the building. Few of us ever completed a night at a concert or a movie without "dropping in to see what was doing," on the off-chance we could become involved in whatever it was. "The long-and-faithful element," in Ross's

* Quoted by Brendan Gill in *Here at The New Yorker* (New York: Random House, 1975), p. 360.

words, may not have counted for anything with the Siftons, but it did with us because most of us regarded our association with the institution as a lifetime commitment. With us it was almost as if we had been "called" to journalism, the way Protestant preachers are "called" to a career in the church. The strength of that religious commitment to the *Free Press* was never the same after our experience with Victor Sifton in the spring of 1937.

5
What Did You Do in the War, Dad—and Mom?

Now what? What do we do now?

It was Friday morning, September 1, 1939, and it was more than fitting that a people who for five years had been drifting aimlessly, leaderless, conscienceless in a sleepwalking trance should have been awakened with a crash. The world we had known in the 1930s ended that morning, with exploding bombs and the crashing of tanks and artillery, as the armies of Nazi Germany crossed the border into Poland. The news of that end was being shouted from the streets by newsboys hawking their "Extra! Extra! Extra!"'s.

The process of awakening varied across the prairies. For rural residents, the war news came mainly by way of the railway-telegraph operator to the telephone operator, and thence out over the telephone party-lines. Occasionally an alert radio announcer would pirate the headlines from the local newspaper for the benefit of his breakfasting listeners. Bedside radios were only then being invented, and news as a marketable radio commodity was still a long way down the road in western Canada. The newspapers enjoyed their monopoly as purveyors of spot news of the world, but across the prairies they differed widely in the way they handled the onset of the cataclysm. In Winnipeg, the papers agreed that midnight would be the deadline for putting out extras. If the Germans did not march before twelve o'clock, the extras would be withheld until 6:00 A.M. so as not to intrude upon the slumbers of their subscribers. In Calgary, the *Herald* was on the streets at 3:00 A.M. with its first extra and followed with a second extra three hours later. The *Albertan* had its first extra out soon after, followed by a second and an unprecedented third extra edition at noon. Elsewhere, most papers were satisfied with single extra editions, though in Lethbridge the *Herald* added special editions on Sunday and Monday to its Friday extra.

It was a shocking awakening and yet there were few indeed who were really surprised by the news. The invasion of Poland had been signalled two weeks earlier by the signing of the Russo-

German non-aggression pact, which turned out to be a secret deal to divide Poland between the two dictatorships. But long before that, with the rape of Czechoslovakia after the Munich agreement, the world was beginning to recognize that Hitler meant what he had written in *Mein Kampf* about conquering the world. Nevertheless, as the news of the invasion sank in that day, there was a lot of grasping after the glimmer of hope that maybe, by some miracle, this would not be it. After all, though Germany had invaded Poland, no war had yet been declared by Britain and France against Germany, or by Germany against Britain and France . . . or, for that matter, even against Poland. Perhaps Hitler's invasion of Poland would be like his invasion of Czechoslovakia, over before it started, and there would be no war. There had been such Nazi excursions before—into the Saar, into Austria, into Czechoslovakia —and there had been no war. Perhaps . . .

The last hope vanished when Britain and France declared war on Germany on Sunday morning, and across the beds and the breakfast tables, over fences and along telephone party-lines, between neighbours, relatives, and friends, there began an endless refrain: "Well, this is it, what happens now? What will Canada do? What will we do? What will you do?"

The question moved from the general to the particular with the speed of sound, for the omnibus questions were only the wind-ups for the ultimate, the fundamental: "What am *I* going to do?"

As the news sank in, the single unemployed in the relief work camps looked at each other and began the process of making up their minds as they packed their clothes; young wives cast sidelong glances at their husbands and wondered what was really going through their minds; mothers of maturing sons recalled the First World War and nervously wondered what their sons would do.

Few there were who seriously doubted what Canada's course of action would be, though a charade of sorts would be played out for the next week. The era of pusillanimity was over for the Anglo-Saxon world community, save for the United States and Ireland. Across Canada, for one and a half million men of military age, "What am I going to do now?" became the question of the hour, and of the days and weeks and months that were to follow. For some it would become an ulcerating, sleep-disturbing dilemma. For others it would be dismissed with no more than a shrug of concern. There were those to whom the thought of volunteering for military service had never occurred. There were those whose British roots still grew near the surface, to whom enlistment was a simple matter of duty, as it had been for the British for four hundred years. There was a war on. You were in it. It was expected of you, by your family and friends as well as by your King and country. Fathers stood a little taller and mothers shed prideful tears as their sons went off to the recruiting offices. For the majority who comprised neither group, time would become the crucible in which character was formed. The steady building of subtle pressures would make it easier for some to enlist than to stay out; for others, it would build into irresistible excuses to stay out.

During the first couple of weeks of the war, the straws in the wind blew every which way. In Edmonton, the manager of the newly opened T. Eaton Company store announced an incentive plan for all employees who enlisted in the armed services. The company would make up the difference between a married employee's regular pay and the pay and allowances provided by the army. Single employees would get subsidies to bring their pay up to seventy-five per cent. In Calgary, the city council voted to provide similar bonuses for enlisting civic employees, but limited the duration to one year. In Winnipeg, the city council was less open-handed on behalf of its taxpayers. It voted all enlistees a cash bonus of fifty dollars. The *Edmonton Bulletin* developed an interest in marriage statistics. It noted that the outbreak of war brought a sudden flurry in marriages; from an average of two or three a day, the numbers vaulted into the fifties. The paper speculated on the reasons, but came to no firm conclusion. Some of the bridegrooms might be marrying to avoid military service, or they might be marrying "to have someone to fight for" prior to going off to war.

Regardless of attitudes towards military service, the answer for the overwhelming majority of Canadian Anglo-Saxons would be deep involvement in the struggle against Hitler, though the nature and extent of that involvement would be endlessly debated. For French Canadians, on the other hand, the extent and nature of the involvement would depend on varying perceptions of the seriousness of the threat of the Nazi Germans to the soil of Quebec. For the majority, the perception was that the threat ranged from minimal to non-existent, and they passively resisted all efforts to involve them in anything more than employment in war industry. That France was involved and occupied meant no more to French Canadians than British involvement.

For the sons of Ukrainian, Polish, and German immigrants, the question was loaded with particular torment. Their parents had come to Canada, in substantial part at least, to escape wars and the omnipresent threat of being conscripted into the armies of Austria, Germany, or Russia. The Germans, moreover, were caught in a special bind all their own. For almost ten years they had been subjected to blatant and sophisticated pro-Nazi propaganda and they had joined pro-Nazi German–Canadian Bunds by the thousands. Even some who were born in Canada were browbeaten by the Nazis into registering with German consulates to be called to Germany for military service if the need arose. None was ever called, but the Bundists did persuade several hundred Canadian Germans of military age to return to Germany for service in Hitler's legions. Where in this struggle would the sympathies of German Canadians lie? The Hobson's choice offered young Germans was one of horrendous alternatives. Those who opted for joining the struggle against Hitler courted ostracism by family and friends; those who did not courted persecution from their non-German neighbours and possible internment at the hands of Canadian authorities.

For the Ukrainians, the declaration of war brought only an intensification of the struggle between the Reds and the Whites that had been disrupting the Ukrainian communities in Canada for almost twenty years. The Whites were the religious, anti-Communist majority who were dedicated to freeing the Ukraine from Russian domination. The Reds were the Communist minority who followed the Moscow party line regardless of its twists and turns. Until the rise of Hitler, Moscow had been pro-German and anti-Western democratic. With the victory of the Nazis, the Ukrainian Communists became noisy advocates of a united front against Hitler and promoters of the League Against War and Fascism. After the outbreak of the Spanish Civil War, they became enthusiastic recruiters of Ukrainian Canadians for the Mackenzie–Papineau battalion, which fought for loyalist Spain. With the signing of the Hitler–Stalin pact that preceded the attack on Poland, the Communists switched sides and denounced Britain and France. When Russia invaded Poland, they became advocates of a negotiated peace with Hitler.

As if the internecine political warfare was not disturbing enough, the Ukrainians suffered from severe culture shock. Of all the immigrant peoples, only Doukhobors and Mennonites had a deeper antipathy towards military service. Because all had been dumped on the western prairie to root-hog-or-die in their own bloc settlements, their assimilation into Canadian society had been slow. No agency of the Canadian government had ever made the slightest effort to acquaint the new arrivals with any aspect of the Canadian way of life. They could live and die, for all anybody cared, without ever becoming privy to a single fact of Canadian history. In the cities, the Ukrainians, like the Jews and Germans and Poles, found the doors bolted against them when they tried to move into the

Canadian mainstream, culturally and economically. It was small wonder that, in the working-class districts of the cities and in the ethnic enclaves in the country, the Ukrainians had more difficulty than anybody in making up their minds about the course of action they should take.

Among all the Canadian ethnic groups, only the Jews had a quick and ready, almost automatic answer. Ben Malkin was the token Jew on the *Free Press* news staff. He had no difficulty with "What do I do now?"

"For us there's no problem," he said when we gathered for coffee the following Tuesday. "We've been talking about fighting Hitler for the last ten years, almost. In the North End that is about all we've been talking about for as long as I can remember. Okay. So the way you fight Hitler is with guns, and the bigger the better. The guys were talking about it yesterday and it looks to us as if the best deal is to get into the artillery. We hear that a couple of field batteries are being mobilized at McGregor Armouries, so we'll be on our way to enlist as soon as we get the word." The word came and Malkin was the first active-service enlistee from the *Free Press*.

In the interval, Malkin had been subjected to an impassioned recruiting sales pitch from Burt Gresham, who was a lieutenant in the Winnipeg Grenadiers of the non-permanent militia. The Grenadiers were also expecting imminent mobilization for active service, and Gresham tried his best to enlist Malkin, as he tried to persuade all the rest of us. But the Grenadiers were an infantry regiment, and Malkin kept insisting that his feet were not made for marching; the war he was proposing to fight was the one he could get to sitting down.

But for every Malkin or Gresham, there were many hundreds of young Canadians for whom the decision was a far more agonizing affair. They ranged from the out-and-out pacifists and conscientious objectors like the Mennonites and Doukhobors, through the political left to the political right. On the left were substantial numbers who were tentatively convinced that Canada's contribution to the struggle against Hitler should be to supply the material with which the British and French would do the fighting. In the catch-phrase of the time, Canada would become the "arsenal of democracy," which would produce the guns, tanks, planes, and ships for its allies. At the other extreme were the vestigial colonials, whose blood reaction was that nothing mattered in war except armies and navies. They rushed to the recruiting offices without a backward glance, while their elders mounted vociferous political campaigns to conscript everybody else for immediate military service. Finally, there were the ideologically and ethnically un-committed, who had no burning zeal to be killed in any kind of war, who, indeed, had a positive distaste for the idea. They would delay answering the question until internal and external pressures compelled an answer.

The advice that came to us in the *Free Press* newsroom from the publisher was: play it cool and wait and see. It would take some weeks before Canada's role in the war would become clear, before a balance would be struck between the various manpower needs of the country. There would then be time enough for each of us to search his conscience to decide what action he would take. This generally was the gist of the advice other employers were dis-pensing, and it was eminently sound and sensible. It was designed to prevent round pegs, whose skills would be vitally needed else-where, from rushing into the square holes of one or the other of the armed services.

The word that came to the nation from the government during the next week was that Canada would become both an arsenal for democracy and a fighting ally in the struggle against Hitler. Armed forces would be mobilized to defend Canada, the air above the country and the seas around it, and an army of volunteers would be dispatched to England immediately to join those already fight-ing. Under the National Resources Mobilization Act of 1939, the industrial plant and the manpower of Canada would be directed into war production. A system of national selective service would be inaugurated to direct eligible Canadians into industrial pro-duction or home-defence training units as and if the need arose. Meanwhile, the militia units would be brought up to strength; volunteers would be actively sought for overseas service, and every airport across the country that had a flying club would be trans-formed into a pilot-training centre which would help to turn out pilots at the national rate of twenty-five thousand a year.

For the footloose and fancy-free seventeen- to twenty-five-year-olds, the God of war had waved his magic wand and transformed their world of hopeless stagnation into a candy store in which they were invited to pick and choose among mouth-watering alterna-tives. They could join the air force and acquire the skills that would send them zooming through the skies with machine guns blazing, or quietly acquire the skills that would turn them into airmail flyers when the war was over. They could join the navy and see the world. Or they could, if the worst came to the worst, join the army and footslog their way through the fleshpots of London and Paris and ultimately Berlin. Or they could look around for the highly paid war-industry jobs that were soon to develop.

But for the encumbered twenty- to forty-year-olds with wives and children, the wait-and-see advice only prolonged the agony of uncertainty. Some were driven, in varying degrees of intensity, by an almost irresistible urge to get into uniform and into the fighting war, but were held back by inescapable family encumbrances. Others, restrained from enlisting by a deeply felt revulsion against the horrors of war acquired between the wars, were being pushed to join by the prickings of conscience reinforced by peer pressure. For some, the pull-push pressures were ended by turning wives and children over to families and friends and heading for the recruiting offices. Sometimes the decision was taken after prolonged tarrying in beer parlours with recently enlisted friends; sometimes it came after months or years of indecision. For a half-million, the decision was eventually taken out of their hands, for some by the selective-services call-up, for others like myself by a snap judgment by a medical examiner.

That I should ever have been among those who agonized over enlisting certainly contradicts the theory of the dominance of environmental influences. A boy of eight when the First World War started, I had my childhood enthusiasm for war and the trappings of military display neutralized, rather painfully at times, by the anti-war attitude of my father. A one-armed, forty-five-year-old father of three, he would have been conscription-proof if the German navy had sailed up the Red River to Winnipeg. Yet he was adamantly opposed to the war from the beginning, and as it went on he became addicted to attendance at anti-conscription mass meetings. Though he was forever being warned by my mother to keep his views to himself when abroad in the city, he paid little attention. He subscribed to an American weekly paper and occasionally it would arrive with pages missing. He blamed that on the censors, and fumed and fussed over the outrage until at last he would fling the paper from him in disgust. The schools of the First World War were handy disposal sites for leftover propaganda, and I soon learned that the better part of valour was never to let my father catch me with it. He even muttered his disapproval of my mother's knitting socks for two of her brothers who had gone overseas with the first Canadian contingent.

The extent to which my father's jaundiced view of warfare rubbed off on me is difficult to assess. Certainly I never quibbled over any of the patriotic exercises that marked my passage through the school system. But in the process of growing up I was at least susceptible to the pacifist arguments that engulfed the world after the awful slaughter of the First World War. If the Second World War had broken out in 1932, I would undoubtedly have found myself marching in the protests against it. But the 1930s were a decade of vast intellectual ferment as well as political upheaval, and few of us left it with the intellectual baggage we carried into it, or indeed much that we had picked up in passing through the Great Depression.

The mood of the Depression years was probably best capsulated by a witness before the McCarthy Committee's Washington witch-hunts, who said something like this: "During the Depression, we were all Communists of one sort or another, if we had any sense or sensitivity towards our environment." From the revolution to the Wall Street crash, Communist Russia had been the pariah of Europe. But with the onset of the Depression, the pariah came to resemble the great white hope for the dispossessed of the Western world.

On the prairies, disenchantment with the working of the capitalist system ran very deep indeed. Little as they were ever inclined to listen to the preachments of Canadian Communists, the urban unemployed and destitute farmers found a lot to admire in what they were hearing about Communist Russia. Russia, we were told, had solved the problem of unemployment. Millions of rubles were being poured into housing construction; Russian farms were being mechanized at a fantastic rate, and production of all kinds of food was being encouraged. Railways were being extended into remote areas; new mines were being developed. Russia's problem was not unemployment but a scarcity of workers of every kind. While the Western world futilely wrestled with the contradiction of millions starving in a world glutted with food, Russia had blown out the roadblock separating consumers from food supplies.

Most of us were content to admire Russia from afar, and to enthuse over what Russia was doing as an example the rest of the world should be copying. Hundreds of others in the United States, England, and France went much further; they actually migrated to Russia to become volunteer workers in the great experiment. The benefits that Russia provided its industrial workers were used as baubles with which the Canadian Communist agit-props sought to attract factory workers, miners, and the masses of the unemployed to their party. Finally, Russia and its five-year plans for economic mobilization became the mecca for hundreds of British and American journalists, professors, educators, and just plain junketeers, who returned home chorusing hosannas for the Russian experiment. Sir Stafford Cripps and Sidney Webb made pilgrimages from London. John Dewey became as ecstatic over what he saw of the Russian experiments in education as historian Scott Nearing did over the economic innovations. Soon the newspapers and magazines of both countries were publishing laudatory articles by the sightseers, and the lecture platforms rang with paeans of praise for the new Jerusalem. The pollen from all this intellectual cross-fertilization drifted into Canada on the prevailing media winds.

All this served to obscure the fact that Stalin's forced-draft collectivization of agriculture was turning out to be the most appalling example of manufactured starvation in modern history. Millions of peasants lost their lives and hundreds of thousands of others were transported from their farms to Siberian slave-labour camps. On closer examination, the industrial miracles turned out to be miracles of mismanagement, waste, and incompetence from top to bottom. News of the horror that Russia had become as Stalin destroyed his rivals seeped through the Russian censorship, in the United Press and *Christian Science Monitor* dispatches of Eugene Lyons and William H. Chamberlain. Canadians became privy to the facts when these, and similar reports later carried by the *New York Times* and *Chicago Daily News* syndicates, found space in Canadian newspapers. As the horror intensified it was documented in a cascade of books, among them Lyons' *Assignment in Utopia*, Trotsky's *Revolution Betrayed*, and Boris Souvarine's *Stalin*.

If ever there was a social order that should have lived up to its press notices, it was the Soviet Union. If ever there was a time when humanity needed an institution to venerate, to give it hope, it was in the 1930s. And it was just when both seemed to be coming together that the masks were stripped away to reveal the utter depravity of the Stalin regime. First there was the liquidation of the entire body of old Bolsheviks who had made the revolution. Then came the slaughter of the army chieftains, the mass murders of the intellectuals and scientists, and finally the liquidation of the liquidators.

But not even the Stalin reign of terror could compete for attention with Hitler's Germany for long. If Stalin was an Attila reincarnate, Hitler's was the sophisticated enormity of the mad scientist, who had clearly enunciated his formulae for populating the world with his master race, and was hell-bent on a program to achieve it while the world looked on in disbelief. He had the Reichstag building burned to the ground and used that as an excuse for launching a reign of terror against his political opposition; his gangs set fire to Jewish synagogues, then forced the Jews to collect the fire insurance and pay it over to the government in fines, in recompense for the cost of putting out the fires; his gangs wrecked Jewish stores and the government heavily fined the Jews for causing the disturbance; he added whole new columns to the lexicon of terror, with such words as Gestapo, blitzkrieg, storm trooper, concentration camp, collective guilt, fifth column, rubber truncheon.

For the *Free Press*, Hitler and the Nazis held a special fascination. Already in 1938 and 1939, a short-wave radio had been installed in the newsroom, and Paul Ausborn, one of Winnipeg's very few authentic anti-Nazi Germans, used to come in and do a running translation for us of Hitler's speeches. But somehow, even halfway round the world, so much of what Hitler said did not need translation, for his voice dripped such venom that its meaning was unmistakable. From the 1933 burning of the Reichstag onward, a week seldom passed without the movie newsreels giving space to some new Nazi atrocity. If it were not the burning of synagogues or the wrecking of Jewish stores and homes, it might be parades of brown-shirted gangsters masquerading as soldiers, massive party demonstrations, Nazi riots in Austria, or the seemingly endlessly repeated film clips of the fear-dazed faces of refugees seeking escape from the violence within Germany.

On most political issues, the practising cynics of the *Free Press* newsroom were inclined to strike a blasé pose where the paper's editorials were concerned. The paper strongly supported the Bracken provincial government, but if there was a single vote-casting adherent of that regime on the news staff, he remained well hidden. In the 1935 election, when the Liberal slogan was "King or Chaos," we toasted the election at the Okum Inn coffee breaks with, "Well, here's to chaos," and most of us voted accordingly. But from the Munich crisis onward, ranks closed steadily behind the editorial conviction that, unless Hitler was stopped by collective action, he would conquer the world. Sooner or later some country would choose to fight and the rest of the world would be drawn into the war. As Ben Malkin had observed, the only way in which Hitler could be stopped then would be by people with guns.

In the weeks after Munich we had whiled away the after-deadline doldrums discussing the alternatives we would choose or reject when war came. There would be an obvious need for war correspondents and several of us thought we would opt for that. Before Munich, even before Austria, Burt Gresham had been an enthusiastic drum-beater for enlistment in the militia. When the war came, the only question to be decided, he said, was where you served and how. The people who enlisted in advance of the war would become the nucleus of the officers' corps in 1939 or 1940. And if we were all going to get killed anyway, it would be a hell of a lot better for everybody's dependants for us to get killed as lieutenants, or as captains and majors, than as privates. Officers' pay started at five dollars a day for lieutenants and went on up from there. Privates were paid $1.45 a day. Allowances and pensions for dependants of casualties were based on the pay schedules, so in fact the colonel's lady and Judy O'Grady were by no means sisters under the skin financially.

On the question of pay and allowances, the old sweats of the First World War conceded that Gresham had a point. But they challenged him on the officers-versus-privates issue. They pointed out that privates followed and officers led, which meant that the officers were first off the mark and prime targets for every sniper within sight and range. "Kill the officers and you stall the advance" was the slogan of every sniper in the business, and of the machine-gunners as well. The veterans challenged Gresham on another point—which branch of the service to join. They agreed that the worst of all possible worlds was the world of the infantryman, to which Gresham's unit belonged. Never mind what the army told you about the new transport division that would carry you into battle in trucks, and forget all this talk about blitzkriegs and tank spearheads and pincer movements. The infantryman would still march till he wore his feet off to the ankles, and sleep in foxholes full of mud. No, if it was action you wanted, take the air force or even the navy. And so the argument went, not only in the *Free Press* newsroom but across the whole country. The antipathy of the First World War veterans towards service in the infantry so muddied the army's image that it was always the third choice of most enlisting Canadians.

The academic aura that coloured our conversations fell away with the invasion of Poland, and we were nose-to-nose with reality. Any remaining trace of my father's pacificism had long since disappeared, probably with the onset of the Spanish Civil War. Faced with the necessity of choosing, I rejected the air force out of hand, for I could get airsick thinking of flying. The navy was attractive only because I would be stationed in Canada and could get home on leave. But seasickness was akin to airsickness and I wanted no part of it either. That left only the army, and the question of when.

Unlike Gresham and Malkin, who were both single, I had a wife, a daughter, and a house under construction. By that September I had managed four raises in pay and was one of the senior reporters on the *Free Press* news staff. On the strength of my last raise, I had talked the paper into lending me four hundred dollars with which I negotiated a $3,600 National Housing Act mortgage. When the war broke out, I was in the midst of contracting for the construction of a three-bedroom home, which we miraculously completed well within the original estimate. In addition to a wife and daughter, building the house became an impediment to immediate enlistment. As a private soldier I would have received $1.45 a day. If I signed over $20 a month to my family, the government promised to add $35 a month. When the house payments of $30 a month were deducted from her $55, Kay would have had $25 a month on which to keep our daughter Pat and herself. The alternative to trying to live on $25 a month would have been for her to get a job, but in September 1939 the idea of married women working was unheard of, for there were still many hundreds of unemployed single girls on the relief rolls and few employers would hire married women.

Economics so confounded patriotism that the possibility of my enlisting faded into the maybe-next-year category, and the publisher's advice to play it cool and wait and see was eminently acceptable—for about six weeks. Then the dilemma was again placed front and centre by the blandishments of a local alderman. Hugh Mackenzie, a moving-and-storage entrepreneur, was in his first term on the city council. He was also the commanding officer of the Queen's Own Cameron Highlanders non-permanent active militia. He had been alerted by Ottawa that his unit was listed for early mobilization, so he was enthusiastically preparing for that happy day.

"We're going to start recruiting any day now," was his invariable opening gambit, "so why don't you come into the Camerons with me and I'll get you a commission." To my response, that with a house under construction and a wife and daughter, I could not afford to join, Mackenzie had a quick answer.

"Look, come here, sit down, and I'll show you something." We sat down at a long committee-room table and he got out pencil and paper. "All right, you go in as a provisional lieutenant and as soon as you complete training and are attested a lieutenant, you will get $5 a day. That's $150 a month. Suppose you sign $100 a month over to your wife. That means she will be getting $135 a month. That's all hers, remember. You won't have to take out lunch money and carfare and cigarette money. On top of that her household expenses will go down because she won't be feeding you. I'll bet if you go home and seriously put pencil to paper you'll discover she'll actually be better off all around with you in the army!"

It was the same pitch I had heard from Burt Gresham so many times: get in on the ground floor, and you will have a jump on everybody else in the struggle for a place on the army escalator. Mackenzie's argument somehow sounded different than Gresham's had. Arguing with Gresham had been an objective, theoretical exercise, something quite remote from taking any action. But with

Mackenzie it was suddenly a very personal thing that involved me and put everything into a different and slightly distasteful light.

It was one thing for me to do my own arithmetic and come up with impossible numbers. It was something else for me to do it with Mackenzie, and come away with the feeling that the struggle against the plague of Naziism could be reduced to a haggling over dollars and cents. And aside from the arithmetic, the idea of going into the army as an officer offended my sense of the fitness of things. It wasn't cricket! It smacked of dirty pool! I would not have to demonstrate my ability to advance from the ranks; I would only have to know the right people and pull the right strings. In this respect, the army was no different from anything else in our society. Nevertheless, I took Mackenzie's numbers home to show Kay and get her reaction. She almost went into hysterics, and the next day I carried my turn-down of his offer back to Mackenzie.

"Oh, I am sorry," Mackenzie said, "because I've been talking to several other reporters and I'm sure you'll find that most of them will be coming with the Camerons." He had indeed. Before the Cameron mobilization was completed, he had enlisted three *Tribune* reporters and two from the *Free Press*. All were friends of mine; most were married and fathers of young children. The fact that they had joined up and I had found excuses not to did nothing for my peace of mind, nor did it make living with myself any easier.

It took the Germans and Russians only five weeks to complete the conquest of Poland. On the surface, the shooting war ended and the 1939–40 "phoney war" set in. It was a hiatus during which the Germans and Russians digested and consolidated their conquests and the Germans prepared for the next assault. In Canada, the early rush for the recruiting offices settled into a slower-paced march of young men into the organizing army, navy, and air force. Both the navy and the air force attracted hundreds more recruits than they could absorb, until their stocks of ships and planes were doubled and redoubled. The army had sent its first division to Europe and the blueprints and contracts for massive expansion of airfields and shipyards and munitions factories were pouring out of Ottawa. With the need for men for the services temporarily satisfied, the internal pressure to enlist diminished. With the British and French armies resting comfortably behind the Maginot Line, and the Germans doing the same behind the Siegfried Line, the war settled into a non-war of desultory token bombing raids and ripostes. Then the Germans launched their invasions of Norway, Holland, and Denmark, and crushed the French and British armies in two weeks with shattering hammer blows, and only the miracle rescue at Dunkirk saved the British from utter destruction.

In the ensuing panic, the pressure on the eligible civilians to enlist became irresistible. It came, not so much from the government, although conscription for home defence was imposed, as from peer pressure. As a small boy I had sat on the curbstones on Portage Avenue in 1915 and watched as the bands led recruiting marches along the street. On almost every block, young men left the sidewalks and fell in behind the marchers to wind up at a recruiting table in the Osborne barracks. Unsubtle things like marching bands helped make up thousands of minds in that war. There were no marching recruiting bands in the Second World War. But wherever we turned, there were reminders nudging at us. In the *Free Press* itself, the ranks were thinning as younger, unattached reporters drifted into the services.

One June evening in 1940, apropos of nothing I could identify, I found myself marching around the Minto Armouries parade ground with the 19th Field Battery militia unit which was soon to be mobilized. Who commanded it I never knew, for my military career lasted less than a month. We paraded twice a week and each evening we shed some of our clumsiness under the command of a permanent-force corporal. Each evening, too, we were introduced to new lieutenants in freshly "store-boughten" uniforms, who followed behind the corporal until, towards the end of the parade, he permitted them to take command and wheel us back and forth across the parade ground. Young lawyers, accountants, businessmen, they were getting into the army by the commission route, and when the unit was mobilized for active service they would be dispatched to an officer's training corps as provisional lieutenants and temporary gentlemen.

My military career ended before it officially began. We were not to sign official attestation papers until we had our physical examination. When I turned up for my physical, I discovered that the examination doctor was Norman Book, our family physician. It took him a moment to recognize me when I stood before him in the altogether. He picked up my enlistment form in disbelief. Then he exploded.

"Jimmy Gray! What the hell are you doing in this man's army. At your age! With your TB history! My God, look at you! Get on the scales!"

Somebody snickered. I was nudging 5'11" and weighed 134 pounds. Book drew his pen across my enlistment form, tossed it into a wire basket, and said, "Get the hell out of here and don't come back."

Well, at least I tried, I told myself as I caught a streetcar and went home. But had I really tried, or had I taken the easy way out?

Once the doubt was implanted, it remained for the duration of the war and a good deal later. In the end I became pretty well convinced that I had chickened out, that I could indeed have made it if I had persevered, if I had challenged Book to find anything organically wrong with me, for I knew that the evidence of tuberculosis was gone from my X-rays. And if the army could not use me, why had I not tried for the air force or the navy? I looked around for servicemen who were older than I, and no more robust, and found enough of them to make odious comparisons.

My reaction to the Nazi triumph of 1940 was shared by thousands of other young men in similar circumstances. But what of the reaction of the girls and women of western Canada? Not one man in ten thousand ever gave that question a second thought. Women's place was in the home, and if not in the home, certainly on the home front knitting socks, rolling bandages, or nursing the wounded. The idea that there would be a place for women in the war against Naziism never occurred to anybody running the war effort, least of all to the military establishment.

That the emergency was grave enough to require the service of women as well as men in the armed forces was an idea whose time had come. Its inevitability was demonstrated spectacularly when one woman was impelled to ask a seemingly silly question off the top of her head at a Winnipeg School Board meeting on June 18, 1940. The question was:

"If we are going to have cadet-corps training for the boys in our schools, why not cadet training for girls as well?"

The questioner was Gloria Queen-Hughes. That she should have been the one to ask it dramatized the complete about-face in public opinion that had occurred between Munich and Dunkirk in western Canada, as it had everywhere else outside French Canada. Gloria Queen-Hughes was the daughter of John Queen, Winnipeg's socialist mayor, a CCF founding father, and a once-jailed leader of the Winnipeg General Strike of 1919. Gloria had followed her father in politics and was a CCF member of the Winnipeg School Board. As the war clouds gathered in 1939 and the conservatives on the board tried to institute cadet training, Mrs. Queen-Hughes denounced the proposal and the motion was voted down. A year later, the idea surfaced again, this time under the sponsorship of a delegation of army officers from Military District 10. The Germans had completed their conquest of Denmark, Holland, and Norway, and were wiping up France and beginning the air war against England. Ottawa was embarked on a forced-draft campaign to expand Canada's own war effort, and was soon to impose military conscription for home defence. The time could come, the school trustees were warned, when Canada might have to conscript sixteen-year-olds from the high schools. It would, therefore, make but elementary common sense to institute cadet training in the schools so that the rising generation would be familiar with the fundamentals of army training when the call came. Mrs. Queen-Hughes joined the rest of the board in its unanimous decision to make cadet training a part of the physical-education program.

She was compelled by conscience to vote for cadet training, particularly with her husband now on active service with the Winnipeg Grenadiers. But she did not have to like the idea, and she was appalled by the notion of teenagers being taken into the armed services before they had at least had the chance to complete their education through grade twelve. As a dedicated feminist, she was also disturbed by the notion that only males could play a part in the defence of Canada.

The question she posed—why not cadet training for girls too—was probably no more than the instinctive response of a committed fighter for women's rights. It evoked no reaction save amused half-smiles from the all-male cadet sponsors. Ignored it was, but it did not go away. She kept mulling it over long after the question was settled, and it grew out of all proportion in the process. Was the recruitment of high-school students really the last resort? Should children be jerked out of school with their education incomplete? If and when the government ran out of grown men for its armed services, why would it not turn to its million able-bodied adult women before it started recruiting schoolboys? Why not, indeed? There must be thousands of jobs in the military establishments that could be done better by women than by the men occupying them. Utilizing the service of women would release thousands of paper-pushing servicemen for actual soldiering. Not only paper-pushers. What about all the soldiers working in kitchens, waiting on tables, driving officers' cars, operating telephone switchboards?

Why not, Gloria Queen-Hughes kept asking herself, and anyone else who would listen, a women's Canadian army corps which would take over all the "women's jobs" the army was filling with men? Did the British not have just such an organization in which women in uniform were driving trucks and ambulances and manning air-raid shelters and anti-aircraft guns? They had indeed. Even in Winnipeg there were already ad hoc women's groups taking lessons in truck driving. A half-dozen women had recently been reported trying to find some way of getting to England so they could enlist in the ambulance service.

In the month that followed the school-board meeting, Gloria

Queen-Hughes pursued the idea through the feminist establishment. She interviewed women doctors and business girls. She located a couple of old soldiers who would be interested in doing some drilling. She negotiated with the school-board administration for the use of schools for training purposes. By mid-July she was ready to test the waters of public opinion; she carried her idea into the *Free Press* newsroom and presented it to Pearl L'Ami, the editor of the women's page. Mrs. L'Ami did a short story on her plans and then had second thoughts about it. It looked more like a news-page story than a social note, so she took it over to Howard Wolfe, the city editor. The reaction of the male-chauvinist news staff was predictably raucous and lewd. The idea of an army of Amazons in barrack rooms struck us as the funniest story of the day. It reminded almost everybody of sexist jokes, and imagining the efforts of girl soldiers to accommodate themselves to the adjectival and adverbial over-use of four-letter words in army jargon drew rounds of hilarity. We imagined the spectacle of a girl sergeant shrieking: "Come on, you effing deadbeats, get that effing truck the effing hell back on the effing road and the effing well out of here!" The joking ran its course, and then Howard Wolfe and Abbie Coo, both veterans of the First World War, turned serious. Coo said:

"You know, it ain't all that bad an idea, Howard, when you remember the thousands of sons-of-bitches that fought our war back in headquarters offices, kitchens, and officers' messes!"

"Yeah," Wolfe replied, "and remember in the last war they used to say they needed five men in support for every front-line soldier. I'll bet this time the odds will be ten to one, what with all the PR types, counsellors, recreation officers and the like they've recruited."

They talked for a while and Wolfe called one of us over to rework Pearl L'Ami's story. "Get in touch with Gloria, see what else she had in mind, and see if you can make this into a story. And ask the brass out at Osborne what they think about it." The story appeared on the front page of the *Free Press* next day under a three-column head.

FIGHTING FEMALES

Plans for a Regiment of Women
Revealed by Mrs. Queen-Hughes

Winnipeg may yet have Canada's first all-women fighting regiment. Such a unit became a possibility Friday with the announcement by Mrs. Gloria Queen-Hughes that registration of women interested would begin at the Commercial Girls' Club, 309 Power Building, at 10 o'clock Monday morning.

While the amount of training that will be undertaken by the unit would depend largely on the number joining, present plans included training in the use of firearms, rifle drill, signalling and general military discipline, Mrs. Queen-Hughes said.

"We are trying to look ahead," she said.

Mrs. Queen-Hughes pointed out that the time might yet come when the need for women overseas might leave it up to the women of Canada to guard their nation. The reserve would be for that purpose. No sanction for the force had been received from M.D. 10, she added. Male instructors would be used in the preliminary stages.

Official comment on the reserve was not available at headquarters at Fort Osborne Barracks, Friday.

The reaction of the women of Winnipeg to the story was instantaneously enthusiastic. It could be summed up as: "Hey, brother, this is our war, too, and we want in!"

When Mrs. Queen-Hughes arrived at the Power Building to greet the volunteers, the hall outside the Business Girls' Club was jammed with women. The main entrance to the building was so full of women that the regular tenants of the building had trouble getting in and out. Outside the building itself there were several hundreds more. In her wildest flights of fancy, Gloria Queen-Hughes had hoped a couple of hundred women would turn up. She was greeted by more than two thousand. Instead of the registration taking a couple of hours, it had to be extended over a week.

A *Free Press* reporter who was on hand for the sign-up noted that the first woman in line was the wife of a recent volunteer in the Princess Pat's. When the second woman in line said that she owned a .22 rifle and was an experienced shooter, the reporter did a spot survey on the number of women who had actual experience with rifles. The result of the survey was a surprising twenty per cent. The women who waited in the stifling, above-100° weather to register were split about evenly between young single girls and young marrieds. Here and there were greying survivors of First World War British volunteer groups. There was also a lone male veteran of the Ulster Volunteer Corps who came along to offer his services as a drill instructor.

Gloria Queen-Hughes had her Women's Volunteer Force battalion. In fact, she had three battalions. What did she propose to do with them? She had only the foggiest idea, but fortunately there was helpful advice in the offing. Colonel H. J. Riley was the recently appointed commander of the Manitoba Volunteer Reserve Force, and he was in full sympathy with her proposal. So he provided outlines for procedures that would enable her to organize her women into groups. He put her in touch with George Hewett, a retired drill-master of the Princess Pat's Canadian Light Infantry. Hewett took over responsibility for putting a cadre of drill instructors together. With the help of Riley, she was able to break her volunteers into special study groups. One group specialized in food handling; another went into communications and took instruction in Morse-code telegraphy; another went into automotive units and was instructed in how to drive trucks. There were also groups in clerical work and even in a provost corps.

All this, however, was to come later, much later. For the first couple of months, the girls spent two nights each week on the physical jerks of the parade squares and, in the end, Hewett and his helpers could boast that they had taken gaggles of sloppy Josephines and converted them into precision marchers who would have put college bands to shame. Queen-Hughes took the boot-training along with the rest, but her days were spent running rather than marching. She persuaded the owners of a downtown business block to provide some rent-free office space, and the telephone company to install some free telephones. Then she got a score of city business firms to volunteer the use of their trucks and drivers to teach the girls how to drive the multi-geared vehicles. She got R. James Speers to donate the use of the Polo Park racetrack as a truck-driver training site so that the students could make their mistakes without danger to civilian life and property. The owners of two large General Motors and Ford garages not only gave the girls free run of their repair shops after work, they set up mechanical instruction courses for them with their foremen doing the teaching. The CNR and CPR provided volunteers to teach the girls telegraphy and the telephone company provided instructors in that branch of communication.

One of the questions uppermost in the minds of the volunteers was: When do we get uniforms? They got uniforms eventually by paying for them themselves. Ben Jacob of Jacob and Crowley had his dress designers whip up a navy-blue skirt, blouse, and jacket combination that the girls could buy for fifteen dollars. The Winnipeg Cap and Hat Company designed a cap to match the uniform and Mitchell and Copp designed a brooch and suitable insignia for the lapels and shoulders.

The one thing Queen-Hughes and her fellow officers could not do was attract favourable notice from the officials in Ottawa. They organized letter-writing campaigns to their members of Parliament. They wrote provincial and municipal politicians. They lobbied the upper echelons of the services themselves. In an effort to help them along, the *Free Press* had one of its Ottawa correspondents needle the military establishment about finding a place for the women in the services. He struck mud. It was officially announced that a survey had been made, and it had been determined that in the entire armed-services establishment, there were only fifteen hundred positions that could be filled by women. It would not be worth the disruption to put women into these positions.

That statement might well have meant the end of the women's-army idea except for one thing. The original Queen-Hughes story had been picked up by other papers across the country, and in all the major centres women were following Queen-Hughes' example and getting into the act. Within days, the Winnipeg post office was being flooded with Queen-Hughes mail. Some reached her at the school board, some at home. Some of it came addressed to her at the *Free Press*. The mail was almost form-letter in content: How do we go about doing what you are doing, and what advice can you give us? Then the form changed, as more and more prospective recruits from country points across the prairies and down into the United States wanted to volunteer for enlistment in the Winnipeg group.

Everybody wanted to get into the act somehow. And it seemed that everybody did in the fall of 1940. Ethel English called for volunteers in Calgary, and the military district put Mewata Armouries and several drill instructors at her disposal. Leona McIlvena in Lethbridge and Helen Rankin in Regina were close behind in getting groups on to parade squares. In the beginning, the efforts of the women were treated as a big joke by the male population, who turned out to stand on the sidelines and jeer at the antics of the girls trying to form threes and march in column of route. The jeers and smart cracks from the sidelines were gradually stilled by the persistent refusal of the women to be intimidated.

The rejection of the women by Ottawa brought a serious, though temporary, impairment of morale. Some of the volunteers gave up and turned their energies elsewhere. But so widespread an appeal did the project have, on the prairies at least, that pressure on Ottawa to change its mind grew steadily until, in June 1941, it gave in. The Department of National Defence announced that, beginning in September, it would be recruiting volunteers for something called the Canadian Army Women's Auxiliary Corps. But it was not going to be the honest-to-God kind of army Gloria Queen-Hughes had envisioned. It would be more like the ladies' auxiliaries of charitable hospitals or the Loyal Orange Lodge. Emphasis was on auxiliary, pointedly so when the corps was placed under the wing of General L. R. Laflèche, then in charge of all volunteer services and soon to enter the Cabinet as Minister of National War Services.

From its recruitment procedures, Ottawa seemed to be looking for groups of vestal virgins who would assist the army in performing certain of its duties with gentility and poise. Each prospective enlistee, for example, was required to provide three written character references. When the local enlistment office had completed a personal dossier on each applicant, the file had to be sent to Ottawa, where a sight-unseen judgment would be made on the suitability of the volunteer.

When Mrs. Queen-Hughes discovered how deeply the regulations were tinged with madness, she high-tailed it to Ottawa to try to get them changed. Eventually she got through to General Laflèche, himself a courtly gentleman who exuded both charm and a massive antipathy towards the whole idea of having women within howitzer range of the army. To her protestations against the idiocy of demanding three character references, he replied that, without such restrictions, the women's army would be overrun by every prostitute in the country. To which she replied that it seemed to her the recommendation system would have the same effect.

"After all," she countered, "who is better acquainted with all the best people, and hence able to provide the best recommendations, than are the prostitutes?"

Anyway, said Laflèche, the whole idea of a women's auxiliary was preposterous. And it would be outrageously costly. The first thing the government would have to do after it brought women into the army would be to build a string of maternity homes across the country. The general unquestionably reflected a fairly common attitude among the aging brass of the service establishment, and among the reverend clergy as well. But, as Mrs. Queen-Hughes argued, putting uniforms on women by itself could not transform chaste and upright girls into promiscuous bed-hoppers. Of course, what H. L. Mencken defined as "the biological urge and the right season" did produce complicating liaisons, but hardly to a greater extent than happened from the mixing of the sexes in business and industry.

Naturally, during the beginning phase of getting the women's army organized, it attracted some card-carrying whores and persuadable amateurs, but hardly in greater proportion than the army had attracted petty thieves, pimps, gamblers, and jailbirds during its first recruiting drives. In any event, the disciplined lives of the CWACS would have discouraged most of the whores from enlistment, and few self-respecting prostitutes would have given the corps a second thought after they discovered the miserly pay scale the Defence Department had established for women—two-thirds of the pay offered male recruits, or 95 cents a day compared with $1.40. On enlistment, the women got a special bonus, however—fifteen dollars with which to outfit themselves with underwear, stockings, and cosmetics. Thereafter they received one dollar a month for cosmetics, payable quarterly.

The establishment moved very slowly in putting the women into uniform. Instead of working through the volunteer corps that had sprung up everywhere, it turned recruitment over to the military, and the commandants in each district looked around for eligible women leaders of local groups to bring into a nucleus of an officers' corps. They set up the registration of volunteers, collected the character references, did their own background checking. Ottawa, meanwhile, located a boot camp for the girls at Ste. Anne de Bellevue, Quebec. Processing the applications in Ottawa took months.

As the time passed, the delay enabled the army to have second thoughts about the women's corps. It abandoned the auxiliary idea and decided to make the women a part of the army itself. It abandoned the titles of subaltern and company commander it had chosen for women officers and reverted to regular army titles. It renamed the body the Canadian Women's Army Corps, and by February 1941, the first officer and non-commissioned-officer candidates were en route to Ste. Anne's. Naturally, the group included the leaders of all the provincial volunteers corps—Gloria Queen-Hughes and Daisy Royal from Winnipeg, Helen Rankin from Regina, Leona McIlvena and Ethel English from Alberta. Included in the Alberta group was Mary Dover, who was given command of the Ste. Anne's training camp when Queen-Hughes and the others returned west to take command of local CWAC units. When a much larger facility was later established at Kitchener to train women from all over the world, Mary Dover was promoted to the rank of major and given that command, while Daisy Royal replaced her at Ste. Anne's.

As things turned out, it was evident that the antipathy of the Laflèches towards the enlistment of women was not confined to the general staff. When the units of the corps were at last in operation, they encountered a good deal of open hostility, even at the common-soldier level. By the time the recruitment of women was seriously undertaken, the Manitoba volunteer groups had run more than three thousand volunteers through the basic army-training courses. The women took the same instruction as the men in communications, map reading, truck driving, food preparation, and so on, and passed the same exams as regular army recruits. But when they began to appear in numbers to take over the jobs of "A" and "B" category soldiers, they ran into resentment and occasional sabotage. Thus, at Fort Osborne barracks, girl drivers of vehicles discovered that ignition systems were tampered with to prevent efficient starting and operation.

By the end of 1941, the flood of volunteers that had responded to the opening of recruiting convinced the Defence Department that it was on to something important. Upward of fifteen thousand women had volunteered for the two thousand places it expected to fill. The air force got into the act with such enthusiasm that it was able to drain away several thousand volunteers from the army. And all this despite conditions that would have sent any self-respecting royal commission on women's rights into conniption fits. Despite the fact that the women enlistees did the same work as the men they replaced, often, as in the case of the clerical work, doing it quicker and better, they were still paid less than men in all categories. Periodic protests in Parliament changed nothing until, late in the war, the women's scale was raised to eighty per cent of the male scale.

The situation was unfair enough in the years before the Canadian forces got into action in Europe. Then it became nothing short of a public scandal. When the women volunteered, it was for service anywhere in the world for the duration of the war, and more than two thousand did see service in Europe. This was in contrast with upward of fifty thousand male conscriptees in Canada who refused to serve outside the country. So CWAC's serving with the army in Italy, frequently very close to the fighting, did so for twenty per cent less pay than the so-called Zombies in Canada received. Nor was that the only discriminatory treatment they suffered. Many thousands of the women in the services were wives of soldiers. As such, in civilian life they had received dependant's allowances of thirty-five dollars a month to go with their soldier's assigned pay. When they enlisted, they lost their dependant's allowances!

Discrimination against women in terms of pay and allowances applied with equal force in the Royal Canadian Air Force Women's Division and in the Women's Royal Canadian Naval Service. Of the three services, the RCAF probably reacted most enthusiastically to the enlistment of women. By the war's end it was rivalling the army both in numbers of women recruited and in the variety of jobs it had found for them.

The Royal Canadian Navy, probably reflecting the Laflèche view of women at war, resisted the enlistment of women until 1942, and then decided to import British women instructors to tell it how to organize the Women's Royal Canadian Naval Service. In the five years that elapsed between Gloria Queen-Hughes' launching of the women's army and the end of the war, more than 45,000 women enlisted in the three services: 21,625 in the CWAC, 17,018 in the RCAFWD, and 6,781 in the WRCNS.

In a speech to the House of Commons in March 1943, Colonel J. L. Ralston, the Minister of National Defence, said that the response of the women of Canada to the first appeal for volunteers had provided him with the greatest satisfaction he had experienced as head of the Defence Department. There is no question, as Colonel C. P. Stacey pointed out in his history of the armed services, *Six Years of War*, that without the women, the conscription crises which kept tearing the country apart would have been much more serious. Certainly, the women more than made up for the men who disappeared into the underbrush when they received their calls to report for military service overseas.

But whether the conscription crisis of 1944–45 would have come sooner if it had not been for the women is highly unlikely. It arose over concern for the lack of adequate reinforcements for the army in Europe. This lack did not become apparent until the unexpectedly heavy casualties suffered during the storming of France and Holland in 1944. In any event, conscription was much more a blood-and-guts issue than an argument over numbers.

The government had gone into the war with the most explicit and firmly made commitments that there would be no conscription for overseas service. The French-Canadian Cabinet ministers were unanimous in supporting the government's declaration of war, but only with the guarantee that there would be no conscription. That had been the issue which tore the country apart in the First World War, and there was overwhelming support for the conviction that it should not be allowed to happen again.

But as Joseph Stalin pointed out during the war, there is no logic as powerful as the logic of things. The thing that unhinged the no-conscription pledges was the attempt by Canada to do too much, to make too great a contribution to the war effort. That, and a gross miscalculation on the part of the general staff of the reinforcements that would be required by the Canadian infantry in the conquest of Europe.

Despite massive war-production undertakings that included everything from production of tanks, guns, planes, and ammunition to artificial rubber, chemicals, trucks, merchant ships, and naval vessels, there seemed no limit the general staff was prepared to place on the size of the Canadian army. Moreover, because it was to be Canadian from top to bottom, it required an under-structure of clerks, paper-pushers, planners, and so on, that would have been appropriate for a fighting force twice the size. By the time the war ended, more than one million men and women had been enlisted by the three services—730,000 in the army, 250,000 in the air force, and 100,000 in the navy.

Once the unemployed and the eager youngsters had been enlisted, the army began to run out of volunteers, even though both the air force and the navy had long lists of recruits waiting to join. With the triumph of Hitler in Europe in 1940, the government imposed conscription for home defence. First, all single males under forty-five became eligible to be called up for a month's army-camp training. The period was quickly extended to four months and then for the duration of the war. At the same time, both other services soaked up their waiting lists and began calling for volunteers as well. Here peer pressure and the herd instinct came into play with ever-increasing force. Naval and air-force trainees home from boot camp became persuasive salesmen among their friends for their branch of the service. But with full employment, good pay, and marriage prospects, the youth of 1941 became more given to weighing alternatives than the youth of 1939 had been.

The calling up of the seventeen- to twenty-five-year-olds was not universally applied, of course. Certain jobs in key war industries and in food production were categorized as essential. University students were exempt, as long as they enrolled in the Reserve Officers' Training Corps and signed up for enlistment on graduation. So men in university in 1938 did not become eligible for compulsory service until 1942. Married men were also exempt. As time passed, young males without exempting jobs or other qualifications developed a formula of sorts to govern their behaviour. First they canvassed the services, picked the one they preferred, and relaxed while awaiting their first call-up notice for service in the army. The navy and air force were restricted to volunteers. Ordinarily, the first notification was followed by a postponement of several weeks. The second call meant immediate induction into the army. So the procedure was for the inductees to wait until their second call was about due and then to rush around to the navy or air force and enlist as volunteers. Others collected their girl friends, put a marriage licence to work, and escaped induction by getting married.

Eventually the selective-service administration closed those loopholes. They blocked enlistment in navy or air force to those who had already received first draft orders. They arbitrarily picked a date in June 1942 after which all who married would be considered single for purposes of the draft boards.

Despite the plebiscite in April 1942, which gave the government authority to impose conscription for overseas service, it refused to do so until the war was almost over. There was conscription for home defence in the army, but only those who volunteered for overseas service were sent abroad. The country, however, had far more men in uniform than it needed for home defence and a great many less in service abroad than the army brass considered they needed to provide adequate reinforcements.

As time passed, the Canadian army at home became split into two antagonistic factions. There was the "A" for active group, which had volunteered for overseas service, and the "R" for reserve group, which had not. The way to solve the reinforcement problem was for the active force to persuade the reserve force to volunteer. Within that reserve force, however, were tens of thousands of very stubborn young men. The majority were French Canadians who would not budge an inch from their home-defence-reserve status. There were the conscientious objectors and conscientious conscriptionists. The latter claimed to regard the refusal of the government to conscript for overseas service as gutless hypocrisy. "If they need me and want me somewhere else, then it is up to them to send me there. I'll go. I'll fight anywhere. All they have to do is take me to where they want me to fight and give me a gun!"

The army mixed the groups in roughly equal numbers and, officially, let moral suasion by the "A" group work its magic on the "R" group. It did not work worth a damn. Physical persuasion worked somewhat better, if reinforced by the infliction of every practical joke an army camp could devise. Like the Jews in Germany, the Zombies, as the "R" group came to be called, were required to wear special insignia, a red maple leaf, which identified them on sight to the army and civilians alike.

There was little that was original in the persuasion-by-humiliation tactics used against the Zombies—sand dropped into shoes on route marches, clothing tossed into showers during the night, purgatives secreted in sandwiches or dropped into beer, gang fights, thievery. More subtle were the ways of the administrators—transfers to remote posts, assignment to special exercises, and so on. In the early months of conscription, gentler forms of persuasion undoubtedly diverted many thousands of conscripts into the active army. But as time passed, there was a build-up of hard cores of the tough-minded, so that towards the end of the war, even special appeals for volunteers brought little response.

Before the 1942 plebiscite, I had been transferred from the news department to the editorial page. The *Free Press* under Dafoe had firmly established an anti-conscriptionist stance, and as a result we got many calls from relatives of Zombies protesting against the treatment of sons or brothers within the army. One winter day, a tearful woman brought in a letter from her son, who complained that his feet had been severely frostbitten as a result of being forced to go on a route march in socks freshly retrieved from soaking in a latrine.

I had never found the stories endlessly circulating about the games played on the Zombies very amusing. This time I thought maybe a sub-editorial mildly rebuking the army authorities would be in order. I composed one and took it in to George Ferguson. He reacted angrily.

"For Christ's sake, don't you think we've got trouble enough with Victor over conscription? Want to run this and get us all fired?" He threw the editorial away.

6
When Wage and Price Controls Were a Way of Life

The heroism, folly, and patriotism of war have all been well celebrated in poetry and prose, but a search of the anthologies and books of quotations for any celebration of war itself is usually fruitless. And rightly so, for war is the ultimate act of human folly, and never before had humanity paid so frightful a price as it did in the Second World War. The crowning human irony is that nothing so forged a people into a solid, cohesive unity as did the Second World War for the people of western Canada. It is hardly an exaggeration to describe those war years as the golden age of the prairie West. Not in economic terms, of course, for prairie agriculture remained in a sadly depressed condition throughout most of the war, and the prairies fell further behind central Canada in industrial development. For prairie farmers, the war years were a season of prolonged frustration and struggle against depressed prices, equipment scarcity, and shortage of essential help. But in terms of unity of spirit, nothing like the Second World War had happened before—nor has it since.

The spiritual unification of the people of the prairies came to pass almost imperceptibly with Winston Churchill's accession to power in Britain on May 10, 1940. Three days later, from his "blood, toil, tears, and sweat" speech in the House of Commons, we got our first hint of the magnitude of the British disaster in France; three weeks later still, we got the full import of it from his "we will fight on the beaches; we shall never surrender" speech as the Germans were beginning to marshal their forces on the beaches of Normandy in preparation for the invasion. Whether Churchill's defiant rhetoric came to us directly from the radio, or was transmitted by Charles Jennings and Lorne Greene on the CBC evening news, we identified so completely with Churchill and with his leadership that anything our own leaders had to say became almost anti-climactic. As a result, when our own government reacted to developments in Europe and took certain actions, our responses tended to be on the carping side, not to quibble about whether the action was needed, but to question whether it was sufficient, whether we were being asked to do enough. That was the way the public reacted to the first war budget of June 1940, and kept on reacting to war budgets as long as there were war budgets.

Until June 24, 1940, the Canadian income tax was a mere fleabite to the overwhelming majority of Canadians, who earned under $2,400 a year. In the West, skilled tradesmen who earned that much were very much in the minority. The banks refused their ledger-keepers permission to marry until they were earning one hundred dollars a month, and a country bank manager with a salary of $150 a month was two or three brackets ahead of the school principals, town clerks, and general storekeepers. Only urban mayors, city treasurers, department-store managers, bank superintendents, railway vice-presidents, and utility heads managed to penetrate the $4,000 to $10,000 brackets. The pre-war tax bite of a childless couple's $4,000 income was only $84, while the couple making $10,000 paid only $781. It was only when the income got into the six-figure range, and nobody's did on the prairies, that the tax became onerous. Thus a $100,000-earner had a Depression-era federal tax bill of around $39,000.

The first wartime budget let the bottom income brackets off lightly. In addition to the income tax itself, a special war tax of two per cent was levied on all wages above $700 a year for single people and $1,200 a year for married taxpayers. If the concept of a poverty level of income had existed in 1940, it would have been represented by those figures. So the law provided that in neither case was the tax to reduce the income of those earning less than $700 or $1,200. This provision was retained for the borderline incomes throughout the war years. In 1940 people in the $2,000 income bracket were assessed a tax of $75. Where the pre-war federal tax on a $4,000 married income had been $84, the 1940 budget raised it to $355, to which an additional $100 was added by provincial income taxes. The tax on $10,000 incomes jumped from $781 to $2,170 plus another $400 for the provinces. In case any $100,000-a-year fat cats developed, the federal tax went to $51,000, to which Manitoba would add $10,000; in Saskatchewan and Alberta, the additional impost was $26,000. A Canadian Press analyst pointed out that anybody in Saskatchewan unlucky enough to earn $500,000 would owe the two governments $538,000.

The urban newspapers all did surveys of reader-reaction to the budget. In 1940 none of the reporters in Winnipeg, Calgary, or Edmonton could locate a single complaint against the imposts. Indeed, a common comment in Winnipeg was that the budget's impact was too light rather than too heavy.

During the Depression, the conventional wisdom of the best

economists was that the 18-per-cent tax on corporation profits had reached the point of no return and was inhibiting risk-taking and investment. When it was raised to 40 per cent in 1940, and an excess-profits tax of 75 per cent imposed on top of it, the business community accepted it with barely a murmur of protest. A special 10-per-cent sales tax on radios, phonographs, and cameras was as readily accepted by those involved as was the 10-per-cent tax on $700 automobiles and an 80-per-cent tax on all cars with an over-$1,200 wholesale price tag.

This universal acceptance of levels of taxation that were burdensome, even horrendous by any previous yardstick, was just as apparent in the reaction to the post-Pearl Harbor budget two years later. In the 1942 budget, the government added a compulsory-saving feature to the increased tax rate. A married man with an income of $2,000 was assessed $231 in tax and $200 in compulsory savings, refundable after the war. The provincial tax put the couple into the 25-per-cent tax bracket. The combined federal and provincial tax and compulsory savings on a $10,000 income exceeded $5,000. Even the corporation taxes contained a compulsory-savings feature. The excess-profits tax was raised to 100 per cent with 20 per cent refundable after the war.

It was along about here that the expression "take-home pay" came into common usage. By 1942, my own pay was up to fifty dollars a week but, with the income-tax deduction, the compulsory-savings deduction, the war-bonds deduction, the Red Cross deduction, and so on, we seldom had even forty dollars to spread on the kitchen table. As everyone else seemed to be doing, though, we got along very well on our take-home pay, thanks in part to wartime shortages of consumer goods. When it was the done thing to get another year's wear out of an overcoat, there was no pressure to replace it until it was downright disreputable. "Making do" had become an acceptable way of life, and made living comfortably on our take-home pay easily possible.

There was not, of course, any massive stampede by the citizenry to impoverish themselves in support of the war effort. Employers and employees alike sailed as close to the legal limit as the law allowed, and the natural tendency was always to interpret the law liberally in the interpreter's favour. As the war went on, the tendency towards paranoia over real or fancied income discrimination increased. People frozen in essential industry boggled at the unfairness of being deprived of a chance to work in higher-paying jobs. Sellers of scarce commodities took what advantage they could of market conditions. In business and commerce, great promotional activity went on "in support of the war effort," but quite often the commercial interests of the companies were much more deeply involved. Thus, the H. J. Heinz Company trumpeted the news that the use of tin cans for fruits and vegetables would soon be a thing of the past. But not to worry, on two counts: the company was already searching for substitute container material, and there were still large enough stocks of cans on hand to keep store shelves pleasantly burdened with Heinz products. General Motors, with no cars or trucks to sell, kept its trademark before the public with a campaign to instruct truck owners how to make their trucks last longer. The skin Palmolive loved to touch might now encase the frame of a girl at a lathe in a machine shop, but it was still eminently touchable, thanks to Procter and Gamble.

Nevertheless, the onset of the Battle of Britain became the wellspring for a surge of altruism across the West, and it increased in power and intensity as months stretched into years. When the Red Cross put out an urgent appeal for blankets for Britain, people all across the prairies not only ransacked their closets for spares, they stripped the store shelves and donated their purchases to the cause. Later, the drive for aluminum scrap saw thousands of pots and pans collected in a matter of hours. Every city, town, and hamlet had its women's volunteer bureau, all of which were embroiled in a frenzied search for things to do to advance the war effort.

In all these respects, the situation contrasted sharply with the First World War. There had been patriotic fervour then, too, but there had been a strong undercurrent of opposition to the war itself. A radical anti-war wing of the trades-union movement, centred in the West, was in continual dispute with the pro-war leaders of the international craft unions. Marxist socialists dominated many of the local unions in the West. Their line was that the war was between rival capitalist-imperialist powers and was one which did not concern the working class. The radical unionist sentiment was neatly summarized by Dick Rigg, a labour member of the Manitoba legislature, in his speech during the bitter conscription debate of 1917. Charles Lipton quotes him as follows:

When people cry aloud for reforms and threaten capitalist profits, the capitalists start a war. When people cry for old age pensions, women's suffrage, workmen's compensation acts, the capitalists start a war. The working men of one country have no quarrel with the working men of another country. The common enemy the world over is the capitalist class.*

* Quoted by Charles Lipton in *The Trade Union Movement of Canada 1827–1959* (Montreal: Canadian Social Publications Limited, 1967), pp. 169–70.

When Rigg completed his speech, A. V. Thomas, the *Winnipeg Tribune* legislative reporter, was so moved that he arose in the press gallery and cheered Rigg at the top of his voice. He was fired out of hand by the paper when he returned to the office. In 1917, local unions all across the West were passing resolutions calling for a general strike to oppose conscription.

Nothing like this happened in the Second World War. Even the Communists, whose boisterous anti-Nazi crusade became an anti-British crusade when Russia joined Germany in devouring Poland, confined themselves mainly to advocating a negotiated peace. But, when Russia itself was invaded, they became the loudest advocates of a total war effort. There was, of course, more than enough rancorous political debate. The CCF wanted Canada's war effort confined to making armaments for somebody else to shoot. The Toronto Tories wanted conscription from the outset and kept clamouring for it within their own party and on the hustings as well. All opposition parties in the West joined with the western Liberal members in a long and acrimonious struggle to get parity prices for agricultural products. But this was all political controversy about means and not ends. About the war itself, there was no argument. Out where the people lived, the question resolved itself into something as simple as, "Okay, what else would you like me to do?"

The difference between 1914 and 1939 was undoubtedly the determination on the part of all members of Parliament, and indeed of all other public bodies, that the evils of 1914–18 would not be repeated. There would be no profiteering on war contracts, no price-gouging of the public, no one class profiting at the expense of another. Above all, there would be no post-war inflation to compare with that which followed the First World War.

Of all the instruments the federal government established to achieve its purposes, two were of pre-eminent importance. The first was C. D. Howe's Ministry of Munitions and Supply. The second was the Wartime Prices and Trade Board presided over by Donald Gordon. A self-made construction millionaire, Howe was off and running before the first shot was fired in 1939. His campaign to conscript the leaders of Canadian commerce, industry, and finance for his massive war-production machine stripped Canadian capitalism of much of its key personnel and chained them to government desks for the duration. Not only did they devise production programs and set production targets, they drafted foolproof contracts which protected the government against profiteering and quality dilution. During the first six months of his ministry's operation, Howe told the House of Commons, it had put out fourteen thousand contracts, mostly to public tender, and let more than $300 million worth of work. This included everything from building airports to building airplane engines, from designing troop carriers to designing minesweepers, from supplying shirts, socks, and boots by the hundred-thousands to the supplying of quadruplicated forms by the carload. In the sharpest contrast to the history of the First World War, no breath of scandal touched Howe's wartime operations. Snafus there were, things got botched, there were delays galore, but crimes of commission or omission for private gain there were not. And the determination of the government to keep wartime profits within reason was demonstrated by the imposition of the excess-profits tax in its first budget.

Under the War Measures Act, the federal government set up the Wartime Prices and Trade Board and gave it almost total power to control and regiment the Canadian economy and everybody in it. Because Depression conditions prevailed well into the war, the impact of the board on the economy was minimal, until the Depression surpluses of manpower and material were worked off. Howe's whopping demands helped to soak up most of the surplus manpower in the country's industrial heartland, but it took a lot longer in the West. For one thing, the sustained depression of farm income through the fixing of sub-marginal prices for grain and livestock, coupled with an absence of war orders, retarded western recovery. There were still five thousand farmers on relief in 1941. Wages remained low, and it was not until the summer of 1942 that the Manitoba government got around to raising the minimum salary for rural school teachers from fifty dollars a month to seventy dollars.

By the midsummer of 1941, however, the business-as-usual phase of the war had about run its course. Until then, women could indulge their newly acquired taste for nylon stockings and nighties, and men who could afford them could still get new cars. Food and clothing of all kinds were plentiful and prices were reasonable. There were plenty of building materials available for housing construction, along with electrical and plumbing fixtures and cooking utensils. Nevertheless, the inhibiting effect of the unbroken litany of bad news from the war fronts was weakening the public's appetite for material things. The purchase of luxury items was more likely to evoke the question "Don't you know there's a war on?" than envious murmurs of admiration.

Until the prices of food and rent started to rise, the activities of the Wartime Prices and Trade Board were confined mainly to controlling rents in a few congested localities, which included

Calgary, Brandon, and Edmonton in the West, and in trying to persuade housewives to go easy on the use of sugar. The board ordered retailers to limit sales to eight ounces of sugar per person per week and made it a criminal offence for anybody to accumulate or withhold from sale any necessities of life. The voluntary restraint worked reasonably well for two years, but as summer passed into fall in 1941, it became apparent that prices were on the rise, scarcities were developing, and more muscle was needed behind the Wartime Prices and Trade Board. In October, it got all the muscle it would ever need when Donald Gordon, the deputy governor of the Bank of Canada, was appointed czar of the Canadian economy. A month later, on November 6, the Honourable J. L. Ilsley, Minister of Finance, announced the imposition of an all-inclusive ceiling on all wages and prices in the country. At the same time the powers of the Prices Board were expanded, so that it could step into foreign markets, buy needed import goods, and move them into Canadian consumption at prices consistent with the prevailing ceiling. In short, it could subsidize the price of imported food to Canadian consumers. In December the Japanese bombed Pearl Harbor, and complicated the job of the board beyond anything imaginable.

In a matter of weeks Canadian consumers of just about everything were put on a total war basis. The original sugar-ration books, only recently distributed, were called in and exchanged for multiple-coupon books which could be used to ration other items in short supply as the shortages developed. An end was quickly put to the production and sale of automobiles for civilian use. The sale of tires to civilians was prohibited except in the most unusual circumstances; for a doctor or a clergyman to get a new tire required that he turn in his discard. Nylon and silk hosiery disappeared from the market completely and the ladies were forced back into the rayon stockings they had abandoned so gleefully when nylons were invented. Eventually the hosiery makers were granted minimal quotas and nylons came back on to the market, but only in minuscule quantities that enabled retailers to build Brownie points with favoured customers by doling them out from under the counter.

The impact of the Wartime Prices and Trade Board on the Canadian economy was all-pervasive. The board stepped in and ordered manufacturers of just about everything people used to change their mode of doing business. It restricted the sizes and shapes of the products they made and the containers they used. It reached down into such things as the number of buttons on the sleeves of jackets and the number of pockets in women's coats. It ordered the dropping of straps from the backs of men's vests; it ended the use of elastic in women's girdles, zippers on pockets, flaps on pockets, and cuffs on pants. Electrical fixtures disappeared from the market as whole factories were converted overnight to war production.

Most important of all, women were turned into peripatetic computers. As the months passed, shopping for groceries began to approach a full-time job. Not only were such staples as tea, coffee, sugar, butter, and meat rationed, but the values attached to each commodity coupon frequently changed. Colour coding made it easier to keep track of the various items, except of course for the colour-blind. But a purple butter coupon that was worth half a pound one week might be reduced to six ounces the next. How did they get six ounces of butter when butter only came in pounds, half-pounds and quarter-pounds? They gave up four coupons, which had been worth thirty-two ounces of butter, in return for twenty-four ounces in three half-pound packets. Eventually the government put out pressed-paper disks which the storekeepers were able to give out for fractions of ration coupons. These disks came to be more valuable than money when meat rationing went into effect in 1943.

How valuable I discovered on arrival home from work one afternoon to a family crisis. Alan, who was born in September 1940, was then going on four, and Linda, who arrived in January 1942, was nicely into the "terrible twos." They had gotten into Kay's purse and were amusing themselves with the meat-ration disks she had accumulated. During the game the disks had become mysteriously coated with peanut butter and jelly and were devoured in a series of gulps by Perky, our fox terrier, to the vast amusement of the children. With the disks went the roast for our Sunday dinner. When none of the neighbours had any spare meat-ration coupons we could borrow, Kay had to settle for beefsteak and kidney pie, with heavy emphasis on unrationed kidney and light on the stewing meat masquerading as steak.

It was not long before a universal one-on-one barter business sprang into existence, as varying family appetites created surpluses and scarcities. A family that packed lunches to school or work tended to run short of butter. A family with two or three small children could have more butter than it needed but was short of jam or jelly. One family would be long on tea and short on coffee and vice versa. Everybody at first was short of meat. That was gradually overcome by over-using unrationed meat like liver and kidneys and saving up beef coupons till they would buy a good roast.

Keeping track of the ration coupons became an endless headache for every merchant in the land. They had to collect all their different coupons, sort them out, and turn them in to their suppliers' banks in order to replenish their stock. The meat packers and other wholesalers likewise had to account for enough tickets to balance shipments to their customers. With such a massive use of loose, stamp-sized ration coupons, it was inevitable that leakages would develop. Indeed, it was almost impossible for large processors and wholesalers to account precisely for their incoming and outgoing commodities. Retailers, too, could go wrong in their counting and there were no ration-coupon registers to remove temptation from clerks the way cash registers did. And, of course, there was always a black market of sorts, where wily law-breakers could convert ration coupons into cash. Burglaries did not by any means end with the war, and a few of these soon convinced business people that the place for ration tickets was locked in the safe, not filed in a tin box on the bookkeeper's desk.

Inevitably, as the public became more accustomed to the ration-coupon economy, the board had more cases to prosecute for violation of the rules. Nevertheless, the system itself had the overwhelming support of the people because it was *prima facie* proof that a fair distribution of scarce essentials of life was being attempted. When an average housewife encountered overt efforts on the part of friends or neighbours to beat the ration system, the reaction was frequently to make an angry call to the local ration board. Difficulties in collecting evidence that would stand up in court usually meant that little could be done about the law-breakers and rule-benders. But every now and then hoarders were prosecuted and examples made. That happened early in the ration era in Calgary, when a prominent oilman was convicted of illegally hoarding several large bags of sugar in his basement. The conviction earned him the sobriquet he carried to his grave, as his friends, neighbours, business associates, and total strangers lost track of his given name and knew him only as "Sugar" Schultz.

Despite the obvious difficulties of enforcing such a multiplicity of complex regulations of wages, prices, and supplies, there is no doubt whatever that the Wartime Prices and Trade Board largely achieved its ultimate aims. The first was to avoid both the adulteration in quality and the massive rise in prices that wartime scarcities would cause. The second was to prevent the runaway inflation that created such economic havoc after the First World War. The statistics put together by the Dominion Bureau of Statistics for the board's 1947 annual report demonstrates the measure of the board's success.

During the First World War and the post-war reconstruction period—six years—the Canadian cost-of-living index rose almost 100 per cent and the wholesale index 150 per cent. Between 1939 and 1947, the increase was only 30 per cent in the cost of living and 35 per cent in the wholesale index. If the comparison is confined to the period when prices and wage controls operated, between 1941 and 1947, the cost-of-living increase was only 20 per cent, the lowest of any belligerent. The statistics of some of the cost-of-living components are striking. Food prices rose 200 per cent between 1914 and 1920 but only 45 per cent between 1939 and 1947. Clothing rose 240 per cent compared with 30 per cent; fuel rose 50 per cent compared with 10 per cent; miscellaneous needs were up 60 per cent compared with 20 per cent, and rents rose almost 40 per cent compared with 10 per cent. In the First World War soles fell off shoes with the first rainfall. Expensive clothes shredded in wash tubs. Men's blue-serge suits turned a sickly purple in the prairie sun. Pork sausage often contained more fillers than meat. Nothing comparable happened during the Second World War. Indeed, because of restrictions imposed on manufacturers, the quality of many items actually improved.

Nevertheless, despite the success of wartime *prices* policy, a dichotomy in public attitudes developed as the policy was evolving. There was a general acceptance, except for farm prices, that the wartime freezing of prices and wages was necessary, desirable, and working reasonably well. There was unanimous support for the rationing system, based on the recognition that the system was working out about as fairly as human ingenuity could make it. There was an acceptance of the fact that the needs of the war effort had to get first priority, and if there were minor privations to be endured they were as nothing compared with the sufferings being endured by the people of Britain and occupied Europe. The rapidly expanding list of wartime austerity measures being imposed stirred scarcely a murmur of discontent, even when some things seemed a little ridiculous, like the regulation that required the depositing of empty toothpaste tubes when new tubes were being purchased, when tinfoil was banned from cigarette packages, metal lipstick containers were abolished, and the manufacturing of curling irons, dustpans, and pencil sharpeners was outlawed for the duration.

On the other hand, it came to be regarded as downright unpatriotic to allow ration coupons to go to waste. If you did not pass your surplus tea or coffee or sugar coupons along to needful friends, you lived with the guilty feeling that you were unfairly depriving them of necessities of life. This attitude reached its fullest flower when gasoline and booze came under the rationing restrictions.

The imposition of gasoline rationing on a nation-wide scale in April of 1942 was an indication of how far the government leaned over backwards to maintain the appearance of fairness in its approach to rationing. Ever-increasing numbers of German submarines, hunting in packs along the Atlantic seaboard, were taking a frightful toll of the oil tankers supplying the United Kingdom and Canadian seaports. Service stations east of Montreal were out of gas for their pumps more often than they had gasoline for sale. On the other hand, Turner Valley was ready, willing, and able to keep the cars of the prairies well supplied with fuel. In the interest of fairly sharing and equality of sacrifice, the Canadian government opted for a uniform, national gasoline-rationing system. The first gasoline ration books distributed to all private car owners across the country contained sixty coupons, each worth five gallons of gasoline. Doctors, ministers, travelling salesmen, and assorted business people were categorized separately and were given larger allotments.

The three hundred gallons a year would be enough to get urban dwellers to work and back, but at first glance the indicated ceiling of six thousand miles a year left little leeway for much pleasure driving. Habitual driving to work, however, had not yet become general across the prairies, and the two-car family was virtually unknown. Indeed, less than a third of prairie families had even one car. And it was still the general practice of most motorists to lay their cars up during the winter. Because ethylene-glycol was in extremely short supply, expensive, and generally risky to use in the leak-prone cooling systems of the cars of the era, winter motorists tended to rely on alcohol-water mixes that boiled away at the slightest provocation. Finally, car heaters and defrosters were seldom equal to prairie winters. So ration coupons were hoarded over the winters for summer vacations and pleasure trips. Indeed, many motorists who did not drive during the winter found themselves with more coupons than they could use during the summer and gave them to needy friends.

As the war went on, there was a vast expansion in the British Commonwealth Air Training Plan. A serious gasoline shortage developed on the west coast, and the pinch was felt on the prairies as well as in the Maritimes. In 1943 the board cut the ration to four gallons a coupon and launched a campaign to discourage coupon swapping and chiselling by commercial book holders. The police set up checkpoints along highways to the beaches and on roads to duck-hunting blinds. Commercial travellers caught using their cars for pleasure lost their preferential status. With the new ration books came coloured stamps that had to be stuck to windshields to enable the service-station operator to check the category of the car with the allowed gas ration. Finally, the filling stations were required to confiscate any loose gas coupons tendered for fuel. But none of the restrictions ever overcame the urge of one neighbour to help another, not as long as gasoline could be siphoned from one gas tank and into another with a white rubber enema hose.

The idea of unrestricted boozing during wartime offended the sensitivities of some members of Parliament. They periodically enlivened proceedings with temperance speeches, and were consistently howled down by the patrons of the press gallery's resident bootlegger. The ultimate rationing of booze was foreshadowed in December 1942 when the government ordered thirty-, twenty-, and ten-per-cent reductions in the production and sale of alcoholic spirits, wine, and beer respectively. The provincial governments put their own rationing systems into operation in the spring of 1943.

The alcohol-rationing regulations were severest in Alberta and loosest in Quebec. On the prairies the systems were fairly uniform in detail. In order to obtain booze by the bottle, each adult was required to purchase an annual permit. In Manitoba it took the form of a cardboard-covered twelve-page booklet. Each page was made up, calendar-style, with a space opposite the date, in which to mark purchases of liquor, wine, and beer. These permit books had been in use since the repeal of prohibition in 1924, and were a de facto system of restricting the purchases of the citizenry. In February and March of 1943, the provincial governments simply reduced the ration from one bottle a day to one bottle a month. The beer ration was also reduced from a case a day to two twenty-four-bottle cases a week in Manitoba, two cases a month in Saskatchewan, and to a dozen quart bottles or two dozen pint bottles a month in Alberta. The following August, Alberta cut its ration in half, to a single thirteen-ounce bottle of booze a month and twelve pint bottles of beer. This mass weaning of Albertans continued until October 1944, when the allotments were returned to the level of the other provinces. The immediate effect of the rationing of liquor was a stampede for liquor permits on the part of every adult on the prairies, male and female alike. In Alberta the number of liquor permits in circulation jumped from 149,000 in 1941 to 400,000 in 1943.

Until liquor rationing was introduced, boozing on the prairies had been a male monopoly. There was no by-the-glass consumption

1. Where western Canada's oil history began: Turner Valley Royalties No. 1 in June 1936.

2. The R. A. Browns, père et fils, earned well-deserved reputations as the complete promoters.

3. Captain Gloria Queen-Hughes of Winnipeg first advanced the concept of a women's army corps.

4. Winnipeg volunteers wait to enlist, September 1939.

5. Captain Daisy Royal
of Winnipeg

6. Major Mary Dover
of Calgary

7. The extent of the regimentation of Canadian life during the Second World War is illustrated by these government advertisements of 1943. An order of the National Selective Service made it illegal for single male Canadians to be employed in scores of occupations, ranging from entertainment to used-car dealing. The second order sets forth regulations for marketing new and used tires.

8. More valuable than money were the ration coupons that became an integral part of civilian life during the Second World War. Here are three of the most prized possessions of the era. *(top)* The ration book held tickets for sugar, meat, tea, coffee, and other staples. The round composition discs were given as change when the amount of meat purchased was less than permitted by the ration coupon. *(bottom)* The gasoline ration book contained coupons without which gasoline was unobtainable. *(middle)* The form of the liquor ration varied from province to province. Perforations in the permit foiled attempts to doctor written ration records.

MEAT

RATIONING EFFECTIVE THURSDAY, MAY 27TH

After midnight May 26th, it is unlawful for a consumer to buy rationed meats and for anyone to sell rationed meats to a consumer except on surrender of valid ration coupons.

WHAT MEATS ARE RATIONED?
Beef, Veal, Pork, Mutton and Lamb.

WHAT MEATS ARE NOT RATIONED:
Poultry and Fish are not rationed. "Fancy" meats such as Heart, Tongue, Liver, Kidneys, Brains, Sweetbreads, and cooked sausages such as Wieners and Bologna are not rationed. Meat cuts containing 50% or more of bone such as spare-ribs, oxtails, and pigs' feet are not rationed.

HOW MUCH RATIONED MEAT AM I PERMITTED TO BUY?
An average of two pounds per week per person. You get less of meats containing no bone and more of meats containing considerable bone. See the chart of coupon values below.

WHAT COUPONS DO I USE WHEN BUYING MEAT?
The brown Spare "A" coupons from your No. 2 ration book—the book you are now using to buy tea, coffee, sugar, and butter.

HOW OFTEN CAN I BUY MEAT?
Two coupons become good each Thursday. The first pair of No. 1 coupons become good May 27th. Each coupon is good for ⅓ of one week's ration.

HOW LONG DO COUPONS REMAIN GOOD?
Coupons becoming good before the 15th of a month are good until the end of that month. Coupons becoming good on or after the 15th of a month are good until the end of the following month.

DO I HAVE TO USE THE TWO COUPONS AT THE SAME TIME OR IN THE SAME STORE?
No. You can use a coupon at any time during the period in which it is valid, and in any store you wish.

CAN I BUY ONLY ONE KIND OF RATIONED MEAT WITH A COUPON?
No. You can buy whatever rationed meat is available and as many kinds as you want providing the coupon value is not exceeded.

MEAT COUPON VALUE CHART

GROUP A - ½ LB. PER COUPON

SMOKED MEATS	PORK CURED	COOKED MEATS
Back Bacon (Sliced and Rindless)	Boneless Back (Sliced, or Smoked or Cooked)	Butt (Boneless)
Side Bacon (Sliced and Rindless)		Ham (Boneless)
Side Bacon (Sliced Rind on)		Any Uncooked Group "B" Cuts — when Cooked

GROUP B - ¾ LB. PER COUPON

BEEF - FRESH or CURED	LAMB or MUTTON FRESH	PORK - FRESH	PORK - SMOKED
Chuck Roast or Steak (Boneless)	Frontquarter (Boneless)	Back (Boneless)	Back Bacon (in the piece, Boneless)
Flank Steak (Boneless)		Belly (Boneless)	Cottage Roll (Boneless)
Hind Shank Meat (Boneless)	**VEAL - FRESH**	Butt (Bone in)	Ham (except Shank End, Bone in)
Minute Steaks and Cube Steaks (Boneless)	Cutlets and Fillets (Bone in)	Ham (Boneless)	Ham, Skinless (Boneless)
Neck (Boneless)	Front Roll (Caul Wrapped, Boneless)	Ham, Centre Cuts (Bone in)	Picnic (Boneless)
Rolled Rib (Boneless)	Leg Roll (Caul Wrapped Boneless)	Picnic (Boneless)	Pork Roll (Boneless)
Round Steak or Roast (Bone in)	Round (Bone in)	Picnic Skinless (Boneless)	Side Bacon (in the piece)
Sirloin Tip (Boneless)	Stewing Veal (Boneless)	Tenderloin	
Stewing Beef (Boneless)	Tenderloin	**PORK - CURED**	**COOKED MEATS**
Tenderloin		(Not Smoked or Cooked)	Any Uncooked Group "C" Cuts—when Cooked
		Back (Boneless)	
		Belly (Boneless)	
		Ham Butt Roll (Boneless)	
		Ham Centre Slices (Bone in)	
		Pork Roll (Boneless)	
		Shoulder Roll (Boneless)	

GROUP C - 1 LB. PER COUPON

BEEF - FRESH or CURED	LAMB or MUTTON - FRESH	PORK - FRESH	PORK - CURED
Brisket Point (Boneless)	Centre Loin Chops (Bone in)	Belly Pork (Bone in)	Ham, Butt End (Bone in)
Flank (Boneless)	Loin (Flank off, Kidney and Suet out, Bone in)	Ham, Butt End (Bone in)	Ham, Shank End (Bone in)
Front Shank Meat (Boneless)	Patties (made from Necks and Flanks, Boneless)	Ham, Shank End (Bone in)	Ham, Whole (Bone in)
Front Shank (Centre Cut)		Ham Trimmed (Bone in)	Picnic, Hock On or Hock Off (Bone in)
Hamburger	**VEAL - FRESH**	Loin, Centre Cut Chops (Bone in)	
Plate (Boneless)	Blade (Bone in and Neck off, Shoulder Knuckle out)		**PORK - SMOKED**
Porterhouse Steak or Roast (Bone in)	Loin Chops (Centre Cut, Bone in)	Loin, Centre Cut (Bone in)	Ham, Shank End (Bone in)
Rib Roast or Steak (Bone in)	Patties (Boneless, made from Shanks, Necks, Flanks)	Loin, End Cuts (Bone in)	Ham, Whole (Bone in)
Rump (Round and Square End, Bone in)	Round Bone Shoulder (Bone in)	Loin, Whole (Bone in)	Picnic, Hock On or Hock Off (Bone in)
Sirloin Steak or Roast (Bone in)	Rump (Bone in)	Picnic, Hock On or Hock Off (Bone in)	
Short Rib Roast (Bone in)	Sirloin Roast or Cutlet (Bone in)		**COOKED MEATS**
T-Bone Steak or Roast (Bone in)			Any Uncooked Group "D" Cuts — when Cooked
Wing Steak or Roast (Bone in)			

GROUP D - 1¼ LBS. PER COUPON

BEEF - FRESH or CURED	LAMB or MUTTON - FRESH	VEAL - FRESH	PORK - FRESH
Blade Roast (Bone in)	Flank (Bone in)	Breast (Bone in)	Hock (Bone in)
Brisket Point (Bone in)	Front (Bone in)	Flank (Bone in)	Sausage
Chuck Roast (Bone in)	Hind (Bone in)	Front Shank (Bone in)	**PORK - CURED**
Front Shank, Whole or Knuckle End (Bone in)	Leg (Bone in)	Hind Shank (Bone in)	Hock (Bone in)
Neck (Bone in)	Loin, Flank on (Bone in)	Leg, Shank Half (Bone in)	Mess (Bone in)
Plate, Brisket (Bone in)	Rack (Bone in)	Leg, Whole (Bone in)	Short Cut Back (Bone in)
Round Bone Shoulder Roast (Bone in)	Rib Chops (Bone in)	Loin, Flank on (Bone in)	**PORK - SMOKED**
Sausage, Fresh		Neck (Bone in)	Hock (Bone in)
Short Ribs (Braising, Bone in)		Rack (Bone in)	
		Rib Chops (Bone in)	

9. A coupon value chart dated May 27, 1943, details meat rationing regulations.

10. J. W. Dafoe at the entrance of the *Free Press* building, 300 Carlton Street, Winnipeg.

11. The *Winnipeg Free Press* building, decorated for the Royal visit of 1939.

12. The *Free Press* newsroom in 1942: (left to right) Frank Morriss, Howard Wolfe, Stan Blique, Cora Hind, Ted Dafoe, J. W. Dafoe, Abbie Coo, George Leyden.

13. Editorial heads together: J. W. Dafoe, George Ferguson and Jimmy Gray.

14. Frying eggs on a sidewalk during the 1937 heat wave: (left to right) Jimmy Gray, Albert Booth, Jeff Hurley, and Earle Beattie.

15. The reporter, on assignment in the forties, interviews schoolchildren.

16. & 17. A strike of Winnipeg printers in 1945-46 necessitated the publication of joint issues of the *Winnipeg Free Press* and the *Winnipeg Tribune*. The first issue of the photo-set paper, bearing dual logos, was published on November 10, 1945. The editorial page is taken from the November 12, 1945, edition.

18. J. W. Dafoe

19. George V. Ferguson

21. Grant Dexter

20. Victor Sifton

in bars or lounges because there were no bars or lounges. In each province, beer by the glass was available only in hotel taverns, and only in rural areas of Alberta were women permitted to accompany men into the pubs. In Alberta cities, women beer drinkers were confined strictly to ladies' taverns. Neither facility was available to women in Manitoba or Saskatchewan. Nor were women by any means a common sight in the liquor-commission retail outlets, where male customers outnumbered women by thirty or forty to one. This latter statistic moved very close to sexual parity with the institution of rationing. It was not that any mad female rush developed to acquire a taste for forbidden juice once it became hard to get. Rather, it was simply that male drinkers were taking defensive measures to protect their supplies. Husbands with permits escorted their wives to the vendors to apply for permits and thus doubled their monthly ration. Employers did the same with their secretaries and other office help.

Prior to the war, the purchase of hard liquor was very much an occasional thing for the overwhelming majority of the population. The practice of having liquor available in the home was confined to the upper crust, and for one very simple reason: money. It cost a carpenter, store clerk, or bookkeeper at least a day's pay to buy a bottle of rye and almost two days' pay for a bottle of $7.50 Scotch whiskey. With wages pegged at the lowest level in history by the existence of mass unemployment throughout the pre-war decade, booze was an unaffordable luxury. It was something that people saved up to buy for the celebration of Christmas, New Year's, Burns' Night, and St. Patrick's Day.

In such an environment it was not too difficult, after rationing came in, for members of the managerial class, who were mildly addicted to before-dinner martinis, to put habit-supportive infra-structures into place. Neither Kay nor I were drinkers, so when George Ferguson discovered that we were permitless, he quickly took action to have us purchase permits so that we would be able to provide him with a bottle a month each. A couple of other staff members did likewise, so that the Fergusons were able to indulge their thirsts to the extent of half a dozen bottles a month. When the arithmetic was done, it actually amounted to about 150 ounces a month or, with allowance for a little sharing with friends, about one modest drink a day.

It was Gerry Gaetz, the manager of the Sifton radio station CKRC, who came up with a solution to ease the impact of the drought. Freshly returned from a broadcasters' convention in Quebec, he enthusiastically reported on his discovery of the gaping holes in the liquor-control dikes. Quebec, too, had rationing, but when a visitor stepped up to the liquor-store counter, presented his permit, and gave the clerk his order, he carefully exposed the corner of a two-dollar bill under the permit. The clerk slipped out the bribe and returned the permit, unmarked, with the liquor. It was an easy matter for a visitor to acquire a whole case of booze by repeating his visits at judiciously spaced intervals. Armed with this information, when I next covered an assignment in Quebec I was able to return with enough booze to keep both the Ferguson and Gaetz households afloat for a month.

In all this there was no sense of wrong-doing. The law provided that every free-born Canadian adult was entitled to his and her monthly ration of booze and beer. No law required the purchaser to consume the liquor or beer himself. We may have been playing fast and loose with the intention of a government at war. Certainly the money spent on booze would have been better spent on war savings certificates. But it was spent on booze without a qualm or a backward glance. As the war went on, some of the wilier drinkers turned their attention to ways to outwit the regulations and get an extra bottle or so a month. Chemical ink remover judiciously applied could remove the scrawls on a permit book and make the acquisition of additional supplies possible. Alberta quickly put an end to that gimmick. Its liquor-store clerks were supplied with ticket punches with which to punch holes in the permits and make tampering impossible. In Winnipeg an imaginative printer counterfeited a number of sheets which could be inserted into a permit book after the used sheets were removed by unfastening the staples on the spine. Surreptitious distribution of sheets was barely underway, however, before the authorities got on to the scheme, laid traps for customers presenting doctored permit books, and put an end to the swindle.

Beer addicts had less difficulty in slaking their thirst than liquor consumers. The ration in Manitoba was generous enough to satisfy all but the greediest. Even in Saskatchewan it amounted to almost two bottles a day. Only in Alberta was it downright skimpy. Moreover, beer drinkers could supplement their home consumption with libations in the beer parlours. The trick was to get there when the taverns had beer for sale. And that was not always easy, given the way in which hotel allocations were computed. It was a system that seemed almost designed to intensify shortages. Hotel purchases were limited to seventy or eighty per cent of the quantity their beer parlours had sold the previous year, month by month. The system made no allowance for increased population resulting from the expansion of wartime activity. Nor did it take cognizance of the increase in the money in circulation as a result of full employment. Assured of the sale of all the beer they could get, the hotels, in the interest of economy and increased profits, cut back sharply on their hours of service. Instead of opening before noon, they opened at 2:00 P.M. and closed at 10:00 P.M. In Alberta, the taverns even closed during the supper hour. Many hotels set their own daily quotas and shut off sales when the quota was reached. That enabled them to maintain more or less regular daily hours. Had they done otherwise, they might have been forced to close completely a couple of days a week. This shutting-off of service, however, was a monstrous inconvenience for the drinkers. And for many it posed a painful dilemma: should they use precious gasoline coupons on a town-to-town pub crawl and risk finding the taverns closed when they got there? The pre-war, payday custom of dropping into the nearest parlour for a couple of beers was replaced by a lot of preliminary scouting to locate the pubs most likely to have a stock that would last until the thirst was assuaged.

Nevertheless, in general across the West, the combined price ceiling, rationing, and materials-allocation system worked reasonably well. The notable exception was in Edmonton and northern Alberta, where the sudden influx of thousands of Americans made mincemeat of all of Ottawa's supply-and-demand projections. The Americans came in such numbers in 1942 that Edmonton's population jumped from 90,000 to 120,000 in a single year. The city became the materials and manpower base for the construction of the Alaska Highway and for the Canol pipeline to Alaska. It was the assembly point for fleets of aircraft airlifting defence material to Alaska. And it was the headquarters for the United States military forces in charge of all these projects.

The United States army and air-force messes were bountifully stocked with American beer. The servicemen, however, frequently preferred to slake their thirsts with the stronger Canadian beer in the Canadian pubs and unwittingly intensified the supply stringency of the Canadian watering holes. The mass descent of a company of American GI's on a neighbourhood beer parlour would run its taps dry long before closing time. Complicating the situation even further was the periodic influx of scores of Alaska Highway construction workers for a week on the town.

The hard-nosed construction bosses kept their road camps Sahara-dry most of the time, for nothing disrupted their fourteen-hour work days like booze in the bunkhouses. To counteract the drought, the highway workers frequently deserted in droves on paydays for week-long carousals in the nearest fleshpots. Such proclivities put an impossible strain upon the hotel and beer-parlour accommodation everywhere, from Edmonton to Fort

Nelson and beyond. The road and pipeline workers, although they were loaded with spendable money, nevertheless fought a losing battle with the U.S. army and the air force for female preference. What good was money when the chubby-cheeked boy-colonels of the United States Air Force could provide a damsel with a purse full of nylons and half a case of fresh oranges after an evening of dalliance in and out of the officers' mess?

The American invasion complicated the ration situation in both the demand and the supply aspects. It was not long before good old American know-how had Edmonton, Grande Prairie, Dawson Creek, and Fort St. John awash in contraband American cigarettes, whiskey, coffee, fruit, vegetables, and sugar. Cigarettes from the American canteens flowed in such volume through the beer parlours that more expensive Canadian smokes became a drug on the market. Towards the end of the invasion, it was not uncommon for smokeshops to carry contraband American cigarettes for under-the-counter sale to steady customers. Displaced Americans, after being guests for Sunday dinner in Edmonton homes, were often known to send thank-you notes in the form of ten-pound roasts to their hostesses.

In addition to the semi-permanent Americans in residence, thousands of others floated in and out of northern Alberta on weekly or monthly visits. Noticeable among this flotsam was an incursion of hundreds of American servicemen's wives on conjugal visits. The American colonels and their ladies so monopolized hotel accommodation in downtown Edmonton that ordinary wayfaring drummers, sports writers, reporters, travelling bureaucrats, and unwary tourists counted themselves lucky to find a cot for the night in a hotel sample room. On one assignment to Edmonton at the peak of the invasion, I shared a King Edward Hotel sample room with two commercial travellers from Montreal and a highway engineer fighting off a mild attack of delirium tremens. When one of the drummers joined with me in a demand on the night clerk for alternate accommodation, the clerk's only suggestion was that we move our cots out into the hall. Which we did.

The impact of the American service wives on the Edmonton marts of commerce created an unparalleled merchandising bonanza. One merchant told a *Calgary Herald* reporter that his record sale was $130 worth of lingerie to one woman. Other women cleaned the stores out of pre-war stocks of English china, jewellery, knick-knacks, and watches. For a period in June 1943, Edmonton was sold completely out of Kleenex. Why Kleenex, of all things? Nobody knew. According to legend, Americans simply rushed in and bought it by the armload.

In no place was the American influx more disruptive than in the restaurant business. Waiting in line for an hour to get a place for lunch became so common that Edmonton offices began releasing employees an hour earlier, when they only had to wait forty-five minutes. Businessmen themselves either went on diets or ate at their desks rather than face the congestion and the delays. And, of course, the vast increase in restaurant eating made the allocation of scarce commodities to northern Alberta centres all the more difficult. Shortages that were unknown elsewhere on the prairies were a common occurrence when the construction of the Alaska Highway, the Alcan pipeline, and the Alaska staging route were all underway at once.

As the Wartime Prices and Trade Board noted in its annual reports, enforcement of wartime rationing and price controls was difficult. Black markets did develop, but never on the scale that might have been expected, given the nature of man and wartime conditions. The essential ingredient for a successful rationing and price- and wage-control system was public acceptance and support. That there was. Another factor helped to make the system work. There was not really a big enough profit in violating ration laws to attract wholesale criminal activity. The profit from diversion of a carload of sugar into the underground market might have been attractive if there had been large markets available to absorb the contraband. In most areas, however, controls were so extensive that black markets on a wholesale scale seldom had a chance to develop. As a result, most of the trafficking in rationed and price-controlled goods was at the level of petty larceny. The exception after Pearl Harbor was in automobiles, both new and used.

After ten years of Depression on the prairies, the built-up surplus of used cars, combined with the shortage of people who could afford a car at any price, slowed the development of a buyers' market. As late as the midsummer of 1941, the *Free Press* was still carrying three or four columns a day of classified used-car advertisements at prices scarcely higher than they had been the year before. Then came the Canadian government's shut-down of auto production and ban on sales for civilian use, Pearl Harbor, and the rapid conversion of the American automobile industry to war production. By the middle of 1942, most dealers were out of late-model used cars; price advertising faded from the want-ads, and the used-car business was dominated by freelancing individuals dealing in one car at a time. In addition to restricting severely the rights of people to buy from the hoarded supply of new cars, the government ultimately brought all cars, new and used alike, under the price ceiling. As time passed, it became easier to get a government permit to buy a new car than to find a dealer who would sell one at the ceiling price.

A car had no place on our list of priorities until I moved to Ottawa for the *Free Press* in 1946. To cover the capital a car was essential and on my arrival I set off to get one. While the war was over, all the wartime controls and restrictions were still in place. Each day the *Journal* and the *Citizen* carried an advertisement or two for a used car; the trick was to get to the home of the advertiser before the car was sold. I must have spent twenty dollars in taxi fares on wild-goose chases before I finally got to an advertiser before he had sold his car. The car was a ten-year-old Buick sedan with spare tires set in fender wells. The owner was a Mounted Police constable just returned from a family holiday in Manitoba. He had driven there and back in the Buick. That fact testified to its durability, and the fact that he was a Mountie into the bargain convinced me that I should buy the car. Without giving it a road test, I gave him a cheque for twelve hundred dollars and drove off.

Driving home, it seemed to steer very heavily, and I decided it probably needed greasing. After taking the family joy-riding over to Hull and around the Experimental Farm, I drove it to the Buick dealer to have it oiled and greased and the steering checked. We got the bad news when the car went up on the hoist. The brackets that held the front coil springs in place were so badly worn that they were both bound up with wire. When I thought of speeding along the Aylmer Road in a car literally hay-wired together, I almost threw up. It would cost half as much as the car was worth to replace the front end, even if the parts were available, which they definitely were not. The mechanic had seen a hundred similar examples, and worse.

"I wouldn't worry too much about it," he said. "Just don't drive too fast. If the wiring comes unstuck any mechanic can put some more on and hold it together. It isn't really holding it together, it's more or less just keeping it from rattling. But don't drive too fast."

What to do? Most of our life savings were now invested in that useless junk heap. I went back to the Mountie to demand my money back. He was at work and would not be back until the next day. His wife volunteered that I could not hope to get my money back anyway because most of it had to go to repay a loan her husband had negotiated to buy the car in the first place. Anyhow, she said, the car could not be all that bad. Her husband had only bought it the previous month and it had taken them to Manitoba and back. Her door-closing advice was succinct and to the point: "If you want your money back, do what we did. Sell it."

I telephoned an ad to the *Journal* and sold the car for what I paid for it to the first of seven people who rang our bell during the interval between soup and dessert the following evening. By 1946 there was hardly a car on the road in Canada that had not been on the road continuously for from ten to twenty years. The city of Ottawa, for example, was still using a fleet of 1920 model-T trucks in its winter snow-clearing. All this made the used-car market the most hazardous for anyone to get into. But that did not discourage any of the army of potential buyers from champing at the bit for cars. Nobody expected anything from the cars except that they would start and run, and by the war's end few of the advertisers bothered lying about the condition of the engines. What they lied about was tires. New tires were even harder to get than new cars after the Japanese cut off North American access to natural rubber, and it took months for the tire makers to perfect the substitution of artificial rubber in both tires and inner tubes. Only the most gullible were taken in by the outward appearance of tires. What appeared from the absence of tread wear to be sound and service-able casing might enclose yards of interior booting and patching, and inner tubes that became porous with the onset of winter.

The Buick experience cured me of fooling around in the used-car market, and there wasn't a new-car dealer in Ottawa who had the time of day for new customers, although the car plants were all back in business, turning out slightly changed 1942-model cars with the machine tools they had saved and stored five years before. A colleague in the press gallery mentioned that he had heard that a member of Parliament from Manitoba had a piece of a car agency back home and had in fact obtained a car for a friend in Ottawa. I rushed off to see the member to twist his arm on behalf of a deserving fellow Manitoban.

"Yes," he said, "I can probably get you one, but it might take a couple of months." I was floored by his casual confidence and was all set to close the deal, when he asked: "What did you figure on paying?"

"Why, the ceiling price, of course. What is it down here, about $1,200?"

He almost blew up in my face. "What? Are you crazy, man?"

It was perhaps a measure of my naïveté that I had never considered the possibility of a member of Parliament operating in the automobile black market.

"Well," I answered, "the war may be over but the ceiling is still on car prices."

He snorted and, as I made for the door, fired a parting sally. "Enjoy your walk," he said.

Another suggestion from a gallery colleague bore fruit. He had heard, he said, that the car makers had put all their dealers on quotas; sometimes those in the smaller centres had fewer customers they were beholden to and actually had cars without a line-up of customers waiting.

I immediately contacted my brother in Galt, Ontario, who owned a lumberyard and was into house building. It so happened that there was a Mercury dealer in Galt who owed my brother a favour, because he had supplied him with some hard-to-get building materials at a critical time. My brother called for a repayment of the favour. Within a month, I got a car at the ceiling price. Only it was shipped to Galt without tires, because the Canadian tire plants, like the Canadian steel plants, were all on strike. I got on a bus and headed for the States and got as far as Albany, New York, before I found a tire dealer with a stock of the right-sized tires for the model-114 Mercury.

Though wild tales of adventure in the new- and used-car marts became embedded in the folklore of the times, public preoccupation with cars rated far behind concerns for other things. For every car addict who could not live without wheels, there were dozens of others getting their occasional highs from the anticipation of acquiring other items on their post-war priority lists. Everybody had lists of things on which they proposed to spend their war bonds and compulsory savings once the war was over. By the end of the war, not spending money had become enshrined as a great public and private virtue. The best antidote to spendthriftery was a list of things to be saved for. Two items usually topped such lists. One was a Bendix washing machine and the other was an electric refrigerator. If there was anything left over, it could go for a mixmaster, an automatic toaster, an electric gramophone, or an electric train.

Prior to the war, most washing machines came equipped with a washing tub and an electric wringer attached to an arm that swung across the top. Between the washing and the rinsing and between the rinsing and the drying, the wash had to be manhandled out of the tub and through the wringer into another tub. Not only did the wringers pull the wash through a set of rubber rollers; the rollers frequently caught the housewives' sleeves or wisps of their hair and pulled them tightly against the revolving rollers. Late-model machines advertised "touch-release" controls, which enabled the trapped women to shut off the machine quickly, but never before it had inflicted painful bruises to the arms and pulled out hair by the roots. Then there followed the painful business of pulling sleeves and hair backwards out of almost-impossible-to-turn rollers.

To the delight of every housewife within sight, the Bendix corporation patented a washer that would banish the wringers from kitchens forever. The Bendix spun-dried the clothes within the washing compartment and presented them to the housewives ready for hanging on the clotheslines. It had, however, barely appeared on the prairie market before it became a war casualty and went out of production. But it was never far from the minds of the women as they hauled the scalding wash into and out of wringer machines, and the visions of drudgery-free washdays with a Bendix made it easier to keep Canadian women buying their war savings certificates and victory bonds.

Everybody had something to save for, from bicycles and electric trains to furniture, cars, and on up to houses. The progress towards the goals was marked with anticipatory relish every payday, and the higher the savings mounted, the greater the satisfaction. Only those who have done it can ever imagine the thrill that comes when the goal is reached, the bank is emptied, and the objective stands glistening in its pristine newness in the possession of the purchaser.

The wartime propagandists knew full well how to play upon these acquisitive instincts in order to promote savings through the purchase of war bonds. In case the desire for some special goody was not enough, other ways were devised to discourage consumer spending. In 1941, the Prices Board moved in on instalment selling. Car purchasers were required to deposit a fifty-per-cent down-payment and pay the balance within a year. Department stores had to abandon both low down-payments and extended instalment plans. The order required a third down-payment and balance within fifteen months. All charge accounts had to be paid in full every month. The extent to which the easy-payment plan diminished as an adjunct to the Canadian way of life may be gauged from the fact that, between 1941 and 1943, department- and furniture-store instalment sales dropped by sixty-two per cent and furniture sales by seventy-two per cent.

Across the country as a whole, the government had less success in controlling wages than it did prices. Under the War Measures Act, Ottawa was able to take control of labour-management relations in a way that would have been impossible in peacetime. Under a National Labour Relations Board, it got nine provincial boards functioning in areas of provincial jurisdiction to enforce the wage-ceiling orders. In the interest of labour peace, these boards also took the power to certify unions and force employers to bargain with unions, many for the first time in history. The result was a massive growth in trades-union membership, and with unionism came drives for higher wages and other fringe benefits. By the time the wage freeze was ordered in the fall of 1941, wages had advanced somewhat from Depression lows. Provision was made in the freeze procedure to enforce payments of cost-of-living bonuses to all workers, if and when the cost of living rose.

From $26 a week in 1939, the Canadian average weekly wage rose to $28.41 in 1942 and to $35.71 by the end of 1946, when the ceiling came off. In addition, the workers were entitled to a minimum of $2.25 per week cost-of-living bonus up to a maximum of nine per cent of their weekly wages. Because of the concentration of war industry in central Canada, wages rose higher there than in the West, where there was a paucity of wartime manufacturing. Thus, by June 1946 the wage index for manufacturing was up 61 per cent above the 1939 level; logging was up 68 per cent; services were up 47 per cent. The best comparison for the prairies would be in the construction trades, where the increases ranged from 20 to 25 per cent.

Such statistics, however, do not accurately reflect the improvement in the general standard of living that occurred on the prairies. In addition to full employment at improving wage rates, there was also a widespread movement out of low-paying into higher-paying jobs. Employees in department stores, restaurants, beauty parlours, barber shops, used-car lots, and other service jobs, were directed into employment in essential services. Many were trained to take skilled and semi-skilled jobs. Overnight, after Pearl Harbor, women ceased to be the outcasts of the economy, and wives of soldiers and married women generally were actively recruited for war jobs and for jobs vacated by people being transferred to essential services. Two-income families made their appearance for the first time in the Canadian economy. As a result of such changes, an overnight housing famine developed. The thousands of families who had lived in single rooms on unemployment relief became rent-paying tenants of the vacant houses and apartments. The housing congestion reached horrific proportions in Edmonton, Winnipeg, Calgary, and Regina, and in two dozen smaller centres where the British Commonwealth Air Training Plan establishments were located. A program of rushed construction of wartime houses was launched but it never began to catch up with the demand. An ironic insight into the impact of the war on the economy was provided in Winnipeg when the now-empty Unemployment Relief Administration office on Elgin Avenue was converted into emergency living quarters for the families of servicemen who could find no accommodation in the city. Ten years before, the premises were used to dispense relief to more than 6,500 unemployed families in the city.

One of the intriguing imponderables of wartime economics was the effect of the excess-profits tax and the high level of taxation on corporate wages and salaries. To the entrepreneurs in the excess-profits bracket, it made no difference whether they raised their employees' wages. It was simply a choice between giving increased earnings to the government or the workers. Resentment against confiscatory taxes might have motivated an open-handed wage policy, but an eye to post-war profit margins might have been a restraint upon largesse. What tipped the scales towards the employees was probably the scarcity of skilled help and the need to avoid work stoppages. Certainly strikes were almost unheard of on the prairies during the war. In 1942 there was a total of twenty-seven such stoppages, involving 5,000 workers for only 7,000 man-days. In 1946 the figures were thirty-three strikes and 9,308 man-days time lost. But 6,500 of those man-days were accounted for by a one-day strike of Alberta miners against the chairman of a conciliation board. When disputes did develop, they were cooled slowly by the maze of procedures that had to be threaded before a strike could take place. Anyway, if an employer was determined to raise the pay of a key employee to keep him on the premises, there were lots of ways of doing it, of which the easiest was reclassification. The tradesmen who were promoted to sub-foremen, assistant supervisors, and assistant sub-foremen in hundreds of establishments across the West simply went on doing the same work as before.

Perhaps the most imponderable of all imponderables about the wage-control system was this: how could the Wartime Prices and Trade Board, even with double its army of employees and super-sleuths, have fine-combed business records and ferreted out all the cases where employers and employees had combined to make mincemeat of the wage-ceiling regulations through reclassification and job switches? There was no answer except this: wage and price controls alike were only possible in an industrial democracy with the consent of the governed, even in wartime. And in wartime Canada that consent was given, wholeheartedly.

7
Barefoot into the Brains Department

During the decade of the Great Depression, the *Free Press* news and editorial staff changed hardly at all. What it gained by recruitment it lost to attrition. With the onset of the war, everything changed. Copy boys disappeared into the armed services with such regularity that they were replaced by girls. The reporting and copy-desk staffs were decimated by enlistment and better-paid jobs elsewhere. Peter Whittall and Bill Metcalfe almost doubled their salaries by jumping to the CBC news department. John Sweeney and Bill Ellis did almost as well by moving to Ontario. The army took, or would soon take, Ben Malkin, Burt Gresham, Orton Grain, George Thurston, and Norton Anderson; the air force got Gordon Sinclair and Albert Booth; and Phil Lee and Frank Walker were ticketed for the navy. Burt Richardson had been posted to Ottawa and Chester Bloom was Washington-bound. Victor Sifton himself was in Ottawa as Master General of Ordnance, and Dick Malone, his executive assistant, was a lieutenant on the staff of Hon. J. L. Ralston, the Minister of National Defence. Malone would end the war as a brigadier and aide-de-camp to Field Marshal Bernard Montgomery.

By the summer of 1941, when Howard Wolfe looked up from his city desk in search of an experienced reporter from his pre-war staff, he would have seen Leslie Bishop, Theodore Hart, Cy Louth, or Jimmy Gray and, as he put it, damn all else. In June of 1941 he was down to Hart, Louth, and Bishop, when I was transferred out of the newsroom and on to the editorial page. The promotion was great news on two counts. It brought with it a ten-dollar-a-week raise in pay to fifty dollars a week, and it marked the achievement of a goal I had been aiming at since I got my news-side job six years earlier. I was convinced, without much evidence to support the conclusion, that my forte was in the world of ideas, that I was better qualified to participate in the intellectual ferment from which public policy emerged than to report the events which the policies produced. As a reporter my services must have been more than adequate, because I was promoted from beat to beat and rewarded with modest raises in pay en route. But as time passed I came to realize that I had a cast of mind that prevented me from ever becoming the sort of reporter who became a fixture on any particular beat. The essence of reportorial skill is the cultivation of news sources, which ensure that the reporter always knows what is going on so that his paper is never scooped on routine developments. I discovered early on that I had small talent for making friends easily, and a large talent for seizing on off-pattern story angles that made enemies. Three episodes illustrate what I am getting at.

When I was covering the labour and suburbs beat, it included the St. Boniface police department and the St. Boniface city council. I had gone to the mayor's office one afternoon to pick up some sort of routine announcement and dropped down to the basement to check in with the police department. There was no one around so I wandered into an adjacent basement courtroom where a trial was about to begin. The prisoner, a vagrant of some kind, was shuttled into the courtroom, pleaded to some minor offence, and was being remanded a week for trial when he began shouting a protest. He pleaded with the magistrate to try the case at once and not to confine him any longer to the cells in the basement of the city hall.

"This is the lousiest jail I've ever been in!" he screamed. "Look at me. I'm bitten from head to foot. I've even got bedbug bites between my toes!" The clerk, the magistrate, and the attending jailor all looked at the prisoner's bug bites and then the jailor nudged him back into the jail.

There is something contagious about an itch; see someone else scratching and one has an irresistible urge to scratch. I felt itchy and started poking around in the seams of the courtroom bench I was sitting on. Sure enough, I discovered a couple of little bugs which may well have been mini spiders, woods bugs, or other harmless insects. But I went back to the office, wrote a three-paragraph story about the prisoner's complaint and the bugs in the court room . . . and all hell broke loose. The mayor of St. Boniface got mad, Magistrate LaCerte got mad, the chief of police got mad, the attorney general's department was mildly provoked. The next day when I went back on a routine call I was noisily ejected from the police department and ordered not to return. The premises smelled strongly of disinfectant. I wrote that story, too, and the St. Boniface boycott of the *Free Press* was on until I was replaced on the beat.

In the spring of 1937 I was assigned to replace Cy Louth on the city police beat while he went off to watch the coronation of King George VI. That was a very quiet spring and little was happening on the crime front. So there was a lot of sitting around in police court, in hopes of getting a few paragraphs of not-very-exciting news. One day a prisoner was ushered into the courtroom and Andy Moffatt, the crown prosecutor, rose before the prisoner was asked to plead.

"This is the case, your worship, I spoke to you about before court. I am informed we have not yet heard from out of town, so it would be in order to have a remand for forty-eight hours."

The magistrate was R. B. Graham, a former prosecutor himself. He mumbled something about "so ordered" and the prisoner was led back to the cells. The episode had taken less than a minute, but it got me to wondering. What was the magistrate doing discussing cases with the crown prosecutor in the privacy of his office before court opened? What was becoming of the notion that judges were supposed to be impartial? For the next week or so I made it a point of stationing myself in the corridor outside the magistrate's office. Sure enough, every day before court Moffatt took his docket into Graham's office and they could be heard discussing some of the cases coming up that morning. It was a cosy arrangement that undoubtedly saved a lot of back-and-forth palavering in court.

In most cases the accused persons did not even have to make an appearance. Moffat would read off a string of remands or appointments for trial, and the magistrate would nod concurrence.

It offended my sense of the fitness of things, so I talked it over with Howard Wolfe and wrote a story about it. The reaction this time was more restrained. The attorney general said that if the practice of consultation between the magistrate and the crown prosecutor was going on it should be stopped. It was. But the friendly detectives, morality inspectors, and deputy chiefs who had been so accessible, suddenly were too busy to see me, and I began to get scooped on routine city briefs. Wolfe found another reporter for the police beat.

The third example had to do with a series of articles I wrote from city hall on the way several aldermen were eking out a profit doing business with the city. Winnipeg had taken back thousands of building lots for taxes during the 1920s and was desperately trying to unload them on prospective builders at bargain prices. The chairman of the city finance committee was chairman of the land-sales committee which approved the lot sales. He was also a prominent realtor and was paid a commission on each lot for which his firm acted as broker. He and another alderman were also selling contract-fulfilments bonds, which contractors building sanitary sewers and sewage-treatment plants for the city were required to have. My stories so outraged one of the aldermen that he spent almost an hour at one council meeting denouncing me by name.

I had expected that these articles and the alderman's reaction would encourage civic employees to bring other material to me. Instead, just the reverse happened. People stopped giving me even the time of day. It had been the practice for some departments to provide us with advance copies of reports going to council so that we could get our work done in advance on difficult subjects. It was always understood that we would never turn any of our copy in to the papers before the city council or its committees got the reports. That understanding was never breached. But in the months that followed, I never encountered less than the severest difficulty in getting advance access to reports.

From these and other experiences I concluded that journalists and bureaucrats are natural-born enemies. I think it was Bertrand Russell who once wrote that the objective of all bureaucrats is to exercise the maximum amount of power with the minimum risk of personal criticism, and both ends are achieved when he says "no!" That is the essence of the art of the bureaucrat, having an automatic "no" on the tip of his tongue for use on every occasion. The only time a civil servant feels safe in leaking tips to journalists is when inter-department or intra-department feuding has reached the blood-letting stage. At all other times, the attitude is, "What's in it for me?" and the answer is likely to be, "nothing but trouble." And trouble is what civil servants dedicate their lives to staying out of.

Though getting news beats, scooping the opposition, is the milk in every reporter's coconut, most news desks prefer the steady, reliable plodder to the showboat scoop producer. The news scoop has a life span of one edition. What the paper needs is a steady flow of copy that covers all the essential stories to be developed on the various beats. It is axiomatic, from what I have said above, that the reporter who scores a spectacular scoop today may himself be scooped, not once but several times. So in other times, and under other circumstances, it might have been that my promotion to the editorial page was a kicking upstairs of a reporter whose off-beat scoops caused more trouble than they were worth. But that was hardly possible during the wartime shortage of skilled hands.

Like winning an election, or an LLD, the achievement of a long-held ambition is a euphoric experience that usually lasts only long enough to give rise to honest doubts. Was it, I wondered, a sort of consolation prize for being refused a war-correspondent's posting?

As I settled comfortably into a semi-private office in "the brains department," I could not still a small voice which kept asking: "What the hell is a guy like you doing in a place like this?"

The *Winnipeg Free Press* under J. W. Dafoe was committed to the proposition that only the divinely inspired Liberal party was worthy of being charged with governing our country. The only good Tories were opposition Tories whose purpose on earth was to serve everlastingly as whipping boys for their undeviating wrongheadedness on the issues of the day. When the paper found it necessary to chastise the backsliding Liberals, it was always more in sorrow than in anger, after the fashion of a doting father woodshed-bound with an erring son. During the Great Depression the *Free Press* had been as devoid of constructive suggestions for dealing with mass unemployment and the agricultural disaster as the Liberal party itself, that is to say, totally. Its standard solution for all economic problems was restoration of world free trade. And here was I, a Roosevelt New Deal liberal, who had reached thirty-five years of age without ever casting a federal Liberal vote, joining such a writing team.

Indeed, the cleavage went further than mere disagreement over political parties or economic theories. During the ten years I had spent trying to read my way through the public library, I had blundered into a book, by Alfred Marshall, *Money, Credit and Commerce*, that made more sense to me than anything else I had read on economics. It was his theory of marginal utility which demonstrated how very small surpluses or scarcities of commodities could unhinge the pricing structure of massive quantities of commodities.

We had seen during the Depression how a surplus of less than two per cent in the world's wheat supply had led to a seventy-per-cent reduction in the value of all the wheat in the world. Similar disastrous drops had taken place in other raw commodities as a result of the impact of small surpluses. On the other hand, minuscule deficits in supplies had at other times forced prices up as much as fifty per cent. The classic laissez-faire solution to the surplus of Canadian wheat was to dump it on the world market for what it would bring, just to get supply back into balance with demand. That was Liberal policy in 1936 and 1937, and it was staunchly supported by the *Free Press*. In the United States, President Roosevelt had tried to do what industry did to achieve balance. When the supply of cars exceeded the apparent demand, factories were shut down and prices held steady till the demand caught up. On a world scale, international cartels of manufacturers were organized to divide markets and control supplies rigidly, so that surpluses could not develop to depress prices. Only in the world of agricultural production were the producers left to the buffeting of laissez-faire economics. President Roosevelt tried to bring the country's domestic food supply into balance with demand by subsidizing the farmers to feed fewer hogs and to grow less wheat. That solution also failed, but it came closer to solving the problem than anything else that was tried.

How could I ever accommodate or reconcile my views with those of the *Free Press* on matters of trade? It was obviously impossible, so, in the crunch, something would have to give. Curiously enough, that crunch did not come for six years, and when it did, we went our separate ways. Our association lasted that long for several reasons, of which the most important was that there was a war on. In times of war all newspapers, to a greater or lesser extent, become propaganda arms of the war effort. Media criticism of the actions of governments focuses always on the way the government is prosecuting the war. It almost never takes the form of opposition to the war itself, because such opposition is seldom tolerated by a government once it goes to war. So the first question every editorial writer in the country had to face when he placed paper in typewriter was, "Does what I am saying advance the war effort?"

In a very real sense, the war solved all other problems for editorial writers everywhere. If something came up that led to a pronounced difference of opinion, it could be shunted to the back burner and attention turned to some war-related subject of more pressing concern. On the *Free Press* editorial page, however, there were few areas of even mild disagreement. For one thing, disagreement was hardly possible when communication was at a minimum. Harold Moore and I shared an office for almost five years, and during that time I cannot recall our having a serious discussion about anything, let alone finding anything to disagree about. And there was even less communication between either of us and the other editorial writers. All this was a result of the way the structure of the editorial-writing team had evolved over many years. People either were chosen for the specialized knowledge they had to contribute, or acquired special fields of expertise after becoming members of the team. Thus Moore, who was a major from the First World War, did most of the writing on military topics and aviation generally. Kennethe Haig, a deep-dyed political Tory and pioneer women's libber, covered the whole education and welfare fields. Benson Guest was the resident expert on both civic and provincial affairs. Bill Mathers, the agricultural editor of the *Prairie Farmer*, was a regular contributor of editorials on farm subjects.

Above and remote from us all was J. W. Dafoe, the editor-in-chief, and George Ferguson, his alter ego. Together they produced the bulk of the political writing on the page. The idea of having an editorial conference to discuss the subjects to be covered and the line to be taken never occurred to anybody on the *Free Press*, least of all to Dafoe or Ferguson. Those two men were so attuned to each other's minds that a few sentences were all that needed to pass between them. As a result, it was almost as difficult for insiders as it was for outsiders to tell which of them had written a *Free Press* leading editorial. When Dafoe was absent for long stretches, the tone and the theme of the editorials that Ferguson wrote were indistinguishable from what Dafoe would have written. There were differences in prose style, of course. Ferguson's was tighter, more compact than Dafoe's, for as the old man frequently pointed out with a grin, "I seem to have let myself run on a bit this time."

George Ferguson's official title was "managing editor," but he spent little time managing because his main interest was in the editorial page. The day-to-day operation of the news side was left pretty much to Abbie Coo and Howard Wolfe. Ferguson ran the editorial page with a very light rein, taking it for granted that everyone would keep abreast of developments in his area of interest and collectively turn in enough copy to fill eight columns of space, six days a week. He selected what went into the page each day and edited all the copy. For someone who had never worked on a copy desk, he was the fastest and most skilful copy editor I ever encountered. Misspelled words, redundant phrases, misplaced adverbs and adjectives, hanging clauses, and illogicalities leapt off the pages for him and his pencil would dart through them almost as quickly as he could turn a page.

When he felt the need to assign an editorial, he did it with a disarming diffidence. "You saw the story about the fight over City Hydro profits again at the council meeting? Do you think we ought to run another sub-edit? Or perhaps it's worth a page piece. Whatever you think. Anyway, we should have something on it for tomorrow." In another direction, I was sure Ferguson always had his antennae out for the individual sensitivies, convictions, and prejudices of his staff. Like: "How'd you like to do a sub-edit saying something nice about old so-and-so who got that award the other day? I'd ask Kennethe Haig but she hates his guts. He's not really a bad guy, even so, and anyway a short piece about him would please the Dogans."

Knowing my deep-seated agnosticism, he never asked me to do a Christmas or Easter leader, chores he normally farmed out to the reverend clergy but sometimes did himself. Newspapers in those days had not yet begun to take the easy way out by simply plagiarizing a chunk of the New Testament.

In addition to the Winnipeg-based writers, the editorial page was the repository of streams of copy from Grant Dexter and Burt Richardson in Ottawa and Chester Bloom in Washington. Richardson had been sent to Ottawa in the summer of 1940 to assist Dexter, who, except for a short stint in London during the Munich era, had represented the *Free Press* in Ottawa since 1922. Dexter was the ablest political reporter Canada ever produced. He had literally grown up with Mackenzie King's governments. The civil servants who were minor clerks when Dexter arrived moved steadily upward in the government service until, by the time war broke out, they were monopolizing the deputy-minister chairs. There was not a government department in which Dexter did not have friends and acquaintances of long standing. What was true of the civil service was also true of the political wing of government. The backbenchers of the 1920s and 1930s were the front-benchers on both sides of the House of Commons in the 1940s, and Dexter was on a first-name basis with most of them.

When the cabinet was making up its mind, Dexter's sources were such that he could feed J. W. Dafoe a stream of memos on who was advocating what lines of action and what the ultimate decision was most likely to be. By the time of the conscription crises of 1944–5, he was privy to more Cabinet secrets than many of the Cabinet ministers. But being a human conveyor belt of back-room gossip was only a pastime, for he was a tireless producer of three- and four-part articles on developing issues. In person Dexter was, withal, a complex loner tormented by the ulcerating conflict of his hard-shell Baptist upbringing and his devotion to Miltonian liberalism. He once confessed to being driven to despair trying to decide whether to forbid or permit his teenage son to smoke.

Burt Richardson was a perfect complement to Dexter. Like Ferguson, he was a prairie minister's son and had worked his way through the University of Saskatchewan and on to a master's degree in economics from Cornell. He went from the *Leader-Post* in Regina to Edmonton in 1935, and over the next three years covered the Social Credit revolution in Alberta. He did it with such competence that he was the natural choice for the Ottawa posting in 1940.

Where Dexter's interest was primarily in politics, Richardson's was in economic and social development. Like a couple of alley cats, he and Dexter mutually decided that the course of wisdom was to keep out of each other's way. Dexter detested Jimmy Gardiner, the Minister of Agriculture, and had little use for C. D.

Howe or Donald Gordon, the czar of the Wartime Prices and Trade Board. Richardson cultivated all three and became a foremost chronicler of the miracle of production that Howe and his department accomplished during the war. Not only did he cover the general news beat in Ottawa, but he was a prolific producer of superb editorial-page articles.

This, then, was the environment into which I settled easily and comfortably. What was my job description and what was I expected to write about? Nobody said. Indeed, I suspected that I had probably written for the page for several weeks before Dafoe himself knew I was there. It was assumed, I later pieced together, that I had been a devoted daily reader of the editorial page and in the process had absorbed its flavour and ideological bent. The editors, for their part, had assessed my own style and attitudes during my service as a reporter and had concluded that I had the cast of mind that would fit in nicely on the editorial page. The closest I got to specific direction was a suggestion from Ferguson that I should consult with Benson Guest and take some of the load off him by working into civic affairs. My adventures with John Hladun had sparked an expanding interest in everything Russian, so for starters I became the resident expert on Russia, and on trades unions, by default. Almost as an after-thought, Ferguson told me to be forever on the lookout for something light to write about.

"This is the deadliest, dullest editorial page in all Christendom, and has been ever since D. B. McRae left for Regina," Ferguson said. "Everybody is a goddam pundit, so for God's sake see what you can find to write about to take the curse of dullness off the page. And if you ever feel a sentimental urge to do an emotional piece, let yourself go, boy, as far as you like."

As it turned out, the first major pieces I wrote never got into the paper. Rumours were persistent in early June that Hitler was preparing an invasion of Russia. I got out my books on Stalin's purges of the old Bolsheviks and the officers' corps of the Russian army, and did a two-part study on the effect the purges were likely to have on Russia's fighting power and civilian morale, particularly in the Ukraine. My conclusion was that the slaughter of the innocents had been so pervasive that the country's will to resist would be seriously impaired. The articles were in type and ready to run in the edition of June 23, 1941. On the day before, a Sunday, Hitler marched and Ferguson called me to say we'd have to throw out the Russia piece and find something else. We met at the office and I worked out a substitute piece in the form of a gloating, we-told-you-so letter to the local Communist party.

The invasion of Russia was the first good news we had had in two years. As Ferguson pointed out, we at least had an ally who could bleed some of the strength away from Hitler before he regrouped his forces for an assault on England. We would soon be called on to ship supplies to Russia as well, and were undoubtedly heading into a critical stage of the war. So we had better start thinking of Russia as a fighting ally rather than as an enemy, and do what we could to turn public opinion around in that direction.

Unhappily, neither of us gave any thought to J. W. Dafoe, who was writing the leader in the quiet of his office. In his second paragraph he let go with these sentiments: ". . . the two most detestable regimes on earth are now at grips with each other. May they do much to devour and destroy each other and thus make it possible for people to live in peace with the world." And then, almost in mid-sentence, he began to have second thoughts. "From our point of view the news is good. The accretion of strength to the anti-Hitler camp is welcomed, be it great or small no matter whence it comes." Obviously he was anticipating Churchill's we-will-ally-ourselves-with-the-devil-if-he-fights-Hitler attitude.

In the first weeks of my editorial writing, I tried to find an occasion to make known my qualms over the reactionary editorial line of the *Free Press* prior to the war, when it never had anything good to say about any suggested reform. But the chance did not come and the need to raise the question gradually faded. The fading started one afternoon when I got word that Dafoe, "the chief," wanted to see me. I had written a longish piece on post-war objectives as a sort of answer to the often-asked question: Besides beating Hitler, what are we *really* fighting *for*? In the article, I pointed out that we already had adopted unemployment insurance and that we must look forward to better medical care, improved old-age pensions, and vastly improved employment opportunities. These were about as rock-bottom minimal as one could get in cataloguing our war aims. But it should be remembered that the weight of the Depression still rested heavily on our minds, and Roosevelt had not yet enunciated his four fundamental freedoms.

Ferguson had shown the article to Dafoe, and obviously they had been discussing its theme when I came into the room. The old man was half-hidden in his great black leather chair that stood at the side of his desk. A lifelong sufferer from asthma, he spent his nights half awake, half dozing, propped up in his bed and sometimes in a chair by the bed. It had been his practice to augment his rest with short naps in his leather chair, and now that he was in his seventy-sixth year, the naps were more frequent. But neither age nor infirmity had blunted his mind, which sometimes seemed to get sharper with age. Ferguson waved me to a chair and I waited for the old man to say something about the piece I recognized as my own in his hand.

"A good piece, Jimmy," he said at last. "A good piece. I said to George we should perhaps talk about it because it is something we must be doing. But we must do it in a way that does not detract from the war. We are not fighting this war for this slogan or that; we are fighting it to rid the world of the worst pestilence ever to afflict it. But we are not going back to the way things were before the war either, not in this country. We are not going to treat the boys who come home this time the way we treated their fathers. They'll see to that, I'm sure. That's why we mustn't neglect getting the commisson's report adopted to make post-war planning possible. So, I guess what we should do is be on the watch for ideas that we can take up and discuss. If they are any good, we can put them aside for the right moment. We should be writing pieces like this. But we should not get carried away with them until the time is ripe."

A door was beginning to open. Dafoe was a voracious reader of the newspapers of the world. Thereafter, whenever he ran across an item on a social theme, he would scissor it out and send it to me. One day he came into my room with a copy of the *Economist* in which there was an article on a subject I had never heard of— family allowances. It was described as a method by which the state could share with the family the burden that children imposed upon family income. The *Economist* saw in family allowances, paid in cash monthly for each child, an instrument that might ease the upward pressure on wage rates. Wage rates could then be based more on the productivity of workers and less upon the needs of their family for more money for the necessities of life. The *Economist* supported the idea and the British trades unions vigorously condemned it. In a country like Canada, where four-fifths of the workers did not belong to unions, family allowances seemed to me a useful way of assisting families to carry the added cost of children. I wrote the first of several pieces on the subject.

Some months later, Dafoe sent me in a book entitled *Poverty and Progress, a Second Social Survey of York*, by B. Seebohm Rowntree, an heir to the British chocolate fortune. The Rowntrees were socially conscious Quakers, and forty years earlier Seebohm had undertaken a massive study of the incidence of poverty in the city of York. He had hired a score of researchers to visit thousands of families with a questionnaire that would have done justice for completeness to the census takers for the Domesday Book. This study demonstrated that the primary pauperizing influence on the working class's standard of living was having children. Married couples who got by nicely without children fell far below what he defined as "the poverty line" once children began to arrive, and Rowntree proved that they stayed there until the eldest children reached working age and began to augment the family income. The larger the family, the deeper the plunge into poverty, and the longer it took to get out. In 1936 Rowntree repeated his survey and found substantial improvement in general conditions. Children, however, still dragged workers below the poverty line in the same way as they had forty years before. As a substantial increase in minimum wages was out of the question, Rowntree came out for a system of family allowances. So did the *Free Press*, long before the federal Liberals made it part of their program.

Obviously, Dafoe was no longer the social reactionary his 1935 editorial attacks on the Bennett New Deal had seemed to indicate. I gossiped with Ferguson occasionally about the old man, and he said that Dafoe's membership on the Rowell-Sirois Commission had had a profound effect. In 1937 and 1938, the commission had travelled the breadth of the country hearing testimony on the state of the fiscal and social health of the Canadian nation. Briefs were presented by governments, learned economists, professors, welfare groups, and sundry crackpots. He came home from these sittings convinced that the conditions under which thousands of Canadians lived in the Maritimes and in the West were a national disgrace. As he saw it, it was not that the country did not generate enough wealth to provide a decent level of social services and a decent standard of living for its people—he was convinced that it did— but that too large a proportion of it was siphoned off into Ontario and too little was left for the other governments. What was needed was to establish a national minimum level of social, medical, and educational services and to devise a re-allocation of revenues to the have-not provinces to enable them to provide these services.

"Maybe 'the road to Damascus' is putting it too strongly," Ferguson said, "but the Rowell-Sirois thing sure as hell nudged him off centre. The only trouble is, I think he has a gut feeling that favours a lot of the kind of things Coldwell talks about, but the fact that the CCF advocates anything drives him in the opposite direction."

Ferguson's assessment made obvious sense. With Dafoe, ideas were purified or contaminated by the company they kept. Thus, the idea of nation-wide unemployment insurance was anathema when it was part of Bennett's New Deal, but something to embrace enthusiastically when the Liberals adopted it at the outset of the war. More than that, I think he was victimized by the like-attracts-like syndrome. His Sanhedrin of Winnipeg cronies might well have been described as the cream of the town's economic royalists, to borrow a Rooseveltian phrase. They included Frank Fowler, James Richardson, and "Fire-Sale Jim" Murray, all Winnipeg Grain Exchange stalwarts; Tom Crerar, Edgar Tarr, J. B. "Bogus" Coyne, and John MacAulay, super-establishmentarians to a man. He had no contact of any kind with the new breed of farmer-leader whose constituency was the great co-operative movement of the prairies. Thus he remained a drum-beater for the great free-trade crusade of 1911 and 1920, long after the farmers who had marched in those parades had veered away to the music of different drums. If he was aware at all of the gulf that divided his thinking from theirs, I don't think he much cared. His primary concern was with the world order, with the shape the League of Nations would take when peace came, and with Canada's place as an independent nation in the post-war world. Primarily, that is, after his dedication to the political interests of the federal Liberal party.

As the months passed and I became the shuntee of many of Ferguson's minor chores—editing copy, reading proofs, making up the page, listening to disputatious readers—my contact with Dafoe increased, but on a very casual basis. If Ferguson was ill or away, I would discuss the make-up of the page with him, see that he had proofs of everything we had written, make sure he knew what articles we had ahead. But there were weeks at a stretch when I never saw him, and I never came close to getting to know him.

Among the chores which I took over from Ferguson was Archie Dale, our once-great cartoonist. We ran at least three and usually four Dale cartoons a week on the editorial page, and for years this had been the feature of the paper to which thousands of our readers turned first. It was agreed by common consent that the most fetching example of nature imitating art was the way R. B. Bennett grew more and more to look like Archie Dale's caricature of him. There were many who even believed that Dale's barbed cartoons had helped undermine the Tory prime minister's credibility as a political leader. With Bennett gone, Archie turned his comic genius on William Aberhart, Mitch Hepburn, Hitler, and Mussolini. But nobody approached Bennett in Dale's affections and he regarded Bennett's departure from power as his greatest personal affront. By the time our paths joined, however, Archie Dale was long past his prime, which had peaked when J. B. McGeachy moved from Washington to Winnipeg in 1931 to provide Archie with the ideas for his cartoons.

"Hamish" McGeachy was the renaissance man of Canadian journalism. A superb pianist, devotee of Gilbert and Sullivan and Shakespeare, collector and reciter of bawdy limericks, he was an incurable rhymester and parodist. Scottish-born and -educated through matriculation, McGeachy had graduated from the University of Saskatchewan while still in his teens. Legend has it that he was bound for Oxford on a Rhodes scholarship when he changed his mind and opted for a scholarship at Princeton instead. Expelled from that institution for some outrageous caper, he obtained employment with a wealthy New Yorker as a part-time tutor of the millionaire's children in English, French, and dramatics. When that job blew up, he returned to Saskatoon and a job on the *Star*. He was the editor of that paper when it was acquired by the Sifton family in 1927. McGeachy wrote the most beautiful prose of anybody on the *Free Press* staff, or in Canadian journalism for that matter. And it poured from his typewriter.

Urbane, handsome, witty, chain-smoking, McGeachy was an iconoclastic hedonist who might have stepped straight out of the pages of Rabelais or Balzac. He had a wild and bawdy sense of humour he was barely able to keep in check. When the legislature was in session, he wrote an editorial-page column called "Under the Dome," dedicated to puncturing the pomposities of the legislature. Between sessions, he wandered the country with royal commissions and reported their doings with a mixture of pithy summarization and incisive comment. At other times, he shared an office with Archie Dale and kept him supplied with superb cartoon ideas. With the onset of the war, McGeachy was posted to London, but soon left the paper for a brilliant career as the BBC's nightly broadcaster in the overseas service. For thousands of Canadians, bedtime came only after we had listened to Lorne Greene's voice-of-doom recital of the daily disasters, followed by McGeachy's superb baritone catching the unflappable atmosphere of London under siege.

With McGeachy gone, Ferguson took up the burden of supplying Dale with ideas, a chore he hated and did rather badly. When I came along I inherited Archie, and my first job four days a week was to search the news stories frantically for a glimmering of an inspiration for a cartoon. I was no better at it than Ferguson, and the quality of the cartoons never again reached much above mediocrity. When McGeachy was supplying the ideas, letters asking for the gift of the originals flowed into the office in such volume that it was not unusual to get half a dozen requests for a drawing. With Ferguson or me doing the inspiring, the flood declined to a trickle before it dried up completely.

Frustration with Archie Dale, however, was such a minor thing that I quickly concluded editorial writing was the high heaven to which all journalists must aspire. When I broke through Ferguson's dour and caustic crust, I discovered a kindly, considerate, and thoroughly attractive personality. Soon I found myself able to read his mind, to empathize with him as easily as he did with J. W. Dafoe. The boss's glove he wore was of the softest suede, and there was rarely an occasion when he exercised his authority by getting his back up. The close personal friendship we established was to last a lifetime. So every day brought new zest and new challenges, but never new problems. There was time for reading, as much time as you wanted to take. There was time for reflective writing without deadline pressure or copy-editors grabbing running copy from your typewriter. Late-afternoon and evening assignments were gone forever, and Kay could now make supper plans in reasonable certainty that I would be home on time. In 1939 I had borrowed the down-payment from the *Free Press* for a house I built on Glenwood Crescent. Eighteen months later, we sold the house for a two-thousand-dollar profit and replaced it with another five blocks up the street. By then I was sufficiently settled into editorial writing that I easily found the time to supervise the sub-contractors on an almost daily basis. Nobody ran herd on the time *Free Press* editorial writers spent at their desks.

Unlike Dafoe, Ferguson, Dexter, and Richardson, I contributed nothing of lasting importance to the editorial page during my stay on it. Nothing that I ever wrote will provide any future historian with a point-making quotation or footnote. But I must have written a thousand sub-editorials on local issues of passing moment, and it reached a point where I could write war-loan leaders in my sleep. In addition to the other routine chores, I represented the paper on such worthy causes as the Canadian Aid to Russia Fund, the Canadian Aid to China Fund, the Canadian National Committee on Refugees, and various national scrap drives. I attended all the annual conventions of the national labour organizations and expatiated—learnedly, I thought—on their proceedings.

For my own pleasure I concentrated on finding off-pattern and light-hearted themes to write about and sometimes succeeded rather well, though the output was dishearteningly meagre. Finally, I shared with Ferguson the task of putting together a weekly radio commentary on the course of the war in Europe, which we did for CKRC, the Sifton station.

The Russians put out little in the way of progress reports on the German invasion, but the news agencies had listening posts in London and Stockholm which monitored all the radio stations on both sides. The *Free Press* library had fallen heir to a *Times* of London gazetteer which was replete with superbly detailed, large-scale relief maps of eastern Europe. The German invasion of Russia tended to follow the railways. There was hardly a whistle stop anywhere in Europe that was not pinpointed on the *Times* maps. When unheard-of places turned up in dispatches, we were able to locate them, identify tactical break-throughs, and alert our listeners to the names to watch for in the up-coming news stories. The way we plastered our walls with maps must have convinced in-coming strangers that they had bundered into an outpost of the strategic air command.

Along about the time I was mastering the technique of pronouncing such Russian place names as Kotelnikovsk, Dniepropetrovsk, and Borisoglebsk, Ferguson decided I ought to get to know some thing of Ottawa and Washington. If I was going to be writing about them, I ought to know how governments functioned at national levels. He suggested that I should plan to spend three or four weeks in Ottawa about the time the House re-opened at the end of January 1943. With another manpower crisis brewing between war production and the armed services, it could be exciting. Dexter, of course, would be on to the politics of it and I might be able to give Richardson a hand with whatever he was involved with.

En route to Ottawa, I was as excited by the prospects of seeing Parliament at work as any newly elected member of the House. Here, I assumed—quite mistakenly of course—was where things happened and where the ultimate decisions were made. With the up-coming crisis in manpower, there would be more of the kind of debate that had preceded the plebiscite and the introduction of Bill 80 the year before. So I was eagerly hopeful that I would get there in time for the casting of the votes. My introduction to the House of Commons was a disillusioning anti-climax.

I arrived late one afternoon after the question period was over. Down in one corner, a member was making a speech to row on row of empty seats. Of the score or so of members present, no one seemed concerned with the speech. This was Parliament? It was impossible to believe, but it was true. And for reasons that made sense. The great decisions on vital issues, as I should have known, were made by the prime minister and his Cabinet committees, then stamped "approved" by the full Cabinet, and then, but only if thought important enough, filtered through the caucus of the party in power. By the time the issues got to the floor of the House of Commons, the decision, with very rare exceptions, had already been made. So proceedings in the House of Commons were not duels between soaring intellects trying to reason together, to convince or be convinced. Nobody ever listened to anybody else, save to ferret out points for rebuttal. The speeches made with such passion were not directed to other members but to the public beyond, who, it was hoped, would carry around what was said in memory until the next election. And vote accordingly. The way the House of Commons functioned, it might well have been devised to destroy the faith in democracy of everyone contemplating the spectacle.

As I was to discover in the weeks that followed, members did not spend time in the House when they had anything better to do, though most turned up regularly for the question period with which Parliament began its daily sittings. What happened when the questions were over and the Speaker called the orders of the day depended on who was expected to speak. When the prime minister, the leader of the Opposition, or important Cabinet ministers were likely to be speaking, the bulk of the members remained in their seats. Listening was always an ordeal, for the acoustics of the place were gawd-awful. To hear Prime Minister King reading his speeches required absolute aural concentration.

When no stars were to perform, few of the members stayed, though protocol dictated that members of each opposition group should remain and applaud when one of the group was speaking. Otherwise, there was a mad rush for the exits when the question period was over. The press gallery was split about evenly over which member could clear the House quickest by rising to speak— Tommy Church, a Tory member for Toronto, or John Blackmore, the Social Credit member for Lethbridge. Torchy Anderson, the cynical correspondent for the Vancouver *Province*, had a much-quoted piece of advice for newcomers to the press gallery. "When you get to the point where you discover you can understand either of them, it's time to go on the wagon as far as listening to the House is concerned. Your sanity is being threatened."

The members who were kept in the House by party discipline mainly spent their time writing letters, reading newspapers, or visiting back and forth. When a francophone member was speaking, order was completely lost. The English speakers became involved in audible conversation, to the extent that the Speaker was forced every few minutes to call "Order! Order!" Sometimes he had to rise to his feet and make his call three or four times before he got the attention of the noisemakers. And when the parliamentary drunks had been too long into the sauce, things got hopelessly out of hand.

I had assumed that Grant Dexter and Burt Richardson would take me in hand, show me the ropes, and give me some news or editorial assignments to cover. Nothing of the kind happened. After twenty years of a lone-wolf existence, Dexter was incapable of directing anybody to do anything. That a newcomer would require introductions and advice never occurred to him. Instead, he invited me to lunch at the Rideau Club with Wilfrid Eggleston. I spent the noon hour being cross-examined about my personal history and we parted without a word of advice. During my stay in the capital, however, Dexter had me out to his home for dinner several times, where he again went on prying expeditions into my personal history. The Dexters seemed fascinated by our misadventures on unemployment relief during the early thirties. Both he and Alice seemed suitably shocked by the vision I conjured up of thousands of families living three or four people to a room in lodging houses, while houses were standing empty of tenants. The commonplace experiences that happened to everybody who lost their jobs and went on relief were unknown to the Dexters. It occurred to me that he had spent five years of his life in Ottawa during the Bennett administration writing thousands of words almost daily on the unemployment-relief crisis, and yet had never become aware of what unemployment relief meant to the people on relief. At last, when we had about milked the subject dry, Dexter made a comment that almost gagged me as it went down. His exact words are lost to memory, but the sense of his comment was: "I guess it only goes to show what happens to people when economic nationalism rules the world."

It seemed to me that this was as staggering a non sequitur as I had ever encountered. I had expected that we might have gotten into discussing measures to make the impact of job-loss less degrading to the unemployed, or to talking about measures that could be devised to shield western farmers from price collapses which made it impossible for them to get enough for their live-stock to pay the freight to get them to market. Instead, Dexter was off on a reverie about the disastrous impact of Bennett's trade policies on Canada. As he talked, it dawned on me that he really and truly was a fundamentalist believer in the gospel according to Adam Smith, that only free trade and the unfettering of the law of supply and demand could save the world. What happened to people in the process was wholly incidental, even irrelevant. What was important was principle and it was only in the adherence to sound principles that the best interests of the people could be served. We got away from economics and back to me before I had a chance to bring up Marshall's principle of marginal utility as a modifier of Smith.

Dexter became downright expansive over my prospects. He was delighted, he said, that I was now on the road that would ultimately lead me to the editorship of a Sifton newspaper. That anyone had considered me potential editor material came as such a shock that

I must have blushed to my hair roots, but he did not appear to notice. I had done my time on the routine news beats, he said; now I was getting experience in the larger world. The progression was from civic politics, through provincial politics, to national politics, and then into world politics. Only when one had had the experience of the Ottawa press gallery, then Washington, and finally London, was one qualified to become an editor.

Dexter's proposition seemed rather academic to me and my mind raced around picking up exceptions to his rule. I pointed out that neither Dafoe nor Ferguson had undergone any such training regimen. Dafoe had missed Washington and London, of course, but he had absorbed all the other experiences, Dexter answered. As for Ferguson, he was sure that George was profoundly aware of the disability he suffered from never having had news-side experience. There was no substitute for the experience one got covering the day-to-day proceedings of the legislature, of Parliament, of Washington and London. It gave you a feel for politics, for developing issues, that was absolutely essential to an editor. I should think of myself as following after Richardson, who would be going to Washington and London in a year or two to complete his training. He was sure that I would be an outstanding success.

I scoffed at the whole idea. The notion of leaving Winnipeg had never occurred to me, and I said that that was the last thing I ever wanted to do. Besides, I added as a clincher, I had the best job I could ever want to have right now. He seemed shocked by my lack of ambition and desire to stay put, until I added:

"You should know how I feel about Winnipeg, Grant. You've got the best job in the world right here in Ottawa, and I bet all the tea in China would not move you out of here!"

He seemed to be nodding agreement. But it was not until four years later, when we were deep into the war of the Dafoe succession, that the import of Dexter's theorizing became clear. He was not talking about the qualifications I could acquire to become an editor. He was talking about his own qualifications to become the editor of the *Free Press*.

Though he was swamped with work, Burt Richardson was much more helpful. He made up a list of people I might get in touch with on stories he had been unable to get around to. He introduced me to Bill Bennett, C. D. Howe's executive assistant, and to Don Allen, who performed the same function for James G. Gardiner. It would be good orientation, he said, to go into the House each day for the question period, and I could track down some answers on questions previously asked. It might also be half-useful, he suggested, to wander around and introduce myself to the members from Manitoba and Saskatchewan. It was not.

Thoreau might well have been thinking of the private members of the House of Commons when he coined the phrase about the mass of men leading lives of quiet desperation. If the bulk of the members of Parliament had little useful function to perform in the House of Commons except to vote when called on, they had less outside. A trickle of mail from their constituents made minimal demands on their time; they could attend occasional committee meetings and take what action they could on requests for patronage. Sometimes, as had happened mid-way through the year before, the western members could cause such a row in caucus about the depressed level of wheat prices that the Cabinet sat up and listened. In between, there were days stretching into weeks of simply putting in time with no sense of accomplishment. Curiously enough, members of the Opposition had a better life than supporters of the government. They were often divided up into groups to study projects and issues with which their parties felt they could make some political yards. They could paw around in the underbrush and come up with embarrassing questions to fire at the government. They could force Cabinet ministers to provide statistical answers they could use in form letters to the folks back home. Occasionally, they even got their names in home-town papers by the questions they asked.

In those wartime winters, Ottawa was a singularly unlovable place. A succession of gloom-laden skies alternated with a day or two of bright sunshine, which brought a biting damp cold that ate through Winnipeg-type winter clothing as if it were cheesecloth. The city was being overrun by a sour-pussed army of occupation scurrying ant-like in all directions, overcrowding everything from taverns to streetcars to hotel rooms and rooming houses. The people who knew anything were too busy to be interviewed, or too circumspect to unburden themselves to a bird of passage like me. By the end of my second week in town, I had taken such a scunner against the place and all its works that I could hardly wait to get back to Winnipeg, Archie Dale, our temperamental oil burner, and the warmth of life in our 40°-below weather. In my month in Ottawa I had been able to produce only a handful of usable copy, despite Richardson's friendly efforts to get me started.

One of Richardson's off-hand suggestions turned out to be a touchdown for me. He mentioned that Arthur Irwin, the editor of *Maclean's* magazine, had been around looking for somebody to write an article on the Steep Rock iron development in western Ontario. To do the article would necessitate a trip to the mine itself, which was remotely located on a branch line near Fort Frances. Irwin had been unable to locate anybody in the gallery who could spare the time to do the job.

"I've got some stuff on it in my files you can have, and if you're interested I'll see if Irwin is still around and you can talk to him. It's worth a couple of hundred bucks, and you might also peddle the story to Sanford Cooper at *Time* magazine."

Richardson introduced me to Irwin; I got the assignment and, after I got home, got some time off to visit the mine and write a five-thousand-word article for *Maclean's*.

It was an exciting story of how human ingenuity was able to overcome monumental natural barriers to get at a rich ore body lying under three lakes that had to be drained. I did a workmanlike job on the making of the mine, and with the article I sent along a memo of my conversation with R. J. Moore, a cynical mining engineer who represented the Reconstruction Finance Corporation of the United States. Thanks to the lobbying skill of Cyrus Eaton, the Canadian-born Cleveland tycoon, the RFC had agreed to lend the promoters five million dollars to bring the mine into production. Moore contended that, as a result, the entire project was being developed for the benefit of Cyrus Eaton, whose firm would have a monopoly on marketing the ore to lower-lake steel mills on a royalty basis. It was, he said, a heads-I-win, tails-you-lose proposition if ever he had heard of one, and he had been looking at mining deals all his life. I spelled out the complicated details of Moore's thesis for Irwin because I felt it essential for him to have this background to assess the worth of the article itself. To decide, even, if he wanted it rewritten in a more critical way.

Arthur Irwin was so impressed by the article and the memo that he telephoned immediately and offered me a job as the *Maclean's* correspondent in Ottawa at one hundred dollars a week plus expenses—double my *Free Press* salary. I was staggered by the offer but had no difficulty saying thanks but no thanks. My brief press gallery experience had been more than sufficient. I was repelled by the town itself, by the parliamentary charade, by the press gallery, and by the monstrous size of the government apparatus one was expected to cover. A random phrase from the *Rubáiyát* of Omar Khayyám clattered into my head: "I often wonder what the vintners buy that's half as precious as the stuff they sell." I had a home of my own on the Red River, a job I liked with people I admired, and enough money, with my freelancing income, to spend the rest of my life in complete comfort. I broke the news of the offer to Ferguson this way:

"George, do you remember a cold winter day in January 1935

when the *Free Press* offered me twenty dollars a week to become a reporter after I was offered a brokerage-office job by George Mc-Cullagh in Toronto at fifty dollars?"

Ferguson nodded and covered his eyes in mock embarrassment.

"Well," I continued, "this is where we came in eight years ago. It's happened again." I told him about Irwin's proposition. He sat staring at me, saying nothing until he asked: "I'm really afraid to ask, but what was your decision this time?"

"The same as before, of course. I told him I wouldn't move to Ottawa if he gave me the magazine, though I was polite and said how flattered I was at the offer."

Ferguson almost exploded out of his chair.

"Goddam it, Gray, you are the biggest goddam fool I have ever known. You damn well know you could fill this job for Art to the King's taste. Sure you'd have to work your ass off. But you do that around here. And you know, and I know, it will be years before Victor would ever part with that kind of money for you. For Christ's sake, don't you ever think of your family? When Kay hears of this I hope she cuts your effing throat."

I never before or again saw him explode so angrily. I left his office and went down to the Okum Inn for a cup of coffee and some cigarettes. When I returned he had cooled down; he came into my room and apologized, and we went out together for another coffee. If I was worth one hundred dollars a week to *Maclean's* I should be worth that much to the *Free Press*, he said. But it didn't work that way if you were Victor Sifton. Put it up to him as a choice between paying or losing your services, and he'd shake you warmly by the hand and wish you on your way. Sifton by this time was back from his Ottawa stint as Master General of Ordnance and reinserting himself into the management of his publishing empire. Ferguson said he would talk to Victor, but first of all he'd talk to Bill Lord, the de facto general manager, and see what could be possible under the ceiling to get me some more money.

When Sifton was apprised of the offer, he bounced enthusiastically into my room and, in Ferguson's phrase, shook me warmly by the hand. He said that I would understand the *Maclean's* offer was to represent the magazine as Ottawa correspondent. The *Free Press* might meet that salary for an Ottawa correspondent, though hardly for an editorial writer in Winnipeg. He added, however, that he was sure the time would come when that position would open for me, and in the meantime he was pleased that I was staying with the paper in Winnipeg. At the very least I expected some sort of increase in pay, but none came. Ferguson, however, kept working, and later that summer he got my category changed from editorial writer to political correspondent and my pay raised to $325 a month. To cover our tracks in case there was trouble with the Wartime Prices and Trade Board, I was sent for another familiarization jaunt to Ottawa that fall, and to Washington the following spring.

Meanwhile, developments in Winnipeg made me happier than ever with my refusal of the *Maclean's* offer. J. W. Dafoe had become impressed with a young economist who had worked with the Rowell–Sirois Commission by the name of John Deutsch, a German–Canadian Saskatchewan farm boy and Queen's graduate. He had told Deutsch that, if he ever tired of working for the government, he would like him to join the staff of the *Free Press*. Deutsch came to work on the page that fall. At the same time, Sifton had been out bird-dogging himself and hired Bruce Hutchison to become a full-time contributor to the page. Bruce had been selling us pieces on a freelance basis for a couple of years, and we got to know and like him when he blew through Winnipeg three or four times a year on brain-picking safaris to and from Ottawa and Washington. He wrote with a sparkling touch that none of the rest of us could match, and we looked forward eagerly to the lightening of the page with an increased contribution from him, though he would remain in residence in Victoria. A third newcomer was the most charming of all. He was Clifford Sifton, the only son of the late Harry Sifton, then in his late twenties and under death sentence from the Sifton disease, which had carried off his father and his uncles in the prime of life. He had arteries of vulcanized rubber and blood-pressure that cardiologists expected to see only in almost dead men. Married to a luscious redhead, he had returned to Canada from London and came to our page in preparation for his later appointment as editor of the Saskatoon *Star-Phoenix*. Aware that theirs was a marriage on borrowed time, Gerry and Clifford Sifton lived an hour at a time in such a way that they charmed the pants off everyone they met. What was more, Clifford wrote with a natural flair, so he too became an ornament, all too briefly, of our editorial page.

With Deutsch providing articles of basic economic analysis, Hutchison flooding us with insights into the Washington scene, and Dexter and Richardson in Ottawa, we had the highest-powered editorial-page team in the country, even if Ferguson and I and the others, including J. W. Dafoe, never wrote a line. And we were all blithely pouring out copy without pause, and doing so in ideological harmony and man-to-man empathy.

It all blew up in our faces on January 9, 1944, when J. W. Dafoe took to his bed and died of a heart attack in his seventy-eighth year.

8
Scooped on the Biggest Story since Creation

The "war of the Dafoe succession," a phrase that came to us some years after the dust had fallen on the struggle, was more closely akin to something from *Alice in Wonderland* than to the realities of Canadian journalism, or of Canadian capitalism. Its source—the War of the Austrian Succession—was the result of King Charles VI's dying without an heir and making no provision for what was called "the imperial dignity." Dafoe, too, died without indicating who among his protégés should succeed him. It was seemly and proper that he should have done so, because the appointment of his successor was not his prerogative. The newspaper was owned lock, stock, and barrel by the Sifton brothers and the estate of Harry Sifton. The owners had every right to name whomever they wanted to the office of editor-in-chief.

What set the *Free Press* apart from all other newspapers was Dafoe's impregnable prestige, which had enabled him to dominate the paper's ownership in violation of the principle that he who pays the piper calls the tune. The *Free Press* came into the hands of Sir Clifford Sifton, Laurier's Interior Minister, in 1901, and he hired Dafoe away from the *Montreal Star* to be its editor. Already a Liberal fundamentalist, Dafoe was to provide the Liberal party with a voice in Manitoba and to become the spokesman for the interests of its constituency—western Canada at the dawn of western expansion. At the same time, Sifton, who had a cyclopean eye for profit, hired a pint-sized financial genius named E. H. Macklin to run the business side of his publishing firm. Sifton and Dafoe did consult on editorial policy, though the latter by all accounts was promised a free hand in developing the paper's editorial positions. The paper zoomed to immense profitability on the wings of the western boom, and Dafoe's reputation grew with it, both as a voice to be heard in the Liberal party and as the voice of western Canada, particularly of the interests of prairie farmers. As western interests collided with those of tariff-protected eastern industry, Dafoe became the undeviating advocate of free trade and laissez-faire economic principles.

When he quit the Liberal Cabinet in a huff in 1905, Sir Clifford moved to Toronto to better husband the substantial fortune he had built during his decade in Ottawa. And he moved spiritually as well as physically, for he was soon a confirmed protectionist. As a result, in the reciprocity election of 1911, he came out just as strongly against Laurier and free trade with the United States as Dafoe came out in favour of it. That was the first of several occasions when Dafoe found himself in ideological conflict with his employer, stood his ground, and committed the newspaper to policies to which the Siftons were resolutely opposed. During the First World War, Dafoe's growing reputation as a leading Canadian nationalist reached the point where Sir Robert Borden invited him to attend the Paris peace conference as part of the Canadian delegation. His support of the winning Progressives in 1920 and his switch to the winning Mackenzie King Liberals thereafter created the impression that Dafoe was not only the authentic voice of the West but a moulder of western public opinion to boot.

With the death of Sir Clifford, the inheriting sons had a titan on their hands, and a prickly one at that whenever they sought to influence his editorial judgment. During the Depression, the brothers urged him to ease off on his attacks on the Bennett administration because they were costing the paper advertising revenue and subscribers. Dafoe refused, with the comment that newspapers were like rose bushes, which thrived best when pruned back occasionally. During the Second World War, the brothers tried to persuade Dafoe that George Drew, the Ontario Tory premier, was an ideal leader for a national wartime government. He wiped out their arguments with a single sentence: "He's a son of a bitch!" He then wrote an editorial rejecting the idea of a national government similar to the one put together for the First World War. This was the "imperial dignity" of J. W. Dafoe in action.

In his ability to dominate the owners of the paper he worked for, Dafoe was unique. Elsewhere, in case of disagreement, it was always the owner or his publisher who called the editorial tune. So the *Free Press* was a mutant, a sport in the garden of Canadian journalism. That fact, curiously enough, went completely unrecognized by the denizens of the *Free Press* brains department. To a man our concern was with how best to carry on the Dafoe tradition and Dafoe policies. We naïvely believed that newspaper subscribers (a) read and (b) ingested the opinions expressed on editorial pages. So we regarded it as our patriotic duty to dictate what the *Free Press* reading public was invited to think. It was a concern that ignored the very existence of the owners of the paper. It did not occur to any of us that Victor Sifton would have anything constructive to contribute to *Free Press* editorial policy.

In the days that immediately followed Dafoe's death, there was considerable speculation by the staff about who would be named to succeed him. The overwhelming consensus was that the position would go to George Ferguson. He had been Dafoe's alter ego for more than a decade and had, as noted, functioned in Dafoe's place over long periods. In Winnipeg itself, even when Dafoe was alive, the public had long identified Ferguson as the editor to whom complaints, appeals, and suggestions should be directed.

On the page itself, we would not have been surprised if Grant Dexter had assumed the post. He had served as Dafoe's eyes and ears in Ottawa for twenty years. While the dedication of the rest of us to the interests of the Liberal party were casual, to say the least, Dexter was perhaps more committed to federal Liberalism than Dafoe himself. And he was far more doctrinaire a Liberal than the chief, who, as I have said, was profoundly influenced by the pleadings before the Rowell–Sirois Commission.

The decision on the successor to Dafoe eventually filtered down to the editorial page and the staff through me on the Sunday following Dafoe's death. I was in the office that evening, finishing making up the page, when Sifton wandered into my room looking for Ferguson. I said that George would not be in, and asked if there was anything special he wanted or anything I could do.

"We must change the masthead," he said, and I recalled that, the day after Dafoe's death, we had taken his name off the top right corner of the editorial page. The box there had identified J. W. Dafoe as president and Victor Sifton as general manager of the Winnipeg Free Press Company Limited. Sifton handed me the slip of paper he was holding with four names typed on it:

Victor Sifton, Publisher
George V. Ferguson, Executive Editor
Grant Dexter, Associate Editor
Bruce Hutchison, Associate Editor

I glanced at the list, expecting to see Ferguson's name as editor-in-chief, and managed to disguise my disappointment by reacting as a mechanic. "You've got a problem with space, Victor. There won't be room to list the names one over the other unless we increase the depth of the box. However, you could fit them two to a line, I'm sure."

He wrestled with making a choice for a while and then said,

"Put George and me on the left and Grant and Bruce on the right."

Instead of leaving, he stood staring into space as if waiting for me to say something. I asked the obvious question: when would Grant and Bruce be moving to Winnipeg?

"Hah," he said, "that's the rub. It will take a little time. Both insist they are *not* coming here, that they are too valuable where they are. So that for the moment is where they'll stay. But they'll come, they'll come. Grant will come and if Grant comes, Brucie will come. It's just a matter of time."

It seemed to me, I said, that it was plain crazy to try to edit a newspaper in Winnipeg with one editor in Victoria, another in Ottawa, and a third in Winnipeg. Victor agreed cheerfully and said that it was just a temporary arrangement and would solve itself once Grant and Bruce came to their senses.

The more I pondered the arrangement, the less sense it made, and I could foresee endless technical difficulties with communication and the production of the page. The next morning I hoped I might get several things clarified when I went in to see Ferguson and offer my condolences for his not being appointed Dafoe's successor. He abruptly ended our conversation.

"My God, Jimmy, you weren't stupid enough to think that Sifton would ever want *me* as his editor-in-chief, were you?" He turned his back and reached for the telephone.

An hour later he came into my room in a better mood and we went out for coffee. He explained the new set-up. He would continue to function as before with a new title. Grant, seemingly, had dug in his heels and refused to move to Winnipeg unless Bruce would move, and nothing was ever going to get Hutchison permanently out of Victoria. Each of the three was to be equal in status and in pay, though when he had left the meeting, Bruce and Grant were arguing that, with Ferguson carrying the heavier load in Winnipeg, he should get a higher salary. And what, I asked, was Victor Sifton's function to be?

"What it has always been," Ferguson said. "He can go on terrorizing the janitors and printers and bookkeepers, spend the summer riding to hounds in Brockville, the fall at the Royal Winter Fair, and the winter fancy skating at the Winter Club. And just to humour him, we'll do our best to help him to feel he's part of the team."

In his book *The Far Side of the Street*, Bruce Hutchison wrote that Ferguson "and Victor shared a mutual respect for each other's abilities but never a true friendship...."* The plain truth was that

---

* *The Far Side of the Street* (Toronto: Macmillan, 1976), p. 197.

they hated each other's guts. On Ferguson's part, his repugnance for the Siftons went back over a decade to a conspiracy on the part of E. H. Macklin and Jack Sifton to get rid of Dafoe. They had called Ferguson in, told him that Dafoe had outlived his usefulness and was impairing the solvency of the property, and offered his job to Ferguson if he would join their cabal. Instead, he carried the offer to Dafoe, who exploded into Sifton's office in a towering rage. Macklin fired Ferguson on the spot for betraying their trust. When told of the firing, Dafoe rehired Ferguson and defied the Siftons to do anything about it. Ferguson was convinced that Victor, though still in Regina at the time, must have been a party to the move to fire Dafoe because of the closeness of the Sifton family relationships. It was inconceivable to Ferguson that Macklin and Jack Sifton would have moved without the approval of Victor and his brother Clifford. And he was certain that Victor never forgave him for exposing their plan to Dafoe.

As for Victor Sifton, he was never comfortable with Ferguson. He had an office adjoining Ferguson's, but the connecting door was always closed. When he came into Ferguson's room, he would get on with whatever had brought him there and leave. He was never given to drawing up a chair and engaging Ferguson in small talk.

The unhappy truth was that Victor Sifton and George Victor Ferguson had nothing in common except being born in Queen Victoria's Jubilee Year and being named in honour of the British queen. Ferguson was the only son of the superintendent of Presbyterian home missions in western Canada, which gave him a modest bump of social consciousness; Victor was as devoid of social consciousness as a praying mantis. Sifton was a teetotaller and Ferguson was a first-class drinking man, a fact that gave both Sifton and Dexter undue concern. Ferguson was a speed-reader who could devour a book at a sitting. Sifton seldom read anything at all, least of all his own newspaper. He had lost one eye in the First World War and, as he explained, he found even moderately prolonged concentration on reading an ordeal. Ferguson had a mind that was always in overdrive, and he was weighing conclusions while slower minds were still plodding through preambles. He had no patience at all with slower minds like Sifton's, which had to work methodically through all the byways towards a conclusion.

In the face of such monumental incompatibility, the mystery was why Ferguson was not given the golden handshake the day after Dafoe died. The explanation lay in part in the intransigence of Dexter and Hutchison in refusing to move to Winnipeg. Ferguson represented continuity with the Dafoe tradition. Dexter and

Hutchison had undoubtedly argued strongly that Ferguson's presence in Winnipeg was essential if they were to function as associate editors. As for Ferguson, he was so firmly attached to the paper through his ideological umbilical cord with Dafoe that he never considered leaving. Like the others, he assumed that the triumvirate would fill the Dafoe void and that Sifton would go on being concerned with his counting house and only passively interested in the editorial page.

That Victor Sifton had no such notion was immediately made abundantly plain. He moved into Dafoe's old office as soon as it had been stripped of all Dafoe's memorabilia. He sent word around that an editorial conference, the first in *Free Press* history, would be held the following morning in his office. In attendance were Dexter, Deutsch, Hutchison, Moore, Guest and myself. Ferguson did not attend. (The shock of Dafoe's sudden death, which could not have shattered him more had he been a member of the family, brought all his emotions to the surface. In an obvious effort to get himself together, he set off at once for London to, he said, straighten out some problems that had arisen in the London Bureau.) In a few days Dexter went back to Ottawa and Hutchison stayed in Winnipeg to pinch-hit until Ferguson returned. The editorial conferences gradually settled down to Hutchison, Deutsch, Sifton, and myself. I was included because I was responsible for the mechanical business of getting the articles to fit and putting the page together.

Under Ferguson's pressure, when he returned, the editorial conference was changed from morning to after lunch. Instead of lengthy palavers over what we would write, we wrote the editorials first and ran the finished copies past Victor for his approval or comment. Then we'd tell him what we planned for the following day, discuss news breaks from the war fronts, Ottawa, and the West briefly, and that would be it.

Except . . .

Victor Sifton, who abhorred alcohol, was a tea addict. He liked to conclude his conference with tea and what he thought was light conversation. Ferguson had a straight-black-coffee man's contempt for tea drinking. One day, after a string of rather tedious hours with Victor, Ferguson called me into his office.

"Gray," he said in mock seriousness, "as the executive editor of this here newspaper, I do solemnly appoint you henceforth and forevermore to the exalted and elevated position as babysitter to the publisher." Then his voice and manner changed to dead seriousness. "Look, Jimmy, I have had all this horseshit I can take, even though I keep reminding myself of J.W.'s definition of an editor's function. The primary function of an editor, he used to say, is to get along with the publisher. He did it by giving in on the little things and digging in his heels on the big things. Well, this tea thing is no big deal. But it's getting to me. So from now on I'll come along as often as I can for the sake of appearances. But I'll get in and get out and you can sit around listening to Victor until the tea gets cold."

So for the next eighteen months, whenever Dexter and Hutchison were not around, which was most of the time, I had afternoon tea with Victor Sifton. For thirty or forty minutes, as I listened while Sifton talked, I became persuaded that, an essentially very lonely man, he valued these conferences mainly because they gave him a chance to talk to someone, anyone, and not to have to make any decisions. During those eighteen months I think I got to know Victor Sifton better than anyone except his family and Dick Malone.

Curiously enough, few of our conversations were ever concerned with editorials. For one thing, I was reluctant to discuss policy questions with him in the absence of Ferguson or the others. And whenever he broached such subjects, it often caused us to get at cross-purposes. In his circulation through Winnipeg social circles, at the Manitoba Club or at the Winter Club, he would be set upon by pleaders for special causes and frequently he would be impressed with their importuning. After such a meeting, he would suggest that we should be giving the cause some editorial support. Most of the time we would already have written something and I would have to let him down as lightly as possible.

"You're quite right, Victor, it is a worthy cause. As a matter of fact, I think we had a piece on it last week. You must have missed it; perhaps it was in while you were away. I'll dig out a copy and let you see it. Then perhaps we should do a follow-up, if you think so." Put to him this way, he was never embarrassed at having missed reading our editorial page. Sometimes the omission was a blessing in disguise for him and for us. That happened when he had taken a strong stand with someone against supporting some cause, unaware that we had already run approving editorials.

In the beginning, Sifton talked mainly about public affairs, about his recent experiences during his stint in Ottawa as Master General of Ordnance, in which he had shaken the stuffing out of the aging peacetime army bureaucrats. As time passed, we wandered much farther afield, and ultimately got deep into Sifton's boyhood. Needless to say, there were times when we got on to some pretty sticky wickets. I knew that Victor was a spiritualist and believed he was in contact with his long-dead mother through a sparrowish spinster who combined poetry writing with spirit communicating. How spiritualism first got into the conversation I have long forgotten. I only recall that Sifton was chagrined by my comments that spiritualism was the plaything of charlatans, that Harry Houdini had challenged them to produce a single manifestation of spirit activity he could not duplicate by fraud. Nobody ever had. Sifton's answer was in question form: Leaving spiritualism aside, would I not concede that "contemporary second sight" was a well-proven form of psychic phenomenon? I had never heard of it, and he went on to explain that it was a gift his mother had possessed and of which he had personal knowledge.

Once, he said, when Sir Clifford and Lady Sifton were in London in 1916, his mother awoke screaming with the news that Ottawa was on fire. Sir Clifford managed to pacify her until morning, when the delivery of *The Times* to their suite broke the news that the Parliament Buildings had burned down during the night. That was "contemporary second sight," and, according to Victor, Arma Sifton frequently astounded her family with similar, though less spectacular, examples of her psychic powers. But unlike the spiritualist mediums, she could not turn it on and off. It came to her only in her sleep. Once I had stubbed my toe on his spiritualist convictions, I tried to stay out of conversation about it at all costs, but it tended to creep in inadvertently.

Sifton obviously worshipped his mother. His response to his father was something else. Last-born of Sir Clifford's offspring, Victor seemed to have languished in last place in both his father's affection and esteem. In the Sifton family confabs, the conversation was always dominated by Sir Clifford and his sons Winfield and Harry. Victor variously described them with such clichés as "sharp as tacks," "bright as new pennies," "minds like steel traps."

"Whenever I'd try to get a word in edgewise, they'd all come down on me like a ton of bricks," he once told me when we were discussing the contrasting travail within families of the eldest versus youngest sons. He was much given to philosophizing over the plight of youngest sons, particularly those growing up in the stately homes of England, and more particularly in homes dominated by strong-willed, successful fathers like Sir Clifford Sifton. "It has been my great good fortune, or misfortune if you like, to have lived most of my life in the shadow of two great men, first my father and then J. W. Dafoe."

While Clifford, Jr., and Victor were off at the First World War, Sir Clifford was busy getting his other sons established in business and the professions. In the early 1920s Winfield was in business in England; John was understudying E. H. Macklin in Winnipeg; and

Harry was practising corporate law in Bay Street, where he managed ultimately to get his fingers caught in the Beauharnois scandal that helped to unseat Mackenzie King in 1930.

For Victor, success was indeed the bitch goddess who eluded his every clutch. After the war, he and brother Clifford had gone into the export business in Toronto, and had been saved from bankruptcy only by the intercession of Sir Clifford, who straightened out their affairs and wound up the company. Victor had then been sent to New York to learn the financial business in the office of a Wall Street broker. That didn't pan out either, even during the hectic boom days of Coolidge prosperity. Victor abandoned the brokerage business for a career as an export broker in Shanghai. He was barely settled into that niche when Sir Clifford bought the Saskatchewan papers and Victor was recalled to Regina to take charge and to learn newspaper publishing from the top down. His enthusiasm for the move may be gauged from the fact that the way he took home was the longest on record: from Shanghai he went to Vladivostok and then to Moscow by way of the Trans-Siberian Railway, with subsequent stops in Berlin and London before sailing for Canada. In Regina, however, he made the best of it, for he bought the largest country house in Saskatchewan. Then he had a carload of horses shipped out from Toronto and was an enthusiastic participant in all the horse shows in the area. He was barely settled into his publishing apprenticeship in Regina when the Great Depression hit with its full force in that centre of the Palliser's arid triangle, and seemingly marked him for another strikeout.

All this, of course, I picked up in bits and pieces at a couple of hundred afternoon tea parties. The natural sympathy which anyone could develop for a "poor little rich boy" who had nothing going for him but an inherited fortune was tending to soften the dislike I had developed for him during our confrontation over pay raises seven years before. I never developed a genuine liking for him, but I did get to dislike him a lot less. Out of all this palavering, I came to the conclusion that what Sifton wanted and needed most was recognition. The triumvirate scheme gave him the self-esteem he wanted because he fancied that he was now the editor of the *Free Press*, and that the prestige that went with the office would accrue to him. He was something like a rich man who buys an honorary LL D with a handsome endowment to a university. He cared nothing for the engraved address that came with the degree, but he wanted to keep the cap and gown to wear around his office so that the public would recognize him as a man of eminence. Even as a figurehead, he could make up for the rebuffs from his father and the feeling of inferiority he had acquired during his years of living, as he said, in the shadow of two great men.

As time passed, he became increasingly impatient with the prima donnas on his editorial team. With mounting desperation, he wanted to have Dexter in Winnipeg. To a lesser extent he also thirsted after Hutchison's presence. But neither would budge an inch in their determination not to leave home. To top it all, he discovered that I was equally stubborn in my refusal to leave Winnipeg for Ottawa. What, he must have wondered, was the use of being Midas-rich if you could not buy people the way other employers seemed able to do.

The honeymoon period for the triumvirate arrangement lasted about six months. During that time, Dexter and Hutchison were back and forth to Winnipeg frequently, and I found myself becoming increasingly involved in their Fort Garry Hotel strategy meetings. Dexter and Hutchison seemed to think that they were working together so well that Sifton was weakening in his insistence on their moving to Winnipeg. I, of course, knew better from my tea party conversations, but I could not convince them. As far as Hutchison was concerned, it did not matter what Sifton thought. There was no way he was ever going to move to Winnipeg. Not ever. Nohow.

Towards the end of the summer of 1944, it was becoming clear that relationships were beginning to deteriorate in all directions, particularly between Sifton and Ferguson, as the conscription crisis developed over the infantry-reinforcement situation in Europe. The Siftons were confirmed conscriptionists and had been from the declaration of war. So, in fact, was Dafoe, in theory. But he was forever mindful of the way conscription had divided the country along ethnic lines during the First World War and was determined that such a division should not be repeated. In this war, the issue was more than an English–French cleavage. There were substantial pockets of ethnic Canadians in the West who were as emotionally opposed to conscription as the French Canadians. The plebiscite of 1942 had demonstrated that. So, as the fighting intensified in Europe and the infantry-reinforcement problem arose, the question of conscription for overseas service became increasingly relevant. Long before, however, Dafoe had taken the position that the *Free Press* must follow and not attempt to lead the government. In the autumn of 1944, that was the established *Free Press* policy and one with which Sifton avowed agreement.

The *Free Press* would support conscription but only after the government became convinced that there was no other alternative. As keeper of the Dafoe flame, Ferguson had summed up our position as, "we will go over the hurdle when the government does, but we cannot go over before it does and become party to a campaign that will split the country." Time and again Sifton had concurred with that position. But time and again, he allowed his impatience with the backing and filling of the government to detract from his commitment. Left to his own devices, he would have had the *Free Press* in full cry for conscription by the end of the summer of 1944. As each new crisis peaked, he stormed into the office in anticipation that this was the time to take the hurdle. But always there was Ferguson, and sometimes Hutchison, to say him nay. On one such occasion, Hutchison challenged him to get a new set of editors if he did not like what they were doing. Sifton backed down. But most of the time there was nobody to face up to Sifton but Ferguson, and the facing-up soured relations on both sides. But this was only part of the problem. Sifton seemed incapable of retaining a collection of ideas for more than two weeks at a time. Thus some things had to be argued about and resettled every time the subject came up. It was something that baffled an orderly mind like John Deutsch's and drove Ferguson into fits of temper. Once he came into my office fuming, and tossed an article on to my desk for editing.

"Nothing," he said, "is ever settled with this bastard! We've been through this time and again and he's always agreed. But I just now ran this past him for the sake of letting him see it and he acted as if he had never heard of it before."

The subject of the editorial was of little importance. It was true, and terribly frustrating, that nothing was ever settled with Sifton. Least of all the conscription tactics. So the relations between Sifton and Ferguson deteriorated steadily.

I was caught in the middle as relations between the executive editor and his associated co-equals also deteriorated. The sand I contributed to the gears came from the making-up of the editorial page. Hutchison lived in fear that we were always in imminent danger of running short of copy. As a result, he tended to over-produce, particularly on American political themes. A subject worth one article might be worried through three or four. Occasionally a couple of writers might overlap on a subject. Frequently we had a surplus of twenty-four-inch articles and a dearth of the sixteen-inch articles we needed to put a page together. The solution was to cut something out of the longer articles. Sometimes the cutting meant dropping several paragraphs: sometimes it only meant cutting a few lines. Neither Dexter nor Hutchison had any appreciation of the problem, nor any willingness to understand that there were pressing local issues that occasionally had a better claim on the space than their pieces. When their articles were edited to size, held out, or even thrown away when they became outdated, there were angry protests, often relayed to me through Victor.

The effect of these bothersome difficulties only increased Sifton's determination to assemble his editors permanently in one place, Winnipeg. And despite his protestations to the contrary, Grant Dexter was behaving as if this was his objective as well. Whenever he came to Winnipeg, he increased his efforts to persuade me that what I needed most in the world was to become an Ottawa correspondent. He seemed not to be listening when I argued that this would undermine his own argument for staying in Ottawa. When I remained unreceptive, he started to work on Kay and our daughter Pat, who was soon to graduate from high school. Neither were any more enthusiastic than I was. More important, however, than any of this was his intrusion into an area that could best be described as Ferguson's Achilles' heel, the *Free Press* news department.

Putting out any kind of a newspaper in wartime was a daily ordeal that got worse with each passing month. The problems of staff decimated by enlistment were complicated by newsprint shortages and mounting demands on steadily shrinking space. On his visits to Winnipeg, Dexter found the content of the news columns utterly inadequate. In Ottawa, of course, he had access to almost anything he wanted to know about anything by dialling his telephone, plus all the political news in two Ottawa, two Montreal, and three Toronto papers. His vexation was shared by Hutchison, who would turn up full of enthusiasm for the latest Washington furor and find nothing in our news columns on which to hang a five-part series. In Winnipeg, they found only condensations of Canadian Press stories out of Toronto. So whenever either was in town, there was a lot of arm-waving and good-natured banter with Victor over the total incompetence of the *Free Press* news department.

Unhappily, neither had any inkling that their criticisms of the news department were music to Victor's ears. When he had first come down from Regina and started heads rolling in the business and mechanical departments, he had also set his sights on the news department. Dafoe and Ferguson interceded, and Victor had backed away from a confrontation that would have led to wholesale firings.

My pointed and repeated urgings for Dexter and Hutchison to lay off our news department fell on deaf ears. If Dexter's criticism had been confined to negative arm-waving, it might not have mattered as much. But Dexter could not resist the urge to offer con-

structive suggestions of people who might be considered as possible
hirelings for the news side. The first time he ran some names past
me, I said something noncommittal, and when Ferguson returned
to his desk, protested strongly against what was going on.

"Grant tells me," I said, "that you are looking for people to
replace Howard and Abbie. But how the hell can you do that while
Bennie Malkin, Orton Grain, Frank Walker, and all our guys are
away at the war?"

I was still not finished when Ferguson almost leaped out of his
chair. "Grant told you what?"

I repeated the conversation I had had with Dexter.

Ferguson's anger subsided, and he said quietly: "Obviously, I
will have to have a talk with our Mr. Dexter and straighten him out
on the facts of life on this newspaper."

Whatever Ferguson said to Dexter, it did not stick. Some weeks
later, when Ferguson was again off some place, Dexter, at an
editorial conference, raised the subject of another candidate for
the news department. I stuck my neck out a yard and appealed to
Sifton not to do anything until our own staff returned from the
war. Surely, I said, we had a duty to keep all avenues of promotion
open until they got back. Dexter, who was unacquainted with any
of them, started to argue about whether they would be able to fill
the bill after being away for so long. Victor cut him off with the
comment that I was absolutely right, that we owed our own people
first call on promotions. But, he added, that did not mean we
should not be on the lookout for people we could use after we had
fulfilled our obligations to our war veterans.

Victor's added comment made it a Mexican standoff, so, after the
meeting, I tackled Dexter, pointing out that he was cutting his own
throat with his criticism of the news department. That department
had been Ferguson's responsibility for fifteen years and its short-
comings had to reflect on Ferguson, because it was he who had
prevented Coo, Wolfe, Frank Avery, and the other editors from
being fired when Victor came down from Regina. Dexter's response
was angrily to pursue his criticism of the way the news side functioned and even to insist, despite Victor, that changes could not
await the end of the war. I decided to take matters into my own
hands and went to Abbie Coo to volunteer a suggestion. I gave him
the sense of the criticism and then offered to zero in on what
Dexter and Hutchison were most interested in when they came to
town. Then the news desk could be on the lookout for any relevant
news stories coming in and try to find room for them in the paper.

The arrangement seemed to work, because the carping over news
stories petered out. In the early summer of 1945, the system was to

get its most severe test. With the war winding down in Europe, the government turned more and more of its attention to post-war planning. It resurrected the Rowell-Sirois *Report* and called a Dominion-provincial conference on the report for early August. Johnny Deutsch, who was becoming restive writing editorials so far from the Ottawa action, got a call from Dr. W. C. Clark, the Deputy Minister of Finance, offering a job in the Department of Finance that he could not refuse. His first assignment would be to prepare material for the conference. Deutsch's career in journalism came to a full stop.

As the material began to surface from Ottawa for the conference, I started hanging around the telegraph desk to help Eddie Armstrong, the wire editor, spot the most important stuff. On the morning of Monday, August 6, 1945, the Ottawa Conference opened and the flow of copy monopolized everybody's attention. By noon the composing room was overset. The front-page dummy was already made up when the report started to come in about Premier Duplessis of Quebec denouncing the federal proposals. That, I told Armstrong, was big news for the West, so he got busy rearranging his front-page stories. As he was doing so, the United Press teletype machine began to ring loudly, as it always did when a bulletin was being carried that merited an editor's attention. A copy boy jerked out the print-out and handed it to Armstrong. He glanced at it and gave it back to the copy boy.

"Take it upstairs and get Louie to put a twenty-four-point head on it and find a spot for it on page seven." He went back to Duplessis.

Half an hour later, somebody looked out the window and called over to the news desk. "Hey, look, the *Trib*'s got an extra out!"

A moment later, Mickey Panisco, the street-circulation manager, came into the newsroom flourishing a copy of the extra. Like every other newspaper in the western world, the *Tribune* needed only four words in boxcar type to describe the biggest news story since the Resurrection, perhaps even since the Creation. The words were:

The Winnipeg Tribune

FINAL EDITION
THE WEATHER
FORECAST: FAIR AND MODERATELY WARM

| 56th Year | By Carrier in Winnipeg—25c per Week | WINNIPEG, MONDAY, AUGUST 6, 1945 | Price, 5 cents; With Comics, 10 cents. | No. 187 |

MORE POWER THAN 20,000 TONS OF TNT

Atomic Bomb Hits Japan

The *Free Press* had just gone to bed with Duplessis on page 1 and this story on page 7.

Truman Reveals Use Of Bomb With Largest Blast Power Yet

The newsroom burst into a frenzy of activity as bodies collected around the make-up editor and changes were hurriedly made to recast the front page. Then, the job done, the bodies drifted apart, a hush fell, and we waited for Abbie Coo's expected explosive tirade. It never came. He walked over, patted Eddie Armstrong on the back as he passed, and headed into the men's room and stayed there. I said, "If I had only minded my own goddam business, this would never have happened." Nobody paid any attention. They were savouring the enormity of a disaster only working journalists could appreciate, plumbing a depth of humiliation that was truly too deep for tears. I retreated to my room and began to write an editorial on the significance of mankind's conquest of the atom. That didn't work, either.

9
And Then There Were None

Of all the strikes that occurred in Canada following the end of the Second World War, none made less sense than the Winnipeg printers' strike of 1945–46. The auto workers, textile workers, coal miners, and metal miners struck for things like union recognition, increased wages, shorter working hours, vacations with pay, pension schemes, and so on. None of these were in any way involved in Winnipeg. Of those which had not been conceded long since, the employers were prepared to accept an arbitrator's decision. Instead, it was a strike over a snit that had developed in the United States between the International Typographical Union and various legislative bodies over labour-relations codes.

Until Franklin D. Roosevelt assumed the presidency of the United States in 1933, trades unionism had been confined mainly to crafts in the building trades, entertainment, coal mines, printing, communications, and transportation. Efforts to unionize the mass-production industries were frustrated by goon squads, the National Guard, and club-wielding police reserves. The New Deal brought the full weight of the government behind the trades unions, and employers claimed that the pendulum had swung far enough in the opposite direction to compromise their proprietary rights and managerial responsibilities seriously. Before the end of the war, the trend was swinging back in the direction of restricting many of the rights which, it was claimed, the unions had begun to abuse. This was to culminate in the passage of the Taft–Hartley Act in 1947, after more than two years of bitter debate in the U.S. Congress. Somewhat earlier, the tide had also begun to flow against labour in state legislatures. Early in the war, steps were taken by both federal and state bodies to ban many practices by which craft unions stretched the time taken to complete job assignments. In war industries, prizes were awarded for suggestions to increase output by cutting corners and simplifying procedures.

From its headquarters in Denver, the International Typographical Union contemplated the scene with a bilious eye. It held the newspaper composing rooms, and most of the printing establishments of the continent, in an iron grip. Any reasonably intelligent high-school student, for example, could learn to operate a linotype machine with passable efficiency in a matter of weeks, certainly in no more than the few months it took to learn to operate a typewriter. But the ITU had managed to restrict the entry of apprentices into the trade so severely, through its closed-shop contracts, that it was able to stretch out the learning period for apprentices to five years. It was also able to prevent labour-saving shortcuts wherever it held jurisdiction.

In the cities where there were two or more newspapers in which department stores ran identical advertisements, a great saving of time was possible if the papers divided the typesetting of the ads. Thus, in Toronto, the *Globe* might set the Eaton's pages, the *Star* would do the same for Simpson's, and the *Telegram* would set Dominion Stores. Then each paper would supply the others with papier-mâché matrixes of each ad from which stereos could be cast for the presses. After prolonged refusal to permit these transfers, the ITU at last agreed to allow them, but only on one condition: after the rush in the composing rooms was over, each exchanged ad had to be set in type in each paper, proofread, corrected, and finally thrown away unused. Universally known as "bogus," the practice was regarded with seething contempt by every publisher on the continent, but defended by the union as essential to save the jobs of its members.

Contemplating the passage of restrictive laws that would put an end to these and other make-work practices, the ITU leaders thought they could see a way to circumvent any legislative assault on the union's prerogatives. They would write all the restrictive practices they could think of into its union by-laws. Then, at contract time, the union could force publishers to agree that none of its by-laws would be subject to conciliation or arbitration. The Denver group further stipulated that interpretation of each by-law would be the exclusive right of the union's national office.

Long-sighted leaders of the union could see the rapidly approaching technological revolution, in the printing trades as elsewhere. The telegraphers' union, which had ignored the combining of telegraphy and printing machines, was already marked for extinction. If key-punched ribbons could operate printing machines five thousand miles away, there was no reason why the same ribbons, key-punched by stenographers, could not trigger the flow of type through a linotype machine next door.

Clearly, the way to prevent technological change from making the typesetting craft redundant was to forbid change by union by-law. And that was what the Winnipeg printers' strike, one of the first on the continent on that issue, was all about. But as far as Winnipeg was concerned, there were other issues as well. Twelve years before, the newspaper composing-room employees had revolted against another ITU edict from Denver. It had ordered all its members on to a five-day, forty-hour week in order to spread the shrinking amount of work available to its unemployed members.

In Winnipeg at the depths of the Depression, many of the printers were lucky to get in a day or two a week in the job shops. The newspapers, however, continued to operate with almost full staffs six days a week. Sharing the work might have made it possible for twenty or thirty printers to get an extra day's work each week. The newspaper printers, however, refused to share the work, pulled out of the ITU, formed their own Winnipeg Newspaper Printers' Union, and got closed-shop contracts with the *Winnipeg Tribune* and the *Winnipeg Free Press*.

As time passed, relationships between the papers and their printers deteriorated. With the war came newsprint rationing and a consequent reduction of the size of the papers. Local advertising declined, and that meant less work in the composing rooms. The newspapers were using more pictures, and again that meant less typesetting. On the *Free Press*, changes were made to increase the re-use of type set for the daily in the weekly *Prairie Farmer*. So printers with twenty-five or thirty years' seniority found themselves relegated to the spare board, unsure of a full work-week. Topping it all off was a growing disenchantment with the contracts their union had been signing, contracts providing for minimal wage increases, and sometimes for no increases at all.

The earlier abandonment of the ITU had come about only after the bitterest debate within the union. A number of printers left their newspaper jobs, after building up years of seniority, rather than give up their ITU memberships. Others were lukewarm to the change, but went along with the majority. When the war came and the printers began to have second thoughts about the wisdom of leaving the ITU, the painful process of making up minds to change was repeated, with the same generation of heat. In the end, however, the scale was tipped by two factors. The first was the shortage of printers that was developing in the job shops, and the subsequent improvement in the wage rates the ITU was getting for its members. The second and most important was the excellent ITU pension scheme the newspaper printers had lost when they left the union. So the approach of the pro-ITU printers to the international was: if the newspaper printers applied for re-entry into the international, would the ITU reinstate the pension rights of the status quo ante?

After keeping the dissidents dangling for months, the ITU agreed to allow the Winnipeg newspaper printers back into the union—on one condition. They would have to conclude agreements with the Winnipeg publishers which provided that ITU by-laws were not subject to negotiation, conciliation, or arbitration. The back-to-the-ITU agitation not only split the printers in the *Tribune* and *Free Press* composing rooms; it at first split the units from each other. The ITU group got a substantial majority in the *Free Press* before it gained dominance in the *Tribune*. In 1943, the *Free Press* printers went on strike to force the paper to recognize the ITU. During this short walkout, the *Tribune* printers helped the *Free Press* to continue production. It took another two years of bitter squabbling before the ITU got a majority in both shops and demanded recognition from both publishers. It did not take the publishers' lawyers long to discover that the non-conciliation clause was a violation of the War Labour Relations Act of Manitoba, which required all labour disputes to be so resolved. In any event, the "bogus"-plagued employers foresaw conditions in which they could only bargain on wages and hours and the union would decide everything that could or could not happen in their composing rooms. For them, it was a no-win situation and they refused to sign.

But as far as Denver was concerned, it was a no-lose situation. It had a group of new members in Winnipeg whom the job-shop printers characterized as "whitewashed rats." It could use them to test the Canadian waters and see what luck it could expect with its new gimmick. To get their pensions back, the newspaper printers had no alternative to taking a strike vote when the employers refused, over a matter of weeks, to accept the by-law provisions. They did that on November 9 and shut down the newspapers. For one day.

At other times, in other circumstances, the printers might have gone on strike with the blessings of the editorial people. But not in a working atmosphere where copy editors like Louisa Macdonald came storming down daily from the composing room suppressing squeals about having "had those damn printers right up to here!" We knew what daily life could be like working with printers and their by-laws, and they got no sympathy from us on that count.

Within the newspaper composing rooms, relations between printer and printer deteriorated during the long factional debate about getting back into the ITU. The frayed tempers of the printers inevitably curdled relationships with the news staff. Then everything went from bad to worse when the publishers first resisted efforts to push the independent union out of the composing rooms and accept the ITU contract.

In the nature of newspapers, it was inevitable that a good deal of copy ordinarily went from the newsroom to the linotype machines in less than letter-perfect condition. Letters, words, and phrases were pencilled out and corrections hurriedly scribbled in. The linotype operators could puzzle out illegible writing and catch obvious mistakes as they set the type. It was a simple and friendly thing to do, and it was done out of force of habit. Until, that is, relationships soured. Then the rule became, "follow copy if you have to follow it out the window." No matter how obvious a mistake might be, no correction would be made. Work-to-rule became the order of the day, and the ridiculous lengths to which it was carried frayed tempers and set off bitter man-to-man feuds between editors and printers.

There was hardly a typesetter in the union who could not set a lot more type in an hour than he was required to do to qualify for his journeyman's card. With a tight deadline to meet, the typesetters could put on a spurt and almost double their production. But when the trouble developed, it became a matter of principle not to set a line over the hourly minimum. At the same time, the playful urge to substitute vowels in four-letter words was given free rein in the hope that they would elude the proofreaders and get into the paper. Sometimes they did.

Our problems aside, the printers might have gained sympathy and support from the other departments of the papers if the walkouts had been over bread-and-butter issues like wages, hours, and so on. But they got none because the issue was beyond the comprehension of most of the non-union employees. The only non-printer to stay off the job when the printers went on strike was a carpenter the *Free Press* had been employing to refurbish a bunch of worn-out newsroom desks. Everybody else on both papers went to work. Nor did the strike make sense to any of the other printing-trades unions. Because the stereotypers', pressmen's, and engravers' unions refused to honour the ITU picket lines, the paper was able to resume publishing, after a fashion, after one day.

The *Tribune* moved its editorial staff over to the *Free Press* building and a joint operation was set up in the *Free Press* newsroom, with joint managing editors, city editors, copy editors, and office boys. The heart of the operation was a battery of typewriters set up in the newsroom, where a bevy of stenographers retyped the reporters' copy letter-perfect in newspaper-column width. A couple of staff artists hand-lettered headings for the stories, which were then pasted on newspaper-sized sheets and sent to the engravers to be photographed and made into engravings. Returned to the *Free Press*, they were matted and cast into stereos for the presses. The first joint edition was only eight pages. It contained both *Free Press* and *Tribune* comics, and the papers divided an eight-column editorial page precisely in half. The union treated the bastard publication as a huge joke and was confident that the publishers would have to give in within a week.

They reckoned without Richard Sankey Malone, Victor Sifton's "brigade major," as he liked to describe himself, freshly returned from the war where he had risen from infantry lieutenant to brigadier-general. In the process, he had organized the Canadian Army's information department on the war fronts and had become the liaison link between Field Marshal Montgomery and the Canadian Army. He regarded the printers' strike as a personal challenge on a par with the invasion of Sicily, and he reacted to it with gleeful enthusiasm. He took on the International Typographical Union and whipped it all the way from Winnipeg to Denver and back again. Then, when the ITU repeated its strikes at other Canadian papers, he was the strike-breaking consultant who routed the union again and again.

It took the girls and the paster-uppers several days to work the bugs out of their techniques. But gradually they did so. While they did, Malone was recruiting a crew of returned war veterans to learn the art of typesetting in our composing room. It may have been this gambit which, a week after the strike started, persuaded both the pressmen and the stereotypers to go on strike. Malone and Jack Owen, the mechanical superintendent, and the pressroom foremen of both papers managed to master the stereotyping and press operations sufficiently to bring out the paper unaided. Two days later, the pressmen were ordered back to work by their unions.

Less than a week after the strike began, the raw recruits in the composing room were setting the type for all the headings. A week after that, the department stores were back in the paper with their ads combining illustrations, typewriter copy, and machine copy. Within another week the paper was up to fourteen pages and beginning to run want-ads. At first, circulation of both papers declined, as every unionist in town cancelled his subscription. However, many of them crept back as the advertising began to appear in volume and wives insisted on having access to it. Within a month, the editorial pages were being set in type and the paper was up to twenty pages. Six weeks after the walkout began, the first news pages were being set on the linotype machines.

During the first couple of weeks, the relations between the picketers and the picket-line crossers were downright amiable. We would stop and chat about football, hockey, the weather, personal things. They would ask us, and we would ask them, how things were going with the negotiations, which were broken off, renewed, and rebroken. But by the end of the first month it wasn't fun any more, particularly with Christmas in the offing and the strikers living off strike pay. As Malone was obviously making headway in his recruitment and training of "scab" printers, tempers grew shorter and shorter. And when several strike-breakers were way-laid and beaten insensible on their way home, things became surly on both sides.

By the middle of December, we were being roundly jeered as we arrived for work and as we left the building. A couple of times I got shoved around and once took a painful crack from a picket sign on the back of the head. Within union ranks, the unanimity was beginning to crack and the union leadership was in trouble, as it tried to keep up the confidence of the membership in face of the strides made towards normal production by the publishers. In the week before Christmas I started getting telephone calls at home after supper. Sometimes the callers identified themselves, some-times not. What they wanted mostly was confirmation of the stories they were getting at the union meetings.

It became clear that somebody was either playing fast and loose with the truth or was giving completely incomprehensible reports. One night I got calls from two different men seeking confirmation of the same story. Union leaders had reported that they had had the most successful meeting yet with the employers and were hopeful of a break the following day, or the next. I knew there had been no meeting that day with the publishers. At a meeting I attended, the publishers were becoming incensed by the personal abuse aimed at them in the unions' strike bulletin. Instead of attitudes softening, they were actually hardening. I tried to let my callers down as easily as possible. The best advice I could give them, if they wanted to continue in newspaper work, was to apply for travelling cards from the union and look for jobs out of the city.

It became painfully clear before Christmas that many of the strikers devoutly wished for a return to the status quo. The older men on the picket lines became greyer and greyer of mien and slower of pace. Once I got a call from the wife of one of the oldest printers on the *Free Press* staff. She was incoherent with rage at the publishers, at the union, at everybody connected with the strike. The burden of her complaint was that the strike was killing her husband, that he could neither sleep nor eat, and how could Sifton with all his millions do this to an old employee? I could only sit and wait until she collapsed into silence and hung up the phone.

Being involved in a prolonged strike is an agonizing experience at any time. It was particularly so for the Winnipeg printers, who probably averaged fifty to fifty-five years of age and could turn nowhere else for employment. Their hopes had been raised and dashed so often at union meetings that they desperately needed to bolster their spirits. So there were half a dozen of us on the paper they called in search of assurance that the situation was not as hopeless as the evidence on all sides seemed to indicate. By mid-January, the *Free Press* and *Tribune* editorial pages were expanded to eight columns each. February 1 saw much of the paper except the want-ads set in type. Then the first step towards publishing separate papers was taken when the copy that went to *Free Press* subscribers contained only *Free Press* editorials and comics, and the *Tribune* subscribers got only *Tribune* editorials and comics.

A couple of months later the joint operation ended and the papers reverted to the normal, competitive production. But the strike was not over for the printers. The pickets still put in irregular appearances, and in 1947 the union headquarters provided one hundred thousand dollars with which to launch the *Winnipeg Citizen* to challenge the *Tribune* and the *Free Press*. It lasted but a matter of months, and folded. Yet even that did not mean the end of the ITU's Canadian campaign. It struck two other Southam papers, the Ottawa *Citizen* and the Vancouver *Province*, in an effort to force the *Tribune* to settle. Both these strikes were lost, along with another hundred printers' jobs. The irony was that the campaign of the ITU to hold back technological change in the interest of protecting the jobs of its members had just the opposite effect. The strikes punctured the carefully nurtured myth of the indispensability of the linotype operator. They proved that the trade was one that could be easily mastered, which gave technology such a push forward that the linotype machine itself became redundant and was a casualty of the new technology of printing.

The strike could hardly have come at a worse time for the editorial and news side of the *Free Press*. Each week brought more of our men back from the war, and the long manpower shortage became a period of vexing surplus. Ferguson, Coo, and Wolfe were just beginning to get a handle on their reconversion problem when the strike broke and complicated everything beyond description. The *Tribune* news staff, also swelling with returnees, had to be meshed with that of the *Free Press* at a time when the size of the combined papers was reduced by five-sixths. Finally, the news stories set on typewriters took up twice as much space as did linotype copy. The result was a prolonged period of people sitting around with no assignments to cover, nothing to write, and nothing to edit.

The situation was even worse on our editorial page. Two years before, following the battle of Ortona, George Ferguson had got Ben Malkin released from the army to become the paper's war correspondent in Italy and later on the western front. With the end of hostilities he brought Malkin back and installed him on the editorial page. He did the same with Frank Walker, after getting him out of the navy to become the correspondent in the war against Japan.

Before the strike, Grant Dexter had reached his all-time peak in production for the page. He covered the birth of the United Nations at San Francisco. Then he returned to Ottawa to fight the general election for the Liberals with slashing daily attacks on John Bracken's Tory leadership, and on the CCF, which had scored great gains provincially in Saskatchewan and Ontario.

Dexter's approach to political journalism was a far cry from the dilettantism practised by other editors. He was never content to stand on the sidelines and comment upon issues as the politicians developed them. He functioned as a one-man brain trust for the Liberal party and devoted his energies to developing arguments the politicians could use on the hustings. Thus, he turned out whole series of articles documenting the lunacies that the Tories and CCF had espoused, and contrasted them with the inspired measures the Liberals had undertaken. His greatest delight was to bludgeon his political opponents into pulp with recitals of their own pre-election words and deeds. He was a dedicated documenter of everything he wrote, whether it was a series on the Dumbarton Oaks conferences that predated the United Nations, the Bretton Woods monetary conference, or the succession of abortive Dominion-provincial conferences.

During 1945 he sailed like a homeward-bound clipper ship through series after series, and was laying on the sail for even greater undertakings when the strike brought him to a crashing halt. There was no longer any room on the half-page we were allotted for all the series he knew needed writing. The Dominion-provincial conference, which had broken up in August without accomplishing anything, was to be reconvened in late November. The London Conference on peace with Germany was getting no-where. A lot more writing was needed on the control of cartels. Jimmy Gardiner's floor prices for agricultural production, which had been introduced in August, would be up for debate in January of 1946.

So Dexter fumed and fussed in frustration in Ottawa and made periodic forays into Winnipeg, seething impatiently for a return to normalcy. Being reduced to producing a page of copy every second day, the rest of us shared his frustration, but were reconciled to waiting for time to remedy our problems. It was during one of these visits that Ben Malkin floated into Dexter's orbit, and additional grit went into the gears of the inter-editor relationships.

Dexter took a real scunner against Malkin, who in turn quickly evinced a genius for rubbing Dexter the wrong way. The ideas that Malkin brought back from the battlefields about the way the world should be run were not quite those Dexter had salvaged from the wreckage of the old League of Nations. What the differences were I have long forgotten, probably because they were of little importance. Malkin's mistake was his insistence on arguing with Dexter on a subject the latter regarded as his own personal monopoly.

Dexter's notion of a discussion was to state a case in precise detail and conclude with a challenging sort of "Don't you agree?" Then he would move quickly on to something else before you had a chance to reply. Malkin's habitual response to the question was authentic Winnipeg North End delicatessen—a combination moue-shrug in which the shoulder movement was of a boxer feinting a one-two punch. It was such a disdainful gesture that a stranger might have assumed it meant that his argument was unworthy of a reply. Dexter, being a stranger, must have so assumed. The rest of us knew that, with Malkin, the gesture was only a habit held over from his chess-playing days in the back-of-the-delicatessen booths. It meant only that he was sending up a signal that he understood the point, was considering it, and would reply in due course. And he did, much to Dexter's annoyance.

Worst of all, when Dexter suggested a change in something Malkin had written, Malkin was inclined to argue the point, and Dexter had no patience with quibbling. Dexter obviously concluded that Malkin was someone to be studiously ignored. But it did not end there. To Ferguson he questioned the wisdom of having Malkin on the page at all. Ferguson made it plain that Malkin was going to go on writing editorials as long as he had anything to say about it. So the strain that had been developing between Ferguson and Dexter over his intrusion into the affairs of the news department became complicated by the emergence of personality problems. And it came at a time when Ferguson was up to his ears trying to keep peace between the strike-bound prima donnas of the *Free Press* and the strike-bound prima donnas of the *Tribune*.

Though the news and editorial staffs of both papers had little sympathy for the printers and their strike, ours was generally an attitude of benevolent neutrality towards the publishers rather than one of active support of their position. Becoming involved in a joint operation with each other was, however, as alien to the nature of *Free Press* and *Tribune* journalists as a joint venture between cobras and mongooses. As a general rule, half the noses were out of joint about half the time, and everybody's antennae were out for evidence of favouritism or incompetence on the other side. It was a situation that did violence to every instinct of journalistic workmanship. It was small wonder that nerves were always on edge, and tempers flared over issues that were laughably ridiculous. But the saving grace of humour was one of the first casualties of the strike.

I was involved in the sort of tantrum that plagued Ferguson for the first weeks of the strike. We were still using wartime typewriter ribbons—old ribbons that had been re-inked rather imperfectly. The linen in the ribbons did not readily absorb the second inking, so that the impression made by the keys tended to be smudgy rather than sharp. In addition, the keys tended to become loaded with lint, so that the letters a, e, o, s, all made the same impression on the paper—just black globs. Then, as the ink wore off quickly, the lettering became very light. This produced dark and light contrasts on the sheets and that complicated the photo-engraving process. When the engravers complained, I suggested a solution. I'd go over to Woolworths and buy half a dozen 25-cent toothbrushes that we could tie to the typewriters so that the typists could regularly brush the sediment out of their keys. It was no big thing so it was no sooner said than done.

When I tendered the receipt for the toothbrushes for reimbursement to Carlyle Allison, the *Tribune* executive editor, he exploded out of his chair and stormed into Ferguson's office. Here, he said, was another example of the neglect of the *Free Press* to keep their agreement that all expenditures had to be approved by both papers! What did I mean by buying these brushes without prior approval by the *Tribune*? The strain of the strike was obviously getting to us all.

With Allison glowering over his shoulder, Ferguson came out and laid down the law again about prior consultation with the *Tribune* about everything involved in the joint operation. Then, with Allison, he went off to another daily conference with the publishers, which went on interminably and drove him farther and farther up the wall. And that, to any outside observer, was just the opposite of what might have been expected. The war was over, and with it had gone the conscription issue, the only editorial issue Sifton was ever really concerned about. Sifton's attention was so sharply focused on breaking the strike that he took no interest at all in the editorial page. With the publisher no longer breathing down his neck, the executive editor might have been expected to let tensions relax. Instead, the reverse happened. He resented the publishers' strike conferences even more than Sifton's editorial conferences. Having nothing to contribute, he simply sat and fidgeted at any of the meetings I attended, and always took the first opportunity to leave.

By Christmas the strain was becoming increasingly apparent. Ferguson's temper grew shorter and shorter. For the first time in his life he lost his ability to see the humour in situations, to lighten moods with a wisecrack or a joke. He had no time for small talk. He was writing less and taking less interest in what we were writing. Along about the second week in January, just when we reached the point of restoring the editorial page to its normal eight columns, he announced that he was going to Europe to get a first-hand look at the war damage, the refugee problem, and the problems of reconstruction.

Dexter and Hutchison were appalled by the decision, because neither wanted any part of a Winnipeg winter. In the end they both agreed to come for short shifts if I would hold the fort in between.

Watching Grant Dexter and Victor Sifton functioning after Ferguson left for Europe convinced me that the last thing Sifton ever wanted was to have George Ferguson as the editor of his newspaper. When Dexter was in town filling in, it became clear that Sifton's determination to move him permanently to Winnipeg had been increasing by the hour since Dafoe's death. With Dexter, Sifton's coldness melted to an exuding warmth. He was as completely at ease with Dexter as one man could be with another, in part, obviously, because they thought alike. And, for his part, Grant's mode of operation fitted perfectly with Victor's. In his Ottawa milieu, Dexter came to his writing only after exhaustive discussions with his mandarin friends. Discussion was a part of his writing process, so he never begrudged the time spent "thinking out loud" with Victor. And it was clear that Dexter enjoyed Victor's company.

With the rest of us, however, Dexter was an embarrassment. We thought best at our typewriters. Ideas seemed to work themselves out the way we wanted them only when we were pounding typewriter keys. Conversations with Dexter inevitably got at cross-purposes. When I suggested the theme of an editorial I was going to write, the following exchange would develop:

Dexter: "A good idea, let's talk about it."

Gray: "First let me go work it out, and see how it comes out."

Dexter: "No, let's talk, because I have a point or two for you."

Gray: "No, I think better at my typewriter. I'll show you."

Dexter: "How the hell can you think better without talking about it?"

Under Dexter, the editorial writers would have become merely a team of amanuenses straining his ideas through their typewriters. After functioning under the Dafoe–Ferguson system of free-wheeling licence to work out my own ideas in my own way, I found that intolerable. I also had great difficulty accommodating him on another score. Dexter could have been described as a person of catholic interests within very narrow parameters. He was interested in anything that touched upon federal politics in any way. He was interested in anything related to any aspect of international trade and international affairs. And he was convinced that *Free Press* readers could never get enough of the subjects he was interested in. On the other hand, he knew little and cared less about anything happening in Winnipeg, or about a hundred-and-one other aspects of life on the prairies. Attempting to convince him that local subjects rated higher priorities usually evoked a response of impatience bordering on petulance.

Bruce Hutchison, on the other hand, took neither himself nor his ideas with Dexter's deadly seriousness. He had a fine sense of humour and shared our enthusiasm for lightening the tone of the page with off-beat writing. And if I thought a local issue was worth a leading editorial, it got a leading editorial. Like all the rest of us, he had his own hang-ups. One was a paranoiac fear of the page running out of copy. Another was ever being stuck in Winnipeg for more than a week at a time.

Getting along with Hutchison was never a problem for anyone. After a week with Dexter, I was looking for excuses to get out of town. The weeks I spent with Sifton and Dexter that winter convinced me that there was no future for Ferguson or for me with the *Free Press*, and for Ferguson there never had been since the death of Dafoe.

The editorial triumvirate might have worked had it not been for the mutual antipathy that existed between Sifton and Ferguson. It might have worked if Sifton had been content to occupy himself with his fox-hunting in Toronto and Brockville and managed his fortune from there. It might even have worked if Dexter had been content to leave the news department alone. But with all the ifs negated, the three-editor scheme was doomed, and the sooner an end was put to it, the better.

When Ferguson returned from Europe at the end of February, I was at the station to meet him and to blurt out my conclusion that he ought to get the hell out of the *Free Press* and that I would go with him. Expecting an argument from him, I was astounded to hear that he had come to the same conclusion for himself, but not for me. He had already considered choices of other employment. First, he wanted to write a biography of Dafoe, and he was leaning more and more towards a university teaching job, about which there had been several approaches over the years. He was as relaxed and as enthusiastic as he had been before Dafoe's death.

"But not you, my friend," he said, "you are not going to quit because of me. If you ever have to quit, do it for your own reasons. Never quit because of somebody else."

I replied that I would do it for my own reasons, that there was no way I would be able to function on the editorial page with Dexter as editor. But as I went on to make my point, he interrupted:

"Look, Jimmy, your solution is right before your eyes. Take the Ottawa job. That will get you out of Winnipeg, it will get you a lot more money and give you a chance to establish yourself down there. When you've done that, you can jump in any direction you want. In fact, you might even want to stay with the *Free Press*. Hell, you even get along with Victor. The son of a bitch likes you. And with Grant here and you in Ottawa, I can't see any reason why things might not work out very well."

We talked for an hour in his living room and in the end I was convinced that his advice made the best sense. I went home to break the news to Kay and Pat, and he went down to the Fort Garry Hotel to notify Grant and Bruce of his decision. My decision was greeted with an outburst of angry tears from my wife and daughter. Ferguson's reduced Dexter almost to tears at the thought of having to leave Ottawa. But in the end, he left Ottawa and I left Winnipeg. In truth, neither of us really left home for neither of us cut off our taproots by selling our homes.

Five years later, Victor Sifton's grandiose dream of captaining a team of editors blew up in his face. For Grant Dexter, the move to Winnipeg was as deep a personal tragedy as it was a professional disaster. He was as lacking in administrative ability as any lone-wolf journalist who had spent his newspaper life at the end of a telegraph line. Broken in health and spirit, he returned to Ottawa and his old political beat in 1951. Hutchison, jettisoned by Tom

Kent soon after he came over from London to succeed Dexter, went on doing what he did better than anyone else in Canada, writing superb books about Canada.

Ferguson took the summer of 1946 off and wrote a short biography of J. W. Dafoe. Then, while he was half-considering a feeler from Ottawa to become Canada's High Commissioner to India, he was offered the post of editor-in-chief of the *Montreal Star*, a position he accepted and filled with distinction and satisfaction for the next quarter of a century.

10
Jimmy Gardiner Made a Deal, and I Got Fired

Nobody ever accused me of being the ablest parliamentary press-gallery correspondent of my time. That was an honour that would have gone to Grant Dexter by about the distance that Secretariat won the Belmont Stakes. Far back in the ruck, but well ahead of me, would have come Burt Richardson, Ken Wilson of the *Financial Post*, Blair Fraser of *Maclean's*, Warren Baldwin of the *Globe*, John Marshall of the *Windsor Star*, and Charlie Bishop of the Ottawa *Citizen*. But I was not the worst, either, for that honour went to a benighted group of French-Canadian correspondents who were hived off near Alex Carisse's booze concession and subsisted mainly on the fees they could cadge writing speeches for Quebec members of Parliament. Sandwiched between them and the Anglo majority were the resident lushes who habitually arrived full of resolve to get in a full day's work before they touched a drop, and often stayed dry until ten A.M.

The most interesting meat in that sandwich was Arthur McKenna, the correspondent of Dow-Jones and *The Wall Street Journal*, a walking encyclopedia on Bank of Canada statistics and such esoterica as money-supply fluctuations and index numbers of wholesale commodity prices. A one-armed former lawyer, McKenna was consumed by an ambition to build a perfect pendulum on his basement lathe. The level of esteem at which he held guests to his home was the length of time he would spend discoursing on the structure and function of pendulums. His basement was full of flawed models he had built. They were affixed to posts, hung from walls, beams, and the ceiling. As a prelude to his dissertation, he would give three or four of them a starting nudge and then explain how the time of the swing had to remain constant while the distance travelled declined, and the distance drop in each swing could not be more than the cube root of the square of the weight of the bob. (Or was it the square root of the cube of the weight of the bob?)

McKenna habitually stayed up half the night working on his

pendulums and kept himself going during the day by sipping steadily on a tumbler of Scotch stashed behind the Dow-Jones teletype. By the time darkness was falling, the Scotch would have sensitized McKenna's noise-awareness threshold to a point where the voluble nattering of the French Canadians would trigger a McKenna tirade. He would storm into their discussions with arm waving and eyes glaring, to deliver a stock oration on the genealogically miscegenational ancestry of the entire French-Canadian population.

"Three boatloads of French women," he'd bawl, "that's all there ever were! Three boatloads! And half of them were whores. What did the thousands of soldiers and settlers do? They married Indians and now we've got to put up with five million of you half-breed bastards!" There is no record of Arthur McKenna's ever being punched in the mouth, slugged with a bottle of vin blanc, or shoved down a flight of the Centre Block's marble stairs.

Around the corner from McKenna's desk sat Austin Cross, the press gallery's only other authentic character. Cross was a refugee from the Montreal steamboat beat who had become a railway and highway buff. He had not only ridden on every railway line on the North American continent, he could recite their timetables from memory. His delight was when a new correspondent arrived in the gallery and he could get him into a conversation on railways. His day was made when the newcomer challenged him on an obscure railway line back home. I did that with the Greater Winnipeg Water District Railway.

"Ah yes," Cross said, rising in triumph, "the GWWD leaves St. Boniface on Monday, Wednesday, and Friday mornings, runs to Waugh on the Lake of the Woods, stopping at East Braintree going and coming back. It gets into Waugh around noon and makes the return run the next day. Usually picks up several carloads of cordwood at East Braintree and hauls it to St. Boniface."

Having run out of railroads to ride, Cross was then concentrating on highways. His favourite trick was to drive from Ottawa to Florida and back for a long weekend. There was hardly a highway east of the Mississippi he had not travelled; he carried around a headful of addresses of comfortable tourist homes, and knew most of the speed traps throughout South Carolina and Georgia. Nobody in the press gallery ever started on a longish jaunt without consulting Austin Cross.

My claim to fame was hardly notable, although I probably had the shortest career in the press gallery of any correspondent within living memory. I arrived in June 1946 and was gone by the end of the following March. The cause for my going, however, was unique.

Reporters were sometimes fired for drunkenness, less frequently for incompetence. I was the only reporter in press-gallery history to be fired as a result of a policy disagreement with his editor. The disagreement came over the oldest of all prairie issues—how best to market the prairie wheat crop. It was an issue over which I had stewed periodically from my first entry on to the *Free Press* editorial page.

The Second World War came at the end of a ten-year depression in which farm prices had been driven to their lowest point in three hundred years, in which hundreds of thousands of fertile acres were destroyed by drought and black blizzards, in which more than two hundred thousand people were forced out of the prairie provinces. The drought was over by 1940 and the long struggle to reclaim the tormented land was underway. But the prices of wheat, other grains, and livestock were still near Depression lows.

With Canada's access to world markets drastically reduced by the war, the government embarked on a policy of discouraging wheat production. A floor price of 70 cents a bushel was established and farmers were paid $2 an acre to take crop-land out of wheat and plant it to coarse grains, $4 an acre if they converted wheat-land to summer-fallow. But to farmers who had to depend on wheat for their livelihood, the 70-cent price was ruinous, and in 1941 the outraged farmers staged a march on Ottawa that resulted in the floor price being raised to 90 cents.

The agrarian revolt was manna to the Opposition in the House of Commons, and a steady barrage of criticism was directed against the government's farm policies. It was a barrage in which the *Free Press* refused to join. Yet twenty years earlier, the paper had bolted the Liberal party and supported the rebel Progressives when the interests of western farmers were involved. So I raised the question with George Ferguson whether it made sense for us to allow the CCF and the Tories to usurp the role of defenders of the interests of western Canada. His reply was that, as we had wheat coming out of our ears, there was no point in raising the price to encourage farmers to grow more.

In 1943, events took an unexpected turn. United States farmers began to feed huge quantities of wheat to livestock just when their government launched a scheme to make needed industrial alcohol from wheat. Soon Canada's carry-over was cut in half by exports to the United States. American demand pushed the price of wheat well above the Canadian Wheat Board floor price. That attracted the speculators into the market, and, in a matter of days, the price was up to $1.25 a bushel, the highest it had been in years.

To farmers with wheat to sell, it looked as if the millennium had arrived. It was a short look. The government stepped in, closed the Winnipeg Grain Exchange futures market, and set a ceiling price for all wheat at $1.25, at a time when American farmers were getting 50 cents a bushel above that price. The *Winnipeg Free Press* had always regarded the open futures market of the Grain Exchange as the ideal vehicle for marketing the prairie grain crops. And it regarded the wheat pools, which came to dominate the trade in the years between the wars, as festering boils on the neck of the economic system. Worse, it blamed them for antagonizing the British millers and losing overseas markets for wheat. But in 1943, the paper justified the closing of the Grain Exchange on the grounds that it had to be done to prevent the anti-inflation restraints from being blown away.

The farmer-supporters of the wheat pools were, of course, delighted to see the Grain Exchange closed down, and a compulsory Wheat Board established to take delivery of all the wheat crop. But to have it happen just when prices were, at long last, returning to the 1920 level was regarded as a not-so-minor outrage. Then insult was added to injury by an unexpected blow from the Department of National Revenue. As a result of a propaganda lobby by the private grain trade, the department reversed a policy it had followed for twenty years and decided to subject the entire co-operative movement to corporation taxes. It thus reversed a ruling it had made, for the third time, as recently as 1940. And for the Wheat Pool, the department had a particularly bitter pill. It was going to assess them for taxes for the previous five years, or back until 1938.

This ruling went unreported by most Canadian newspapers; when I stumbled over the story in the *Western Producer*, I worked up quite a head of steam over such an arbitrary exercise of power by the Ottawa bureaucracy. If they could do this to the co-operatives, there was not a business in the country that was secure from being similarly shafted and even bankrupted.

Ferguson agreed that it was outrageous conduct, but added that the wheat pools were phoney co-operatives anyway and should have been taxed long ago. He used the news story as a peg on which to hang an editorial calling for an examination of the entire income-tax system. In 1944, shortly after these events, electors of Saskatchewan went to the polls and, concentrating on federal issues, angrily drove the Liberals from power by electing CCF candidates in 47 of the 52 provincial ridings.

When the co-op leaders of Quebec joined with the westerners to blast the flip-flop of the Revenue Department, the government held its ground but agreed to appoint a Royal Commission on Co-operative Taxation—the McDougall Commission. While growing up in Saskatchewan, Johnny Deutsch had ingested a good deal of the co-operative ideology, so he and I did considerable soul-searching about the extent to which our editorial page was out of touch with the agrarian West. Eventually, we came up with a leader on co-operative taxation that was about as objective a piece of writing on a complex problem as the page had ever seen. When the McDougall Commission came to grips with the subject, I was assigned to cover it for the editorial page.

The hearings of the commission were a post-graduate course in prairie socio-economic history. It quickly became apparent that the co-operative movement, which had flourished and expanded in the inter-war years, was as much a revealed religion as an economic system. It was this intensity of religious conviction that enabled the wheat pools to become the dominant wheat-marketing agency in the country, and sparked the growth of the dairy pools and the poultry pools into million-dollar businesses.

Co-operatives were founded on the principle of providing service at cost to their members. They could not, therefore, earn profits. When, in the course of providing service, they misjudged costs and wound up with a surplus, it was never called a profit or a surplus. It was defined as "savings" and returned to the members in the form of dividends based on patronage. As the co-ops thrived and spread, however, their need for additional capital increased beyond what could be provided by membership shares. It could be obtained only through increasing the price of shares, or selling more shares, or persuading members to return their patronage dividends to be held in reserve. Eventually the co-ops devised a system of paying only part of the savings back as patronage dividends and crediting the rest to the members' "reserve" account. These reserve deposits could then be used as working capital and for expansion, and were only repaid to members when they retired from the co-op, or died. From the inception of the Income Tax Act of 1917 onward, the Department of National Revenue had consistently ruled that these savings of the co-operatives were not income within the meaning of the act.

Nobody paid any attention to the co-operatives' exemption from corporate taxation in the inter-war years, when the standard rate of taxation was only 17 per cent. But with the onset of the war and whopping increases in all rates of taxation, plus the excess-profits taxes, private businesses competing with the co-ops sat up and took notice. In the new circumstances, they claimed that the tax-free advantages of the co-ops created such unfair competition that private business was being driven out, while the co-ops expanded.

When the Department of National Revenue bought that argument and subjected the co-operatives to regular income tax, the reaction on the prairies was akin to the emotion that would have been aroused by an attack on holy writ. And with reason, for the co-ops were the bootstrap answer of the prairie communities to price gouging on the one hand and lack of service on the other.

As the royal commission moved across the West, it discovered from a steady parade of witnesses that the co-op was everybody's answer to everything. When the farmers in a community could not get coal delivered when they needed it from a company that enjoyed a local coal-selling monopoly, they formed a co-operative and brought a carload of coal from a mine and unloaded it into their wagons on a siding. From such beginnings grew a province-wide network of coal sheds, then a co-operative purchasing organization to supply coal. When the mines, reacting to pressure from the Retail Merchants' Association, refused to sell coal to the co-ops, they bought their own coal mine. The same story was told about setting up co-ops to buy and distribute binder twine, gasoline, farm machinery, and fertilizer. When general merchants went broke and disappeared during the Depression, the local residents set up their own co-ops to replace them. When the chartered banks pulled out of the prairie towns and left communities without banking services, the residents and farmers set up their own local banks and called them credit unions instead of co-ops.

At these hearings, it was impossible to remain unimpressed by the spirit that permeated the co-operative movement. It was as apparent in the testimony of spokesmen for the smallest as it was in the witnesses for the gigantic wheat pools. One spoke his piece haltingly and ungrammatically; the other was skilfully led through his story by high-priced legal retainees. But the message was akin to the unity of the peasant and the archbishop avowing their faith.

There was not a co-operative, regardless of whether it was a wheat pool or a dairy pool, that did not trace its origins to desperate small groups of farmers seeking to fill their own needs, not to make profits. The need always came first. Bulk-oil co-operatives were organized to supply gasoline and oil at cost. When the oil companies shut off their supplies, they built small skimming plants to service a group of bulk stations, then small refineries as the need for more oil arose. The ultimate result was a vertically integrated refinery-to-consumer operation that differed in no essential detail from an ordinary oil company. Except one. It was not in business to make a profit.

The co-operators saw a world of difference between a sum of money identified as the savings of the members, and a similar sum of money labelled profits of the shareholders. A mystical aura of virtue surrounded the first and the other was stained by the basest of human emotions—greed. There was scarcely a sitting of the commission at which debates over semantics were avoidable. The decision to tax the "savings" of co-operatives could hardly have been less acceptable if it had been to tax the income of the local churches.

After working in the Winnipeg Grain Exchange for seven years, I left in 1930 with a deeply rooted suspicion that its Monte Carlo machinery was providing the farmers with a sadly flawed method of marketing their grain. But it was not until I discovered from the Turgeon Royal Commission on the grain trade in 1935 that the flour-milling trusts at home and abroad were unanimous supporters of the futures-market system, that I became convinced that the Wheat Pool–Wheat Board system had to be far better, not only for the farmers but also for the people of western Canada as a whole. That perhaps mildly held belief became a case-hardened conviction as I sat through the hearings of the Royal Commission on Co-operatives. So it was probably inevitable, when the Minister of Agriculture, the redoubtable Jimmy Gardiner, rose in the House of Commons in January 1945 to introduce a bill that would establish a comprehensive floor-price system for all prairie agricultural production in the post-war era, that he would set James Gray on a head-on collision course with Grant Dexter. Yet when it came, two years later, the floor-price system was only peripherally involved.

Gardiner's basic argument was that the western farmers had been called upon to make such stupendous financial sacrifices during the war years that they were entitled to protection against falling prices in the post-war era. So he was going to provide that protection with a system of floor prices running until 1950. Dexter thereupon launched a series of attacks on the floor policy. The farmers, he argued, had not lost anything during the war because their incomes had risen well above the pre-war level and they had been able to reduce their debts. There was no security in price floors that bonused the inefficient. What the farmers needed was to increase their efficiency so they could make a profit out of lower-priced wheat. The only hope for Canadian agriculture was to expand world markets by the elimination of tariffs and international cartels. He was back at square one, with the arguments J. W. Dafoe had used to belabour R. B. Bennett in the early years of the Depression.

It was an argument with which I completely disagreed, so I simply stayed out of it. As I have said, nobody on our page was ever required to write in support of anything to which he conscientiously objected. So I followed the McDougall Commission around, attended labour conventions, wrote pretty much what I pleased about things that pleased me to write about. Until, that is, I arrived in Ottawa in June of 1946 almost simultaneously with the British Wheat Agreement, under which Canada undertook to supply the United Kingdom with certain minimum quantities of wheat over a period of five years at prices substantially below current world prices.

To Dexter, the British Wheat Agreement was the betrayal of everything the Liberal party stood for. It was a repudiation of Dumbarton Oaks, the United Nations, and the principle of multinational trade, to which his world was committed. But to Gardiner and the Liberal Cabinet, it was simply a logical extension of the floor-price system it had already adopted. Indeed, it helped the system, because the British government would be helping to underwrite it when it agreed to floor prices over the five years. I listened to the debate, read the bill carefully, spent a couple of hours with Jimmy Gardiner listening to his further explanations, and wound up writing a series of three articles. I sent the articles off to Winnipeg and retired from the argument. None of the pieces was ever used. And for good reason. They objectively set forth the arguments for and against the agreements and came down in the end in favour of them. For the rest of the summer and fall, the Wheat Agreement became Dexter's day-after-day-after-day *idée fixe*. When he eventually wrote himself out on it, he commissioned Senator Tom Crerar to take a hand at worrying the subject to death.

Meanwhile, in Ottawa, I was the veritable cat on the hot tin roof, as I jumped from one crisis subject to another. The Taschereau-Kellock Commission report on the Gouzenko spy probe came out, and that was worth a three-part series. Then I did a series on the report of the McDougall Commission, which had come out in favour of taxing the co-ops but with some escape clauses that took much of the sting out of the decision. I tackled the housing crisis and did a series on why there were no bathtubs and sinks for the house builders. From there I drifted into the combines investigation and did series on an investigation into wasteful disposal of war assets, on labour organizations, and on the production crisis.

That summer, the biggest issue in the country was whether to maintain the wage ceiling or let things blow. The steel workers went on a summer-long strike; the House of Commons became involved, and called everybody for hearings before a special committee. The provinces were negotiating individually with Ottawa over the rental of tax fields, and these had to be reported and commented on.

In addition to grinding out copy, I had to learn my way around the Ottawa bureaucracy, which was changing almost by the hour with the end of the war. I had no files into which I could reach for material. Everything had to be done from scratch, which made everything I wrote at least three times as hard to do. I had never worked as hard before, and never would again. Then one day, Burt Richardson blew into town from Saskatoon, where he had been appointed editor of Sifton's *Star-Phoenix* some weeks before. Instead of the usual friendly greeting, he came at me with fire in his eye.

"Damn it all, Jimmy, what the hell are you doing down here? Here we have the biggest issue in the history of Saskatchewan—the British Wheat Agreement—and we haven't had a word out of you on it. What's the matter with you, anyway?"

I reached into my desk and took out the duplicates of the series I had written and sent to Winnipeg.

"This is exactly what I wanted," he said, when he had read it, and then he turned his anger on the absent Dexter. "Our deal in Saskatoon is that we get everything you write out of here, just as you used to ship around everything we wrote. What right does Dexter have to hold these out on me? He's not editing the *Star-Phoenix*, and we pay the *Free Press* for Ottawa coverage. By God, I am going to stop off in Winnipeg and straighten a few things out with our Mr. Dexter." And he did.

This episode set in motion a train of events that would ultimately get Richardson fired as well as me. After Winnipeg, he went back to Saskatoon and launched a free-wheeling campaign in the *Star-Phoenix* in favour of the Wheat Agreement. It turned into quite a family shouting match, with the *Star-Phoenix* on one side and the *Leader-Post* and the *Free Press* on the other.

Whether whatever Richardson said to Dexter had anything to do with it or not, Dexter came down to Ottawa for a couple of days, and we met in his room at the Château Laurier for as unpleasant a two hours as I have ever spent. It began with his presenting me with a bill of particulars of my errors of omission in my coverage of the national scene. I had paid no attention to certain speeches Bracken had made in the House, which I should have used to compare with what he said as premier of Manitoba. He had provided us with a tremendous opportunity to shoot him down in flames and I had ignored it. There had been questions about the Japanese which would have made good pieces. The *Globe* had a couple of pieces on the steel-strike issues I should have written.

I defended myself as best I could by emphasizing the inherent difficulty any newcomer faces in simply finding out how to go about covering Ottawa. When I came down, I had expected that he would have done what every reporter does when he is being replaced: he takes his replacement around and introduces him to the key people and news sources the new man will need to know. Not only had Dexter never done so, he had never provided me with a single word of direction about what he wanted in the way of coverage. It was obvious that he had expected that I would arrive in Ottawa with only fits and snatches of experience and be able to cover it as well as he had done after twenty years' residence in the place. Indeed, he was affronted by my reference to the fact that I had received no instruction from him on any assignments to be covered. It was not his job to tell me what to cover; it was up to me to know what to cover.

All this, however, was only a preface to his main complaint, which was my lack of assistance to him in his campaign against the Wheat Agreement. He had expected I would pick up the ball from what he had written and provide him with a whole series of articles to supplement his writing. Instead, I had produced nothing but the first three articles, which were the antithesis of what he wanted.

How, he wanted to know, could I possibly have written these pieces if I had read any of the *Free Press* editorials on wheat marketing over the years? Of course I had read the editorials, I told him. But I thought that the readers, and the government, were entitled to a fairly presented case for the Wheat Agreement and a fairly presented opposition criticism of the case. Then an assessment of the weak and the strong points would add to the worth of the presentation. When I completed that project, I considered that I had done my job, and I saw no virtue in returning to the subject and re-threshing the old straw. In any event, I recalled for him what Ferguson had said, that wheat policy was Dexter's baby and I was more than willing for him to attend to it.

And anyway, I continued, I thought his whole argument was tinged with madness. What the hell was the point of blathering about the virtues of multinational trade and the evils of bilateralism when Europe lay in ashes, when there wasn't a single functioning viable economy between the Urals and Brittany? Hundreds of thousands of refugees faced a winter of starvation; the five-year British Wheat Agreement would expire before Europe was back to anything resembling pre-war normalcy, and with that "normalcy" would return monstrous obstacles to anything resembling free trade.

My angry response flabbergasted Dexter. He was obviously shocked to discover that his editorial page was sheltering a dissident who did not subscribe wholeheartedly to his editorial line. It was clear that he was unaware of the wide range of opinion that had always existed within the editorial staff. He was seemingly unaware, even, that neither Ferguson, Hutchison, nor Deutsch shared his fundamentalist commitment to laissez-faire liberalism. He should have been under no misapprehension about my views, for all sorts of wild ideas had been kicked around in bull sessions when he was in Winnipeg.

"Have you forgotten the time," I asked, "when I kidded you for accepting Adam Smith as an authority on the working of industrial capitalism, because his *Wealth of Nations* was written before Watt invented the steam engine or Whitney invented the cotton gin? And how we spent half the next morning tracking down dates on Smith and Hargreaves and Arkwright and Whitney, and you ultimately admitted that I was at least half right about the dates?"

A look of recollection spread slowly over his face. "I remember," he said, "I remember. And you were serious, weren't you?" His tone of voice buzzed with a dawning realization of something that had never occurred to him before. Perhaps he was also recalling some of the discussions we had had about Thorstein Veblen, Alfred Marshall, and Thurman Arnold.

He went to the telephone, got room service, ordered up some coffee and toast, and then sat for what seemed minutes looking out the window. I thought of reverting to the Wheat Agreement argument again, but he embarked on what was almost a reverie, with all the aggression gone from him.

"For twenty years or more, my job in Ottawa was to be J.W.'s eyes and ears. Mind you, I covered Ottawa for the news side, too, and wrote editorial pieces, but most of the time I wrote more memos to the chief than copy for the page. And sometimes he'd send the memos out to George and get him to work them around into pieces for the page. But I was J.W.'s eyes and ears in Ottawa. And in all that time, there was never an occasion, not once, not ever, when I found myself in the slightest disagreement with him. And that was the way I expected that you would function here, that you would be my eyes and ears, that you would swing in behind me and try to take some of the load off me the way I always tried to take the weight off the chief."

He must have talked for the better part of thirty minutes on his relations with the chief. The recollection of one episode during King's early administrations triggered others during the Bennett regime. And it was, he said, because he had accepted Dafoe's judgments in all matters that he had been able to grow into his job in Ottawa, and ultimately prove his indispensability to the chief. This was the kind of relationship he had expected would develop between us, that I would automatically accept his judgment on matters about which he had greater experience, as he had been eager to accept Dafoe's greater experience as the basis for his judgments.

I said that it would probably have helped us both if we had taken the time to clear the air before I came here. For one thing, it would be difficult for me to act as his eyes and ears when, as far as his friends in high places were concerned, Grant Dexter had never left Ottawa. I told him of trying to get to see Ken Eaton, the Assistant Deputy Minister of Finance, and making the mistake of telling his secretary what I wanted to talk to him about. She returned from Eaton with the message that he had already talked to Dexter about that. The indication was that, having talked to the editor, there was no point in wasting time on a reporter.

As we talked, both of us became more relaxed, and Dexter returned again and again to the recollection of episodes in his relations with J. W. Dafoe. I began to try to puzzle out whether Dafoe had fashioned Dexter in his own image, or whether Dexter had cast his own mind in the Dafoe mould. It was probably some of both. Towards the end our conversation became downright amiable, and when I said that I was planning to take what was left of my vacation by going on a bus trip to New York with Kay to enjoy the fall colours, he applauded the idea and suggested routes to take and places to visit.

We parted on the friendliest of terms, and I felt that my right to dissent from the paper's wheat policy had been recognized. During our vacation trip, however, I became more and more preoccupied with the confrontation with Dexter; as I did, I became more and more convinced that Dexter was right and I was wrong about the relationship that had to exist between an editor in Winnipeg and his correspondent in Ottawa. With a newspaper like the *Free Press*, whose main policy lines had become ossified over fifty years, there had to be complete empathy between the publisher, the editor, and the Ottawa correspondent, on all the main policy points. Where I had gone wrong was in assuming that the system would work when I was totally out of sympathy with the fundamental tenets of *Free Press* policy. It was as if a Cardinal had expected to be able to maintain his relations with Rome, and carry on his duties, if he rejected the concept of the virgin birth. Unless I accepted the fundamental tenet, I would be unable to deal with other matters in a manner satisfactory to the editor.

The basic problem was conviction. If the *Free Press* had run a Thomson-newspapers type of editorial page, or a country-weekly type of page, there would have been no problem. Then it would not have mattered what the editors or correspondents wrote, so long as they did not offend advertisers or readers. Nobody was expected to take editorial opinions very seriously, and these editors were under no illusions that their papers moulded public opinion. But the *Free Press* believed that it was a great national institution, a paper of immense influence. It had a tradition of responsibility to maintain, to be the ever-vigilant watchdog of the public interest, to prevent politicians from adopting policies and passing laws that were inimical to the public interest. When it deemed this to be happening, the full force of the institution must be brought into play on the side of right, justice, and common sense. And that could not be achieved to the fullest extent necessary unless I was in complete accord with Grant Dexter on fundamentals. Realizing this, Dexter had come to Ottawa to try to achieve such an accord. He made his position clear and went home to see whether the seeds he had planted would germinate. Unhappily, they had fallen on soil as barren as a cobblestoned street.

Jimmy Gardiner argued from conviction that the farmers of the West were entitled to five years of the kind of prosperity his floor prices would bring because of the disabilities they had suffered during the war. I bought that argument, but my reasons went much deeper. I had experienced those disparities in the 1930s, when the dust storms were destroying the land, when natural disaster had been piled on financial disaster until it seemed that most of the prairie wheat-land was doomed, and the people with it. A five-year period of floor prices was little enough repayment for the ten years of ruinous prices they had suffered, never mind the disabilities of the early war years.

To my mind, it all came down to a very simple question. The farmers of western Canada had earned the right to say what kind of a system they wanted to market their production. It did not have to be the best ever devised by man, or the second best the spur of the moment could provide. It did not matter whether the Wheat Board and the British Wheat Agreement would yield them more or less than the open futures market. It only had to be their choice, and the choice of the producers, overwhelmingly, was a floor-price system and marketing through a Wheat Board.

It took no Gallup polls to demonstrate that fact. The annual meetings of farm organizations became increasingly insistent on some sort of farm-price parity program. The wheat pools preferred an international wheat agreement that would bring some degree of stability to wheat exports and international prices. But they were not prepared to hold their breath until such an agreement was negotiated some years down the road. In the meantime, they were all in favour of the British contract.

All this was a reflection of a two-pronged fear. The first was directly rooted in the First World War, when world wheat prices soared in the post-war inflation and then dropped to ruinous lows in the years of deflation that followed. Weighing even more heavily on the minds of western farmers was their experience during the Great Depression. The improvement in their economic status was rightly attributed to the war, and only to the war. In peacetime the government had been content to maintain the floor price for wheat at, and below, the subsistence level. So the consensus was: the farmers saw an artificially high price of wheat as the forerunner of a disastrously low price. One caused the other. They were prepared to forgo getting all the traffic would bear for wheat sold to Britain if they could be assured a reasonably profitable price in the years to follow.

There was, moreover, no disposition to soak the British with a famine price for wheat. Everywhere in the West there was an appreciation that Canada had emerged unscathed from the war; Britain, on the other hand, was all but bankrupt internationally, her cities in ruins, and was in no position to pay inflated prices for wheat.

Finally, there was the question of whether Britain could have bought Canadian wheat for even 50 cents a bushel under world prices, which was what the $1.58 price of the British contract represented, if it had not been for the U.S. Marshall Plan. Under that plan, the United States government was pouring billions of dollars' worth of industrial equipment of all kinds, along with immense quantities of food, clothing, and medical supplies, into the reconstruction of Western Europe. It also provided the post-war governments with billions of dollars in financial credits so they could buy "offshore" supplies from Canada and other favoured nations. Thus, Britain was able to pay for some of its Canadian wheat and other purchases with Marshall Plan dollars. In addition, Canada had its own "Marshall Plan," and contributed both material and money to the rebuilding of Western Europe. And it did so on a per-capita basis that equalled what the U.S. did.

Without the Marshall Plan concept, the recovery of Western Europe from the war damage might have taken twenty years, and wheat might have piled up in Canadian elevators because of the lack of money in the hands of starving people. Because of the Marshall Plan concept, food moved steadily to the starving and the impoverished, and there was no collapse in wheat prices. Indeed, when the price for the third year of the British contract was negotiated, the $1.58 a bushel was raised to $2.00. By then, the uncontrolled price in the United States was in the neighbourhood of $2.75 a bushel. All of this was to trigger a spate of "I-told-you-so" editorials in the *Free Press*, which became preoccupied with the calculation of the astronomic cost of the Wheat Agreement to the western farmers. But that was to come later.

The sign that Dexter was obviously waiting for as 1946 became 1947 was an article or two from me backing down and supporting his attack on the floor-price system. He needed such a sign, for he was now involved in massive administrative problems for which he had neither experience, patience, nor talent. The sign from me never came. I never wrote a line on floor prices, parity prices, or the Wheat Agreement, because even the idea of writing one was repellent. Instead, I tried to make up in quantity what I lacked in quality. I wrote a series of well-researched articles on post-war industrial-reconversion and -production problems. I did a series on civil liberties in Quebec, one on Dominion-provincial tax negotiations, and others on housing problems and on foreign-exchange control. While Dexter waited with growing impatience for a sign from me, he was embroiled in the problems of an unhappy editorial-page team. Ben Malkin left for a job in Montreal. Hugh Boyd was negotiating for a job in Ottawa; two of the older members retired on pension, and newcomers Dexter brought in failed to measure up to his standards. Early in March, he reached the end of his tether. I got a long, discursive letter telling me how sadly disappointed he was in my performance, that I had fallen far short of what was expected of me, that my default regarding the wheat policy had placed an impossible burden on him. The best course for all concerned would be for me to start looking around for another job.

The letter was a surprise, to the extent that, while I half expected to be replaced as the Ottawa correspondent, I had assumed that some other writing post would be offered, preferably in Winnipeg. But during the early winter I had spent some time wondering what to do if the crunch came and I was fired. One thing I was determined to do was to get out of Ottawa, and Kay shared my objective.

One of the disabilities for westerners coming to live in Ottawa was the feeling of total alienation that engulfed us. It was as if, coming east, one stepped from a floating island on to dry ground, and an instant later the island itself disappeared. One could almost live and die in Ottawa in complete unawareness that western Canada existed. Save for sports scores and natural disasters, no western news was carried by eastern newspapers. Parliamentary issues vital to the West were passed over lightly in the eastern press, if they were noticed at all.

Most devastating of all was my discovery that, as far as influence was concerned, the impact of *Free Press* editorials was, as Omar once phrased it, "as much as ocean of a pebble cast." And the reason was obvious. Nobody ever saw the paper. Nobody, it became clear, ever even bothered to look at the editorial-page proofs we so conscientiously airmailed to them every day. This last was one of Bruce Hutchison's ideas. Second-class mail, he pointed out, was handled so tardily that our editorials were a week old before the papers got to the Ottawa desks of top bureaucrats and politicians. Why not pull up some page proofs, he suggested, and airmail them so that Ottawa would have the benefit of our thinking while the issues were still hot? That surely was the ultimate in ego trips— for us to assume that what we wrote was so important that it could have an influence on the political decisions being made. But it was the trip we took without a second thought. So we had the composing room pull a dozen proofs every day and off they went to Ottawa. Not only that. From time to time, one of us would add a new name of someone we deemed important enough to get the service. So far as I was able to discover, none of the intended recipients ever got the proofs. Or if they did, a paper-plagued staff soon diverted them in the general direction of the public-relations or the clipping-storage department.

To the extent that any newspaper had any influence, the papers that did were the *Ottawa Journal* and the *Citizen*, the *Montreal Star* and the *Gazette*, and the *Toronto Daily Star* and the *Globe and Mail*. The morning papers were read by the members of Parliament and the bureaucrats with their breakfast. In the afternoon, what little attention was being paid in the House to speeches was quickly lost as the afternoon papers arrived. Throughout the establishment, small armies of secretaries pawed over the news columns of the papers in search of clippings that might affect their bosses or their bosses' bosses. Between the politicians and the members of the press gallery, there was a sort of mutual-aid program in operation, and had been for years. A reporter trying to work up a story would get a friendly member to ask a question in the House of Commons. The Canadian Press would report the question, and this would give the reporter a peg on which to hang the story he had already developed. For their part, the politicians would alert their friendly correspondent to the story behind the question they were about to ask. In either case, the member would be likely to get his name in the newspaper back home, which was the only objective of the exercise in the first place.

Among the bureaucrats, the system functioned with a lot more sophistication. The eggheads, the top civil servants concerned with thinking out policies for the Cabinet ministers, used favoured gallery members to launch trial balloons. If an idea seemed to catch on, it could be carried further. If the response of the public was negative, it could be quietly dropped. Penetrating that deeply into the bureaucracy took years, and only the greybeards of the gallery had such pipelines. The flow here, however, was all one way, for there is little evidence that any opinions or suggestions from newspaper editorial pages ever influenced the policy-making of a single Ottawa egghead.

In contemplating my own future, I very early decided that the press gallery was not for me. I developed a kind of claustrophobia from the feeling of constantly working in a vacuum, for there was never any reaction to anything we wrote for papers eight hundred miles away. In such circumstances, the most carefully researched and superbly written article was just so much writing on the ice in a spring thaw as far as the writer was concerned. One solution was to become caught up, as most correspondents did, in the politicking of the partisans of the House of Commons. That was, of course, what the press gallery was all about, but I could find little to become excited about in the hair-splitting over infinitesimal differences between Grits and Tories in or out of power. I found even less to enthuse over in the prospect of the holier-than-thou preachers, teachers, and lawyers of the CCF ever coming to power. So I firmly resolved, when the word was passed that I had been fired by the *Free Press* in a dispute with the editors over the wheat policy, that I wanted no more jobs in the press gallery. (I need not have concerned myself, for none was ever offered. Editors are never prone to go looking for odd-ball writers with a developed flair for flouting their authority.)

Instead, I decided to launch out on a brand-new career. I would return to Winnipeg and become a freelance foreign correspondent in western Canada for eastern newspapers. As far as eastern papers were concerned, that was a lot more foreign than being a correspondent in London, Paris, or Washington. So before I returned to Winnipeg, I made a deal with *Maclean's* to write a minimum of eight articles a year on western developments. Then I made arrangements with the Ottawa *Citizen*, the Montreal *Star*, and the *Windsor Star* to write an article or two each week for them on western themes, to enable the transplanted westerners among their readers to feel a little more at home in their own country. I also counted on doing a broadcast or two a week for the CBC, for the fifteen-minute original news round-up it carried after the national news at night. When I did the arithmetic on all the things I proposed to do, it looked as if I could become a foreign correspondent on the prairies and be twenty-five dollars a week better off in Winnipeg than I had been in Ottawa. It would depend on how hard I worked and how closely I could stick to a schedule with no one looking over my shoulder.

How well it would ultimately have worked I never really got a chance to prove. When we got back to Winnipeg in June, I got a telephone call from Marshall Menzies Porter, whom I had got to know during the McDougall Commission hearings on co-operatives. As the solicitor for both the Alberta Wheat Pool and the Home Oil Company, he owned one of the most lucrative law practices in Calgary. He had heard of my trouble with the *Free Press* from George Ferguson and was full of indignation and sympathy. Then he came to the point of the call. He and two friends had recently acquired the *Farm and Ranch Review*, Alberta's oldest and once the West's best, he said, farm journal. He was in the market for an editor, and Ferguson had recommended me for the job.

Having but recently settled into my new career as a liberated wage slave, I greeted the offer with a less-than-eager response. In fact, I was on the point of rejecting it out of hand when he suggested that the least I should do was to come out to Calgary at his expense for the Calgary Stampede and combine a vacation with a meeting with his partners. Then I could make up my mind. If I decided against it, there would be no harm done and no hard feelings. I accepted the invitation, and my life was never to be the same again.

11
They Came, They Saw, They Carted Off the Country

For his environment and times, Marsh Porter was a very strange character, and for the longest time I had the greatest difficulty identifying the quality that made for his strangeness. Then it came to me. He was an enthusiast, the first honest-to-God enthusiast I had encountered in western Canada in more than fifteen years.

That is only a slight exaggeration, because the climate of those years was not conducive to the germination and growth of enthusiasts of any shape or size. The worldly hopes that three generations of westerners had set their hearts upon had all turned to ashes, and simple day-to-day survival was about all anyone expected of life. It was no accident that the universal western response to a friendly inquiry about one's health, one's economic status, or one's love life, invariably was: "not too bad." It was a response that had been so deeply ingrained into the psyche of prairie Canadians that it was still in common currency after three decades of unparalleled prosperity.

Even if there had been the odd enthusiast on the loose, the chance of any journalist's crossing his path was quite remote. In the nature of things, the trade of journalism must become the exclusive precinct of the nay-sayers. The essence of the craft is indeed to be found in the definition of news as a report of a man biting a dog. News is what is different, and what is different usually is what has gone wrong, what is going wrong, or what will go wrong.

A report that a government department has run smoothly and accomplished everything it was required to do can seldom claim even two paragraphs among the want-ads of any Canadian newspaper. But let a minor clerk mismanage his work sufficiently to justify public notice and the newspapers can build it into a front-page story, even a federal case. A city police force can manage the arrest of thousands of drunks, peace disturbers, wife beaters, shoplifters, sexual perverts, and thieves without number, and nobody notices. Until, that is, one policeman in one incident smacks somebody in the chops with excessive enthusiasm, and the smacker and his company become a *cause célèbre*.

Editorial writers who come up through the ranks of political reporting mature with a finely honed instinct for the destructive. It could not be otherwise, considering the years they spend listening to the litany of criticism flowing from the opposition ranks, whatever assembly they attend. In other areas, local newspapers function as a sort of community-complaints department. Ordinary citizens are conditioned to believe that, when everything else fails, bringing their troubles to the newspaper might be a productive last resort. In small matters, when editorialists have rallied to the side of a put-upon citizen, satisfaction has occasionally been obtained. Most of the time, however, editorial writers have been concerned with poking under their own rocks and viewing what they discovered with alarm.

Renewing acquaintances with Marsh Porter at the 1947 Calgary Stampede was a massive anti-toxin for my own nay-saying. As I remembered him from the McDougall Commission, he had a courtroom presence that reminded me of E. J. McMurray, the famous Winnipeg criminal lawyer and one-time federal solicitor general. Both could dominate a courtroom while half dozing at the counsel table when their pedestrian opponents were supposedly occupying the spotlight. Both were masters of the *sotto voce* aside and the loaded double entendre. Porter, in particular, was never at a loss for a story to sharpen a point he wanted to make, even in the deadly dullness of a royal commission hearing. Away from the commission, he was a master raconteur of ranch-house humour. Although he was in his middle fifties, his sandy hair and lithe build belied his age, and he was as enthusiastic about his acquisition of the *Farm and Ranch Review* as a kid with a new bike, or, more in context, a farm kid with a new pony. His partners in the *Farm and Ranch Review*, and in the Western Printing and Lithographing Co. Ltd., of which the *Review* was a subsidiary, were Gordon Love, the rough-cut owner of radio station CFCN, and R. J. Dinning, the figurehead president of Burns and Company. In the Calgary Shriners– Stampede Board mafia there were no Godfathers, but those three ranked as equals with the highest Dons.

The concern of Love and Dinning, when I met them, seemed confined to the Western Printing Company, the largest job-printing plant in the province and, I gathered, the most profitable. It had been established by Charles W. Peterson forty years before and had grown with the province. The *Farm and Ranch Review*, though a separate corporate entity, functioned as a subsidiary of Western Printing and was Peterson's pride and joy. Through it, he had become a voice of authority in the Alberta farming and ranching community, and he remained so until his death early in the war.

Peterson had married twice, and, with his death, a feud developed between the two families. Porter was brought in by one side and he eventually put a deal together by which he and his partners acquired ownership of the property by buying out the heirs.

With Porter, the motivating force that impelled him to put the deal together was the chance to become the publisher of the *Farm and Ranch Review*, rather than the potential profits from the printing business. Certainly, when I met him, he had convinced himself that his primary interest was the magazine.

Pacing his office, gesticulating with his cigar, Porter was like an evangelist transported as he sketched the future of the *Farm and Ranch Review*. The West, he said, had been crying for a voice since the death of Dafoe, and the Siftons had abandoned the farmers to the interests of the Grain Exchange. There wasn't, he said, an editor in the whole of western Canada, in the dailies, the weeklies, or the farm press, who could locate a fundamental orifice with both hands and a garden rake. In their editorializing they were engaged, to a man, in something analogous to picking fly specks out of pepper. I had sampled these and other examples of his limitless collection of Porterisms at the royal commission hearings, but it was great to hear them come tumbling forth again.

What the West needed now, he said, was somebody like me with the courage of his convictions who would come to grips with the new issues that were facing the country and particularly the farmers. But not only the farmers. The West was on the threshold of its greatest economic boom in history as a result of the oil discoveries at Leduc. Leduc would do for Alberta, and for Canada, what the Smackover discovery did for Arkansas, what Spindletop did for Texas, what Signal Hill did for California and the United States.

At the moment, however, Alberta and Canada were at the crossroads of history, and the policies adopted in the months to come would determine the course of Alberta and Canadian development for generations. Alberta had to make up its mind what kind of a province the people wanted. Did they want a province of poor people and a rich government? Or did they want a province of rich people and a poor government? A government that had to come to the people every year for every dollar it spent would be responsive to the wishes of the people. A government that, through oil income, could get along without taxing authority would be unresponsive to the people and might ultimately become completely dictatorial.

Because of the way the mineral resources had been withheld

from the settlers of Alberta, few of the pioneer farmers would ever profit from the oil discovered on their land. The natural resources beneath the farmlands of Alberta had to be restored to the farmers on the land, to put them on a par with the farmers in Manitoba and in most of Saskatchewan who had received mineral rights with the title to their farms. Then it would be the farmers who got rich and, like the American farmers, they would plough their riches back into the development of the country.

But that was only the beginning. An even greater issue was looming on the horizon. There were still only three or four producers in Leduc, but the inquiries were already pouring in from oil companies in the United States. Scarcely a day passed without his office getting an inquiry from the big American companies about Alberta's land-leasing regulations, tax laws, and so on.

"After this comes the deluge!" he exclaimed. "Once they discover what they can do in Canada with their tax advantage, it will be Katy bar the door! They will be in here slavering after our oil resources like a pack of hounds after a bitch in heat!"

That set him off on a long account of his wartime struggles to convince the Ottawa bureaucrats they should allow ordinary Canadians who invested in resources development to write off their losses against other income. That step alone would attract much-needed capital to oil exploration when more oil was the urgent need of the country. His contempt for the thought processes of the Ottawa mandarins was pungently expressed. The idea of their ever allowing a taxpayer an incentive to encourage risk-taking made them, he said, as palpitatingly nervous as a whore in church.

The *Farm and Ranch Review* could become the means of bringing all these issues out into the open for the farmers of the West. It had a subscription list of ninety thousand and that could be doubled within a year or two. And who could say that it might not ultimately become the *Time* magazine of western Canada and a real power in the land?

To my objections that I knew nothing about farming or ranching, that I knew neither a Hereford from a Guernsey, nor a plough from a harrow, almost, he had an instant rebuttal.

"Look, Jimmy, the woods are full of clean-handed experts telling farmers how to farm. The universities are overrun with the bastards, filling farm boys so full of horseshit that it takes them years to get over it. And the farm magazines are all full of a lot of handy-dandy advice every farm boy already knows before he's weaned, if he has any brains. For the real practical farm problems there are experimental farms full of experts with answers because they have worked on the problems in the fields. There is no problem there.

"As a matter of fact, the less attention we pay to those so-called farm problems the better. What we have to do is raise the level of the farmer's interest in the great issues which are going to beset this country. Get him excited about getting his mineral rights back instead of feeding him new wrinkles on how to pull tits! And not just about our own issues. Let's get him interested in what's going on in the world, because, who knows, we may not have fought the last world war."

As for my ignorance of what the world of oil exploration was all about, he had been intimately associated with every aspect of it for more than twenty years and knew enough for us both. "Tell you what. You go out to Turner Valley to the Home Oil camp and spend a couple of days touring around getting a feel for field operations. Then go up to Leduc and I'll tell you who to see. Meantime, I'll put a lot of stuff together for you—remember that I am here and we can get together for bull sessions. I know that in a matter of weeks, our ideas will begin to meld.

"And one more thing. You. Let's talk about you," he said. "If the capitalist system is worth keeping, it surely must reward people like you who are prepared to stand up for their ideas. We don't want you simply as a hired man in this project. We want you as an equal partner with us. With the income tax the way it is there is no point in making a big issue about what salary you get. The name of the game today is capital gains. We are not in this business to earn more income. None of us needs it because anything more will go to the government. We want to build up a capital asset which, when the time comes to sell it, will give us all a profit we can keep for ourselves and our children. And with Alberta on the verge of a great boom, there is not the slightest doubt of our being able to do just that. And we want you in with us."

But, he hurried to emphasize, what he wanted most from the *Farm and Ranch Review* was not profit but the dissemination of ideas. Indeed, it wouldn't bother him too much if the *Farm and Ranch* didn't show a profit. "The Western Printing plant will make more money than the *Farm and Ranch* can ever lose if it tries," he boasted. With the right direction it could become the bible of western agriculture, and while it was growing into that role, he wanted it circulated into every farm and ranch home in Alberta.

It was heady stuff for a guy who had been through three years of the *Free Press* "situation," and I began mentally to bobble about like the fellow in the Jimmy Durante song who couldn't go because he wanted to stay and couldn't stay because he wanted to go. But I knew that, if I went back and told Kay we were moving to Calgary, there would be a divorce in the family. Her experience with Ottawa had convinced her that she would never venture out of Winnipeg again. But Porter's sales spiel had me—hook, line, and sinker. I was fascinated by the man and everything about him. So we worked out a compromise. I would take on the job for his six thousand dollars a year and a piece of the action if I could commute to Calgary and back each month and put out the magazine, and consult with him about the editorials we should work on. If, at the end of the year, we were both satisfied, we would move to Calgary. Meanwhile, I could go on freelancing to my heart's content. Indeed, said Porter, the new fields I would cultivate for the *Farm and Ranch* ought to provide some excellent articles for eastern newspapers as well.

As we were getting to the end of the interview, I was suddenly struck by the anomaly of becoming editor of a magazine that, up to that point, I had never seen, and had not even heard of before Porter's phone call. At his suggestion, we drove over to the Western Printing Company plant, which also housed the *Farm and Ranch Review* offices. There I met Fred Maxie, the general manager of both enterprises, and Pat Peterson, the son of the founder and the advertising manager. Porter got me a copy of the most recent issue, which contained an editorial he had written on the historic background of the withholding of mineral rights when homesteads and railway lands were passed out to the settlers. I picked up several other back numbers and took them back to the hotel for detailed study.

An agricultural version of *Time* magazine it certainly was not. Indeed, it resembled nothing so much as a catch-all for the releases of every government, implement-company and chemical-company publicity mill. And it was printed on the cheapest, yellow-tinged newsprint on the market. In the hiatus between Porter's first call and my trip to Calgary, I had tried without success to locate a copy of the magazine in Winnipeg. But the search had turned up a number of American and Canadian farm publications, and the distance that separated them from what I saw in the *Farm and Ranch Review* was a yawning gulf. To catch up with the competition, it was obvious that the *Review* would require better content, better typography, better reproduction, and most of all, upgrading of the newsprint. I was making notes of suggestions for improvements all the way back to Winnipeg.

For its size, the *Farm and Ranch Review* was probably the most economically operated magazine in the Western world, never mind western Canada. With a circulation that was to reach 125,000 a month, it varied in size from twenty-four to forty-eight pages, with never less than sixty-five per cent advertising. It had a staff of six—

an editor, an advertising manager, a circulation manager, a woman's editor who doubled as office secretary, a bookkeeper, and an advertising representative in Toronto. Except for the Toronto man, we were all hived away in a second-floor corner of the sprawling Western Printing and Lithographing Company building.

The magazine itself was printed on a one-of-a-kind four-colour rotary press that Peterson had imported from Germany prior to the Second World War. It had been a superb piece of machinery, with a rated capacity of five thousand copies per hour of a forty-page magazine, in four colours, saddle-stapled as they emerged from the press. However, the German pressmen who had come with it all returned home as the war clouds gathered, and its operation was turned over to Western Printing's regular press crew, whose forte was offset printing rather than letterpress. Over the years, since replacement parts were unattainable, the German press developed vexing idiosyncrasies for the pressmen who operated it. Getting out the *Farm and Ranch* every month became a cross they bore with increasing impatience and a complete lack of enthusiasm.

For Western Printing, the magazine was both an invaluable customer, from which it made a juicy profit each month, and a nuisance that could throw its composing-room scheduling out of whack. The primary function of the magazine, to the printing company, was to absorb unproductive composing-room time. When work was slack on government printing, which bulked large in the company's operation, type could be set for the *Farm and Ranch*. In theory, the type would all be set early in the month, prior to the deadline for putting out the magazine. This meant that the spot-news content of the magazine had to be set so far ahead of publication that it would be out of date by the time it reached the readers. But until I arrived on the scene, nobody had worried too much about that. What everybody worried about was getting in all the advertising possible, and if a late-arriving ad delayed publication two or three days, it was of little concern.

Like all new brooms, I raised a great deal of dust around the Western Printing plant when I moved into the editor's office. How the publication had retained its circulation of ninety thousand a month with the kind of reading material it supplied the subscribers baffled me. In addition to the overload of handouts, the writing was uniformly stodgy and the make-up uninspired. The answer came to me when I happened to inquire casually what the subscription rate was and discovered that it was one dollar for ten years.

"My God!" I almost croaked, "what kind of rate is that? It won't even pay the postage! And what interest can subscribers take in a magazine that is given away at that price?"

Pat Peterson had a ready answer. "It doesn't matter what the subscribers think," he said. "It's what the Audit Bureau of Circulation thinks. As long as we can show signed subscription applications, ABC doesn't give a damn about the subscription rate. And why should it? It knows that every magazine in Canada employs sheet writers to sell subscriptions and their commissions are always one hundred per cent of what they collect, plus bonuses if they reach certain sales quotas. And you can be sure that when they get within sight of the quota, a lot of names come off tombstones and out of telephone books on to subscription forms."

That was the first of many chastening experiences. But it did not dissuade me from setting out to revamp the format of the magazine completely. I threw out most of the handout material and did some departmentalizing of interest areas. I set up an environment section devoted to irrigation and reclamation, expanded the women's pages with some new features, and hired a covey of regional correspondents to write monthly columns from Ottawa, Winnipeg, Regina, Saskatoon, Edmonton, and Lethbridge. Then I located some specialists to deal with areas of concern to the various special-interest groups among the farmers and ranchers. My goal, of course, was so to improve the quality of the publication that we would have something to sell to the farmers of western Canada, a magazine they would turn to eagerly each month, through which they would become vulnerable to the ideas we would be developing on the editorial pages.

Having worked with distant editors on the *Free Press*, I had no reason to expect problems editing the *Farm and Ranch* from Winnipeg. I simply had all the special articles directed to me there for editing. A 10- by 14-inch magazine does not require all that much copy, if well over half of it is advertising, and I was able to keep a steady flow of material going to Calgary throughout the month. But when I went out each month to make up the book and put it to bed, deadlines arrived in a frenzy of foul-ups. Copy sent out early got mislaid; articles already set in type were set over again. Ads were delayed going out in proof to agencies. Cuts were lost. And if, by some miracle, the composing room performed without a hitch, the stereotyper got the flu, or the pressroom failed to get the presses started on time. Instead of spending two or three days in Calgary putting the magazine together, my jaunts stretched to a week and beyond.

Two or three months after taking on the job, the first issue for which I had subscribed arrived at the house and I almost wept. Never have I seen such an abortion of a magazine. It was loosely held together by a single staple; several four-colour advertisements were off register; the pages from one deck of plates were over-inked and others were almost impossible to read.

I stuck the copy into my briefcase, and before I started making up the next issue, I got Fred Maxie and Pat Peterson together and spread the copy out for them, expecting that their outrage over the printing job would match mine. Instead, neither showed the slightest concern and simply walked away. I followed Peterson into his office to ask what he thought the advertisers would think when they saw copies like this.

"They'll never see anything like that," he said. "All they ever see are the advertisers' copies we run off specially for them when we are well into the run and the press is running smoothly."

Reality was turning out to be a far cry from the visions of the future that had been conjured up in Marsh Porter's office. The magazine was turning out to be more of a con game on the advertisers and a put-on of the readers than a serious publishing enterprise. But I could see nothing inherently wrong that could not be repaired, so I let production problems slide until I completed my move to Calgary, which was then in the works.

On our return to Winnipeg from Ottawa, we were impressed with the truth of Thomas Wolfe's book title, *You Can't Go Home Again*. In the year we had been away, several of our closest friends had left town, and others were into different groupings. The Winnipeg we returned to was far different from the Winnipeg we had left. In the early spring of 1948, Kay and I drove to Calgary with the idea of locating a river lot on which we could build a new house, one that would be free of the mistakes we had made on the two we built in Winnipeg. But instead of river lots, we became enchanted with the views we got of Calgary from its surrounding hills, and settled for a superb view-lot on the fringe of Mount Royal. The problems encountered in trying to sell a house in Winnipeg on the flooding Red River while building one in Calgary easily diverted my attention from the deficiencies of the *Farm and Ranch Review*'s appearance. And the satisfaction I was getting in chasing the rabbit tracks of new ideas all over the landscape provided about all the mental stimulation one mind could stand.

To make the switch from criticism to advocacy is akin to the change that takes place when the sinner becomes the zealot. Friends of a reformed drunk frequently become so bored with his preachments against alcohol that they wish he would get back on the booze. That, I suspect, was the reaction of my friends in the press gallery and elsewhere in journalism to my sudden emergence as a special pleader of lost causes. In addition to setting the minds of the farmers squarely in my sights, like an instant convert to New Thought or chiropractic, I wanted everybody else to become privy to what I was thinking. So I made up a mailing list of my old newspaper colleagues, press-gallery members, sundry editors around the country, and a selection of politicians. Each month we sent off fifty to seventy-five tear sheets of the *Farm and Ranch* editorials to these alleged moulders of public opinion. I hoped that, if they would not pick up one of the ideas I was belabouring, they might at least think enough of it to start an argument. But none ever did. In fact, there was probably less readership for the reprints of *Farm and Ranch* editorials than there had been for the *Free Press* editorials we had sent off with such dedication. In any event, I never did encounter anyone who had bothered to read them, even among the editors who were buying my foreign correspondence. Worse still, the farmers paid no more attention than anyone else. That none of our ninety thousand subscribers ever took pen in hand to discuss our editorial topics never retarded the outpouring, however.

When it came to the question of ideas, Porter was just about a perfect publisher, once his dominating prejudices and special interests were identified, and properly graded. These areas aside, his attitude towards ideas was that of the lumber-camp cook to leftover stew. Doubts of whether it was edible or not were quickly resolved by trying it out on the camp dog. If it didn't poison the dog, it was good enough for the lumberjacks. Porter's reaction to most of my ideas was, "Let's try it out on the dogs." To wit, the readers of the *Farm and Ranch Review*. One of the ideas I first tried out was an unused leftover from my *Free Press* days.

During John Deutsch's short sojourn on the *Free Press* editorial page, he and I had enjoyed bouncing ideas off each other. One of my pet schemes for solving the vexing railway problem of western Canada was to apply the canal principle to the mileage of both roads through northern Ontario. For fifty years, the people of the West had been paying twenty per cent more for everything they bought and getting twenty per cent less for everything they sold as a result of the long freight haul through traffic-barren northern Ontario. So, I argued, let the federal government treat this sterile mileage as it treated the Welland Canal, which it had built to get lake shipping around the Niagara gorge. Let the government take over the Sudbury-to-Winnipeg mileage and operate it as a public service. Then the railways would be able to reduce their charges for moving eastern goods west and western grain east. There was already a precedent for doing just that. The Board of Railway Commissioners had established what was called an agreed mileage between Winnipeg and the Lakehead. Under that order, the actual 400-odd miles were reduced to 260 miles for the purpose of rate-setting for freight and passenger movement. Even an economist of Deutsch's stature could find nothing wrong in principle with reducing 800 miles to zero, once 400 miles had been reduced to 260 miles by board ukase.

Another railway freight-rate issue pursued with even greater vigour, and even less success, was the campaign to get the Spokane formula adopted in Canada. The people of Alberta, and those of western Saskatchewan only slightly less, were the "white niggers" of Confederation as far as the impact of freight rates on their standard of living was concerned. Freight rates increased, of course, the farther west one got from Montreal, until Calgary and Edmonton were reached. Then everything changed, and the basing point became Vancouver instead of Montreal.

It was far cheaper to ship goods from Montreal to Vancouver by water through the Panama Canal than overland by three thousand miles of railroad. So, in order to enable the railways to compete with the canal route, a special low rate was established from Montreal or Toronto to Vancouver. The result was that everything the railways carried, from window glass and steel products to binder twine and shoes, could be shipped to Vancouver via Canadian railways for about half what the railways charged to ship to Calgary or Edmonton. This created the wonderland in which goods could be shipped all the way to Vancouver and then hauled back seven hundred miles to Edmonton for less than would have been charged to drop them off as the trains passed through en route from Montreal to Vancouver.

In my pawing over freight-rate data, I discovered that the western United States had all suffered the same disabilities. Then the U.S. Interstate Commerce Commission had established the Spokane formula. Under it, the railways could not charge more for moving goods to an intermediate point like Spokane than to a distant point like Seattle. Under that formula, the Vancouver rate would have been the ceiling on most of the freight to everywhere in western Canada west of Regina. This would have run into tens of millions of dollars a year in savings for most of the people of western Canada, and might even have promoted the establishment of some secondary industry in Alberta, but none of the politicians or newspapers could work up any enthusiasm for it.

The refusal of *Farm and Ranch* subscribers to become excited about any aspect of freight rates was perhaps understandable. The subject had been worried to death for forty years by succeeding generations of politicians. But their refusal to support our crusade to get their mineral rights returned to them passed all understanding.

Reserving to the Crown all gold, silver, and precious metals discovered on any granted land had been an accepted practice of the British Crown from the days of Henry VIII onward. Indeed, the Crown did not hesitate to reserve other valuables if the spirit moved it. In some early maritime land grants, timbers of a certain height and girth were reserved to the Crown for use by the British navy. When the settlement of the West began in the decade following Confederation, however, the federal government had begun by following the practice long established in Upper and Lower Canada, where the settlers got patents for the surface of the earth and everything beneath it.

Then, with the construction of the CPR across the West, a number of valuable coal deposits were discovered. That led to concern that, unless the mineral rights were withheld from the homesteaders, they might prevent the development of coal mines which were vitally needed. So, after 1887, both the government and the railways kept the ownership of all the minerals underlying the land when they sold the land to the settlers. Most of the land in Manitoba and eastern Saskatchewan had been settled before that date, and those pioneers got their minerals along with their surface titles. But western Saskatchewan and Alberta were only sparsely settled by 1887, and settlers with mineral rights there were few and far between.

Until Leduc was discovered in 1947, it was a situation that gave no one much concern. The coal deposits were mainly beneath rough land that frequently went unsettled. Here and there, surface outcroppings were worked, and there were actual coal mines in Edmonton before the turn of the century. When eastern capital came in and developed mines at Lethbridge and Drumheller, there was little conflict between surface owners and mineral owners because the mines usually got title to both. During the Alberta oil boom in the 1920s, many farmers did acquire mineral rights to their property, simply by filing a claim with the federal government and paying a small annual rental. When the boom collapsed, most of them simply let their mineral rights lapse.

With the discovery of the Leduc oilfield in the heart of some of Alberta's richest farmland, everything changed. It so happened that the Leduc area contained a fair sprinkling of farms that were first settled in the early 1880s after the CPR had reached Calgary. The mineral rights for all these farms had been passed on with the surface titles. When Imperial Oil was putting its land spread together for its Leduc wildcat, it had to pick up a dozen or so mineral leases from the farmers as well as those it got from the Alberta government. Once the well came in, every farmer for miles around was besieged by oil-company employees eager to make deals for their mineral rights. The lucky farmers who had their oil rights were able to set themselves up for life with the cash bonuses and royalties they got from the oil companies. Across the road, their neighbours on land for which the government retained the mineral rights were lucky to get a few hundred dollars' compensation for the damage done by a drilling site on their land.

When exactly the same situation had developed in Texas on the school land to which the state had retained mineral rights, the farmers and ranchers broke out their guns and threatened the trespassing wildcatters with death unless they vacated their land. When near civil war developed in west Texas, the state opted for discretion instead of belligerence. It rushed through something called the Mineral Rights Relinquishment Act. Under it, the state turned over all but an eighth of its mineral rights to the surface owners and appointed them its agents to negotiate whatever deal they could with the oil companies. Marsh Porter had discovered the Texas precedent about the time I was being hired, and wrote a long editorial urging that the precedent be followed in Alberta. It would be a fitting reward for the farmers on the plains who had stuck with the province through all the lean years of the 1930s. I readily embraced the idea and carried on the campaign.

Albertans, however, were more Caspar Milquetoast than Texan when it came to asserting their rights. Instead of fighting for the oil under their land, they were content to accept the law as it stood and haggle with the oil companies for an increase in the pittances they were offered for the use of ten-acre well sites, and later for the running of gathering lines and pipelines across their land. As more and more wells were drilled, gathering lines built, and pipelines extended, the haggling over compensation increased in boisterousness. To dampen down the farmers' rising indignation, the Alberta government appointed an arbitrator to settle disputes. His bias was ever so slightly in the farmers' favour, but he became so snowed in with work that he soured rather than sweetened relations between the oil companies and the farmers. In some areas, the farmers barricaded access to their land until compensation claims were settled. The government then sided with the oil companies and passed the Right-of-Entry Act, which made it a criminal offence for farmers to bar their land to drilling rigs or seismic crews. The farmers accepted that order without even a whimper.

When the bigger and better Redwater field was discovered by Imperial Oil in 1948 in an area thirty miles northeast of Edmonton, none of the farmers held mineral rights. This was the home base of Carl Stimpfle, president of the radical Farmers' Union of Alberta, and he mounted a campaign to force the oil companies to pay a five-per-cent royalty to the farmers on whose land the wells were drilled. The payment of $25,000, he said, was little enough for the owners of a $5,000,000 well to pay the farmers for the damage to their land. His misplaced decimal did not matter, because nobody, least of all the Social Credit government, paid the slightest heed to Stimpfle's agitation, and it quickly subsided. When the *Farm and Ranch* campaign for farmers' mineral rights failed to bear fruit, I dropped it in favour of an assault on the way government regulations were turning Alberta's petroleum wealth over, holus-bolus, to the American oil industry.

The major American oil companies had been in Alberta off and on since the Brown discoveries in Turner Valley in 1936. Shell came in and blanketed the province with its reservations and then withdrew. California Standard Company and Union of California both did a lot of wildcatting and discovered several small pools during the war years. But it took the blow-out of the Atlantic No. 3 well on the eastern fringe of the Leduc field on March 8, 1948, to rivet American attention on Alberta. Atlantic No. 3 spewed oil into the air at the rate of 14,000 barrels a day for six months. Vast lakes of oil were created around the well, out of which hundreds of tank trucks pumped more than 1,250,000 barrels of oil and hauled it to the Edmonton refineries. Just as relief wells drilled to shut off the wild well were being completed, the well caught fire, and pictures of the flaming oil focused continent-wide attention on Alberta, at a time when the Americans were running out of prospective oil acreage on which to drill. When the Americans discovered the vast exploration acreage available to them for the asking in Alberta, the trickle that had begun in 1948 became a torrent in 1949 and 1950.

For an American wildcatter to sign up enough acreage to put an oil play together in the United States was endlessly time-consuming and frustrating. Negotiations had to be conducted successively with a dozen individual farmers for the assignment of their mineral rights. That had to be done with consummate stealth, for if word got out that a wildcat oil well was in prospect, amateur leasehounds descended in droves in an effort to get a piece of the action. The over-all result was that large, solid blocks of leases could seldom be put together, and spreads were usually pock-marked with leases whose owners hoped to capitalize on the risk taken by the wildcatters. In short, it was fragmentation worse confounded.

In Alberta, the Americans found a landman's Valhalla. Here the government was prepared to hand over a maximum of 96,000 acres in a solid bloc for a nominal fee of $7,500. The oil companies were given two years in which to conduct geophysical exploration and drill whatever wells they considered justified. If they found oil, they were granted one-hundred-per-cent ownership of nine sections —5,760 acres—surrounding the well without additional payment of any kind. Then they were entitled to pick up half the remaining acreage in mile-square units checkerboarded over the original 96,000-acre reservation. The government took back its half and then resold it by public auction to the highest bidders. The nine-section blanket thrown over the original wildcat site would have entirely covered the vast majority of the oil fields discovered in the United States, for there would be room on those 5,760 acres for the company to drill another 144 wells.

Old-time Canadian oilmen were very much like old-time prospectors. The word of an oil strike or a gold strike sent them stampeding for the location of the strike. When Leduc hit in Alberta, most of the Turner Valley veterans were on the ground the next day searching for drilling sites. Thus, Cliff Cross put a handful of companies together to try to do in Leduc what he had done in Turner Valley. Home Oil, Calgary and Edmonton Corp., Anglo-Canadian, Okalta, and Commonwealth, all poured their Turner Valley profits into the purchase of Leduc and Redwater Crown-land leases and whatever freehold acreage they could pick up from the farmers. While they were scrambling for footholds in the new bonanzas, the Americans ran off with the rest of Alberta.

The Leduc and Redwater strikes, following upon thirty years' experience with the Turner Valley, demonstrated for all who ran to see that the sedimentary basin along the eastern fringe of the Rockies was prime petroleum-prospecting land. Instead of trying to elbow into the discovered fields, the American companies rushed for exploration reservations in such numbers that the province was soon plastered with their filings from border to border. Imperial Oil, being first on the ground, took out millions of acres of reservations and was the first to make mincemeat of the province's naïve notion that it could limit the acreage any company could inventory. The regulations stated that one company could only hold one reservation of 96,000 acres at one time. Suddenly, the provincial secretary was swamped with applications to incorporate new oil companies which differed only to the extent of a single shareholder from the major companies themselves. By 1950, the wall of the main hall in the Imperial Oil Company building in Calgary, for example, was all but covered by its list of subsidiary companies, which had been incorporated to get around the spirit of the regulations. The same was true of every other multinational company in town, and they were all in town.

When the Canadians ran out of Leduc and Redwater drilling room and went after some reservations for themselves, the cupboard was bare. Not only was the Alberta government fresh out of reservations, but the Americans had gobbled up so much more than they could possibly develop that millions of reservation acres were in actual default within a couple of years. When the Canadians discovered the defaults, they tried to put pressure on the government to cancel the contracts with the defaulting companies. The government refused, and the Canadians were forced into heads-you-win, tails-I-lose farm-out deals with the international companies. The latter were thus able to get the independents to prove up their reservations at no cost to themselves.

The aroma of all this was sadly reminiscent of what I had smelled in the Steep Rock mine development. Canadians took the major risk in the early development of their resources and the Americans pocketed the lion's share of the profits. The editorial line I pursued in the *Farm and Ranch Review* was that the right to exploit Canadian natural resources should be restricted to Canadians, and that our tax laws should be changed to encourage Canadians to develop Canadian natural resources.

Neither happened, of course, and during 1948, 1949, and 1950, the Americans were pouring into Alberta, and particularly into Calgary, by the thousands. Well-service companies, drilling companies, and geophysical companies clogged the highways with their massive convoys of equipment from as far south as Texas, Oklahoma, and Louisiana. Technical specialists like geophysicists, drilling-mud purveyors, every type of engineer known to the industry, along with geologists from as far away as Borneo and Peru, scoured the town for office space. On a five-minute walk from the Palliser Hotel, you would encounter accents ranging from Louisiana patois to Texas drawl, New England twang, and upper-crust English.

Office space that had remained empty for years filled up, and wartime Quonset huts were converted to storage space for the oilfield-equipment suppliers. A ten-year boycott of Alberta by the mortgage-lending companies following Aberhart's repudiation of the Alberta debt had left Alberta trailing all other provinces in housing construction. Lending was resumed in 1948, but the construction industry was barely back in business when the American influx hit. The house builders could not begin to keep up with the burgeoning demand from incoming Americans. Undeterred by the housing scarcity, the American oil companies simply opened their purse-strings and sent their agents into Calgary's Mount Royal district to buy up the most luxurious houses available for their top executives, eight or ten units at a time. Thus was created a bonanza for everybody with a house for sale, and a headache for every Calgarian who had to rely on rental accommodation, as the house sellers immediately rushed out to buy replacements.

If the American invasion of Alberta was greeted by genuine enthusiasm by the government of Alberta, Ottawa's reaction was much closer to wild jubilation. After a fifteen-year diet of chicken feathers, the Social Credit government of Ernest Manning found itself with nothing but white meat and drumsticks as the millions began to roll in from sky-rocketing oil royalties and sales of proven Leduc and Redwater acreage. Ottawa saw the inflow of American capital as manna from heaven for a government that for two years had been caught up in a currency crisis of historic proportions.

When the pent-up purchasing power of Canadians' wartime savings hit the consumers' markets of 1946, it found a desperate shortage of the kind of goods everybody had been saving for. So the money flooded south to the United States in such volume that the government was forced to impose the most rigid peacetime control of currency ever. An embargo was placed on the importation from the United States of everything from electrical goods to cars and clothing. Travel of Canadians into the United States was severely curtailed through strict rationing of American funds. Price controls were retained or reimposed on a long list of products, ranging from electrical wiring to cement and nails.

With a one-billion-dollar-a-year trade deficit, plus a drain of upward of $200 million a year to pay interest and dividends on American investment in Canada, the post-war Canadian government was caught like a horse player in the clutches of a loan shark. It had either to borrow heavily or to sell off its assets to keep afloat financially. And, as if Canada's assets were not attractively priced as it was, the sudden onset of the Korean War had the effect of cutting prices by ninety per cent. The American oil companies were immediately caught up in the emergency ninety-per-cent excess-profits tax imposed by President Truman.

Under American law, companies could deduct expenditures on natural-resource development anywhere in the world from their U.S. before-tax profits. In other words, they could use U.S.-government tax money to acquire Canadian drilling reservations, and by legalistic sleight of hand could even buy Canadian exploration companies, at prices no Canadian could ever afford to match. They could, moreover, afford to take greater risks because it was the government's money they were spending. The drive for the acquisition of Alberta's petroleum rights intensified in 1950.

As Calgary broke out in a rash of American licence plates,

American cigarettes, and American Stetsons, I began to have an uneasy feeling that something very wrong was happening. Like everyone else who had taken a close look at the production miracles that were worked by C. D. Howe and his Department of Munitions and Supply during the war, I was easily convinced that Canada could become one of the great industrial nations of the world. We had stopped relying on the United States for technical expertise and components. When the Ford company, late in the war, was able to announce that it had built a motor vehicle completely from Canadian-made parts, it was an occasion for much self-satisfaction. By this time, Howe's department's press-release file of important discoveries and developments by Canadian industry was overflowing, because the ingenuity of Canadians had been given free rein during the war.

On top of all this, four hundred thousand young Canadians had returned from the wars exuding a new pride in themselves and their country that rubbed off on everybody at home. And it was a new country, where there was work at a living wage for everyone who wanted it, where the farmers were almost out of debt and able to contemplate the purchase of new machinery and, here and there, even new homes with inside plumbing and other amenities of city life. By any score anyone chose to keep, being a Canadian was demonstrably the best thing in the world to be. We never tired of confirming to ourselves that Laurier had been right, that the twentieth century did belong to Canada, and in the last half of the century we'd demonstrate that fact.

But somehow, what was happening in Alberta did not square with my version of the Canadian dream, of a country pulling itself up by its own bootstraps. But I could not put my finger on the cause of the unease until I came across a statistical contradiction. A newspaper story estimated that Leduc and Redwater had attracted $100 million in American investment in Alberta in 1949. It was estimated that the amount would double in each of the following five years. At the same time, Alberta oil production had reached 50,000 barrels a day, enough to supply the entire prairie region. Worth roughly $50 million a year, the oil plus the American investment had helped Canada's balance-of-payments deficit by $150 million. But when I looked deeper into the figures, that conclusion fell apart.

The $100 million could have represented in large part the value of the drilling rigs, drilling bits, drill pipe, and well-casing that were imported from the United States for use on the 250 successful wells that were drilled in 1949. Alberta, therefore, was creating a minor boom for the oil-well supply business in the United States because much of the so-called American investment in Canada was being spent in the United States. I lugged the problem into Porter's office and discovered that the arithmetic was even crazier than I had suspected. His office acted for several American companies, of whom only the smallest actually transferred American funds to Calgary. The big companies preferred to operate with money borrowed from Canadian banks on the security of corporate debentures. So, in fact, the bulk of the American investment in the purchase of Alberta's natural resources had no impact at all on the balance-of-payments deficit. Except, that is, when the borrowed Canadian funds were converted into U.S. funds to import American equipment. Then the effect on Canada's balance of payments was adverse, rather than favourable. It was from Marsh Porter that I appropriated for my own use a phrase that summed up the situation perfectly. "We're being bought out with our own money," he said.

But there was more to the alienation of Canadian national resources to American corporations than money. We had just emerged from a decade when the forceable seizure of other people's property had become a fact of life in Europe and Asia. That era ended with the war and a resurgence of national self-determination movements everywhere—in China, southeast Asia, India, Pakistan, North Africa, and South America. In many global areas, this new spirit was directed particularly against the foreign exploitation of natural resources. France, India, and Mexico all strengthened restrictions against foreign development of natural resources. In the case of France, the rules applied to its colonial territories as well as to France itself.

There was, of course, no possible comparison between what had happened in Europe and Asia and what was happening in Alberta. No armed legions stormed into our country to carry away our most prized possessions. But the sudden appearance of large numbers of strangers, even unarmed and inoffensive strangers, in the midst of the indigenous peoples has always provoked uneasiness, and frequently, hostility. The Americans who came as friendly allies discovered that in London and Sydney during the Second World War. Concern over the alienation of Alberta's natural resources never surfaced in Alberta. But the uneasiness over the influx of hordes of strangers became apparent very quickly.

Along with the American drilling rigs, draw-works, well-head fittings, and drill pipe by the carload, came a steadily increasing influx of a special variety of the species *homo Americanus*—eager-beaver young junior executives on their way to the top. Or so they thought, as they enthusiastically seized their first opportunity to test their upward mobility on their companies' executive ladders. Many of them were recently retreaded army, navy, and marine-corps officers, and all had been field-tested in the domestic operations of the American exploration, transportation, refining, and service and supply companies.

In Alberta they filled the top executive and supervisory positions of the American branch offices. In some cases, the Americans also occupied the lower echelons, particularly of the smaller companies. But in the main, the Americans followed the policy of recruiting local people for all but the senior positions.

The intermixing of nationalities in the oil-company offices would have created tensions under the best of circumstances. The circumstances that prevailed in Calgary and Edmonton were far from the best. Canada, by definition of the major companies, was just another Borneo, Peru, Saudi Arabia, or Sumatra, as far as personnel policy was concerned. The employees sent to Alberta were entitled to the same "hard-service allowances" granted employees in any foreign-service area. Such allowances, moreover, were paid on salaries that were half again as high as those earned by their Canadian opposite numbers. The Americans drew their salaries in American dollars, on which they collected a ten-per-cent premium when converted into Canadian dollars. They got subsidized accommodation in company-owned houses and were allowed to bring in their Cadillacs and all their household furnishings duty-free from the United States.

It was hardly surprising that the underpaid Canadians viewed their overpaid American colleagues with a bilious eye, and took to muttering imprecations against the "goddam you-alls" in men's-room colloquies. This envious resentment spread gradually through the periphery of the commercial community, as retail merchants took umbrage at the wholesale importations of the immigrants, who gave nary a thought to patronizing local industry.

Curiously enough, when the Americans tried to cultivate Canadian goodwill, they often made matters worse. Many of them, particularly the women, seemed to have graduated *summa cum laude* from a Dale Carnegie course in international public relations. The women, only slightly more than the men, seemed to share a common inclination towards gushiness, in the overblown, southern-states type of drawling politness.

"Oh, my deah, we ah jus' so dee-lighted to be given the oppah-toonity to come up heah to this wunnaful cont-ree of youahs and meet all you wunnaful Canad-ee-uns."

When well out of earshot of the newcomers, Canadians tried to parody the American dialect, but few ever really mastered it.

Occasionally, when the opportunity arose, they did more than mimic accents—like setting up de facto quotas, which kept all but a very select few out of the Ranchmen's Club and the Calgary Golf and Country Club. In the end, the American companies seemed to become cognizant of the situation, and took positive steps to remedy it by Canadianizing their operations. The Americans were gradually called home or re-assigned elsewhere, and Canadians were moved into the executive suites. Twenty-five years after Leduc, everything came full circle as Canadians began to be moved into the pinnacles of power in the international companies themselves.

The early antipathy that Albertans developed towards "those goddam you-alls" seldom focused on individual Americans and never on the American companies that were taking over Alberta. As the government backed and filled, trying to devise the best system of disposing of its resources, it faced frequent threats from the American companies that they would pick up and leave if the government took certain actions considered inimical to their interests. Whether the threats were a bluff or for real, the government never discovered. It was not ever going to risk losing the trickle of gold that would become a torrent by finding out. As for the eager young graduates of the science faculties then hitting the job markets, the American companies frequently paid better and had more to offer than the Canadian companies, and hence were regarded as preferred employers. For Albertans generally, the mere thought of going back to pre-Leduc economic conditions was enough to close all their receptors to suggestions that their country was being sold out from under them.

When our campaign to get their mineral rights back for farmers laid the biggest kind of crockery egg, I turned my editorial pop-guns on two other aspects of the natural-resources problem. My criticism of the wholesale disposal of petroleum resources to foreigners became increasingly strident as it went unread by the *Farm and Ranch* subscription list. Admittedly, these were pretty heavy topics to expect our farm readers, most of whom still lived in powerless and toiletless houses, to become agitated over. But I did manage to get a lot of people stirred up over another issue I just happened to luck into when I was searching through Hansard looking for something else. I discovered the great power-export issue that had blown up along the St. Lawrence River in the decade preceding the First World War.

Front and centre in that great controversy was Sir Clifford Sifton. He was the chairman of the powerful Commission of Conservation at the time when American power interests were hell-bent on getting development of Canadian power sites on the St. Lawrence to generate hydro power for the factories of New York. Sifton rallied the country against the power grab and succeeded in establishing the policy that power could not be exported to the United States until all Canadian needs had first been met. This, it seemed to me, was all the precedent we would ever need to adopt the policy that Canadian natural gas should be reserved for Canadian use in Canada, both as a fuel and as the raw material for a petrochemical revolution.

The editorial nailing the *Farm and Ranch* colours to Sifton's "no-power-export" mast appeared in April 1950, after the passage through Parliament of three bills incorporating natural-gas pipeline-transmission companies. The incorporations came hard on the discovery of some spectacular gas reserves in Alberta and British Columbia, which temporarily overshadowed interest in the oil boom itself. The extent of the euphoria over gas can be gauged by the frequently heard claim around the oil patch that there was enough gas in Pincher Creek alone to justify a pipeline to Seattle. The Alberta Natural Gas Company, indeed, was incorporated to build just such a pipeline. Another company, Westcoast Transmission Company, proposed to take northern British Columbia gas to Vancouver and Washington State. A group of Winnipeggers put together the Western Natural Gas Company to build a pipeline to Winnipeg.

As the Alberta Conservation Board wrestled with the export applications, voices began to be heard for the first time in public opposing almost everything the petroleum industry was proposing. The town of High River went on record as opposing export of gas until all the towns of Alberta were hooked up to a supply of the product. The Edmonton Chamber of Commerce, the Calgary city council, and the companies that supplied the domestic gas needs of the province, all joined the clamour against exports. Ultimately, the Conservation Board decided that exports of gas from the province would only be permitted when it was demonstrated that Alberta had enough proven reserves to meet its needs for thirty years.

The decision dampened down the gas-export agitation for a couple of years; then it broke out all over again with the discovery of several new important gas reservoirs. The Winnipeg promoters raised their sights to include export to Minneapolis and Chicago from Winnipeg. Frank McMahon pushed the Westcoast proposal through the American authorities, and it was left to a multimillionaire Texas oil baron, Clint Murchison, to come riding over the horizon to protect Canadian interests in the natural-gas resources of Alberta. What Canada needed, he trumpeted to C. D. Howe and everybody else who would listen, was the biggest natural-gas pipeline in the world to carry Alberta gas to Toronto and Montreal.

Long before this, however, the American government had given the *Farm and Ranch*'s Canada-First crusade a powerful push forward. In the late winter of 1951, the U.S. Federal Power Commission shut off the shipment of American natural gas into southwestern Ontario, where it had been used to supplement supplies being produced in the Sarnia area. The FPC ruled that there was a need for all the gas that could be carried into the Michigan area, and all American needs had to be met before any exports could be permitted. The decision gave me another peg for an editorial opposing any export of Alberta or British Columbia gas to Washington until Ontario and Quebec needs were fully satisfied.

Though I liked to envision myself as a lone pro-Canadian voice crying in a pro-American wilderness, the truth was that some concern was developing in eastern Canada over the massive inflow of American capital that was taking over Canadian enterprise. Control of several of Canada's largest mining companies had passed into American hands, and control of the CPR was also threatened. The expansion of American branch-plant investment in Ontario was continuing and American insurance companies were growing rapidly. The *Financial Post*, for example, was viewing the whole process with growing concern, not to say alarm.

When I had about written myself out on the natural-resources issues, I got started on the way Canadians financed such projects as the Interprovincial Pipeline by buying the bond issues while ignoring the equity investment. It was a process that enabled the Americans to debt-finance themselves into the ownership of projects mainly financed by the lending of Canadian insurance companies. Marsh Porter was an avid reader of insurance-company annual reports, which he sent along to me heavily pencilled. One day he phoned to tell me of a luncheon he had been to the day before.

"What do you know," he said, "even C. D. Howe is now getting worried about what we've been saying about the Yankees taking over the country. A bunch of us had lunch yesterday with Graham Towers, who's on a tour to reassure us we are all wrong, that eighty-five per cent of our post-war development has been financed by Canadians and only about fifteen per cent by Americans. He claims that we've spent twenty-six billion dollars and Canadians have provided over twenty billion dollars. It doesn't make sense, but he had all the figures."

Over the next few weeks we returned to the Towers thesis several times, and the more we talked, the greater our suspicion became that there was something terribly wrong with his arithmetic. The thing to do obviously was to go and see Towers and get to the basis of his statistics. Now, the unknown editor of an unheard-of farm journal in Alberta doesn't call the Bank of Canada and get an instant appointment with the governor of the bank. So weeks stretched into months in 1953 before the barriers were breached and I was granted an audience in the Bank of Canada mausoleum in Wellington Street in Ottawa.

The interview was over almost before it began because we hardly got beyond definitions. I mentioned Towers' Calgary visit and the figures he had used, and said that, from some rough calculations I had made, the American proportion had to be a great deal more than fifteen per cent. As examples, I cited the immense expansion in the automobile industry, the aluminum and steel industries, and most of all, the petroleum industry.

At the mention of the petroleum industry, the impassive Mr. Towers pursed his lips and said: "No, Mr. Gray, I am sure that you will find that in all these categories, the bulk of the investment has been from Canadian sources."

I could hardly believe what I was hearing and found myself blurting out quite unthinkingly: "Well, if that is true, sir, then there's got to be something radically wrong with our definition of what is Canadian. In fact, how *do* you define 'Canadian' in this context?"

Mr. Towers had been persuaded to grant this interview by his public-relations department, and his impatience showed in the tone of his patronizing answer.

"The figures are those developed by the Dominion Bureau of Statistics, of course, and the definitions are theirs. Obviously, they define 'Canadian' in the only way it can be defined—as citizens of Canada and corporations incorporated in Canada. American investment is by investors domiciled in the United States."

That, except for some fruitless shadow-boxing and the exchange of some forced pleasantries, was the end of the interview. Under that definition, General Motors, Ford, Chrysler, International Nickel, International Harvester, Canadian General Electric, Canadian Westinghouse, Imperial Oil, Gulf, and Texaco were all Canadian. And in a real sense they *were* all Canadian, because all were financing their expansion and business growth with the profits they were earning in Canada. And those profits were like a snowball rolling downhill, doubling and redoubling in size with every turn. How long would it be, I wondered as I left the Bank of Canada, before all the rolling snowballs stripped all the snow from the hill and crashed at the bottom? I caught a taxi to the Dominion Bureau of Statistics to try to start an argument with the statistician in charge of definitions. He turned out to be beyond definition himself, so I came home and wrote an editorial raking the Howe–Towers thesis from stem to gudgeon.

I might just as well have saved the train fare and the trouble of putting words to paper, for the readers of the *Farm and Ranch Review* paid even less attention than I had been able to arouse in the press-gallery pundit corps. And for very good reason: the timing was all wrong.

The first half of the 1950s was no time for a prairie Cassandra to be setting up shop with a stock of prophecies of doom. All of western Canada was too busy living through one of the greatest booms in history. By 1952, even Winnipeg, which had survived the disastrous 1950 flood that might have set it back a full decade, was cock-a-hoop with joy as building permits nudged all-time highs. The construction boom, moreover, encompassed the entire region. It reached such a peak in Calgary that, by the following spring, the telephone company was wrestling with an unfilled-orders file that contained eight thousand names.

Out in the boondocks, things were even better. Five years of uninterrupted farm-production growth reached its peak in 1952, when the prairie wheat crop exceeded 650 million bushels for the first time. Thanks to the British Wheat Agreement and the International Wheat Agreement that followed, the wheat growers were free at last from the uncertainties of wildly fluctuating wheat prices. Saskatchewan farm income that year reached a historic high of $735 million, out of which the Saskatchewan farmers spent upwards of $80 million on new farm machinery to cope with the doubling in farm sizes that was taking place.

It was more of the same the next year. How could anyone be expected to become concerned with obscure economic distortions when the regional and national economies were as unclouded as the political climate? Such was the political serenity of the era that the biggest scandal to surface was the discovery that the armed services had a couple of dozen horses on the payroll.

12
The Deputy Minister Didn't Give a Damn Who Owned the Country

In the world of enterprise, nothing can equal the thrill that comes to an investor when he stands safely off from the wellhead and watches a wildcat oil well in which he has invested being brought into production. *Experto crede!* That was as true of the bringing in of Driver-Rex-Arrow-Kitscoty No. 1, a gold brick of an oil well if there ever was one, as it was of the Dingman well, Turner Valley Royalties, or Leduc itself.

From the time we gathered in Rex Dwigans' used-car office on Seventh Avenue East to examine the cores from the well, there was no doubt in anybody's mind that we had struck oil in our first wildcat. The core box held about ten feet of inch-and-a-half-diameter rock that had been drilled out when the well hit the Sparky sand. The rock was saturated with heavy black and mildly stinking oil. We picked up the fractured segments of the core, rolled them around in our hands. We examined them under Dwigans' ninety-five-cent magnifying glass to evaluate the porosity of the rock, because porosity was the key to the extent of the oil deposit. In the next couple of days, we traipsed from Dwigans' office to Fred Larson's egg-candling shop to Ab MacDonald's taxi office to discuss, not what the next step would be, but how soon it could be taken.

Our reaction to the success of the well was the universal reaction of oilmen the world over whenever a new well comes in, and we were not even oilmen. None of us gave the slightest thought to the profit we might make from that well. The thought at the top of everybody's mind was: when do we drill the next well, and how many more wells will we be able to drill on the lease? That is a reaction that permeates the petroleum industry, from the lowliest speculators to the highest reaches of Jersey Standard, Gulf Oil, British Petroleum, and the Kingdom of Iran, and has done so since the dawn of the industry.

Drilling the next well is what the oil business is all about. At a time in 1977 when the natural-gas reserves of Alberta reached the highest point in history, the province's Minister of Energy was urging the industry to increase its efforts to sell the gas as quickly as possible, so that it would have the incentive to drill for and find even greater reserves. No oilman has ever publicly suggested that, once the industry has proved up enough petroleum to last twenty-five years, a drilling holiday should be declared.

The financial profit to be derived from completion of a successful well is the last thing anybody thinks about. Ultimately, long after a field is completely drilled up, some dullish business-school graduate in the nether reaches of oil-company accounting offices will begin feeding data into a computer. A print-out will tell him how long it will take each well to repay drilling costs, the present worth of the oil that will be marketed five years hence, and the cash flow from the field ten years hence. But the profit the first wildcat will earn and repay to the investors he will never bother to compute. By the time he completes his calculations, his company will have long since committed the cash flow from that field to the drilling of more wells in other fields.

As a concomitant of the drill-more-wells principle, no sophisticated investor has ever bought oil stock on the basis of the rate of return he expects on his money. The dividend rate has always been the last thing considered by an investor, or by any petroleum company's board of directors. The oil company's annual reports are the only ones where the top line—the number of wells drilled, the number of discoveries made, and reserves increased—is more important than the bottom line, which only reports net earnings for the year. The name of the oil-industry game has always been capital appreciation, and the rules for that one were set by people like the Rockefellers and the Mellons almost a century ago. John D. Rockefeller's Standard Oil Company of New Jersey invested a maximum of fifteen million dollars of its own money in the Imperial Oil Company, extracted only minuscule dividends, and let the profits multiply to a point where Imperial was returning fifty million dollars a year to New Jersey on its original fifteen-million investment, while the value of that investment increased a thousandfold.

The pervasive mystique of the petroleum industry was perfectly illustrated by the behaviour of Imperial Oil after its discovery of the Leduc and Redwater fields. Instead of sitting back and methodically and patiently drilling up its immensely rich discoveries with the cash flow from earlier production, it did just the reverse. It sold off its most profitable subsidiary, International

Petroleum Corporation, to get more money to accelerate its drilling program, a program that would ultimately carry it far up into the Arctic Ocean.

For us, as we waited impatiently for the official Conservation Board testing of the well, an endless string of questions bounced off the walls of Dwigans' used-car office. Should we decide definitely where to drill the next well? Should we have preliminary talks with Husky Oil about buying our production? Should we start looking for a trucker to haul the oil, or wait until we had the actual production test? Could we negotiate a bank loan so as to get started on the next well right away, or would we have to wait until the well generated the cash needed for the second well? Should we take a closer look at some of the remote acreage on our reservation to see if there were other favourable locations? Eventually, the word came that the test would take place the following day, so we all roared up to the well site, a dozen miles west of Lloydminster. The well had been equipped with a "Christmas tree" with several valves which would release the oil and gas. The drilling crew had bulldozed out a flare pit, into which the flow of oil would be directed through fifty feet of two-inch pipe which ran from the wellhead to the edge of the pit.

At the appointed hour, the Conservation Board engineer drove up in a half-ton truck, checked the various valves and pressure gauges, and started to spin the wheels that would bring the oil to the surface. The pressure in the Christmas tree began to hum and one of the helpers ignited an oil-soaked sack and tossed it over the end of the flow line. It caught fire with a roar, and a flame shot three or four feet out from the pipe. Then, as the valve was opened wider, the flame increased in length until it was shooting fifteen or twenty feet into the air. The pressure of the emerging gas jet was such that the plume of the burning gas was separated from the end of the flow line by five or six feet of unignited gas, on which the bottom of the flame seemed to be dancing.

The noise of the gas flow was deafening, and we retreated thirty or forty feet farther from the well. We tingled with excitement, took turns shaking hands all round and clapping each other on the back. Gradually, we noticed that the group of spectators had doubled, as the farmers from the general vicinity had been attracted to the site by the roar of the gas and the sight of the flame. The Conservation Board engineer fiddled with the valves, cut back the flow for ten or fifteen minutes, then opened it up again and took readings from his dials. The oil flow we expected never came, but we sure had one hell of a gas well, or so we thought. Eventually the test was completed, the engineer packed up his books and locked up the well, and we returned to Calgary to decide what to do next. What we ultimately did was nothing.

The significance of all this was that the Driver-Rex-Arrow syndicate represented what was fast becoming an endangered species in Alberta, as it represented everything that was good about the way free enterprise once functioned in the petroleum industry in Alberta. We were an authentic cross-section of the doctors, lawyers, merchants, and chiefs of Alberta who had dug under their mattresses for the money that originally found and developed the province's oil resources.

And how did a journalist who migrated to Alberta in 1947 to edit a farm magazine wind up investing in a wildcat oil well? The short answer is that I went to the annual spring horse sale at the Stampede grounds and bought a forty-dollar horse.

In those days, everybody who migrated to Alberta felt an instant urge to own a horse. We resisted the impulse until the spring of 1949, when Alan, who was nine, pestered us into giving in to his pleas for a horse. Like every other greenhorn, I quickly discovered that people never own horses. Horses own people. First I had to find a place to put the horse. Then I had to find somebody to train it. To make sure it was safe enough for a nine-year-old, I had to ride it myself, and I had not been on a horse for twenty-five years. Buying one horse solved nothing. Linda, who was seven, immediately began agitating for a horse so she could ride in the Stampede parade with Alan. The next year we went to the Spence dispersal sale of a herd of American Saddlebred palominos, and wound up with not another horse but what turned out to be three more. The brood mare I bought had a foal at foot and was in foal. The foal would be for Linda, and I would have the mare to ride when she got out of the foal-production business.

Finding a trainer and a place to board my horse brood led me to Rex Dwigans, who had recently bought 160 acres of rough land on the escarpment on the outskirts of west Calgary. I wound up buying twenty-three acres from him for a horse pasture, and in the process discovered the Driver-Rex-Arrow oil syndicate. In addition to Dwigans, the egg candler, the taxi-company owner, and Gordon Plotke, a service-station owner, the syndicate included William Robertson, a clothier, Leon Plotkins, who owned a small oil company, and Clive and Frank Brown, who operated a couple of marginal wells in Turner Valley and had put a new company, Driver Petroleums, together as a stock-promotion venture. Clive Brown was a petroleum engineer and provided what technical expertise the syndicate needed, which was not much. I was persuaded to part with two thousand dollars for a five-per-cent interest. The convincer that tilted me into the deal was the momentary fascination I developed for a doodle-bug oil finder that a fellow named Glen Phillips had invented.

Phillips was a farmer and ham radio operator who lived fifty miles east of Calgary. He claimed to have adapted the use of radio waves to locate oil and gas deposits successfully. He had his gadget wired up in the trunk of his car and, as the car was driven across the surface of the earth, the dials fluctuated when it passed over mineralized strata, underground water, and oil and gas reservoirs. Phillips' interest in oil finding extended from Alberta into Montana, and he was reputed to have located successful wells on both sides of the border.

Dwigans solemnly avowed that he had watched Phillips at work east of Drumheller. They had driven on to a well site where a rig was drilling. Phillips told the crew that they would find no oil under their bit, but, if they drilled a site a mile away, they would find an oil pool. He was proven right on the first count in a matter of weeks, and on the second a year later. On the strength of this and similar reports, Dwigans cut Phillips in for a piece of the action in return for his picking out several drilling locations on the fifty-thousand-acre, soon-to-expire drilling reservation Dwigans had subleased in the Lloydminster area.

An added attraction to the doodle-bug geologizing was the fact that wells could be drilled in the Lloydminster area to the two-thousand-foot pay zone for less than twenty-five thousand dollars. If the first well failed, we would still have the fifty-thousand-acre reservation on which Phillips had spotted several other locations.

On our way back to Calgary from the well site after the test, the only dubious partner in the car was Plotke. He had been involved in more wells than all the rest of us put together, and he was willing to bet Dwigans a new Stetson that we didn't have a well.

But how could that *be*, we chorused. There was oil aplenty in the cores. The depth was right because the Sparky sand was producing oil at Lloydminster. And we had that terrific flow of gas. Maybe all we had to do was go deeper to get oil. But if not, at least we had a gas well and perhaps the next well that Phillips would locate for us would be into the oil zone. Plotke had a feeling about the well, but the rest of us still waited out the Conservation Board verdict with only slightly diminished confidence. Even the official verdict when it came did not discourage us. The board decided that it was a gas well with a productive capacity of around 500,000 cubic feet a day. The thing to do was drill two or three more wells, which we thought we could do by using the income from gas production.

There was only one problem. We were all out of money and there was no market for natural gas. As things turned out, we would not have been able to market the gas even if a pipeline had been available. The pressure in our well was lower than the pressure carried in gas trunk lines. If our well had ever been hooked up to a transmission line, it would have drained gas out of the pipeline instead of pushing it in. We spent a couple of months threshing around trying to find something to do with the well besides leaving it stand as a capped gas well. There was nothing; and so far as I know, it is still standing out there in lonely splendour twenty-five years later. We pocketed our losses and went off about our business.

In a conversation with Marsh Porter some months later, I happened to mention the tragic end of our hopes for the Driver-Rex-Arrow syndicate. When I was finished, he said:

"By God, Jimmy, that's it. You've got the perfect case. You are exhibit A of everything that is wrong with the tax structure of this country. Tell you what let's do. Why don't you go down and talk to Doug Abbott about it. There's been a lot of talk lately about how we have to have American capital to pay for developing our oil resources. Nonsense. There isn't a farmer or rancher or businessman in this province who wouldn't be into the oil business with both feet if the government would give him half a chance. Look at George Ross, who went in hock to the bank to put Neil McQueen and Art Mewburn into business in Leduc. It was the farmers of this country, and the Calgary people, who financed Turner Valley."

He went on reeling off name after name. The problem of individual investors, like me and Frank Fulton and George Ross, was that we had no way to write off our losses and had to pay full income tax on our other income. The oil companies could write off the cost of drilling wildcats from their income, if their primary business was oil. Any American citizen, regardless of occupation, could write off his oil losses in Canada from his American income. There was hardly an American movie star or entertainer who didn't habitually invest in oil and gas exploration because of the tax brackets they were in. If they could not find attractive deals in the U.S., they could send their money to Canada. If they lost, they deducted the loss from their taxes. If they won, they let the income ride to drill other wells, and in the end sold the package out as a capital sale and paid a small capital-gains tax.

"Just give Canadians the same tax break Americans can get in Canada through their tax laws," Porter predicted, "and then just watch how Canadians come into the oil business!"

I wrote to Abbott, who was then Minister of Finance, and asked for a chance to talk to him about the problem when I was next in

Ottawa. I outlined the general tenor of the complaint and he replied that he would be happy to talk any time. When I did see him, he took the offensive almost at once.

"It's a poor time to come talking about tax incentives, Jimmy, because when I got your letter I had the tax people take a look at the oil industry, and we were astounded to discover that our corporate tax income from the Alberta oil industry is practically nil. Alberta may be getting rich, but none of the oil companies are reporting any profits to us."

"Of course they're not making a taxable profit," I replied, "and they won't be as long as they are pouring out so much in exploration. And the reason is, they have the benefit of such whopping write-offs. My point is that individual Canadians who risk their money to develop the resources of the country should have the same rights to share their losses with the government as the corporations do. With most of us, that would not make all that much difference, because we are not in the top brackets. With me, I'd probably be able to reduce my taxes by maybe three hundred dollars on my two-thousand-dollar loss. But that little something might encourage me to take another flier. And it is people like me taking small fliers who develop a country."

In the end, Abbott admitted I might have a point and suggested that I try it out on Ken Eaton, his assistant deputy minister. He had his secretary make an appointment for me and I went over to see Eaton, who had little time for me and less for my ideas. He listened politely enough to my pitch, but I quickly discerned that nothing I was saying made any impression on him.

"I've been listening to this argument spring and fall for five or six years, and it makes less sense to me every time I hear it," he said. "You tell me: Why should we tax the bus drivers and the retail clerks and the secretaries and the garage mechanics of this country so we can subsidize a gang of speculators who had the bad luck to take some losing gambles in oil wells and mining claims? You tell me, and if you can convince me then I'll think further about it."

Eaton knocked me back on my heels, and I must have stumbled and stuttered for several minutes before I could think of an answer. It was not really an answer, for there was no answer to the question as he had phrased it. The burden of my rebuttal was this: It was not a question of one group of taxpayers subsidizing another. The same argument could be made about widows and orphans subsidizing the meat packers and sugar barons through their write-offs. What I wanted was encouragement for Canadians to put their money into developing their country instead of into life-insurance policies and savings banks. I can remember blurting out something like:

"Look, Mr. Eaton, I'm out of money. I've invested all I could afford in that oil well and that is the end of it. But if I had the same advantages the Americans have in Canada, I'd get enough of my two thousand dollars back as a tax deduction so I'd have a nest-egg to put aside for another try."

"And that is just the point I'm trying to make," he replied. "You want the hard-working wage earners of this country to pay heavier taxes to subsidize you to gamble in the oil or mining business. That's where the money comes from, you know, from the taxes somebody else pays."

I insisted that there was more to it than taxes. Resource development led to the growth of a prosperous country. Off the top of my head I mentioned that the resource-development industries that Carnegie, Rockefeller, and Guggenheim had developed had returned a thousand dollars to the U.S. government in taxes for every dollar in incentives they had obtained in the beginning. I lost that one when he pointed out that their industries had been founded before there was any such thing as income tax, and they therefore had no tax incentives.

Getting nowhere, and running out of things to say, I wound up my argument with: "Well, it seems to me that, if nationality has any meaning at all, it ought to mean that a Canadian should have an advantage in his own country over any foreigner who comes in to develop the country's natural resources. I ought to be able to compete on even terms, at least. But look at what is happening in Alberta. Every American who comes in has so many advantages in his tax write-offs that you hear it described as spending ten-cent dollars."

Eaton's reply was that he had trouble enough with the Canadian income tax without worrying about the American tax system. But, he said, Canadians had one advantage the Americans did not have. Americans had a capital-gains tax, and if they cashed in on any success they had in Canada, they'd have to pay a U.S. capital-gains tax on their profits. "Any profits you make on your investments in Canada, you keep. You're asking us to subsidize your speculating and let you keep all your profits if you win. How long do you think we could live politically with that kind of a proposition?" To my reply that perhaps we should have a capital-gains tax in Canada along with the incentives, he held up his hands in horror. "God forbid!" he said. "God forbid that we should ever become involved in that administrative nightmare, that mare's nest!"

"Well, I know one thing for sure," I said as I got up to leave. "If things keep going on as they are going now, the Americans will wind up owning this country. You think you've got foreign-exchange problems now with five billion dollars of American investment in Canada? Wait till you see the trouble you'll have when that five billion becomes fifty billion, as it will the way it is growing."

He only smiled. "Mr. Gray," he said, as I left, "I don't give a damn who owns this country, as you put it, as long as we have the power to tax, because whoever has the power to tax calls the tune! And don't forget it."

I could hardly believe my ears. What kind of a country could we ever have when the top financial advisor of the national government didn't care who owned its resources? Surely he could not believe that. Perhaps it was just an unhappy lapse into hyperbole. But that could never be proved by the fiscal policies of successive Canadian administrations.

Half a decade later, on a trip to Washington, I picked up an enlightening footnote to that visit with the Assistant Deputy Minister of Finance. It was provided by a cynical gnome I encountered in the basement of the Capitol, when I was trying to discover how the Western Hemisphere Trade Corporation taxation amendment affected American oil companies operating in Canada. That amendment to the United States Internal Revenue Code was passed in 1942, to provide American corporations with an incentive to expand their trade with Latin America and to assist in the development of those countries. Companies that set up subsidiaries to invest in Latin America were granted a thirty-per-cent reduction in the taxes they would pay on any profits earned outside the United States.

Some years later, in the middle 1950s, there was a noticeable flurry of name-changing by American oil companies operating in Saskatchewan and Alberta. For example, the Standard Oil Company of Indiana's Canadian subsidiary was Stanolind Oil and Gas. It was renamed Pan American Petroleum, to identify it as a western-hemisphere company and to make it eligible for the lower American tax rate. By this time, it had become an important Canadian oil producer from its large holdings in the Pembina field west of Edmonton. The change of names, logic dictated, must have meant that the American companies were nearing a taxable-profit stage, so they were being tidied up, corporatively, in order to take advantage of the western-hemisphere tax rate. But how could that affect a company that would be taxable in Canada and come under the reciprocal taxation treaty Canada and the United States had made to govern cross-the-border companies?

Nobody in the Washington office of the Independent Petroleum

Association could supply an explanation; in the end, they made an appointment for me to see the man who, I was assured, knew more about corporation taxation and all its implications than anyone else in Washington. He was the assistant secretary of the Permanent Joint House and Senate Committee on Corporation Taxation. That committee's function was to iron out the differences that developed between the two legislative bodies on amendments to the Internal Revenue Code. As the committee was meeting infrequently that year, its permanent officials had lots of time for visiting firemen.

The name of the assistant secretary is gone from my memory, but the burden of what he told me that day is permanently embedded. He was a fascinating character in his mid-thirties, with a dishevelled and preoccupied aura, sitting in the midst of the messiest ten-by-twelve-foot room in Washington. He sat at a desk surrounded by paper. Reports and books overflowed from a table to stacks on the floor and to piles on a chair by his desk. He made room for me on the chair by starting another stack on the floor, and we talked for the better part of the afternoon.

"The reason you don't understand what is going on," he said, "is because you are thinking like people who draft tax laws. You are looking in the wrong end of the telescope. You are all like kids at a magic show; you are looking at the results of something else, and the magician's craft is to keep you from seeing that something else! Standard of Indiana can have a dozen reasons for putting its Canadian subsidiary into a western-hemisphere company; none will have anything to do with Canada. The tax treaty, which prevents double taxation, takes care of that. But it may be doing all kinds of things in Venezuela or Peru or in Brazil or Argentina, where there are no tax treaties. I'd have to look that up to be sure. But anyway, it, or any other company, can move things around between subsidiaries and come up with some whopping tax gains.

"The WHTC is typical of hundreds of amendments to the IRS Code that have been rushed through in the last twenty years. Suddenly the government discovers it's got a new problem. Okay, we solve the problem by amending this or that tax law. It's almost automatic. The only thing is, the people doing the amending have never demonstrated an ability to run an ice-cream concession in a Washington heat wave. They know nothing about how business works and never think of the long-term consequences of what they are doing. All they want is to get rid of a problem, no matter how.

"The big problem that led to the WHTC amendment back in 1942," he said, "was Adolf Hitler. All the tin-pot dictators in South America were playing footsie with Hitler, or threatening to. Okay. So we bribe American corporations to pour some millions into the development of those countries in the hope of getting them on to our side. And what happens? All the companies who have been doing business with Latin America all along stampede to get in under the WHTC umbrella and get that thirty-per-cent tax cut. Coffee companies, fruit companies, sugar companies, oil companies, and mining companies all get themselves involved. And you can stick the real development that results from the tax change in a pig's eye. So who knows what Indiana Standard has in mind when it converts a subsidiary away up in Canada into a WHTC company?

"I can tell you who knows," he went on. "The tax department of Indiana Standard knows, and if you don't think tax lawyers are more important than sales managers or plant managers, take a look at the tax departments all the major international companies maintain right here in Washington. They are immense. They have to be, because they keep track of the tax laws of all the states as well as the national government. And you want to know something about the tax laws of Australia, Patagonia, or Finland? Call the Jersey Standard tax department, and there'll be a guy there who can tell you.

"I don't know how things are in Canada, but in this country we've got a genuine horror about paying taxes. And that applies to the biggest corporations as well as to the newsdealer across the street. So there is a kind of guerrilla war going on among all the taxers in all the national, state, and local governments and agencies and all the taxpayers in all the states. And it is a war that has been going on for almost a hundred years. And if you want to know why the American international companies are engulfing the world, it is because they are applying on a world scale the lessons they learned avoiding taxes in the forty-eight states. Let me get at this by stating the principle that has emerged from this experience. The principle is: No state can raise its corporation tax rate above the level of other states and hope to increase its tax income from interstate companies over the long term.

"There are still lots of knuckleheads in state capitals who have never heard of that principle, and wouldn't subscribe to it if they had. But you can bet on this: the corporations not only accept it, they live by it! If you want to extend it internationally to countries like Canada, you could say that no country can raise its corporation tax rate above the American level and expect to benefit in the long run on its income from international companies. Sure, they can manage some quick profits, but only until the companies catch up and take remedial action.

"The name of the explanation is cost allocation, which is just accountants' jargon for saying we'll charge out our costs in such a way that we will show the highest profit where we pay the lowest taxes. Take General Motors, for example. It has assembly plants in a dozen states and component plants in another dozen. Suppose Texas raises corporation taxes and California lowers them so that the difference is important. GM can cut its taxable profits in Texas by a hundred methods of increasing its costs and diverting profits elsewhere. Or it can even transfer a market that was being serviced by its Texas subsidiary to a California subsidiary. The financial press is loaded with reports of intra-company switches of functions and service areas, and if a tax angle was not the positive factor in the move, it was certainly not a negative factor that prevented it being made.

"Internationally, take Jersey Standard for example. Its crude oil is produced in Venezuela by a Venezuela subsidiary, moved to England in a tanker registered in Liberia, refined in its English subsidiary, and sold through its same subsidiary. Where will the bulk of the profit on the transaction be made? By the subsidiary which will pay the lowest taxes, of course, and how can any of the other countries determine how the costs were artificially inflated or deflated when Jersey keeps the books?"

How indeed? And how indeed, I wondered later, could any country cope with the kind of manoeuvre Gulf Oil was able to make as a result of expertly manipulating the corporation tax laws of two countries?

Gulf Oil had become a substantial shareholder in British American Oil Company during the early war years, and by the early 1950s had most of the company's directors in its corporate pocket. It had arrived, corporatively, in force in Alberta in 1947, and soon had millions of acres under reservation. It made a number of spectacular natural-gas discoveries, including the Pincher Creek field. Under the forced-draft compulsion of President Truman's Korean War excess-profits taxes on its American income, Gulf was able to run its Canadian investment to eighty million dollars by 1955. Most of it, had it not been spent in Canada, would have gone to the U.S. government in taxes.

Gulf Canada, however, kept its own set of Canadian books; because it had no profits in Canada, the company had been able to accumulate its tax losses here, and would write them off all over again when the income from its oil and gas discoveries showed a profit. Instead of waiting for that to happen, it did a deal with British American Oil Company directors. It sold its entire Canadian holdings to British American and set off a flurry of public exultation on the editorial pages of Canadian newspapers. The deal,

Canadians were told, marked a new high point in Canadian enterprise. Here was a Canadian company buying out a giant American company, just the reverse of what had been happening. It only went to show the strength of Canadian enterprise.

It did nothing of the kind.

Nobody thought to ask: buying out Gulf with what? The purchase had been made, not with money, or even with interest-bearing debentures. It was made with the common shares of British American Oil Company, 8,335,648 of them, worth more than $240 million at then current market prices. What actually happened was that Gulf Oil, with those shares, was able to gain complete control of the largest Canadian integrated oil and natural-gas company in Canada and turn it into a wholly owned Gulf Oil subsidiary. As for British American Oil Company, it acquired all of Gulf's tax losses along with its new oil and gas reserves. That put it in a position where, despite a spectacular growth in earnings, it could just about stop paying taxes on its corporate profits. Between 1956 and 1962, BA earned a total of $210 million in net profits, on which it paid $16 million in income taxes.

I wondered a lot in those years about Ken Eaton and his lack of concern over who owned Canada. I wondered, in particular, how he would have explained the monstrous tax advantage conferred upon Gulf Oil to his retail clerks, taxi drivers, and auto mechanics, who were being taxed to make up for the losses suffered because of the way Gulf Oil juggernauted through the tax systems of two countries. But by this time, the era was long past when egg candlers, used-car salesmen, and editors of farm magazines could find room in the oil business for their curbstone syndicates. The land-leasing policies of the Alberta government had seen to that, and made the argument over tax concessions to Canadians, to enable them to compete with Americans, highly irrelevant.

13
Like a Silver-tongued Orator at a Deaf-mute Convention

Save in the wackier fringes of the Hollywood milieu, divorce proceedings are seldom begun as soon as the honeymoon is over. And that was true of my involvement with the *Farm and Ranch Review*. The honeymoon phase had about run its course by the end of my first year in Calgary. During that period, it became clear that the gaudy prospects held out in the courtship stage would turn out to be as ethereally unreachable between editor and publisher as between swain and light-o'-love.

Our honeymoon ended when I became convinced that, as far as the goals of the *Farm and Ranch Review* were concerned, Marsh Porter and I lived in different worlds. His interests began with the editorial page and ended with the bottom line on the profit-and-loss statement, and there was a complete void in between. My interest was in creating the kind of publication that would be recognized by its readers as the outstanding magazine of its kind in Canada. In the process, it would take me on an ego trip which would be exultantly capped by my being recognized as the latter-day Dafoe of the Canadian West. That dream died, not with a bang but from malnutrition, yet it was many months before the idea of divorce became inescapable.

It was once axiomatic among newspaper people that the readers of their paper always thought they knew better how to publish newspapers than the people who were doing the job. This was evidenced by the unending flow of advice from the sidelines about what to put in and what to leave out of the finished product. Fortunately, the readers' ideas tended to divide about equally between those who were outraged because something was published and those who were outraged because something was not. Editors thus felt safe in ignoring the clamour from the sidelines and going their own merry way, frequently with very elastic standards for guidance.

It did not take me long to discover that Porter, like readers everywhere, had some queer ideas about publishing and publications. It seemed obvious to me that, in order to achieve any goal, either of profit or of prestige, we had to turn the *Farm and Ranch* into a magazine the farmers would subscribe to because of its intrinsic worth to them and to their families. The opportunities for improvement, in what was really little more than a junk-heap for throw-away material, were almost limitless. Once we had the product, we could launch a subscription campaign that would put us right up there with the *Country Guide* and the *Family Herald.* Porter regarded all this as doing things the hard way. The way to increase circulation was simply to hold another contest. And this in fact was what was done. A guessing-game contest was held with a total of five thousand dollars in prizes, and it brought in twenty-five thousand new subscriptions and renewals at the regular rate of ten years for one dollar.

There was never to be any material evidence that my complaints about the slipshod and tardy production of the magazine were heard. The idea of improving the quality of the paper on which the magazine was printed was rejected, on the grounds that we were better off using the lowest-grade newsprint because the farmers eventually would file the magazine on a nail in their outdoor privies, where it would be available for perusal, as well as . . . Nor did Porter attach any importance to getting the magazine to its subscribers on a regular schedule each month. If the interests of the Western Printing operation dictated that it should be delayed, he accepted that as sufficient reason for the delay. No amount of complaining on my part changed anything at the printing end of the operation. To Porter, the only things that mattered were the editorials. The rest of the magazine's forty pages were intrinsically inconsequential and were simply a convenient carrier to get the editorials to the readers. If any of the delegates to the Alberta Wheat Pool annual meeting mentioned having read our editorials, he was easily convinced that the farmers of western Canada were hanging on the fenceposts waiting for the *Farm and Ranch Review.*

Any editor given as free a hand to roam the world of ideas as I was would, of course, have shared Porter's enthusiasm for the editorial page. It was not long before I was filling not one, but two pages a month. And a month seldom passed without a sharply barbed answer to the arguments of the *Free Press* in its everlasting pillorying of the Canadian Wheat Board and the British Wheat contracts. If it had become the unpaid propagandist for the Winnipeg Grain Exchange, I willingly played the same role for the western wheat pools.

As the West turned into the 1950s, a good eighty per cent of the farm homes of Alberta were still without electrical power or inside plumbing. And the province, alone in Canada, was without any kind of government cost-sharing rural electrification system; farmers who wanted power on their farms had to form their own co-operatives and buy their electricity from the Calgary Power Company. Thus, our farm-power crusade ran head-on into the powerful Calgary Power Company and the Social Credit government. And, of course, the strictures against Alberta's anti-Canadian resources-development policies did nothing to endear the magazine to the Manning government. But for the first years of my association with the *Farm and Ranch Review*, my main priorities were elsewhere than the editorial page. I was convinced that the key to the success of any magazine had to be in the wide net of interest it cast to attract its subscribers to its columns. Much of the editorializing was pretty heavy and remote stuff for subscribers who, overwhelmingly, were still mired in a pioneer environment, and still read by Coleman lamps. To entice them into looking at the editorial page, we had to bait the rest of the magazine with material that hit them where they lived. That was a concept as old as journalism itself.

Once, in a journalism textbook, I encountered a story, probably apocryphal, about the late Arthur Brisbane when he was the editor of the New York *Journal*. After hectoring his news editors over the pedestrian dullness of the writing of the *Journal*'s reporters, and getting nowhere, he took matters into his own hands. He ordered a canvas sign with letters five feet high and had it stretched along the wall facing the reporters' desks. It read:

THEY DON'T WANT TO READ IT.

Brisbane's message was that, unless great skill was used to attract the reader's attention to their stories, lazy-minded readers would not bother to read what they were writing. They would glance at the headlines and ignore the rest. The test of a reporter's art was not alone in his writing; it was also in the state of mind he brought to his story, his skill in devising imaginative ways of telling it.

My problem at the *Farm and Ranch*, however, was more difficult than Brisbane's at the *Journal*. His readers had plunked down their money and picked up their paper with the firm intention of reading something in it. In the main, our subscribers were people who over many years had been getting the magazine because they had filled in a coupon in a circulation contest. There was a difference. How great a difference I discovered inadvertently when I wandered one day into a country post office to get the address of a farmer I was looking for.

Most country post offices in those days kept a large cardboard carton on the customers' side of the counter near the wicket as a convenient receptacle for junk mail. To my chagrin, I noticed that one carton was half full of the latest issue of the *Farm and Ranch Review*. I retrieved a handful and was examining the address labels when the lady postmistress said:

"Oh, that darn nuisance!" She pointed to another carton on her side of the counter containing several more copies. "These are the dead people," she said. "It's like the acne, that magazine—once you get it, you can't get rid of it even after you die. They subscribe to it and then never read it when it comes in. No wonder. One family out here subscribes to six copies. If I didn't have that box out there, we'd be up to our knees in them every month."

At that moment, it was easy for me to resist the temptation to introduce myself as the editor of Canada's least-wanted monthly magazine. Instead, I said something about people cancelling subscriptions they did not want. The postmistress said that she had once taken the trouble to cut off a bunch of address labels and send them to the office with "dead" written across them. She couldn't understand why the magazine kept coming. I could have explained that advertising rates were based on subscription lists, and what the advertisers did not know never hurt the *Farm and Ranch Review*'s advertising income. I could have explained, but I didn't.

The memory of that cardboard carton became a recurring nightmare. It danced in front of my typewriter and triggered a succession of "what-the-hell-is-the-use" fits of depression, a mood that was heightened by the fact that I was consistently unsuccessful in evoking a response of any kind to the editorials I was writing. It was probably true that for every copy of the *Farm and Ranch Review* discarded in post offices, a score were taken home and looked at, if not read. That somebody was reading part of it was demonstrated by the response we got to several of our features. But months would pass without a single response to any of my editorials, and this was probably what contributed to the development of my trash-box syndrome. On my trips around the country, the post offices became irresistible magnets that pulled me in for a masochistic inspection of the junk-mail receptacles, in search of copies of the *Farm and Ranch Review*. I was seldom disappointed.

So how do you reach the subscribers who habitually throw your magazine away unopened? I decided that it could be done by word of mouth after the magazine became loaded with articles that would perk the interest of those who at least glanced through it. So I set out to recruit a large stable of regular contributors whose expertise in their fields was widely accepted. I got Harry Hargrave of Lethbridge to contribute pieces on irrigated pastures; Jack Stothart of Lacombe, the authority on swine breeding, reported on his experiments; J. W. G. MacEwan, a farmer-professor of animal husbandry, became a monthly contributor on livestock; Bert Harp of Morden, the horticultural expert, provided a regular gardening column. Then we had such expert farm writers as Tom Leach in British Columbia, Frank Steele of Lethbridge, and Jack Denhoff of Saskatoon covering general farm subjects. Ben Malkin did a monthly column on world affairs; Harry Boyle wrote nostalgic pieces from Ontario; and Kerry Wood was the nature contributor from Red Deer.

Porter's contribution to the stable of writers was the Reverend Frank Morley, the pastor of the Grace Presbyterian Church in Calgary, whose theology Porter greatly admired. I found it incomprehensible, but for the duration of my tenure, Morley was a regular contributor to the magazine. It was Morley who inadvertently set off the greatest controversy in the magazine's history. He had done a piece on Heaven and Hell in which he argued that the universal yearning for Heaven which imbued all mankind was in itself a proof of immortality. Or something like that.

In my efforts to stir up interest in our letters-to-the-editor page, I had occasionally stooped to the old newspaper trick of writing a "Mother of Eight" letter designed to start an argument when dropped on to the page. In the early spring of 1953, I produced such a teaser that mildly challenged Morley's thesis, signed it James Henry, and date-lined it Lloydminster, where, I had been careful to make sure, there were no James Henrys in the phone book.

Any doubt about Alberta's being the Bible Belt of the western world was quickly dispelled by that fake letter. The replies flowed in at the rate of twenty to thirty a day. For the next couple of months I could have filled the magazine with them. It was the first and last time in my editing career I found myself having to select one letter for publication out of every twenty received. The abuse that was poured on me for running such a scurrilous letter was wondrous to behold. At least eighty per cent of the replies quoted scripture to confound our devil's disciple.

It was a chastening experience, for which I was completely unprepared. I was convinced I had been writing about issues that vitally affected the farmers where they lived. But the response from the letter writers indicated that they could not have cared less about getting back their mineral resources, about the way in which their country's natural resources were being alienated to foreigners, about farm electrification, about the threat of the egghead fraternity to the experimental-farm system that had served them so well, about the threat of the educational egghead fraternity to the educational system, even, indeed, about the threat that legalization of margarine posed for the dairy farmers. But Heaven and Hell? Now *there* was an issue that got the farmers' hearts to pounding and outrage to flow from pen to paper!

Outranking all of the writers I recruited in the importance of their contribution to the magazine over the long pull was Joseph Fitch, a maverick agronomist at the Swift Current Experimental Farm who wrote under the pseudonym of Joseph Paul. He contributed series after series of superb articles on soils management. He anticipated Rachel Carson by a full decade in a series attacking indiscriminate use of chemical herbicides and insecticides. His greatest feat was the war he started with the Science Service bureaucrats who were then reaching out to devour the experimental-farm system.

The Dominion experimental farms had been established in the 1880s to discover the best varieties of crops the settlers could grow on the open prairies of western Canada. As the name implied, the farms experimented not only with plants to grow but with varying ways of growing them. Thus at Morden, Manitoba, the farm developed hundreds of varieties of fruits and vegetables that ultimately were planted and grown all over the West. Indian Head did the same with trees and shrubs. Swift Current was the great soils laboratory; Lethbridge was the centre of irrigation experimentation; Lacombe was the place where new varieties of swine were developed, and so on.

At each of these farms were men whom the farmers of the West came rightly to regard as the fountainheads of wisdom in their specialties. W. R. Leslie at Morden, L. B. Thomson and Grant Denike at Swift Current, and Asael Palmer at Lethbridge were all glittering stars in the agricultural firmament. Not only did the farmers come from miles around to consult with them, and leave loaded down with advice, but the experimental-farm people ranged far and wide to bring the fruits of their experiments to the farmers on the land.

Then, with the departure of Edgar Archibald from the experimental farms' directorate, winds of change of cyclonic proportions began to blow through the institution, winds that would eventually turn the entire institution into a gigantic boondoggle for PH D's. Like so much else that happens in Canada, this disaster was triggered in part by a mild dispute between the provinces and the Dominion over constitutional jurisdiction.

During the 1930s, it was the experimental farms which mounted the intensive drives that ultimately nailed down the blowing soil and reclaimed the drought-damaged western crop-lands. Working through direct mail and the country papers, the experimental farms drifted into the publishing of informational bulletins for the assistance of the farmers. That ran afoul of the empire builders in the provincial departments of agriculture. Ottawa, they chorused to each other, is invading our sacred jurisdiction—education. These informational bulletins are just as much educational publications as any textbook! What Ottawa should do is tell us what they are doing and we'll take it to the farmers through the brand new agricultural-representative networks we are organizing all across the provinces!

And this, curiously enough, was also the argument of the people running Science Service, an offshoot of the experimental farms wherein scientists hived away in Ottawa laboratories occupied their time with fundamental research into various obscure and esoteric aspects of plant and animal life and death.

Incredibly, J. G. Gardiner, the plain-dirt farmer-Minister of Agriculture, and Gordon Taggart, the Deputy Minister and one-time head of the Swift Current Experimental Farm, both bought these arguments. The word went out from Ottawa that relations between the farm press and the Dominion experimental farms were to be broken off. Even worse, so were all relations between the experimental farms and the farmers on the land. Even the business of supplying farmers with experimental seedlings to test under farm conditions was abolished. Naturally, the instructions in the beginning were honoured more in the breach than in the acceptance. But all the while, the egghead bureaucracy in Ottawa was agitating for the conversion of the whole experimental-farm system into regional laboratories for "fundamental research."

What was wanted was no longer the out-on-the-farms kind of testing that had saved the West in the dustbowl years. The name of the new game was to be massive production of scientific papers for the journals of the various disciplines, papers which could be listed on the experimenters' résumés when they put in for promotion but which otherwise gathered dust on the ever-expanding library shelves of the bureaucracy.

I got to know the Morden Experimental Farm well early in my newspaper career, and when I moved to Calgary, one of my first steps was to search through Morden and all the other farms for possible contributors to our pages. It was not long before I became caught up in the struggle between the Science Service test-tubers and the people dedicated to growing things. By 1952, the ultimate victory of the campaign of Science Service to absorb the experimental farms was becoming inevitable. For example, Dick Painter, head of the entomological laboratory at Lethbridge, was booted upstairs to a high-sounding but quite meaningless liaison job. That was his reward for the twenty years he had spent touring the prairies, winter and summer, showing farmers and ranchers how to protect their livestock against warble flies and other insect pests, instead of publishing papers in the entomological journals.

With the help of Joe Fitch, the *Farm and Ranch Review* mounted an editorial campaign against the Science Service take-over of the farms. Writing under his pseudonym of Joseph Paul, Fitch delivered a stinging, four-part attack on the Science Service paper-chase, while I wrote editorials urging that it be abolished and its research programs turned over to the universities where they belonged.

But what was all this activity worth if the subscribers to the *Farm and Ranch Review* never opened their magazines? An opportunity to needle them into changing their habits came from a chance conversation with Arthur Milton "Scotty" Shoults, who was running the James Lovick Advertising Agency in Calgary. By some wily manoeuvre, he had latched on to the Massey-Ferguson local advertising account in Alberta, at about the time Gordon Love began pressing vigorously for some sort of melding of the interests of the *Farm and Ranch Review* and radio station CFCN. Love was intent mainly on finding a way of mounting a campaign through the magazine to attack the CBC for the way it was curtailing his radio station's profit-making appetites. That was one issue on which I dug in my heels and wrote nothing. It was Shoults who came up with the proposal that I might satisfy Love by doing a couple of CFCN radio programs a week on farm topics for Massey-Ferguson.

That was the beginning of the series "I'd Rather Be a Farmer!" which we put together twice a week for the next two years. My interest in everything involving agriculture had ballooned since coming to Calgary. I became friendly with Charles Yule, the general manager of the Calgary Stampede and the outstanding beef-cattle judge of his time. I followed him around the livestock barns and tried desperately to absorb his patient lectures on how to tell a good cow from a poor one, how to identify the qualities that made one bull a prize-winner and another roast beef. Likewise, when I discovered that Rex Dwigans was one of the best judges of horse-flesh around, I picked his brains to a fare-thee-well. Then, on my twenty-three acres of horse pasture, I did some experimenting with plots of registered seed and reseeded the prairie wool to tame grass. From Halloka Gloria, the Saddlebred mare I had bought at the Spence sale two years before, I raised a superb palomino colt which the Alberta government shipped to the Royal Winter Fair; I came home with the reserve junior-championship rosette, to say nothing of a photo of my colt on the cover of *Saturday Night* magazine.

Left to my own devices, I'd gladly have chucked my journalism career to become a full-time farmer, because I was fascinated by everything about production from the soil. But that would have taken resources beyond my reach, so, in 1952, I settled for talking about it on the radio, and replaying the editorials and articles I was running in the *Farm and Ranch Review*.

Those who knew my limitations rightly regarded my performance as an exercise frequently flawed by fraud. But the response from CFCN listeners was a pleasant ego massage; the money was good, and the program attracted a lot of attention to the *Farm and Ranch Review*, particularly when several other Alberta radio stations picked it up. Unhappily, my career as a radio spieler came to a crashing halt the following year, after a change of sponsors and for the most improbable reason on record. Crows.

Nudged in the direction of organic farming by Joe Fitch, I had become an avid reader of the gospel according to Friend Sykes and Newman Turner, the British natural farmers. From them and from their American counterparts, I had gained an almost limitless supply of ideas for broadcasts that led me far afield from the prosaic contents of the farm press. I discovered that once one starts doubting conventional wisdom, all sorts of strange thought processes begin to emerge. A developed interest in the value of weeds as the saviours of wind-threatened soil led naturally to an interest in the value of predators to the maintenance of ecological balance. Almost without being aware of it, I found myself taking public umbrage at the antics of the southern Alberta sportsmen who were waging a war of extinction against coyotes. They were destroying them with lethally explosive bait, hunting them from airplanes, and running them to death with half-ton trucks, wolfhounds, and killer dogs unleashed on the exhausted animals. Defending predators is like eating peanuts—once you start, you cannot stop. Having set myself up in business as the radio defender of coyotes, I also took crows and magpies under my wing.

This was in the days when Alberta offered bounties of a nickel a pair for crows' feet, to encourage farm boys to slaughter all the crows in sight with their .22 rifles. Having just had several water troughs perforated by boys hunting crows and gophers with .22's, I did a broadcast roundly condemning the crow hunters for the destruction of a species that was an indispensable part of the ornithic kingdom. The broadcast was heard by the leaders of the Alberta Fish and Game Association, who rushed immediately to the sponsor of the program, the makers of Red Head gasoline and lubricating products. Their message was short and to the point:

Get that guy Gray off the air or we will organize a boycott of your products all over Alberta!

The owner of the Red Head company got the message. After my defence of the crows, I never did another sponsored radio broadcast. But it was my radio deal with Shoults that led ultimately to my divorce from the *Farm and Ranch Review*, which inevitably took an unconscionably long time to happen. The satisfaction I was getting from my new fascination with all phases of farming and ranching was diluted each month by the struggle to get the magazine out to the readers in presentable shape, and by my sense of the futility of trying to achieve a public impact through its effect on the minds of prairie farmers.

What I failed to realize was that the economic climate in which our readers existed bore no resemblance to anything they had ever experienced before. Certainly, it bore no resemblance to conditions of life I had come to know through the royal commissions of the 1930s and 1940s. For one thing, it was becoming possible to grow profitable crops under climatic conditions which would have spelled crop failure fifteen years before. For another, the Second World War had turned everything else around. From an economic environment in which nothing the western farmers produced could be sold at a profit, markets had developed for everything they could produce, and at prices which, at the very worst, earned them a return for their labour.

By common consent of the headline writers, the 1930s were "the Dirty Thirties" and the 1940s "the Roaring Forties." For the prairie farmers, the dirtiness of the thirties was not only related to the economic collapse that reduced them to penury; it also identified the succession of black blizzards created by wind-blown topsoil that obscured the sun and drove uncounted thousands of farm families off their farms and out of the country. And the roar of the forties was not only the cacophony of exploding shells in the worldwide holocaust; it was also becoming the new sound that was heard across the land from the roaring engines of rubber-tired tractors hauling the newly invented tillage and harvesting equipment that was revolutionizing agricultural production. And that roaring of the late forties was very much the direct result of the dirtiness of the thirties, and of the exertions of the prairie farmers under the leadership of as superbly dedicated a team of agricultural scientists as one country ever produced.*

* The story of the conquest of the prairie dustbowl is the theme of my book *Men Against the Desert* (Saskatoon: Prairie Books, 1967).

It was generally believed, as the dustbowl developed in the early thirties, that the western wheatlands had simply lapsed into another cycle of dry years, similar to many in the past. So it was assumed that, when the drought lifted, the dust storms would pass and timely rains would again produce bumper crops and bountiful harvests. But to a coterie of Dominion experimental-farms scientists, led by Asael Palmer at Lethbridge, L. B. Thomson at Swift Current, and E. S. Archibald in Ottawa, the truth lay elsewhere, in the cultural practices the farmers had been following since the time of Joseph in Egypt—ploughing under the topsoil after each harvest and cultivating the seedbed to acceptable tilth.

It was a practice that was carried to an extreme on the western prairies, where the annual rainfall was insufficient to sustain a viable agriculture. Nineteenth-century agronomists, however, had discovered that the moisture deficiency could be overcome by using two years' precipitation to produce one year's crop. This entailed leaving a third or a half of the land out of crop each year to store moisture for the following year. That, however, required that the fallow fields be cultivated throughout the summer to keep weeds from using up the stored moisture. Repeated cultivations turned the surface of the soil into a fine dust mulch, and this finely powdered soil was supposed to seal the surface and prevent the sun from sucking out the moisture.

Long before the dust storms came with the 1930s, however, Asael Palmer began to have doubts about the dust-mulch theory. In the high-wind country around Lethbridge, it became apparent that the best farmers, who were the most conscientious summer-fallow cultivators, had the worst wind-erosion problems. Conversely, the poorer farmers, who left the stubble on their fallow and neglected their cultivating, had the least problem with wind erosion. Ergo, the rougher the soil surface was kept, the less damage the wind could cause. Palmer embarked with such vigour on a crusade to stand the whole science of agronomy on its head that he soon earned the nickname of "Trash-cover" Palmer.

Two of Palmer's earliest converts, Sidney Barnes and W. S. Chepil at the Swift Current Experimental Farm, put together a series of soil-moisture tests that completely demolished the dust-mulch theory and demonstrated that the black blizzards were more a man-made than a natural phenomenon. The three, as early as 1934, were able to put together an authoritative text on the measures that had to be taken to control wind erosion. Their manual became the guide, over the next four years, for the massive counter-attacks that were mounted against the soil-destroying winds at hundreds of localities in Alberta, Saskatchewan, and Manitoba.

Emergency measures like ridging the fields across the wind stopped the deserts from spreading. But what was to prevent them from recurring if the farmers continued to plough and disc and harrow as they had in the past? The answer was nothing short of the development of an entirely new system of tilling the soil. That in turn meant the need to invent new equipment, which would make it possible to plough the land and leave the stubble on the surface to protect it from the wind.

This need for something better set off a veritable frenzy of tinkering and experimenting across the prairies. Farmers, university professors, blacksmiths, auto mechanics, agronomists, all became embroiled in experimental orgies in the small-town blacksmith shops, garages, implement sheds, and farmyards. They experimented with chisel ploughs, duck-foot ploughs, disc ploughs, but mostly they tinkered with one-way discs. It took them a full decade to perfect the discer to a point where the implement companies became sufficiently interested to appropriate their models and put them into production. They came on to the market at the close of the war, with the rubber-tired tractor, without which the big one-way discers could not have done the job for which they were designed.

With the discers came the Noble blades, which cut a four-foot swath inches below the surface of the soil and left the stubble-covered topsoil undisturbed. The one-way discer and the Noble blade were destined to revolutionize grain-production methods, not only in what John Palliser had called the northern tip of the Great American Desert, but clear down to the Gulf of Mexico and ultimately to the semi-arid areas of the world. And all this began to happen just as the farmers were emerging at last from the economic morass of the 1930s on to the high ground that unlimited wartime demand for their production had built.

That change came not from any recovery of farm prices from the Depression levels. Indeed, in 1944, farm spokesmen could claim with justification that the price ceiling the government imposed on wheat alone had cost the farmers more than $1.2 billions. It was volume production that did the trick, that and the return of the rains that made volume production possible. Farmers were exhorted to get into the production of chickens, turkeys, beef, and hogs as a patriotic duty. And they did so with a vengeance. Between 1939 and 1943, they doubled their hog production, trebled poultry and egg production, doubled milk production. With positive encouragement from the government to switch from wheat to coarse grains for livestock, the farmers responded so enthusiastically that they produced an annual wartime average of almost $300 million worth of oats and barley compared with the $50 million worth of 1938. Just about everything else was in proportion. Between 1937 and 1945, the income of prairie farmers jumped from under $300 million to almost $1.1 billion. As important as the growth of income was the fact that they got to keep a larger proportion of it than ever before. Thanks to the decade-long operation of the Farmers' Creditors Arrangements Act, the debt load the farmers had been carrying for twenty years was drastically reduced, when it was not wiped out completely.

So throughout the war years, the farmers could afford to tinker with machinery, and to visit around and exchange ideas with each other. When the new tillage, haulage, and harvesting equipment rolled off the assembly lines after the war, they were able to queue up at the implement dealers' order desks. Between 1946 and 1951, they placed orders for more than 80,000 new tractors, almost 40,000 new combines, and 55,000 new farm trucks.

They did all this without the outpouring of rancorous umbrage that had been an agrarian characteristic from the earliest days of settlement. The wheat growers now had the Canadian Wheat Board to market their grain instead of having to rely on the Grain Exchange futures market. The import duties were abolished for farm implements in 1944. Prices were high enough to provide even moderately efficient farmers with a comfortable living. It was a condition of life that the rebellious Progressives of the 1920s would have regarded as the achievement of Nirvana. The fires of agrarian revolt that had been stoked to white heat through the eras of Ed Partridge, R. C. Henders, young Tom Crerar, Henry Wise Wood, Louise McKinney, Jim Weir, A. J. McPhail, Jack Wesson, Aaron Sapiro, and Colin Burnell were doused forever. It was hardly surprising that there was not a farm leader on the horizon in the 1950s who could attract a big enough crowd of outraged agrarians to fill a woodshed.

If all the old issues had been eroded by time, there were clearly new issues developing that should have aroused the farmers. I seized upon one which I was sure would reverberate through the rural communities. That was the beginning of the California educational mafia's take-over of the prairie educational systems.

In the early 1950s, the newest gimmick of the educationalists was the intelligence test. In Calgary, children were being "streamed" into academic and vocational careers as ten- and eleven-year-olds on the basis of intelligence tests. I had to fight the system clear up to the superintendent of schools before I was able to change my children's streaming. And it was only done to the accompaniment of the direst warnings against the disasters that were inevitable if I persisted in my wrong-headedness. None of the predictions ever came to pass. My own experience made me particularly receptive to the message of Dr. Hilda Neatby's book, *So Little for the Mind*. In it, she took on the whole educational bureaucracy, which was beginning the process of overloading the system with hordes of administrators, specialists, resource people, technicians, and God knows what else, to the everlasting detriment of the learning process.

I seized upon the Neatby book as a launching pad for my own editorial crusade, and expected that it would produce a blizzard of letters from concerned parents, teachers, and school trustees. The response would have comfortably filled a gnat's eye. It consisted mainly of carping letters, like the one from a Saskatchewan Bachelor of Education who was delighted to discover some grammatical mistakes in the editorials I had written.

The frustrations of a rebel without a cause, difficult as they are to bear, can hardly compare with the mental turmoil to be endured by a crusader without an audience. As the years passed, I began to feel more and more like a silver-tongued orator who had blundered on to the podium of a deaf-mutes' convention. The solution to my dilemma was, of course, simple enough—quit and do something else. Occasionally I would make a tentative move back towards daily journalism, but as that always involved moving some place else, I always backed away. I once actually tried to revive the radio broadcasts, with the prairie wheat pools as sponsors. But all three had reasons for rejecting the proposal.

The problem solved itself in 1954, when Marsh Porter was rewarded for his service to the Liberal party with an appointment to the Supreme Court of Alberta, and Scotty Shoults came up with an offer to me to take over the publication of the *Western Oil Examiner*. In the hiatus between the two, Porter and Dinning sold their interests in the *Farm and Ranch* to Gordon Love. When I asked them about my promised share, I was told by each of them separately that the only way you can realize on a capital gain is to sell out. I was still employed by the *Farm and Ranch*, and hence would have to look to Love for my arrangements. Love denied all responsibility.

Clearly, as Stanley Holloway's Ramsbottoms said after the lion ate little Albert and his cane with the "horse's 'ead 'andle," somebody ought to be summonsed. In my case, somebody would have to be sued. But I could not find a single lawyer in any of the first-flight legal firms in Calgary to take my case, despite a diligent search, so I settled for becoming the editor of the *Western Oil Examiner*. As for the *Farm and Ranch Review*, it was soon caught up in the television revolution, as every advertising agency in the business began diverting all the money available from farm publications to television advertising. Within two years, its advertising was down to almost nothing; the advertising drought eventually carried it off completely, along with the *Family Herald*, the *Saskatchewan Farmer*, and a number of general-readership magazines.

When I took it over in the spring of 1955, the *Western Oil Examiner* was a relic of a far-gone past. It was born during the Turner Valley boom of the 1920s, had miraculously survived the Dirty Thirties, and was on the scene when Turner Valley Royalties blew in with such spectacular results in 1936. Unlike the trade papers that came later to service the technical needs of the oil industry, the *Western Oil Examiner* was an investor-orientated publication purveying the news from the fields to the share-buying public. When I came on the scene, an effort was being made to convert it into an oil-industry trade journal, which would circulate exclusively within the industry and depend on the advertising of the service and supply companies that sold equipment and services to the exploration, pipeline, and refining segments of the industry.

To the job of editing and publishing a trade paper, I brought a massive ignorance, which was in no way a handicap, according to the sales pitch I got from Shoults. He was running the paper, he said, for a group of independent oilmen headed by R. A. Brown, Jr., whose coup in 1952 had nudged Porter and his friends out of Home Oil Company. Shoults said he had shown Brown some of my early editorials on the government's land policies and gas exports, and Brown was convinced that I was the person needed to turn the *Western Oil Examiner* into a sounding board for the independent Canadian companies who were battling to survive in the oil business. It sounded like an opportunity to return to the kind of writing I had been doing in the *Farm and Ranch Review* five years before. And as things turned out, that was what happened, only more so.

To my caveat that I knew nothing whatever about the technical side of the oil business, and had no news sources within the business, Shoults and Brown answered in terms reminiscent of the Marsh Porter of seven years before. Brown had all the experts anybody needed; all I had to do was ask them to help, and they'd give me an intensive course in everything from land-leasing to gas processing.

What neither explained before it was much too late was that there was no place in trade-journal publishing for a magazine with an editor who took sides in the internecine feuds of the industry. What all industries required of their trade papers was the preservation of a monolithic defence of industry interests. The cardinal sin in trade publishing was to become involved in disputes between segments of an industry that weakened the industry's ability to present a united front to the outside world.

It was thus, in blissful ignorance, during the first weeks of my editorship in 1955, that I planted the seeds which led to the inevitable destruction of the *Western Oil Examiner*.

14
Anti-American S.O.B.

There is no convenient metaphor to describe the changes that occurred in the Alberta oil industry between the discovery of Leduc in 1947 and the onset of 1955, when I took over as editor of the *Western Oil Examiner*. The plight of a Canadian mouse co-habiting with an American elephant might have been appropriate enough, if attention was focused only on North America. But when the outside world came into the picture, the American elephant itself became the mouse, a mouse reacting in panic to external forces it could neither understand nor control.

More than a score of new oilfields with over five thousand wells capable of producing more than 450,000 barrels of oil a day were in operation in Alberta. Saskatchewan had more than eight hundred wells on production, and even Manitoba had its own infant oil industry in its southwestern corner. Canadian crude oil was now supplying Canadian needs clear down to western Ontario. There were even those who were enchanted by the notion that California itself might be served by Canadian crude oil, once a loading dock was built in Vancouver.

On the other side of the world, oil development had been paralleling what was happening in western Canada, but on a scale that reduced what we had been doing to mere dribs and drabs. One well tapping into the fabulous Kirkuk reservoir in Iraq was producing more oil than five hundred wells in Leduc. New discoveries in the Persian Gulf were so rich that the world would soon be awash in a flood of surplus crude oil. Kuwait, previously unknown to the Western world, was producing fifty thousand barrels of oil a day when Leduc came in. In 1954, it was up to one million barrels a day and climbing steadily. Iran, whose fields had been shut down during the dispute over nationalization, was coming back into production. Saudi Arabia was up to one million barrels a day. So was Iraq, almost, and the discoveries in the Neutral Zone and the shiekdom of Qatar would soon add to the mounting surplus.

Of the implications for Alberta of what was happening on the other side of the world, no one in Alberta seemed to have more than an inkling. There was only the realization that the trend to ever-expanding markets for all the oil Alberta could produce had been blunted. One obvious development was that more and more oil was being discovered in Saskatchewan, and it was moving into Interprovincial Pipeline's markets ahead of Alberta oil. That forced Alberta to increase restrictions on production, until the province would only be able to find markets for half the oil it was capable of producing. And that surely was a far cry from 1948, when a Saskatchewan refinery bought into the Leduc play in order to obtain an assured supply of crude for its operation.

Not only was the cutting back of flush production hurting the industry, the price had also dropped sharply. As the Interprovincial Pipeline was extended steadily from Edmonton to Regina, to the Lakehead, and on to Sarnia, the price at the wellhead was reduced each time to absorb the additional transportation charges. From a high of $3.47 a barrel in 1947, the price of Leduc crude was down to $2.60 at the end of 1954.

So the oil industry the *Western Oil Examiner* hoped to serve was not exactly at the peak of a boom when I arrived to edit the weekly magazine. The squeeze on the smaller Canadian companies, in particular, was coming from several directions. Many of them financed their drilling programs out of revenue produced from their successful wells. The production was frequently hypothecated to the banks as security for loans to accelerate their exploration. When wells producing 70 barrels of $3.25 oil a day were cut to 40 barrels at $2.50, oil-company executives dodged phone calls from bankers and cut back on drilling commitments. The government, for its part, became uneasy over the hundreds of thousands of acres of drilling permits held by the American companies, which were defaulting on commitments to drill. When the government made small noises about getting on with fulfilling the commitments, the companies threatened to abandon the leases and stop paying rentals on them.

On the other hand, there were Canadian companies who had money to drill with but were frozen out of all the favourable drilling areas by the eighty-four-million-acre blanket with which the major companies had covered the province. To get some place to drill, they were forced to take farm-outs (sub-leases from the major companies), take all the risks, and then cut in the companies on the other side of the deal for the bulk of the production they developed. Home Oil was such a company, for it had the income from eight thousand barrels of oil a day that it was producing from Turner Valley, Leduc-Woodbend, and Redwater. The terms it was forced to accept to get a farm-out of land to drill on in the grizzly-bear country in north-central Alberta was typical.

The Virginia Hills forest 150 miles northwest of Edmonton was as close to being an untouched wilderness area as there was in Canada. Trails had to be cut through the brush to enable men on horseback to get into it, and then weeks were consumed clearing a way in for drilling equipment. Ultimately, the wildcat struck oil at a depth of over nine thousand feet and opened up a vast new area to successful exploration. But the return to Home Oil was never in proportion to the risk taken, for it was required to return two-thirds of the production from the well, and the field it developed, to the original reservation holders. Naturally, the independents clamoured for the government to cancel leases that were in default and turn them over to companies who were prepared to drill. Throughout the 1950s, that was the prickliest of issues for a government that had no stomach for facing up to the international companies on any issue. The long decade of empty treasuries was too deeply etched in the memories of the politicians for them ever to consider antagonizing the goose that had laid more than $580 million worth of golden eggs, from lease sales, rentals, and royalties, during the post-Leduc decade.

So the attention of everybody in 1955–56 was focused on how to increase markets, as it had been for two years. Unless new markets could be found, the drilling up of new fields was going to worsen the financial position of just about everybody in the business. It was at this moment that a crisis situation was developing in Washington, because a similar concern was being expressed in much louder voices by the Texas oil producers. Oil imports were pouring into the huge refineries on the Atlantic seaboard from Venezuela and the Middle East. When the imports topped one million barrels a day, the lobbyists for the Texas and Louisiana oil producers began to cry havoc and let slip the dogs of political warfare at the heels of the Eisenhower administration. It would not be long before the administration would decide that foreign oil imperilled the security of the United States, by retarding the search for new American reserves that the U.S. would need to have instantly available in time of war.

In the hearings called to consider the peril that oil imports allegedly posed to U.S. national security, the battle plans were quickly drawn. On one side were the multinational companies who were developing the newfound oil riches of the Middle East— Standard Oil of New Jersey, Gulf Oil, Texaco, Aramco, Standard Oil of California, and Socony–Vacuum (later Mobil Oil). These companies owned the refineries into which their own foreign crude was pouring, and they dominated the markets for refinery products clear down to the gas pumps of the hinterlands. In addition, none of these giants had oil production within the United States that was at all comparable to their foreign production.

Opposing this handful of major companies was an army of producers who were, collectively, the main source of the United States' domestic oil production. The complaint of the domestic producers was that the imports were backing out their American crude from the eastern refineries, forcing them to cut back on production and take a lower price for their oil. They demanded an end to oil imports, or at the very least a limitation on imports to that part of American petroleum needs which could not be met by American production.

The agitation in Washington, being extensively reported in the trade journals, created a feeling of unease in Calgary. It was feared that any restrictions on imports by the U.S. would be framed in general terms, and hence catch Canadian oil up in something designed only to affect the Middle East and Venezuela. Alberta's exports of a mere one per cent of America's seven million barrels of daily oil consumption could have only a minuscule impact on the U.S. oil economy. But it was a vital part of Alberta's production. Moreover, fear of U.S. import-control was not even the most important aspect of Alberta's problem. Alberta's need was to increase substantially that one per cent, if its own oil industry was to prosper.

At a critical period of the hearings, something completely unexpected happened. Standard Oil Company of Indiana broke ranks with the other members of the Rockefeller sisterhood and came out publicly for the imposition of rigid controls on U.S. oil imports. Since a subsidiary of that company, Stanolind Oil and Gas, was involved in the development of several fields in Alberta and thus was adding to the province's surplus producibility, it seemed to me that the company was doing something inimical to Canadian interests, and I read it a small lecture in an editorial in the *Western Oil Examiner*. I, of course, did so completely unaware that I was thereby setting forces in motion that would destroy the magazine.

On June 5, 1955, the *Western Oil Examiner* went to its subscribers with this editorial:

ECONOMIC PAROCHIALISM TURNS UP IN THE QUEEREST PLACES

When the American government was considering the restriction of imports of oil from Canada and elsewhere it was good to see so many heads of big oil companies stand up and be counted on the side of freedom of trade. Among those who did so were the heads of Socony-Vacuum, Standard of New Jersey, Gulf and Texaco among many others.

Readers of the Western Oil Examiner will remember how we applauded the courage and common sense of the companies involved. Here's where we call attention to the opposite stand being taken, likewise by a company with large holdings in Canada. On a recent visit to Tulsa, Dr. Robert E. Wilson of the Standard Oil Company of Indiana—Stanolind—got off the following pronunciamento:

> For some years imports have supplanted rather than supplemented domestic production.
>
> In the U.S. as a whole today more than one barrel out of 10 crude oil processed is imported. And in 1954, for the first time in five years, U.S. production showed a decrease over the previous year. The rising pressure of imports was one of the responsible factors. It is distinctly not in the national interests that imports continue at anything like the present scale. The effect of imports on this scale can only be to reduce the incentive to find and produce oil in this country.

What goes on here, anyway?

Perhaps the learned doctor was only doing what comes naturally to a product of the environment dominated for so long by the Chicago Tribune school of political economy. Or perhaps he was falling into an all too frequent American error—of thinking of Canada as an American hinterland, as a sort of second-class Hawaii, Alaska or Virgin Islands. When Americans do that, they are always very much surprised when a protest from Canada reveals that Canadian interests are being affected. So perhaps Dr. Wilson was thinking of Latin America or some other benighted but non-Canadian exporter.

We have been told so often that one advantage of having American investment in our natural resources is that it gives us a friend at court. Americans with investments in Canada will be able to put pressure on their government to prevent reactionary trade policies being pursued at the instigation of special interests. It is a sad thing indeed to find such arrant expressions of economic parochialism in the very people we had assumed would be eager to protect their investment in Canadian natural resources.

This, obviously, was not the kind of editorial usually found in trade magazines, whose watchword has always been: "Never make waves within the family." A more circumspect editor might have looked at what he had written and blue-pencilled out some of the phraseology that gave the piece a cranky, even offensive tone. It was, perhaps, an example of one of the faults George Ferguson had found with my writing—a tendency to reach for a meat-axe when a bit of tut-tut might have served as well. But none of these caveats occurred to me. Even less did I suppose that the editorial would be regarded as offensive by the readers of the magazine.

We were so busy getting in ads and setting copy for a forty-eight-page special anniversary edition we were getting out to celebrate Alberta's Golden Jubilee as a province that I gave the editorial no more than a passing thought. The following week, Jack Doupe, our advertising manager, and Rowland Hill, our only reporter, returned from their rounds of the oil offices in a highly perturbed state of mind. The manager of an American oil-well supply company greeted poor Hill so offensively that he was still shaking when he got back to the office.

"He shouted at me," Hill said. "He shouted at me and threw the magazine at me, and said, 'You get the hell out of here and take this dirty rag with you.'"

Hill was at a complete loss to understand the reaction until Doupe came in and reported that the editorial seemed to have been read by every American in Calgary, and the general reaction was that I was an anti-American son-of-a-bitch.

I got out the editorial and reread it, in an effort to see what all the shouting was about. The employees of Stanolind might have taken unkindly to it, but why would the others have reacted so violently? It was beyond me.

Doupe's mind went right to the point. "It doesn't matter too much, I suppose, why the Americans are so incredibly thin-skinned. What matters is that if this kind of attitude persists, we're sure as hell in trouble with our advertising." He was certainly right on that count. Some weeks later he reported that there was an undercover word-of-mouth campaign being waged against us. One of Doupe's customers reported to him a conversation with one of his American customers.

"The guy asked me at lunch the other day what I'm advertising in that goddamn anti-American rag for," Doupe's client said. "I said your magazine never impressed me that way, but he was still hot under the collar about something."

The extent to which the editorial was primarily responsible for our inability to sell advertising would be difficult to assess. The fact was that we never could crack the accounts that regularly went into the other trade journals. Ultimately, we were forced to change the magazine to two issues a month, then to a single issue a month, before folding it completely three years later. The oil industry was, of course, vastly over-served by trade papers. Bankruptcy might have been the inevitable fate of the *Western Oil Examiner* on any count. Perhaps the advertisers refused us support because they concluded that we were publishing a poor product. They could have been right. Certainly it was a different product, with an unabashed partisanship where the interests of the Canadian independents versus the major international oil companies were concerned.

It might, perhaps, have turned out differently if the Americans in the oil business had not become so overly sensitive to criticism as a result of the storm of controversy that raged during those years over natural-gas exports. They found it inexplicable that Canadians could have any objection to their taking home to the United States the gas they had discovered in Alberta. But Canadians not only objected, they became involved in noisy controversy over who should be permitted to promote pipelines to move the gas out of Alberta. One group was beating the drum for a pipeline to Minneapolis, another for a pipeline to Vancouver and Washington State, and another to Toronto and eastern Canada. In each case, American promoters were involved and, when the controversies got into political debate, "American" became a fighting word for Canadian nationalists.

There was within the oil industry itself, and not only among Americans, an all-pervading ignorance of the realities of Canadian politics, even of Canadian history. Not one oilman in a thousand of either nationality had ever heard of Canada's fifty-year-old prohibition against the export of electrical power to the United States or of the reasons behind it. In the bitter political squabbling over pipelines, the Americans were baffled by the nationalist poses Canadians were always striking. But they were no more baffled than were their Canadian colleagues, who were ill-equipped to explain Canada to their American colleagues. Indeed, the Canadians were just as clamorous for permits to export Alberta's gas to the United States as were the Americans. And adding to the bafflement of both was how Canadians could be pressing so vigorously for oil exports to the United States and refusing to permit natural-gas exports, when both came out of the same holes. The Canadian independents, incidentally, were just as boisterously advocating gas exports to the United States as were the Americans. Their only interest was in where they could get the most for their gas the soonest.

Within the oil companies themselves, however, serious cleavages between the American and the Canadian employees had already developed. Wherever one looked within the industry, the chiefs were mainly Americans and the Indians were mainly Canadians. In seven years there had been a tremendous expansion of employment within the industry for young Canadian engineering, accounting, geology, and law-faculty graduates. Scores of young Albertans studied petroleum engineering in Oklahoma and returned to highly paid employment in their home province. And, as the supply of qualified Canadians increased, pressure was put on the incoming American companies to hire Canadians. They did so readily enough, and many companies set up training programs so that they would be able to promote Canadians. However, because Canada was outside the continental United States, the Americans qualified for "hard-service" pay supplements standard for employees on foreign assignment. That meant, as previously noted, that they enjoyed a number of perks that Canadians doing the same work did not receive. So it was inevitable that personal cleavages would develop and lead to the formation of national cliques.

It was an unhappy fact of life within the oil industry that Americans were favoured and Canadians were discriminated against, but not by reason of any active prejudice on the part of Americans against Canadians. It was simply a reflection of the awesome herd instinct of Americans, who naturally thought of each other, and only of each other, when business was being done. Accustomed to dealing with American firms in the United States, they naturally, and unthinkingly, looked around for the same familiar names when they had orders to place in Canada. When problems arose, it was as natural for Americans running oil companies in Alberta to turn them over to American consultants as it would have been if they had still been in the United States. It was an almost universal rule, whenever American and Canadian companies became engaged in a joint venture, that the engineering and legal studies had to be stamped with the imprimatur of American consultants. On the other hand, Canadians, regardless of whether they worked for Canadian or American companies, were notoriously tongue-tied when it came to sticking up for other Canadians in the same context.

The most glaring example of this was in the designing and building of the natural-gas-processing plants in Alberta. The Canadians who had gained experience in the Royalite gas-processing plant in Turner Valley were world-class experts on the behaviour of sour, wet natural gas under frigid Canadian winter conditions. There was in Canada in the early 1950s the nucleus of engineering talent that might have provided Canada with the greatest concentration of gas-plant-design skill in the world, if Canadians had insisted that the design of Alberta's processing plants be done in Canada. Instead, the decision makers, in both Canadian and American companies, ordered the design engineering from specialists in California. It took years for some of the companies to iron out the bugs that the blundering Californians engineered into their designs. Nothing set the teeth of competent young Canadian engineers on edge quite so much as being given to understand that only the Americans knew best how everything should be done.

This, then, was the milieu in which it was possible for a new editor to gain an instant reputation for being anti-American. Once we had our big Jubilee edition out of the way, I turned my attention to devising measures to get me back in the good graces of the Americans. This took on an air of urgency one day when Roland Hill returned to the office with a story that the office manager of a large supply company had ordered the mail clerk to fire the magazine into the wastebasket, instead of distributing it through the staff. A young friend of Hill's had retrieved a copy from the basket, tucked it under his coat, and carried it into the men's room to read it.

We both laughed, but the story was not that funny. This, surely, was no way to run an oil-industry trade journal, and some drastic fence-repairing action was called for. My first step was to try to arrange an interview with George Galloway, the resident manager of Stanolind, and offer him space for a reply to the editorial. At first his secretary refused to let me talk to him, but in the end persistence paid off, and he reluctantly agreed to see me.

In the hiatus between the editorial and the interview, the editorial gave me more cause for thought than it did any of our readers. And the more I brainstormed the Alberta system of pro-rating oil production, the more puzzled I became. Because its fields were capable of producing a third more oil than there were available markets, the Alberta Oil and Gas Conservation Board limited production to the market and established quotas for each well and field within the province. Thus, when all the refineries and pipelines notified the board that they would take a maximum of 400,000 barrels a day for the following month, each well was given a maximum daily allowable, so that the gross production from all the wells in Alberta would not exceed 400,000 barrels a day. Some wells in older and less productive fields might be restricted to 25 or 30 barrels a day, while those in richer fields were allowed quotas of 250 barrels a day.

The prices at which oil was sold were established by Imperial Oil. It was the price leader of the industry and all the other purchasers followed Imperial, for prices at both the field terminals and the retail gas pumps across Canada. Imperial Oil was also the leader in everything else. It was a sponsor of the Interprovincial and Trans-Mountain crude-oil pipelines, and put more Canadian crude oil through its refineries than all the others put together. It took the lead in expanding its own refining capacity across the country to utilize Canadian crude oil. Because it refined a lot more Canadian crude than it was allowed to produce, however, it had a vested interest in lower rather than higher prices for crude oil. Despite its outstanding leadership of the industry, it was, as the years passed, forced to reduce its own production steadily, in order to make room for the oil its competitors were producing from fields in which Imperial had little in the way of production of its own.

Several of the other major companies, like Texaco Canada, B.A.–Gulf, and Shell, had also built new refineries, and California Standard, Shell, and Texaco had expanded into the Washington State market. But the rest of the American companies, and most of the Canadian independents, did nothing to provide markets for the crude they were producing. That, of course, was a common condition in the United States' petroleum industry. Some companies restricted themselves to producing oil for others to refine. Others were integrated from oil field to gas pump. Still others were producers and refiners, but were not retail marketers.

Out of all this, I put a list of some pretty fundamental questions together to ask George Galloway. If Stanolind had no intention of ever taking any of its Canadian crude oil back to the United States, or establishing refineries in Canada, what was its purpose in spending money finding oil in Alberta? Would the small profit it could make selling its pro-rated production at low prevailing prices justify its drilling still more wells to increase the surplus still further? These were questions I could also have asked a score of other branch managers.

I asked them of Mr. Galloway, but never came close to getting an answer. Galloway was typical of the managerial class the American companies had dispatched to Alberta—fortyish, clean-cut engineers or geologists who had stood high in their graduating classes. Able and dedicated to the service of their companies, their eyes were always on the main chance.

As I took a seat across from Galloway and started to begin my questioning, he reached into the drawer of his desk, took out a book, and opened it at a pre-marked page.

"In preparation for your coming, Mr. Gray," he said, "I got down our company manual to refresh my memory on how my function within our organization is defined. I am, I see, empowered to provide the press with information as to our company's operations, policies, and so on, but it does not seem that I can go much beyond that. So, if we can just keep that in mind, I am sure we will get along fine."

My first question, of course, was to inquire about the possibility of having him prepare an answer to the editorial that criticized the president of his parent company. I said he could use whatever space he liked and I would undertake to publish it without any change or deletion. I was, in fact, rather eager to get such a statement, in the hope that it would dampen down the angry reaction of our American readers.

No dice. I was asking him to comment on the policies of his parent company, not Stanolind, and he was not empowered to discuss those policies with the press. Then would he care to comment on the proposal currently under discussion to extend Interprovincial Pipeline into the Chicago area, where Indiana Standard had a refinery? No, he was not empowered to discuss anything of that sort. Then perhaps he would care to discuss what plans Stanolind had for finding markets for the oil it was producing? It had none, because it was strictly an exploration and development company. Well, perhaps he would say what Stanolind was doing in Alberta, if it was unconcerned with finding markets for the oil it was producing. They were here for the same reason everybody else was here, to find oil, sell it to anyone who wanted to buy it, and make money for the company's shareholders.

The interview could have lasted no more than ten minutes and produced not a line of copy that would have helped to fumigate the anti-American reputation of the *Western Oil Examiner*. It was probably Galloway's first-ever encounter with a working journalist, and a discomforting experience it was for us both. But we parted with friendly handshakes, and I went off in search of other steps I could take to obliterate the anti-American label and turn ill-will into goodwill. I never found any that worked.

No publication, and most of all, no trade journal, can survive in an atmosphere poisoned by the ill-will of advertisers towards it. The ultimate failure of the *Western Oil Examiner*, however, could not be attributed to any lack of effort to change the climate or woo the advertisers. In the next two years I ran through three advertising managers, trying to break through the curtain of doubletalk that hemmed us in. I sent one of them on a tour of the head offices of the supply companies in Los Angeles, Houston, and Dallas, to confront the advertising managers in their deep-carpeted dens. They all insisted that their advertising placement depended upon the strength of the recommendation they received from their regional managers. That was just the opposite of the story we got in Calgary, where we were told that all advertising was placed by head offices, and local managers had nothing to say about it.

If there had been any positive support from the Canadians in the industry to balance the antagonism of the Americans, it would have been different. But the flow of advertising from Canadian companies, which Scotty Shoults had promised to develop through his agency, failed to materialize. It was not long, moreover, before we got the impression that the vigour with which ticklish subjects were treated in the *Western Oil Examiner* was as much an embarrassment to the Canadians as it was objectionable to the Americans, as the following episode indicates.

Following the Galloway non-interview, I did a lot of poking around in the economics of the oil industry, trying to make sense out of the behaviour of the major international companies in Canada. There was logic in their pouring American profits into Canada to avoid U.S. income taxes, but nothing else they did made much sense. For example, they were punching down holes in the newly discovered fields at break-neck speed, adding daily to surplus producibility, yet doing nothing to expand market outlets. I talked to a lot of people and ultimately did a long two-part series on major-company operations. It was headed:

> HOW CAN THE AMERICAN MAJORS GET THEIR PROFITS OUT OF CANADA?
> They use their Venezeulan crude to keep Alberta oil backed out of the 75,000,000-barrel Toronto–Montreal market.
> They won't take western crude home to their U.S. refineries as they have been taking home a lot of their other foreign crude.
> How then do they get their Canadian investment home to their treasuries?

The most surprising reaction I got to the series was an angry phone call from an executive of a Canadian company, who accused me of getting the majors so riled up that it would be difficult for Canadians to get any decent farm-out acreage from them.

Far from being intent on antagonizing anybody, I thought the articles would be a constructive contribution to getting attention focused on the pressing problem of crude-oil markets. Following the publication of the articles, I talked to several of the executives of the international companies, and got no more out of them than I had out of George Galloway.

After a while, I began to feel like sensitive bigots must feel when they begin to get the impression that the objects of their prejudices do not like them. I never reached the point of boasting that some of my best friends were Americans, but I did try to make friends with the Americans and to run articles favourable to them whenever an occasion arose to justify such articles. One month I devoted most of the magazine to an essay on Canadian history. It was headed, "A History of Canada for American Oilmen." In it, I tried to explain why Canadians act like Canadians, to the bafflement of Americans who encounter them for the first time. The general tenor of the piece can be gauged from the following sub-headings:

If Canadians seem to tick counter-clockwise, there's a reason—they wind up differently than Americans.

When Canadians start damning Americans the chances are it's the Washington government and not you that got them stirred up.

Washington has been riling Canadians for 90 years, only now it's happily unintentional. But Cleveland and Blaine used to do it on purpose with malice aforethought.

So did the New York shanty Irish who tried to free Ireland by putting the torch to rural Ontario.

I got several phone calls from American immigrants complimenting me on the piece, and one of the callers suggested that I send a copy to his company personnel director. He thought it would be useful background for future immigrants to have. I had several dozen copies reprinted and circulated them throughout the American personnel offices, from which I also elicited several friendly comments. In short, I felt that I was leaning over backwards to avoid giving any more offence. Nothing did any good, however, and as time passed, it came more and more to look as if the dog was stuck with the bad name it had acquired with its first false move. Certainly nothing we did improved our volume of advertising to a point where we could begin to live without periodic injections of capital from R. A. Brown and his associates.

As we moved through the middle 50s, all kinds of issues were coming to a head in the oil business, issues that no magazine pretending to serve the interests of the independent producers could avoid discussing. Having decided to take sides, I was stuck with the decision. One example was the controversy that developed over how the formula for monthly well production limits should be calculated. Some of the major companies were pressing for changes that would have allowed increased production from the high-reserve fields. They regarded it as grossly unfair for some of their wells, capable of producing thousands of barrels a day, to be limited to ten per cent of their capabilities. On the other hand, thousands of marginal producers were permitted to flow at their maximum capabilities of thirty to fifty barrels a day. Most of the smaller companies had their entire production in the poorer fields and had to have the maximum flow possible in order to finance their operations. So the arguments for the retention of what was called the "economic allowance" got full play in the *Western Oil Examiner*.

Another prickly issue was the manner in which the Alberta government granted pipeline franchises. Crude-oil pipelines, particularly those connecting field terminals with refineries or interprovincial lines, were licences to print money, in bills of large denomination. So everybody wanted to get into the act. At first, Imperial Oil built its own connecting lines. Then, as other fields developed quickly, the companies in them clubbed together to build a single co-operative line. That pattern was broken in 1953, when the line from the new Pembina field to Edmonton was awarded to the Fred Mannix Company, one of Alberta's largest general contractors.

The award had created a lot of grumbling in the industry, but it seemed to me that pipelines could provide an opening through which local residents could find profitable investments in Alberta. So I wrote several editorials advocating an end to pipeline monopolies and the opening of fields to anybody who wanted to get in. The money to be made with pipelines would surely attract a flow of money out of savings banks and life insurance.

The proposal drew flak from all sides, but most importantly, from Bob Brown himself. Pipelines, he argued, ought to be owned exclusively by the people who discovered oilfields. They ought not to be parcelled out to fly-by-nights who simply rushed in to take advantage of someone else's enterprise, as Mannix had done after Pembina was discovered. Brown had a point, but I argued that the right to build pipelines in Alberta, at the very least, ought to be reserved exclusively for Canadians. That was the position taken by M. A. MacPherson, QC, on behalf of the government of Saskatchewan in the Westspur Pipeline case. That idea was spurned by the National Transport Commission, which awarded the line to the producers in the field rather than to Canadian Devonian Petroleums, Ltd., the only Canadian independent seeking to build the line.

With Brown looking over my shoulder, I worked out a policy for the magazine. It was that a producer in the field should have first claim on a franchise, but that the company should have to make seventy-five per cent of the equity interest available to Canadian citizens.

The Alberta government had studiously avoided all the advice I had ever given it about how to run its business. But when it put the Alberta Gas Trunk Line in place to make sure that the federal government could never get its hands on Alberta's petroleum resources, it came so close to what we had been advocating that we might have sued for patent infringement. Trunk Line was to be the instrument that prevented any interprovincial gas-line from coming into Alberta. All pipelines were required to accept delivery smack on the Alberta border, and Trunk Line was to be the deliverer of the gas to the border points from all the Alberta field-gates. The government was prepared to allow the oil companies to operate Trunk Line and to supply some of the financing, but its entire 2.5 million shares of equity stock were to be reserved for Albertans who wished to buy them at $5.25 a share.

In the annals of Canadian corporate financing, there has never been anything like Alberta Gas Trunk Line. Weeks before the share offering was actually made late in 1956, the urban brokerage houses and small-town banks alike were being besieged with people seeking shares in Trunk Line, people who had never invested in anything before. When word of the magnitude of the demand and the popularity of the project got back to the government, it had to back off and consider how best to allocate the shares to the public. That only served to whet the public interest.

To tens of thousands of Albertans, the Alberta Gas Trunk Line financing was something akin to getting the Social Credit twenty-five-dollar-a-month-for-everybody dividend twenty years late. The more sophisticated were aware, of course, of what had happened to the shares of the Interprovincial, Trans-Mountain Oil, and Pembina pipelines, and more recently, the Westcoast Transmission and Trans-Canada pipelines. The oil-lines shares had increased seven-, eight-, and nine-fold in less than ten years, and the gas-line companies' shares had doubled overnight. Ordinarily, it was unlikely that workaday Albertans would have recognized a pipeline share if a chinook had blown it into their faces. But by the time the Ides of March 1957 approached, Trunk Line shares were about all anybody talked about. The opening salutation on streetcars, at timeclocks, in bowling alleys, beer parlours, bookie joints, and prayer meetings, and outside confessional boxes was: "Have you put in for your Trunk Line shares yet?"

Those whose reply was negative got a short, sharp lecture on the opportunity of a lifetime they were passing up. Those who replied positively were quizzed about where they had placed their orders and how many shares they hoped to get.

Underlying the burgeoning public demand for the shares, shoals were developing that might wreck the whole exercise. How could the public be guaranteed a fair deal from the dispensing agencies? What could prevent the banks and brokers from passing out thousand-share certificates to their friends, and foisting nothing but job-lots on ordinary Albertans? At first, distribution was supposed to be only through chartered banks. Then the stock brokers, trust companies, and bond dealers were brought in, accompanied by dire warnings of their consequences, if any of the agencies failed to apportion the allotments fairly to all comers.

When it became clear that the issue was going to be over-subscribed, schemes to beat any rationing system bloomed like dandelions along Jasper Avenue and Eighth Avenue. Businessmen sent their wives on shopping excursions through the financial district to place orders with all the banks, trust companies, and stock brokers who would take them. To prevent being swamped with application forms, the issuing agencies then put some new rules in place. First, they limited orders to one hundred shares per customer. The frenzied financiers countered that by ordering hundred-share lots in the names of their wives and children. Then the issuers insisted that all orders had to be accompanied by payments for the full amount of the order.

The application of these rules pushed many thousands of quick-profit investors out of the market. They had hoped to be able to obtain the shares by making a small deposit, and then to sell them at a profit as soon as they got their shares. Certainly, the word-of-mouth advertising the issue got convinced them that the price would rise rapidly once the shares were available. However, the restrictions only momentarily slackened the public's thirst for shares. Friendly bank managers were prepared to lend their creditable clients short-term money to finance the deposits needed to apply for one hundred shares each for their wives and children, because it seemed certain that the allocation of the shares would not exceed twenty-five per cent of the numbers ordered. In point of fact, the cash-with-order rule was strictly enforced by issuing agencies only against total strangers who wandered in off the streets. And, of course, anybody who did walk in off the street to plunk down $525 for one hundred shares could place an order with any branch of any bank or brokerage office.

When the Trunk Line buying binge ended, more than ninety-seven thousand subscribers had signed up for stock in Calgary and Edmonton alone, and the issue was over-subscribed by between four and five to one. As soon as the stock certificates were in circulation, an over-the-counter market quickly developed in Calgary and Edmonton. The $5.25 shares were gobbled up quickly as the price rose steadily to $12 a share during the week of March 7, fluctuating between $10 and $14 a share in the weeks that followed, but never falling closer to the issued price.

In the main, the apportioning of the issue worked out so that each applicant for one hundred shares was able to get a minimum of twenty shares at the issued price. The multiple shoppers who placed orders everywhere for father, mother, and children, could thus wind up with several hundred shares. It was easy, too, for the modest investors to sell off half their holdings for more than enough to give them the other half cost-free. For those who could afford it, the hundred-share Trunk Line stock certificates squirrelled away for their offspring in March of 1957 got them well started through college fifteen years later, when the value of the investment reached five thousand dollars.

In the final analysis, the Alberta Gas Trunk Line was more than a profitable investment for everyone who bought its shares in 1957. Through it, thoughtful Canadians could obtain a fleeting peek at an economy and a country that might have been, if Canadians had been given the opportunities and incentives to invest in the infancy of the post-war oil boom.

Equally important, from the viewpoint of that anti-American son-of-a-bitch who edited the *Western Oil Examiner*, was the fact that a few hundred shares of Alberta Gas Trunk Line made a comfortable anchor to windward as the dwindling advertising lineage of the magazine made its long survival an increasingly dubious prospect.

15
Ruined by the "I'm all right, Jack" Syndrome

The constructive influence that all the editors of Canadian newspapers and magazines have had on national affairs since the sealing of Confederation would probably fit rather comfortably in the corner of a gnat's eye. So, if this chronicle of editorial misadventure is to end on a high note of accomplishment, about all I can claim is that I was personally responsible for setting in motion the forces that ultimately resulted in Canada's National Oil Policy coming into effect. To that statement, candour dictates that a footnote be added: when the nudge was applied, I had not the foggiest notion of what the end result would be. I was only interested in getting three or four pages of copy for the *Western Oil Examiner*. It began this way:

In May 1955, the *Western Oil Examiner* ran the text of a market analysis for Alberta crude oil by F. G. Cottle of Imperial Oil. After considering all the markets available for the steadily increasing surplus crude-oil supply in Alberta, he developed the thesis that the United States offered the best and most secure opportunity for development. He predicted that the markets for Canadian crude would rise from 335,000 barrels a day in 1955 to 573,000 a day by 1960, with 120,000 barrels of the increase coming from additional exports. The balance of the increase would be achieved through the natural growth of Canadian markets and the use of more Canadian crude in the Toronto area.

Some weeks later, I obtained a copy of a notable speech by a young Winnipeg-born vice-president of the Standard Oil Company of California's Canadian subsidiary. His name was G. F. Furnival, and he took the opposite view to that of Imperial Oil. In a well-researched and superbly organized study, he all but wrote off the American export market because of political considerations, and presented the case for extending the pipeline to Montreal, where a market for 200,000 barrels of oil a day existed. The market was not only there, it could be reached by Alberta oil at a price that was fully competitive with oil being imported from Venezuela and the Middle East.

Cottle had confined his study largely to the consideration of the factors affecting the North American supply-demand picture. Furnival's focus was much broader, and took in the impact on North America of the astronomical increases in Middle East production. He saw the United States' protective reaction to mounting imports as an inevitable bar to increasing Canadian exports to that country. In relation to his times, Furnival's exercise was the wildest kind of heresy, because nobody challenged the authority of Imperial Oil on anything. When an Imperial engineer appeared before the Alberta Oil and Gas Conservation Board, it was like Moses coming down from the mountain to present the Commandments. It followed that no neophyte editor such as I could afford to get caught in the middle of an argument with Imperial Oil. But the Furnival thesis stuck in my mind like a fishbone in a craw, and, in the months that followed, I used it to measure the other arguments about markets that were put forward by F. C. Whiteside of Hudson Bay Oil and Gas, who did a couple of studies, a couple more by Imperial Oil, and one by Stewart King of Merrill Petroleum.

Concern over markets was the cause of only half the brainstorming that was going on in the oil industry. The extension of oil pipelines to Sarnia and Washington State, as noted, was accompanied by the lowering of wellhead prices to the lowest point reached since the wartime controls were removed in 1947. Among the independents, a body of opinion was growing that the markets being reached did not justify the price reductions, and the agitation rose for higher prices and even a tariff on imported U.S. crude. Twenty years earlier I had written a series of newspaper articles on gasoline-pricing practices on the prairies, and I used that experience as a springboard for a long article in the *Examiner* on the need for a new system of crude-oil pricing. One of the conclusions I advanced was that the industry ought to hire an economist to do a study of crude-oil markets and crude-oil pricing, and, by doing so, settle the argument about the Montreal market.

John Scrymgeour, R. A. Brown's executive assistant, called me some days later after reading the article. He liked the idea of hiring an economist: why shouldn't the magazine do it? I batted the idea around my industry contacts over the next several months. One of the most perceptive of these was Charles Lee, an English-born petroleum engineer who had come to Canada by way of the Trinidad oilfields and was the head of a toddling company, Western Decalta. He liked the idea, and he was so intrigued by Furnival's analysis that he had assigned a firm of Canadian engineers—Pryde and Flavin—to do a feasibility study on building a new pipeline from Edmonton directly to Montreal. Alex Bailey of Bailey-Selburn and Stewart King also liked the idea, so during the winter of 1956–57, John Scrymgeour and I toured the prairie universities in search of a hireable economist. As it turned out, nobody capable of undertaking the task had yet emerged from the womb of Canadian academe.

The year 1956, however, was a high-water-mark year, when Alberta's production almost reached an average of four hundred thousand barrels a day. That was the year, moreover, when the export of natural gas and the partisan political uproar over Trans-Canada Pipelines in the House of Commons usurped most of the attention from the marketing problems of crude oil. Then came the winter of 1956–57 and the Suez War, and it suddenly looked as if concerns for markets for Alberta crude could be banished forever. The blockage of the Suez Canal had the experts shaking their heads over the possibility of its ever being re-opened. Some even thought that the cost of hauling Middle East crude around South Africa to the United States would price it out of that market. When cargoes of Alberta crude were actually shipped from Vancouver to California, the other trade journals were busy heralding the dawn of a new age for the Alberta oil industry.

So as spring came in 1957, there was less urgency to the controversy over markets, and the search for an economist to do a study was dying on the vine when Charles Lee happened to bump into his old friend Walter Levy while strolling along Fifth Avenue in New York. Levy, a former journalist, had been a petroleum advisor to the U.S. government during the war and had set up a consulting business in New York. In response to Lee's question, Levy expressed interest in doing the sort of survey we wanted, so when Lee came back from New York, he got Scrymgeour, King, and myself together to talk about hiring Levy. Ultimately, Milton Lipton, Levy's partner, came out to Calgary, a deal was done, and work was begun on the Levy report, which would ultimately become the bible of the independent oil producers.

By midsummer of 1957, the Egyptians had got the Suez Canal cleared for traffic, and the bubble was burst for Canadian oil producers. Alberta's production declined drastically as the inflow of foreign crude increased into the Pacific northwest and the Ontario markets. From a record production of 412,000 barrels a day in July of 1957, Alberta's output dropped to 275,000 barrels the following July. Midsummer 1957 also saw the accession to power of the first Diefenbaker administration and brought to the treasury benches a coterie of Tories who had fought the financing of the Trans-Canada

Pipeline to a standstill during the stormy debates of the previous year. The election sent shock waves through the oil industry, and the consternation was hardly allayed by the announcement that fall that a royal commission would be appointed to investigate Trans-Canada Pipelines.

This was the atmosphere of uncertainty that prevailed towards the end of 1957 when Scrymgeour phoned.

"How are you at writing speeches that will knock a bunch of security analysts into the aisles?" he asked.

My reply was that my talents, if I had any, were strictly negative, that I had listened to so many bad speeches in my time that I was certainly an expert on how not to write a speech. But how to put a good speech together was an area I had never investigated.

"Well, Bob's got an invitation to make a speech to the Toronto Security Analysts' club early next year, and you know who's being joed into writing it? Me, of course! So do you want three guesses who I am going to joe into doing it?"

One guess was enough, and I agreed to help produce a speech. The next question was what Bob Brown wanted to talk about. Well, said Scrymgeour, Brown himself was undecided. His preference, he thought, would be to talk about the developments at Swan Hills and Virginia Hills, where Home Oil had made two major oil discoveries. On the other hand, there was also the Carstairs gas find and the implications for Home Oil when Trans-Canada began moving natural gas to Toronto. Scrymgeour and I got together to block out a speech, and I suddenly had a stroke of inspiration.

"I've got a better idea," I said. "Why don't we just rewrite George Furnival's speech on the Montreal market? The way the allowables are dropping, that's far more topical today than it was when Furnival gave it two years ago."

We got out the speech and went over it, and Scrymgeour went off to sell the idea to Brown. It was easily sold, and we were helped in putting the speech together by the arrival of Walter Levy's report on Canada's place in the world oil picture. The burden of Levy's thesis was that the immense profits the international companies would be able to make on their foreign oil production would compel them to use their own foreign crude exclusively in their refinery operations throughout the world. The words for this were "commercial preference," and the commercial preferences of the internationals would dictate that they use their self-produced foreign oil, regardless of price discounts that might be offered them by other producers. Commercial preference was repealing the law of supply and demand, where the supply dictated the price and the price dictated the volume of goods being purchased.

All this, of course, had been demonstrated twenty years before by the Stevens Royal Commission on Price Spreads. Then it had been the department stores which had stocked their shelves with goods produced in their own factories instead of buying from competitors. But the Levy doctrine was revolutionary in the context of the Canadian oil industry, where the major Canadian companies continued to insist that competitive pricing dictated whose oil was used in which refineries.

The Brown speech went off well enough and was greeted with the usual polite applause, while its theme was quickly forgotten by all concerned. The same fate greeted Charles Lee's development of the same theme from an engineering viewpoint two days later to the same group. But there was one man at that January meeting in Toronto who paid particular attention to the content of Brown's speech. That was Robert Arthur Brown, Jr., himself.

"I know how to crack that Montreal market," he said coming back to Calgary. "We'll build that goddam pipeline ourselves!"

Nothing he ever did or said was more typical of Robert Brown than that remark. As a gushing haberdashery salesman might have put it, that was him!

Already plagued, as I was later to learn, with personal financial problems that would have given a plaster saint the colic, and with his company's finances strained beyond endurance by the drilling programs in Swan Hills and Virginia Hills, Brown had committed Home Oil to the investment of more than $12 million in Trans-Canada stock and converted its $8 million in working capital into a $4-million working-capital deficiency. Yet he was prepared to launch himself on the promotion of a $350-million pipeline project that might have given the Shah of Iran cause for momentary hesitation. And he did it with an air of enthusiastic euphoria found only infrequently in winners of million-dollar lotteries. He was the complete promoter.

Bob Brown came by his promotional instincts naturally, by inheritance from his father and by sitting across the desk from his father during the hectic era of Turner Valley Royalties. The momentum, however, was gone from the elder Brown by the end of the Second World War; when Leduc struck and the Turner Valley promoters stampeded for the north and the new oil boom, Brown turned his back. Until his death in May 1948, he concerned himself only with husbanding the income that flowed from his Turner Valley wells into his holding company, Federated Petroleums. With the high rates of wartime taxes, the annual Federated dividend of forty-four thousand dollars was no more than enough to provide the Brown family and Brown's partners with a comfortable living. But it was enough to keep Bob Brown ensconced in a Château Laurier hotel room in Ottawa for the duration while he functioned as a petroleum-supply officer for the Canadian navy.

In Ottawa, and on junkets to the Sydney and Halifax naval installations, young Brown crossed paths with a coterie of other twenty-five- to thirty-year-old eager beavers who fought boredom by exploring avenues of opportunity they hoped would arise for them in post-war Canada. Towards the end of the war, the consensus was that the best gravy train to get aboard would be one catering to the pent-up consumer demand for electrical appliances, or for cars. Aware that the bloom was long gone from the oil business, young Brown favoured the appliance business, and, as his father was to be persuaded to establish a line of credit for the enterprise, everybody else went along with his choice.

The seriousness of the collective intention was indicated when Brown got Northland Automatic Appliance, Ltd., incorporated, and they turned their attention to selecting the best products to handle. They scrounged advice through friends in the Department of Munitions and Supply and settled on two products for which the demand was likely to be without limit. The first choice was the Bendix washer and the second was the Emerson radio, which was bringing car radios to the motoring public. Brown was able to sign up both products for his company while still in the service. When the group hit the bricks on civvy street, they were off and running for South Bend, Indiana, and a concentrated course in electrical merchandising at the main plant of the Bendix Corporation. Then they entrained for Winnipeg, Regina, and Calgary, to await the boxcars filled with washers. And that, for the next six months, was the way they sold them—by the boxcarful—for such was the demand that they were frequently called upon to move them directly from the boxcars to the retailers. In those months, Scrymgeour was more supply officer than Manitoba and Saskatchewan sales manager, for both appliances sold themselves and the main problem was to keep the supplies rolling to customers, not finding customers for stocks on hand.

It all came to a grinding halt midway through 1947, when a plummeting Canadian dollar brought on the foreign-exchange crisis that led to the adoption of an austerity program of unprecedented severity. Foreign exchange was rigidly controlled and an embargo was placed on the importation of all electrical goods from the United States, except for those firms that had previously built up a history of importing such goods. Even those firms were placed on sharply reduced quotas. Northland Automatic Appliance, Ltd., as a newcomer to the business, was one of the first fatal casualties of the orders. John Scrymgeour moved to Calgary to liquidate the company.

With the death of his father soon after the failure of the appliance adventure, Bob Brown was nudged back into the oil business as he took over as president of the now arch-conservative Federated Petroleums. When he got the appliance company liquidated, Scrymgeour joined Brown in Federated Petroleums. At the same time, the secretary-treasurer, alarmed at the prospect of the flamboyant young Mr. Brown steering the company towards bankruptcy, resigned to go looking for a job with more secure prospects. As a replacement, Scrymgeour suggested that Brown try to persuade their mutual friend, William Atkinson, to come over from Saskatchewan to take the job. It was the brightest idea John Scrymgeour ever had. When Atkinson agreed to make the move, it provided Brown, and later Home Oil, with the only authentic financial genius Saskatchewan ever produced.

And a many-sided genius he was. A red-haired, gregarious, fun-loving, beer-sipping practical jokester, he was blessed with a computer-brain with an instant-recall mechanism that fascinated everyone who knew him. A childhood obsession with figures undoubtedly tilted him towards a financial career. But when he graduated from high school in Regina at sixteen, he was two years short of the qualifying age for entering the University of Saskatchewan. So he articled to a firm of chartered accountants for two years and then enrolled. The Second World War caught up with him when he graduated at twenty, and he ultimately wound up at HMCS *Protector*, where he and Scrymgeour became fast friends. Scrymgeour introduced him to Brown, who was intrigued by Atkinson's depth of knowledge of the Alberta oil business. The explanation was simple enough. During a hiatus in his career at naval headquarters in Ottawa, Atkinson had put in his time studying corporate reports and investing in the stock market, with notable success.

In addition to his fascination with figures, Bill Atkinson was a voracious reader almost from infancy. Certainly he could read before kindergarten, and when the Atkinson home ran out of everything else to read, he would settle for the dictionary or the phone book. As he matured, his reading tended to concentrate on the financial press. During his absence from his office, his secretary always stored incoming papers in piles on his table against his return. He would then devour stacks of them at a sitting and seemingly remember everything he had read. There was hardly an Atkinson acquaintance who, beguiled by his memory, had not tried to stump him with unusual questions. They almost always failed.

It was a rare occasion, indeed, when he ever had to look anything up, and, most incredible of all, there was seldom an answer that he could not embellish with more information than any questioner ever wanted to know.

As he circulated through the oil industry, he provided friends and acquaintances with an endless flow of Atkinson stories with which to regale each other. A fellow accountant, for example, once looked up from some working papers to wonder aloud how the prices of used cars in Montreal compared with those in Calgary. Atkinson not only had an answer, he quoted some ballpark figures for makes and models. Flabbergasted and unbelieving, the accountant went out and bought a Montreal paper, looked up the used-car ads, and discovered that Atkinson's figures were right on target. Even when he had become a millionaire many times over, Atkinson delighted in pushing a shopping cart through a supermarket on a weekly comparison-shopping spree, and he always checked the tapes against the purchases.

Trick memories among specialists are perhaps not that unusual. What set Atkinson apart was a mind that became instantly aware of the implications of the figures he juggled. It was this quality that made him indispensable to Brown who, in 1948, was trying to bring order to the chaotic condition of the subsidiary portfolio of Federated Petroleums. There were bits and pieces of royalties, minority shareholdings, majority shareholdings, portfolio investments, well-operating contracts. Brown had to get an accurate dollar value on the holdings so that he could buy out his mother, brother, and sister, and get on with getting the company back actively in the oil business. He turned the entire mass of detail over to Scrymgeour and Atkinson to organize, and went off to try to pry open some major oil-company doors.

His first call was on friends of his father's at Imperial Oil, where he discovered that the company was in the process of selling off some of its assets to raise the capital it needed to finance the drilling of new wells in the Redwater and Leduc fields, and for refinery expansion and pipelines. He carried the news back to Scrymgeour and Atkinson and they went to work at once to evaluate the various companies Imperial had in Turner Valley, to see if there were any they might be able to buy with Federated as security for a loan.

The next day, Atkinson came up with figures that showed there were a couple of Imperial subsidiaries that might be useful acquisitions for Federated if the price was right. Brown scarcely glanced at the individual company valuations. He focused on the aggregate value Atkinson had placed on all the Turner Valley properties.

"Let's buy the whole works," he said, as he collected the financial data and a Federated statement and headed for the bank. That was truly the approach of someone with the gall of a second-storey man, for Federated would have been strained to demonstrate a net worth of three hundred thousand dollars, and the Imperial properties were worth at least three and perhaps five million. Brown had that gall, and he brought off the deal with a three-million-dollar Bank of Commerce loan secured by the production Federated would get from the Imperial–Turner Valley wells. It was the first oil-production loan negotiated with a Canadian bank, though they were common enough in the oil country south of the border. Then Brown went out to try to make a deal with Imperial to buy Royalite itself, the biggest operating oil producer in Canada until Leduc came along. That attempt failed, but in the months that followed, Atkinson and Scrymgeour kept finding other "situations" where judicious purchases turned handsome profits, for themselves as well as for Brown.

One of the most important "situations" they discovered was Home Oil Company, in which none of the directors held more than a handful of shares. As a result, no group of shareholders, or even combined groups of shareholders, held enough stock to control the company. So, with the help of another whopping loan from the bank, Brown was able to move quietly into the market and buy up sufficient stock to enable him to take control of the Home Oil Company in 1951.

Taken together, these episodes underline two of the qualities that made R. A. Brown, Jr., one of the most successful promoters in the annals of Canadian petroleum development. He was as persuasive in recruiting talent as he was in raising money, and he was a master money-raiser. Scrymgeour and Atkinson made a perfect team. Atkinson was overly shy in the company of strangers and diffident in volunteering an opinion, although he was thoroughly outgoing in the company of friends. Scrymgeour was completely at home in any company, and the articulate interpreter of the ideas the pair had put together. As a team, they were able to keep Brown well supplied with projects to work on, and to act as brakes on some of his promotional aberrations.

Once he was in control of Home Oil, Brown moved quickly to flesh out its staff with some of the top talent in the business. He reached down into Casper, Wyoming, and hired Alex Clark and R. W. Campbell away from Shell Oil. Clark became head of the company's geology department, George Blundun was hired away from Gulf Oil to head up the geophysical department, and Bart

Gillespie was brought in from Gulf to manage the production and pipeline divisions. In short order, the Home Oil staff expanded from a half-floor office in the old Lougheed Building to a three-storey and then a nine-storey building on Sixth Avenue.

A few days after Brown and I returned from the security-analysts' convention in Toronto, I got a call that he wanted to see me. It turned out that his statement that he was going to build the pipeline to Montreal himself was being converted into an actual drive to do just that. John Scrymgeour was putting a group of independents together with Charles Lee to sponsor the project, and Brown already owned a pipeline charter which had turned up in the files of Federated Petroleums. It was named, appropriately enough, Independent Pipeline Company, Ltd. He wanted me to wind up the *Western Oil Examiner* and come over to Home Oil as manager of public relations for the Montreal-pipeline promotion. When I hesitated, he brought the full force of his persuasiveness into play. He confided that his ultimate goal was to obtain control of Trans-Canada Pipelines and bring its head office back to Calgary from Toronto, where C. D. Howe had moved it. When that was accomplished, I would become the public-relations director of all three companies—Home Oil, Independent Pipeline, and Trans-Canada.

He was convinced, he said, that with me handling the publicity and press relations for the Montreal pipeline, and he and Ross Tolmie, an Ottawa lawyer, carrying on the political campaign, it was bound to win. And within a year! Getting control of Trans-Canada would take a little longer, but it was also a certainty, and we would both live to see the day when we were sitting on the top of a billion-dollar corporate pyramid in Calgary.

My reward for all this would be a salary of one thousand dollars a month immediately and fifteen hundred a month as soon as his salaries re-assessment was complete, plus an option on fifty thousand shares of his United Oils stock at one dollar a share. United Oils was the holding company in which he had his control of Home Oil, and its shares were then selling for around two dollars.

My head reeled. After three years of struggling to keep the *Western Oil Examiner* afloat with an uncertain, not to say dubious, future, it was intoxicating stuff. The stock option alone would provide a secure future for my family, and the fifteen hundred a month would be almost twice as much as I had ever earned before. I went about the business of finding a buyer for the *Examiner*'s printing equipment and wrote my last editorial. Meanwhile, Brown and his independent group had appeared before the Borden Commission to pressure it to widen its scope of inquiry to include the oil business as well as Trans-Canada and the gas business. If it was to provide the Canadian government with the guidelines for a national gas policy, it should also provide it with advice on the development of a national oil policy.

The Borden Commission agreed; the next order of business involved putting together a submission to persuade the commission to recommend the construction of a new crude-oil pipeline to Montreal. Though he was still nominally working with the other independents, Brown regarded them more as a nuisance than as an asset. He operated strictly on the assumption that, if a pipeline was ever built, it would be Home Oil who controlled it and called the tune. He brushed aside Charles Lee's engineering study and reached down into Oklahoma for the services of the world's largest pipeline builders and engineering consultants—Williams Brothers, Inc. Between times, he was back and forth to New York, to bring Lehman Brothers and the Mutual Life Insurance Company into a syndicate to do the financing.

The case for the Montreal pipeline was based on six propositions:

1. It was necessary to restore economic viability to the Alberta oil industry, which was down to producing at thirty per cent of its capacity, and where more than a third of the drilling rigs in the province were stacked and idle.
2. The reliance of the Montreal refineries on foreign crude was inimical to the security of Canada in time of war, whereas the Montreal pipeline would provide Quebec with an assured and safe supply of oil, regardless of world conditions.
3. The construction of the pipeline would provide $300 million worth of new business for the steel mills of Ontario. Additional thousands of jobs would be created along the route the line would take.
4. The transfer of the Montreal refineries to Canadian crude oil would end the drain on foreign exchange of more than $350 million a year.
5. The creation of the additional 250,000-barrel-per-day market for Canadian crude would increase drilling activity in Alberta and Saskatchewan and lead to the discovery of additional crude-oil and natural-gas reserves for Canada.
6. The new pipeline could deliver crude oil to the Montreal refineries at prices that would be no higher than those charged for foreign crude, and would result in no increase in retail prices for either fuel oil or gasoline.

To achieve all this, no government subsidies or financial assistance was ever sought. The only obstacle to achievement was the fact that the Montreal refineries were owned by subsidiaries of international oil companies, who supplied them with crude from their concessions in the Middle East and Venezuela. And, because the profits of the parent companies were substantial, the Canadian employees of the subsidiaries fought the Montreal pipeline with every means at their disposal.

They appeared before the Borden Commission with briefs which demonstrated (a) that profitable new markets would be developed by them for Canadian crude in the sweet-by-and-by if the producers would just be patient, and (b) that Quebec consumers would be severely penalized if the government forced them to substitute "expensive" Canadian crude oil for "cheap" foreign oil.

The most difficult truth ever to try to sell was that the commercial preferences of the international companies, not the nominal price at which oil was sold, dictated whose oil would be used everywhere in the world. While Brown was trying to persuade Prime Minister Diefenbaker, George Hees, and Maurice Duplessis of the virtue of Canadianizing the Montreal crude supply, I carried the message to the financial editors and editorial-page writers on all the Ottawa, Toronto, and Montreal newspapers. We junketed editors out to Alberta to introduce them to the oil industry and we countered the refineries' arguments with our arithmetic. We produced study after study by Williams Brothers to show the actual cost of building the pipeline. We lined up security-analyst conventions for Brown to speak to.

On Brown's own junketing around, he sloshed the financial writers with booze and plied them with argument. But so far as we were ever able to discover, not a single writer or broker or politician to whom we directed our arguments was ever convinced of the soundness of our case. It foundered on the universal acceptance of Imperial Oil arithmetic. Imperial simply had to pass the word that imported oil was "cheap" oil and Canadian oil was "expensive" oil, and nobody would listen to our rebuttal. The best we could achieve was a Mexican stand-off—most of the writers chose to stay out of the argument rather than support either side. Unfortunately, that was the same as rejecting our project, because we had to generate both public support and political acceptance in order to bring it off.

In the end, I tried a new tack by getting away from arithmetic entirely. Suppose it might cost you a penny or two more for your gas at the gas pump, I conceded. That would cost the average motorist fifteen or twenty cents a week, a mere drop compared to the extra cost Albertans have to pay for the cars and refrigerators and shoes and shirts that we buy from Ontario and Quebec. And that fifteen or twenty cents would provide an immense amount of work in the steel plants and fabricators in eastern Canada.

The reaction to the idea of paying an extra penny or two to help an Alberta industry was universal outrage. It could be summarized in a seriously phrased wisecrack I heard again and again:

"Why the hell should we have to pay more for our gas? To keep a bunch of Alberta oil barons in new Cadillacs every year?"

It was a mass demonstration of the universal insensitivity of the eastern media to the needs and aspirations of western Canada, spread over two years. It underlined so painfully the total lack of a familial attachment among Canadians, and the elevation of the "I'm all right, Jack" principle into a way of life for Canadians.

But the cause was not wholly lost. A new Montreal pipeline was rejected, but the Borden Commission eventually recommended a compromise which, in reality, accepted our basic case. In substance, it told the international companies to find additional markets for Canadian crude equal to what the Montreal refineries could provide, or face the loss of those markets to Canadian crude oil. In February 1961, the recommendation was adopted as Canada's National Oil Policy, and the major companies rushed into action to save their profitable Montreal dumping-ground for their foreign crude oil.

In the months stretching into several years that followed, I re-learned the lesson I had learned so well during the Great Depression and had momentarily lost sight of under the spell of Brown's promotional rhetoric. It was: The job that pays off only in money is never worth having.

The public-relations job at Home Oil melted into nothingness with the collapse of the Montreal-pipeline campaign. Days stretched into weeks and then into months, with nothing to do but attend meetings, drink coffee, and read the papers. Ironically, I even missed the brass ring I had grabbed for, since neither the promised stock option nor the raise in pay ever materialized. Brown's own grab for control of Trans-Canada Pipelines also eluded his grasp, and he lived to see all his promotional dreams turn to ashes in his mouth. On the other hand, John Scrymgeour and Bill Atkinson, who left Home Oil soon after I arrived in 1958, continued to root out special "situations" in the business world like a couple of poodles in a truffles patch. In a little over five years they became the biggest drilling contractors in Canada and were in the process of building the biggest electrical- and plumbing-supply empire the country had ever seen. Once, they came within two months of being able to wrest control of Home Oil away from Brown himself, by the same manoeuvre he had used to gain control fifteen years earlier.

While all this was going on, I was abandoning my dreams of financial security and making arrangements to return to the only thing a writer should ever do, because it is the only thing he can ever do.

Write.

Farm & Ranch
R E V I E W
May ❖ 1950

Don't Miss – Kerry Wood "On The .22 Menace"

Farm and Ranch Review Editorials

Exporting Canadian top soil builds American colleges and hospitals

SUPPOSE that an American enterpriser came into your district and made this proposition to you and your neighbors:

"There is a wonderful market in the United States for top soil. If we can get the right concessions, we are prepared to come to Canada, erect a $5,000,000 factory and process this top soil and ship millions of tons of it to the United States. It will create riches for the farmers who sell their top soil, and it will help Canada to solve her American dollar problem."

Our enterprising friend would be laughed at. There would be a rush to ask him this question:

"It sounds wonderful, but what do we do when the top soil is all gone?"

Yet the really staggering fact about the Canadian economy is this: Our national policies have been directed for many years toward encouraging American capital to export our top soil. We have seen that happen everywhere, only we haven't called it top soil. We have called it paper, oil, copper, gold, nickel. We are preparing, at this moment, to encourage American capital to take possession of the world's richest iron ore deposit. In the end, we will be in exactly the same position as a farm community would be in if it shipped out its top soil. We will be the owners of denuded forests in British Columbia, pumped out oil fields in Alberta, yawning caverns of worked-out mines in the north. And the capital increment from the development of all these resources will have accrued to the people who provided the capital.

It would be easy enough for us to wrap ourselves in a Canadian flag and start a great anti-American crusade. That would also be nonsense. American capital came into Canada to take over the development of our natural resources because we Canadians were not prepared to do it ourselves. We were the ones who thought it would be smart to sell our top soil. In many cases, our natural resources might never have been developed if they had to wait for Canadian enterprise to start functioning.

The prospectors who discovered the Flin Flon copper deposit had to go to New York for money to develop it. If the nickel at Sudbury had had to wait for Canadian capital it might never have been developed, and the world might not have been free today.

We are not interested in stirring up anti-American feeling. But we are interested in this great riddle: What makes our natural resources so attractive to Americans and so repulsive to Canadians? Is it, as alleged, because our taxing laws discourage risk taking and encourage an obsession with security? Is it because we have replaced our free enterprise system with a safe enterprise system? What we would like to do is jar Canadians out of their lethargy and get them interested in the development of their own country.

It is of some consequence to us all that this be done, and quickly. American investment in Canada is rising steadily, as American firms plow their profits back into development. A few hundred thousand dollars invested years ago in an oil company have mushroomed into a multi-million-dollar concern today. The profits earned on these millions go to the United States, and complicate our exchange problem.

American investment in Canada today has reached $4,982,000,000. It takes upwards of $200,000,000 to pay interest on that investment to American owners. Probably less than half the $4,982 millions of Canadian assets now owned in the United States are represented by American funds invested in Canada. But as the investment grows steadily from reinvestment of income, it takes more and more money to provide interest payments. Yet in face of that, there are those who say that the way to solve our exchange difficulties is to encourage more American investment in Canada! In short, export more top soil.

This mushrooming of American investment has arisen in substantial measure through the operation of the Canadian tariff. Through the years Canadian consumers, particularly on the prairies, have paid tribute in the form of higher prices than were being charged for identical products across the line.

All that brings us back to our argument for a customs union. Unless this American investment in Canada is prunned back it will sink our economy. Its growth can be restricted in two ways: (1) Give Canadian consumers and producers alike free access to the American market. By producers we mean not only the farmers but all Canadian manufacturers as well. (2) Overhaul the Canadian taxation system where it is required so that every possible encouragement will be given to Canadians to risk their capital in the development of their own resources.

Then, and only then, would the capital increment that results from the development of capital assets accrue to the benefit of Canadians. The profits earned from the developing of Alberta and Saskatchewan oil and Manitoba mines will eventually build universities and hospitals and highways in our provinces, instead of in New York and New Jersey and California, as they do today.

"Untruthful, unfair, false, irresponsible and mischievous"

EVER watch a clown at a circus when a fire-cracker explodes under him? He screams, shouts, jumps in the air, waves his arms and takes off with frantic haste in all directions.

That seems to be the reaction of Grain Exchange cheer-leaders to the editorial in our January issue. Frankly, we are not too much concerned about this resort to the argument by insult technique. We recall the words of Mr. James Murray, then chairman of the Wheat Board, before a special parliamentary committee in 1936. Reminded that some people had called him "Grain Exchange Murray" and others had called him "Wheat Pool Jimmie", he replied:

"If it makes anybody feel better to call me names, it doesn't hurt me."

That's our position, exactly. When any of our opponents run out of arguments, we hope they will feel free to ease their blood pressure by calling us names. But in the case in question we do feel we are entitled to a bill of particulars. Our friends lifted a paragraph from our editorial and tacked all these labels on it. Here is the paragraph in question, the statement that is untruthful, false and mischievous:

"One of the first acts of the new Liberal Government was to fire Mr. McFarland. He

was replaced by the Murray board which promptly did what the Grain Exchange wanted, sold off the Canadian carryover for what it would bring. And it did it when the new crop was being marketed.

"When, in December, 1935, the Argentine advanced its price overnight 20 cents a bushel, two things happened. The Grain Exchange immediately imposed a three-cent daily limit on fluctuation to prevent the Canadian price from rising. And the new Wheat Board sold wheat to those who had been caught selling the market short, thus enabling them to avoid financial disaster. But from that day to this, there is no record anywhere of a single calculation of a Winnipeg mathematician to show the losses inflicted on Western farmers by the Murray Wheat Board-Grain Exchange policies."

Well, let's see what is true and where falsehood lies.

1. "One of the first acts of the new Liberal Government (in 1935) was to fire Mr McFarland."

Is that true or is it false? The general election was on October 14 and Mr. McFarland was fired on December 3 by order-in-council.

2. "He was replaced by the Murray board which promptly did what the Grain Exchange wanted, sold off the Canadian carryover for what it would bring. And did it when the new crop was being marketed."

Is that true or is it false? In the balance of December and in January, the

(Continued on Page 6)

The Farm and Ranch Editorial Page...

Keep our gas in the ground until Canadians can use it!

IT didn't take long for those interests which seek to export Canada's natural gas to the United States to rush out into the open once the pipe line bills were through the House of Commons. A Calgary newspaper started the ball rolling with a front-page story to the effect that unless Alberta got into the U.S. market right away, gas reserves would be developed in Montana and the Pacific Coast market would be lost forever.

That is it exactly. Vancouver, the alleged terminal for these pipelines was just the lure on the hook. The real market is the Pacific northwest of the United States. Pious promises by promoters that Vancouver would be served can now be filed and forgotten. What will happen next is easily discernible. The Alberta Government and the Conservation Board will be subjected to terrific pressure to declare that Alberta's gas resources are sufficient to permit huge exports. If that declaration can be obtained, it will be used to pry a pipeline permit from the Transport Commission and a gas export permit from the Minister of Trade and Commerce.

It will be a dark day for the people of all Canada if these things should be allowed to come to pass. And they will unless there is an immediate awakening by the people of the prairies to this threat to their future.

As Mr. Gardiner said in his recent broadcast, which we have reproduced in part on page 8, the paramount need for prairie agriculture today is the development of an expanded home market. That can only be done by a tremendous industrial development west of the Great Lakes. Cheap power, from our great stores of natural gas, can create whole new industries out here, industries that will not only provide thousands of new jobs and new markets for our farm produce, but raise substantially our whole standard of living.

But all that will take time. It will take forebearance. It will take patience and above it all it will take a clear vision of the destiny that can belong to the West. Make no mistake about this: With hundreds of millions of dollars involved, every effort will be made to confuse and beguile us into selling our birthright for a mess of pottage. That campaign has already begun.

So long as any doubt remains about our intention, industry will hesitate about locating in the West. American industrialists will be prepared to wait 10 years to see if they can get out gas to Seattle. Yet there is one way to hasten our own industrialization. That is to decide once and for all that Canadian natural gas is to be used for Canadian development. **Let us make it plain that we are determined NOT to permit the export of our natural gas.**

This is the greatest issue that has ever **faced** the West. Let us react to it with such **vigor** and determination that our aims will be achieved. This is something that can be fought on many fronts, and on an issue that can be kept crystal clear. The whole thing can be summed up in a single slogan:

"Keep our Canadian natural gas in the ground until Canadians can use it!"

Every farm organization, every Board of Trade, every municipal council on the prairies can help to win this battle. In Alberta, the campaign must be two-pronged. A counter-attack must be launched at once to strengthen the resolve of the Government and the Conservation Board. In addition, Alberta citizens must join with fellow Canadians in Saskatchewan, Manitoba and British Columbia to carry the battle into the decisive Federal field. Even if the struggle is lost in Alberta, it can still be won at Ottawa.

It is in Ottawa where the final decision must be made. As Mr. Gardiner points out, Ottawa has the say as to whether we export any kind of power or not under the Power Export Act of 1907. Because Canada had the wisdom in 1907 to take a stand firmly against the export of electric power, a great industrial basin was created in Ontario and Quebec. If 1907 history can be repeated now, in preventing the export of our gas power, it can be repeated again in the industrial development of the West.

This is not only an issue that transcends all others in importance to the producers of the West, it is one on which everyone in the West, regardless of where he lives or how he makes his living, can unite to speak with one thunderous voice.

The pipeline debate in the House of Commons at least served the purpose of awakening public opinion to the potentialities of the West and natural gas. It has brought home to the Government the depth of the conviction of the members from the West on this issue. Because the Alberta Social Credit members took no part in the discussion an impression may have been left that the people of Alberta don't care what happens to their natural gas. That must be dispelled quickly because, in plain truth, Alberta will be the main loser if export of natural gas from Canada is ever permitted.

Help the flood victims

EVEN with the most liberal aid coming from the governments, the losses that will be suffered by the people of Manitoba from the worst flood in a century will be terrific. These losses are far beyond the capacity of the people themselves to absorb. So it is heartening indeed to see the whole-hearted and generous response all over Western Canada to the appeal of the Manitoba Flood Relief Fund.

Every organization of any consequence anywhere on the Prairies has swung into, action to contribute and raise money. It is being channeled into Winnipeg through a hundred different avenues. All the radio stations and newspapers are aiding in the collection. The Farm and Ranch was asked to start a fund from its readers and lend a hand in the collection. But by the time that our June issue comes out we know that the field will be completely blanketed.

Of course we will be only too pleased to send along any contribution to the fund our readers care to send us. But it seems to us that it would be much simpler for those readers who wish to contribute to send the money through their local weekly paper, the nearest radio station, or directly to the Manitoba Flood Relief Fund, Great West Life Building, Winnipeg.

Of this there can be no mistake, even if the fund is generously oversubscribed, it will still not begin to cover the losses and misery of so many thousands of our neighbors. That's something to be remembered when we are thinking about giving.

Mr. Coyne talks sense

READERS of the Farm and Ranch are of course aware of the emphasis we have been placing on the need for Canadians to finance the development of their own resources and their own country. Perhaps they will be interested in the fact that this idea is now percolating in the high policy level at Ottawa.

Mr. J. E. Coyne, the deputy governor of the Bank of Canada, in a speech to the Canadian Life Insurance Officers' Association, recently did some most useful embroidery on the same theme.

In the last four years, Mr. Coyne pointed out, thrifty Canadians have saved a total of $3 billions. And they are adding to that pile at the rate of $400,000,000 a year. That money, together with surpluses accumulated by Canadian corporations, would have been sufficient to pay for the whole development programme Canada has gone through. That didn't happen. While Canadians were putting their money into banks, insurance policies, bonds, mortgages, and other allegedly "safe" investments, foreigners were pumping money into Canada to invest in productive enterprise.

Canada's resources are going to be developed, if not by Canadians then by outsiders. The tragedy is that Canadians are not doing it and the outsiders are. The capital increment that will result from the development of our resources will be forever lost to Canada. It will go to enrich the countries from which the money comes. Today, one-half of all the dividends paid by Canadian corporations go to people outside the country.

What's the answer? Mr. Coyne suggested one. He urged the banks and insurance companies, who hold 60 per cent of the savings of the Canadian people, to transmute a greater proportion of these savings into productive investment. It is sound advice, perhaps the soundest that can be given.

Security-mindedness has crept through our whole society like an influenza virus. Losses resulting from the 1929 speculative

(Continued on page 6)

The Farm and Ranch
Editorial Page...

Natural gas exports
and faith in Canada's future

IN the June issue of the Farm and Ranch we ran an Editorial on the natural gas question which took the position that we should keep our gas in the ground until Canadians could use it. For this we were attacked with language usually reserved for public enemies and traitors. As there is no sense in trying to reason with hysteria, we made no effort to reply. Recently, however, it was with some satisfaction that we noted that a prominent and highly respected chemical engineer from Montreal appeared before the Alberta Conservation Board and made the same appeal.

The points made by Mr. J. R. Donald are fundamental to this discussion. And as the whole future of the Prairies is bound up in the decisions that are made in connection with our oil and gas resources, the question is vital to our farmers. Because they must depend so largely on foreign markets, our producers' position in the economy is extremely vulnerable. There is only one escape — in growing food that can be consumed in Canada. That can only be achieved by a substantial increase in our population. Only a great industrial expansion in Canada can give us this population base. In many ways, this question of gas exports is, therefore, more important to prairie farmers than any strictly agricultural problem they have to face.

Mr. Donald made these points:

The greatest industrial expansion in recent American history has been in chemicals. Chemicals have far outstripped everything else.

The greatest expansion in the chemical industry has been in the Texas area, close to the source of natural gas.

The whole history of industrial expansion has been that industry moves to the source of power, that raw materials are brought to power.

In recent years interest has been rising steadily in our gas and oil resources on the part of great American chemical industries. If we have patience and take the long view upwards of $150,000,000 may ultimately be spent on industrial investments near our gas resources.

If export of our natural gas to the north-west States is permitted it will adversely affect us in two ways: Industry that might have located in Alberta or Saskatchewan will locate in Washington or Oregon. Products of Canadian industry will be excluded from the United States by tariffs imposed to protect the north-western industries founded on Alberta gas.

That these suggestions were anathema to the promoters of export pipelines was quickly demonstrated by the efforts that were made at once to discredit Mr. Donald's testimony. But what is important here is not the scoring of lawyer's debating points. It is the whole future of Canada. What is important is not the few million dollars in profits that these pipeline promoters can skim off the top of their operation. It is the long term and noble vision of a Canada with a future. What is important is not a greedy grab by franchise hunters for a quick promoter's profit. It is faith in the destiny of these Prairies and their people.

The United States does not permit the export of its natural gas. The Windsor industrial basin is starved for gas. It is brought all the way from Texas to Detroit. But it cannot be exported to Canada unless and until the needs of everybody in the United States are filled. It would be one thing to trade gas with the United States, for Canada to supply the middle west in return for American supplies for eastern Canada. It is something altogether different for us to give the United States our gas, and get only dollars in return.

True, there has been no great industrial expansion in Alberta yet founded on natural gas. But there was no industrial expansion in Ontario either when Sir Clifford Sifton set out to save Canada's Hydro power resources for Canada. Because, largely through his efforts, these power sites were saved from alienation to American industry, we have a population of 8,000,000 in Ontario and Quebec today. Is a population of 8,000,000 beyond the hope of fulfillment on these prairies if we can retain our power resources now? Not to anyone with a spark of faith in this country!

In plain truth, we are on the threshhold of great new scientific developments. Only recently the magazine Newsweek reported that even greater industrial expansion may take place in Texas as a result of perfection of a Diesel electric plant that operates on natural gas. This plant can generate electricity cheaper from natural gas than it can be obtained in the north-west from hydro-electric plants. Does that item alone not open up glittering vistas for men of faith and vision? Then the scientists are making great progress in the development of the gas turbine engine, in the jet engine, in the piston-free engine.

If there was ever a time in Canadian history when patience, restraint and the long view were needed, that time is now in connection with our gas resources. Time is on the side of the people of Canada. The longer we can hold onto our natural resources, the more valuable they will become. What does a year or five years or ten years mean if, by waiting, we can make sure that the boon of these great natural resources will be used to the maximum ultimate advantage of our country and our people?

*

Confusion over coarse grain prices

ON our letters page this month is a communication from a reader which underlines the confusion that is inevitably created when a Monte Carlo gambling casino is superimposed upon a grain marketing system.

The Winnipeg Grain Exchange futures market is operating on all grains but wheat. Oats and barley, however, are marketed exclusively in interprovincial trade by the Wheat Board. If a producer of Oats wants to use the Grain Exchange to sell his grain, he must first deliver it to the Wheat Board. He can sell his Oats short on the Grain Exchange, if he thinks the price will go lower and then eventually buy back his future. But the actual Oats, the stuff fed to animals as distinct from the paper markers

used in gambling on the market, remains with the Wheat Board for disposal to feeders or other users.

The Wheat Board initial price, the Grain Exchange futures prices, and the selling prices of feed grains at country elevators are all different. So different in fact that there is a great deal of suspicion engendered. It is needless suspicion. The Wheat Board functions as the sales agent of the producer. It seeks to get the best price possible for him. When John Jones delivers 1,000 bushels of Oats to the elevator he gets an INITIAL price and later a substantial dividend.

When the stock feeder goes to the elevator to buy grain, he finds a substantial difference between the grower's initial price and what he is asked to pay. That applies as well to the original producer if he discovers he has sold too much and has to get some back as livestock feed. People accustomed to the old days when they could buy grain at the Fort William price less freight, conclude that somebody is being cheated, mainly them.

That is not so. What we have today is a marketing system by which the grower doesn't get soaked for freight on feed that is sold locally and on which no freight has been paid.

This is no doubt rough on commercial feeders. But it seems to us to be an equitable sort of system. It still permits direct dealing between grain producers and feeders. They can haggle and horse-trade and make whatever deals they like. There is one thing, however, that the producers should keep constantly in mind. The Wheat Board price is the initial price. They are entitled to get considerably more for their grain if they sell direct to people who will feed it to livestock because in that case there will be no subsequent payment

A Merry Christmas to All

The Farm and Ranch
Editorial Page...

As a nation of money-lenders
we are losing our country

THERE was once a time, during the dark ages, when money lending was held in universal contempt. Yet because even the dark ages had need for occasional lines of credit, money lenders existed. They were tolerated as an unfortunately necessary evil, and barely tolerated at that. They were put upon, swindled, beaten-up, robbed and even murdered. And they were victimized very often by the very people who had borrowed their money. The tragedy of Canada today is that we are fast generating into a nation of money-lenders. More, we are being impelled along this road to ultimate disaster by all our best minds and deepest thinkers!

C.P.R. is Going

There was a story in Time magazine recently that points up the facts of this tragedy. Much of the information in this story will be old stuff to readers of the Farm and Ranch — how ownership of our industry and commerce is passing into the hands of American investors. One point is new and important. The ownership of the Canadian Pacific Railway is passing into American hands. Since the war, American investors have increased their holdings of C.P.R. stock from 15 per cent to 34 per cent!

Behind all this is the curse of depression thinking which has glorified security above all else. And behind this thinking is the outrageous delusion that security can be obtained by investing our money in bonds. So Canadians have become a race of bond-buyers, collectors of gaudy colored promises to pay. In so doing, they have become the greatest risk carriers of all, for there is nothing riskier than an investment in a bond.

The Big Pipe-line

Let's illustrate the point by a concrete example. The money to build the great Imperial Oil pipeline from Edmonton to Superior was supplied by Canadians in the form of bonds purchased. They will get a fixed interest on their money, if the pipeline is a financial success. Twenty years from now they will get all their money back, if the pipeline is a financial success. And at that stage, if it is a success, it will be owned by the Standard Oil Company of New Jersey, which owns the majority of the common shares.

But if the line does not succeed financially, what then? Well, then the bond-holders will have to take over and operate something that is losing money. They will not get their annual interest. They will not get back their principal. Even if the pipeline succeeds, and they not only get their fixed interest every year but their money back at the end of the term, what will that money be worth then? The $900 automobile of 1929 cost $2,100 in 1949. The $5,000 house of 1929 cost $10,000 in 1949. What will the $1,000 the bond-buyers get back in 1969 buy in terms of 1949 prices?

We have not the slightest doubt that this pipeline will prove to be a very profitable undertaking. It is too bad that the people who paid for the steel and the cost of installation will never own it. But do Canadians have any inkling of where this mania for security, in the form of bond collecting, is leading them? We doubt it.

Wrong Solution

To reverse this thinking requires a radical change in our thinking in high places. The impact of the times on that thinking was beginning to be felt. Bond yields were declining. That meant that insurance and mortgage companies were being squeezed to keep up their earnings. If the squeeze had become a sharp pinch perhaps they would have been roused from their slumbers. Instead the Dominion Government started machinery in motion to increase income from bonds.

National Housing Act mortgages, for example, which for 15 years had carried interest of $4\frac{1}{2}$ per cent were raised to 5 per cent. But what would have happened if instead of raising interest rates they had been lowered? The big lending institutions would have been driven to investing in productive enterprise, where the returns are substantially higher. They would have acquired a piece of ownership. They would have profited or lost directly by the success of the enterprise. They would have become partners in the development of enterprise, not merely holders of promises to pay that are good only if the enterprise flourishes.

True, substantial changes would have been necessary in our insurance laws.

Those laws were written in a panic, when all lived in terror at the prospect of having an insurance company or a bank go broke. Well, which is worse — to have financial institutions go broke occasionally or have title to all the productive enterprise of this country pass into foreign hands? That is what is happening. Canadians are selling their equities in productive enterprise and putting the money into bonds. The Americans are buying the real ownership and financing their operations by selling bonds to Canadians. American investment in Canada plants has now reached the staggering sum of $7,000,000,000. They are ploughing back their income into expansion at a terrifying rate. In the not too distant future Canada will have to find perhaps $1,000,000,000 a year in U.S. funds to pay out to Americans as interest on their investment in Canada.

Our Real Crisis

Here we face a crisis of historic proportions. It is something that screams for attention. It gets none. The Farm and Ranch has modestly suggested a few things that might be done. One is that we should completely overhaul our whole tax structure so that Canadians would be given irresistible incentives to risk their capital in productive enterprise. Other nations, faced with a similar problem, have taken drastic action to limit foreign investment particularly in natural resources. India has closed the door on outside investors. France will permit foreigners to investment in the development of North Africa only so long as French capital controls the enterprise. Even the banana republics of South America have tightened up their restrictions on foreign investment in their natural resources.

But in Ottawa, any suggestion that Canada even examine its thinking on foreign investment falls on stone deaf ears. The people who both make and administer fiscal policy want no changes made. They can see administrative difficulties. They can see loop-holes. They are afraid that some sharp Canadians might find these loop-holes and use them to build fortunes. The sad truth is that the wise American investors, who have had the benefit of a tax structure that makes enterprise possible and profitable, have found the loop-holes through which they, though not Canadians, can drive whole railway systems.

And Canadians, who will one day awaken to the fact that none of the physical assets that make a country rich belong to them, rush madly about exchanging title to ownership for gaily printed promises to pay!

Our subsidized newspapers
complain about subsidies

IT is axiomatic that the advocates of any cause must come into court with clean hands. In the uproar over the final payments under the British contracts, Canadian newspapers harped endlessly on the "subsidy" angle. Such criticism would have come with better grace from an institution less generously subsidized than is the press of Canada.

For a generation the people of Canada have subsidized our newspapers to the tune of several millions a year on the postage rates. The rates charged all publications, including the Farm and Ranch Review, have been outrageously low. These rates are now being increased by almost $2,000,000 a year. It is about time, but it is not enough!

Then there is the direct subsidy to newspapers through the operation of the Press Gallery in Ottawa. Not only is the press corps provided with a free press room, free desk space and desks, and stationery and 24 hours per day page service in the main House of Commons building, the Federal Government provides additional accommodation in an office building on Wellington Street. This service costs the taxpayers of Canada at least $100,000 a year.

Nothing Happens

Conscientious newspapermen who have rankled at living on Government bounty have been agitating for years to have the publishers erect their own building and take

(Continued on page 6)

The Farm and Ranch
Editorial Page...

Who owns Canada?
Nobody knows in Ottawa

IN the years since the close of World War Two, Canada has undergone an industrial expansion unequalled before in our history. Indeed, probably never before has any small nation expanded its productive capacity so greatly in so short a time as Canada has. And this expansion, unlike any that preceded it, has been done largely from resources and capital within the country. We have not imported capital to finance our growth to any appreciable extent.

It is this last fact, which has been getting very wide publicity in recent months, which has led to the drawing of some very wrong conclusions about this country. Because Canada must depend so largely on its export markets for prosperity, we cannot afford to build up a large external debt. It takes all the money we can earn through the export of food to purchase the materials required to keep this huge industrial plant in operation. Any appreciable increase in our external debt could prove disastrous to our economy if there was any slackening in our export trade.

Aware of this, Ottawa is exceedingly proud of our record in financing our industrial expansion internally. Time and again this statement has been made: Since 1946 we have spent $26,000,000,000 on capital expenditures and Canadians have provided 85 per cent of that huge sum.

For complete and unadulterated balderdash there has been nothing to equal these claims in a generation. It is more than nonsense, it is dangerous nonsense which is being used to lull Canadians into a completely false sense of security about the nature of the ownership of the assets and resources of this country.

What will astound Farm and Ranch readers, as it astounded us when we discovered it, is that there is no factual basis for either of these figures, either the $26,000,000,000 or the 85 per cent.

Let's take the percentage figure first. When it is said that Canadians have financed 85 per cent of our capital expenditures the first question that arises is:

What is a Canadian?

To any ordinary Canadian, that is any easy question to answer. A Canadian is a citizen of Canada. When we say Canadians financed Canada's development we mean that Canadian people either privately or through Canadian-owned corporations did it. But that is not what Ottawa talks about at all. Its definition of "Canadian" for purposes of these statistics is a company that has a Canadian charter.

In short and to the point, all the expansion that has been financed out of the Canadian earnings of wholly-owned and partly-owned American branch plants located in Canada is included in that 85 per cent. Or put it another way: The 15 per cent that foreigners have financed is made up entirely of the new money that has been brought into the country since 1946; it includes none of the old money that has been doubling and redoubling in Canada since it came in before the war.

The history of Canadian industrial growth is this: It has been accelerated by the establishment mainly in Ontario and Quebec of wholly-owned branches of American corporations. These companies have invested a few millions in Canada in their original plants. Profits made from Canadian operations have been retained and plowed back into bigger and bigger plants.

It is no job at all to find many American corporations which now repay every year in the form of dividends more than they originally brought into the country.

Many of them have increased their assets in Canada 10 fold. It has been done out of profits made in Canada, not by imports of capital. But because ownership of these assets remains in the United States, this growth of American capital inside Canada has vastly increased our debt to the United States.

Let's paraphrase it. Suppose the Americans brought in and planted an apple tree. At harvest time, they took home a bountiful load of apples, but they used most of the crop for seed. Soon they had a whole orchard in production. The orchard, like the first tree, is owned abroad. The implications of that ownership are obvious.

As long as things are good, the owner may be content to leave his apples or dollars in Canada. But when and if things get tough, he may want to take all his apples home. Things have been good for American manufacturers. They have not needed their Canadian profits at home. So they have plowed them back in to Canada. Yet even with the plowing back, more than half the dividends now paid by all Canadian corporations now go to owners in the United States.

So the inclusion of expansion by American branch plants in any study of Canadian financing is sheer lunacy. It was done because nobody in the Bank of Canada, nobody in the Department of Finance and nobody in the Department of Trade and Commerce has done any delving into the growth or growth rate of American capital invested in Canada. The plain and brutal fact is that none of the Government's advisers can even guess at what proportion of our capital expansion has been done by Canadian capital. They have no information of which to base a guess.

Nor is their $26 billions figure any more reliable. It is like a drover putting a bunch of cattle, sheep, swine, goats and poultry into a corral and asking a buyer to bid on "a corral full of livestock" sight unseen.

The $26 billion figure indicates to the unwary that times have been so good that we have accumulated that much extra capital in six or seven years. But the $26 billion makes no distinction between long-term borrowing and investment in equities. It does not distinguish between investment in machinery and equipment to produce more wealth and expenditures on capital goods that consume wealth. For example, the $26 billion includes all the money Canadians have borrowed and spent on house and apartment building. That would knock at least $5 billions off the total.

As a general rule, the Americans invest their money in things that will make them money, in production machinery and plants to house them in, in purchasing our oil, gas, copper and iron ore deposits. Canadians tend to buy bonds and put their money in mortgages. This has given the Americans a great help in financing their companies in Canada. They take the common stock and let the Canadians buy their bonds.

The difference between the two operations is one every farmer can appreciate in these terms: The Americans buy bredheifers. Canadians lend money on promises to pay with herds of dry cows as security.

What is so important about this is that ownership not only of our whole productive machine but of our natural resources as well is becoming concentrated more and more in foreign hands. The profits and capital increment that inevitably result will accrue to the foreign investors. Unless that trend is arrested and reversed it can and will ruin this country.

We don't say that the time has come to impose restrictions on American investment in Canada. We can't say that because there is no factual basis upon which to justify it. What we do say is that there is enough evidence everywhere in this country to indicate that it is imperative that we encourage Canadians, through taxation and fiscal policy, to risk their capital in the development of their country. The curse of "security" has laid a dead hand on the thinking of too many Canadians. On the other hand, Americans have seized the opportunities which Canadians have been content to ignore.

In order to devise correctives, the first task of the Ottawa brain trust is to get out the facts. Let's study the way American capital has grown in Canada. Let's find out how much it amounts to. Let's distinguish between equity and mortgage and bond investment. Let's above all, let's stop calling Americans Canadians for statistical purposes.

And until we have done this, let's stop talking through our hats. Only when we have information upon which to make decisions are intelligent decisions possible. When we have it we can proceed to take the steps that are necessary to reverse a course that can lead only to our loss of the ownership of our country.

The Farm and Ranch
Editorial Page...

The educational scandal
is worse than you think!

WHEN a scandal breaks in this country we expect it to explode in either of two ways: in speeches of men in public office or through revelation by newspapers. There is almost no record of a scandal being laid bare by a book. That was true until Dr. Hilda Neatby published her indictment of Canadian education in the new book, "So Little for the Mind".

It is a book which every Prairie farmer who has children in school should buy and read. More, it is a book which every school trustee and member of a provincial legislature should read until they fully appreciate how scandalously they have been taken in by the educational fifth-columnists.

The plain truth is that the socializers have captured the Canadian schools in all the western provinces and Ontario. Whether they are card-carrying Socialists or not is of no consequence. Their aims and objectives are clear, to turn out young people who will fit precisely into a socialist state. It has been the bending of every instrument of education to that end that has created the educational scandal of today.

What is the educational scandal? It is many sided. Its end product is an army of young Canadians graduates of our schools who cannot read or write or spell or do arithmetic, who are unequipped by training for life in a competitive economy, who don't know what they want of life, or how to go about achieving it.

That's one side. Another is the frustration that has made teaching our most barren profession. One has only to read the comments of the teachers in Dr. Neatby's book to understand the depths to which education has fallen in this country. Barred from imposing either physical or mental discipline, condemned to a life of futility in a maze of projects and time consuming nonsense, they surely deserve our sympathy.

This naturally is not equally true of all provinces, or of all school districts within each province. But no one can read Dr. Neatby's book without being impressed by the completeness with which our educational system has been overrun by the modern American theorizers.

Canadian education has been taken over, lock, stock and barrel by educational theorists to whom John Dewey, the American philosopher, was the prophet. Dewey was an able and energetic thinker and an intellectual socialist. He used the obvious defects of our traditional educational system to stand the whole business on its head.

The faults of the old system were many. Discipline was perhaps too strict, perhaps

Not Perfect too much emphasis was placed upon the storing up of factual material out of context. Pupils were forced to learn arithmetic, grammar, spelling, geography, history and literature from rather dismal text-books. They had to pass rigid examinations and those who failed had to take the course over again. So little imagination was shown that the effect of the lessons was often to destroy interest in the subjects, permanently.

Dewey reversed everything. From emphasis on learning it became emphasis on doing — "learning by doing". The formal teaching of the subjects was abandoned and in its place was instituted a system of "arousing interest" of the pupils by means of collective projects.

Dr. Neatby's book is based upon her collection and reading of a great mass of teaching manuals which are the Bibles of our modern school teaching. Throughout them all runs the thread of "arousing interest". It is the most important task the teacher has, to arouse interest in her pupils. She must never teach anything directly, she must waylay and trick them into the acquisition of knowledge.

And this trickery must be practiced always on a whole group. Great emphasis is

The Herd Principle placed on group planning, group activities, group problem solving. Backward pupils must not be flunked because this would reflect on the group and retard the natural blossoming of child personality.

It is small wonder then that time is wasted on outrageous stupidities. In Saskatchewan there are lessons on how to answer a telephone. All provinces favor endless paper chases where children are required to collect pictures relating to lessons. Subjects which could be taught in a few days or weeks are stretched out for years, until they are buried completely is masses of trivia.

To state plainly a simple fact, and force children to learn it, marks a teacher as a "traditionalist" who won't be welcomed in the profession. Thus, in her rating of pupils, she must overlook factual errors and concentrate on the attitude of the pupils. Are they co-operative, are they interested? Old fashioned parents, who think their children must be learning something at school because they pass every year will be shocked by the disclosures in Dr. Neatby's book. The system is to pass everybody, the good, the bad and the indifferent.

Well, how did we get into this mess? Largely, we suspect, by infiltration, the way the Communists get into positions of power in society. The Dewey disciples got into the provincial educational departments. In no time at all, the main jobs were filled by other Deweyites. Today the infiltration has taken over the faculties of teacher training courses in colleges. Dr. Neatby, who is professor of history at the University of Saskatchewan, reserves her most trenchant criticisms for the texts used in the teacher training courses. If there is little for the mind in our public schools, there is even less for the mind in the teaching courses.

We will concede that this system, the collectivist approach to education, would be

Good in Russia

ideal for a collective system like Russia's, or one envisioned by Marx or Lenin or even by milder socialists like those in Canada. But if the aim of education is to provide young Canadians with a foundation upon which they can build a useful life with alert and lively minds with which to meet the challenge of the times, this system is alien to Canada.

How, then, does it happen that it was foisted upon us? Largely because the people who are primarily responsible, the members of our legislatures, were asleep at the switch. They were hornswoggled by the gobbledegook of the administrators who parroted catch-phrases like "we don't teach subjects, we teach children."

The legislators left the curriculum to the experts and concentrated only on the financial problems of education. The experts, the civil servants in provincial departments of education, are mainly responsible for the mess we are in. How little attention has been paid to education may be illustrated by this single fact (it is NOT in Dr. Neatby's book):

Some years ago one prairie province hired a certifiable mental case with a galaxy of bogus college degrees as deputy minister of education. A couple of years passed before the government discovered the swindle and fired the imposter!

No one who reads Dr. Neatby's book can help being convinced of the urgent need for action to get our educational system back on the rails. Her book comes at a very appropriate time. It comes when the parents of this country are stirring uneasily about the obvious failings of our school system. In Alberta, the teachers themselves are speaking out against the major lunacies. The time for a real house-cleaning is at

(Continued on page 6)

A Merry Christmas to All

Farm and Ranch Editorials
Bring foreign policy
down from the clouds

ELSEWHERE in this issue our readers will find a condensation of the submission to the U.S. tariff board by Mr. George McIvor on the proposal to bar Canadian oats from the American market. It is the sort of able presentation western farmers have come to expect from Mr. McIvor.

What surprised us about the brief, as we believe it will surprise most Farm and Ranch readers was Mr. McIvor's statement that Canada imports more food from the United States than the U.S. imports from Canada. Mr. McIvor mentioned this in the process of arguing that the United States should recognize the facts of life of trade with Canada. To all of what Mr. McIvor said so well we may well add — "Amen".

(Continued from page 5)

hand. To bring it about will need pressure on the trustees and legislatures by an aroused citizenry.

Dr. Neatby has quoted chapter and verse in her indictment. It provides us with all the factual ammunition we need to force a house-cleaning of our departments of education. We've had enough of their nonsense, their pseudo-psychology, their double-talk. It is time for the people to insist upon the adoption of a useful educational system in which there is something for the minds of young Canadians.

In saying all this, we are not urging a return completely to the traditional system of 30 or 40 years ago. **Fundamental Needs** Its errors were obvious and important. Nor should all of Dewey's theories be completely discarded. There is much in them that can still be useful. As Dr. Neatby points out, Dr. Dewey would quickly repudiate many of the crimes committed in his name. But of this we are certain: We must retrace our steps to a point where a hard core of fundamental subjects are made an imperative part of the curriculum. We must restore discipline to our class rooms, and bring back the element of competition so that our young people will be prepared for entry into the competitive society in which we live.

Meanwhile, we have a constructive suggestion to offer. When you start shopping for Christmas, put a copy of Dr. Neatby's book on your list. (It costs $3) Send it to your school trustee after you've read it yourself, or to your member of the legislature. No book published in Canada in many a year deserves a wider reading.

But it seems to us that this fact about food trade should be drilled home at Ottawa, too, so that we can devise a more realistic approach to trade problems with the United States. In order to safeguard our interests we have got to widen our methods of dealing with the Americans. Our contacts with the Americans are at too high a level. The Canadian ambassador talks to the State department and vice-versa. That isn't at the level at which policy is made. American policy is made in Congress where sectional, regional and economic interests often collide head on.

Obviously, in such collisions innocent by-standers can get badly mangled. In the American system, national interests are very often made subservient to parochial interests. When the corn growers get excited about imports of Canadian oats, they never consider the fact that by importing Canadian oats the United States is enabling Canada to import Florida and California fruit, Texas vegetables and Louisiana and Mississippi vegetable oils and cotton.

Now, surely the logical way for Canada to safeguard her interests is by making certain that the Congressmen, from the States that have profitable markets in Canada, are aware of the fact. It should be somebody's responsibility to get acquainted with the representatives from all these areas and acquaint them with the facts. What they do with the material will be their decision. But we have a feeling that the Congressmen from these areas would be just as concerned to protect the interest of their constituents as the Corn Belt Congressmen are to protect theirs.

Ottawa's unofficial reaction to this proposal was that it might lead to charges that we were meddling with the internal affairs of the United States. We see no validity to this objection. It comes from the state of mind which works harder to find excuses for not doing something than it would to actually do the job. The fact remains that unless we understake some such educational campaign, we can hope for no aid from the State department. It, like our own external affairs department, can only talk of lofty generalities. Congress deals with actual cases, with realities that are important back home.

In a real sense, the difficulties we are in are the natural result of entrusting diplomatic negotiations to career diplomats. They are experts on how diplomacy works from the inside, but are completely without experience in the outside world. Our problems with the United States are practical. They will never be solved by negotiations at the diplomatic level.

And it is right here that we think our External Affairs department could do with a change in emphasis. It is concerned, as it should be, with the affairs of the United Nations and the North Atlantic Treaty Organization. But too much of its top level thinking is concerned only with that. Devising means by which the world may be saved from a third World War is important. Our relations with the United States are also important. It is becoming increasingly apparent to all Canadians that these relations are getting roughed up, that merely passing notes back and forth between ambassadors is not enough. Our guess is that things will get worse before they get better.

If that is so, then surely some serious attempt should be directed to methods of pursuing policies by other means. We have suggested one. It may not be effective. But at worst is far better than sitting back and doing nothing constructive to make some friends for Canada where friendship counts most — inside the American Congress.

*

A good appointment

IN the appointment of Mr. Earl Robertson to the position of assistant commissioner of the Canadian Wheat Board, the government has indeed acted wisely.

The Wheat Board is one of the biggest businesses in Canada, ranking right up with the railways in both its importance to the welfare of Canada and in the complexity of its operation. So it is vitally important to its successful operation that it be served by men of the highest technical competence. Mr. Robertson's ability is well known throughout the grain trade and the Board was fortunate in obtaining his services.

He is, as well, the nephew of John I. McFarland, the father of the modern Wheat Board. The farmers of Western Canada have a special place reserved in their hearts for Mr. McFarland who, more than any other Canadian, laid the foundation on which the present Board was built. He combined an all-inclusive knowledge of the grain business with a deep concern for the interests of the farmers and certain knowledge of how these interests could best be served. We have no doubt that Mr. Robertson will serve the interests of prairie farmers not only with competence but with the distinction we would expect from a nephew of John I. McFarland.

*

Savings are not profits

AS this was written, our Prairie Wheat Pools were concluding their annual meetings. As usual, they all enjoyed splendid years both financially and in the volume of grain handled.

Unfortunately, and this is an old complaint with us, when the reports of these meetings get into the press and onto the radio the emphasis always seems to be on the "profits" earned by the Pools.

None of the Pools earns a profit. The surplus that is left over at the end of each year's operation belongs to the pool members and is distributed to those members as patronage dividends. Unlike the private companies, which are in business only to make profits, the Pools exist to provide service for their members. Earning a surplus or a profit is only an accidental minor incident in their operation.

There are some who don't worry too much about what the yearly balance of the Wheat Pools is called. They like the idea of a large balance because it will make a nice talking point when patronage dividends are paid out. However, there is another side to the story. Because these savings over the years came to be identified as profits, it was easy for special interests to distort the picture and, through persistent pressure, force legislation subjecting the Pools to taxation similar to that paid by corporations. So we insist that a name is important when it comes to describing the savings made for members by all co-operatives. They are not profits and we should stop referring to them as profits.

WESTERN OIL EXAMINER

Per Copy, 20c

Saturday, January 15, 1955

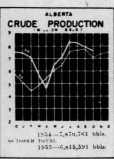

ALBERTA
CRUDE PRODUCTION
(MILLION BBLS)

1954—7,870,761 bbls.
OCTOBER TOTAL
1953—6,815,591 bbls.

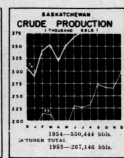

SASKATCHEWAN
CRUDE PRODUCTION
(THOUSAND BBLS)

1954—550,444 bbls.
OCTOBER TOTAL
1953—267,146 bbls.

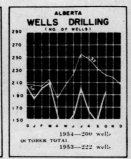

ALBERTA
WELLS DRILLING
(NO. OF WELLS)

1954—200 wells
OCTOBER TOTAL
1953—222 wells

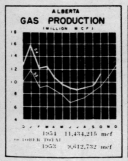

ALBERTA
GAS PRODUCTION
(MILLION M C F)

1954 11,434,215 mcf
OCTOBER TOTAL
1953 9,612,732 mcf

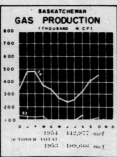

SASKATCHEWAN
GAS PRODUCTION
(THOUSAND M C F)

1954 442,977 mcf
OCTOBER TOTAL
1953 109,666 mcf

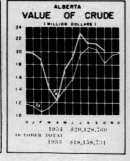

ALBERTA
VALUE OF CRUDE
(MILLION DOLLARS)

1954 $20,128,769
OCTOBER TOTAL
1953 $18,158,731

Crude Production Drops During Month In Alberta.
Drilling Activity Jumps.

WESTERN OIL EXAMINER

editorial

Access to natural resources is Capitalism's "fifth freedom"

One of the obvious virtues of the capitalist system is that it enables people to grow, opens ways for the poor to get rich and the rich to get richer and for nations to thrive and prosper as their enterprisers prosper. Under our system, the little shots of today become the big shots of tomorrow, if they have what it takes to grow into big shots.

Throughout history there has been one sure course through which both individuals and nations have grown rich. That is through the development of natural resources. It has been almost as if a "fifth freedom" existed which was vital to our economic development, the freedom of access to raw natural resources to develop.

Because of the operation of the "fifth freedom" in the oil business, small enterprisers of 50 years ago have grown in the United States into corporations with assets running close to the billion dollar mark. In a thriving capitalism, the minor Independents of today can become the major operators of tomorrow. And when that cannot happen there is something radically wrong with the system. That describes us today as far as the Canadian Independents are concerned.

Under the Canadian leasing system, the door of access to our oil and gas reserves is open only to the highest cash bidders. The American companies, who have grown enormously through development of their own resources are able to pay millions of dollars, cash in advance, for Canadian mineral rights. Canadian Independents, who are just as eager to develop these resources, are barred from the bidding because they lack the resources, because they have not had the time in which to grow and accumulate reserves.

There is this point on which most economists agree: It is best for a country to have its own people develop their own resources and keep the capital increment of such development at home. It is imperative, hence, that something be done to enable Canadian Independents to gain access to our resources; not to the exclusion of foreign interests but in competition with them.

How can this be done? We do not know, though we are confident that if we can pool our intelligence a solution will be possible. It is not enough for politicians to extol the virtues of our free enterprise system. One of their primary responsibilities is to see to it that it stays in working order. Our leasing system may have resulted in an accelerated development of our oil and gas resources in the West. But no system can operate without change, without modification with the times. If substantial changes are needed to get the Canadian Independents back into the oil business, we should not hesitate to make them.

In other words let's take a real good look at that "fifth freedom" and get it back into operation again in our oil and gas industry.

editorial

The pipeline franchise racket is finally reduced to absurdity!

The sheer lunacy of having pipeline franchises distributed by Government ukase was surely demonstrated in Ottawa this week. Three separate companies appeared to ask for the right to construct a pipeline along an almost identical route from the Midale field in Saskatchewan to the Inter-provincial pipeline at Cromer, Manitoba. The authority, in this case, was the Board of Transport Commissioners.

The Board has at its disposal all the technical help it needs in making railway, waterway or highway decisions. It is obviously not set up to decide between rival claimants for pipeline monopolies. How, then, does it get into the picture? Because jurisdiction over inter-provincial pipelines has been placed with the Transport Board.

Clearly there should be some control over pipelines in the public interest. But that control should be confined to protecting the public from harm as a result of careless or inefficient installations. Public control should be confined strictly to public safety. That could be achieved by formulating a set of regulations for pipeline construction and maintenance and letting nature take its course from there.

How in the name of common sense can the Transport Board be expected to decide which one of the three claimants is best able to construct a suitable pipeline to move Saskatchewan crude? A far better judge, as we recently pointed out, would be to have the decision made by impartial dollars. Let whoever can build the line and then whoever gets the oil to put in the line will prosper and whoever fails to get oil for a line will go broke.

To attempt to choose between the applicants will put the Board in the preposterous position of conferring a rich plum on one group and with-holding it from another. That, surely, is no part of the function of the Transport Board.

Neither, we submit, should it be part of the function of provincial Conservation Boards. In provincial cases, in the past, it has often been possible to argue the merits of different routes. That may have served to becloud the issue. There is no chance of that in the Saskatchewan-Manitoba line. The fact that they are taking the same route surely must focus attention on the ludicrous position we have got into in connection with pipeline franchises.

WESTERN OIL EXAMINER

editorial

Canadians can draw a melancholy moral from the ancient Incas and Indians

Perhaps the strongest reason we have for being saddened by the gradual decline in importance of the Canadian Independent in this: The capital increment that results from the development of our natural resources will go elsewhere.

A great deal of guff has been peddled about the value of oil investment as a maker of jobs for Canadians. One of the major companies devoted a lot of space to that notion in a newspaper advertisement some weeks ago. To us, this argument is completely specious. It can be demolished easily by a couple of examples from history.

The Spanish Conquistadores could certainly have argued that their plundering of the wealth of the Incas gave work to the natives. Certainly the enterprise of the Hudson's Bay Company gave the natives of Canada work in trapping and shooting the wildlife of the continent. But when the once almost boundless resources were depleted, in South America and on the Great Plains of North America, where was the native prosperity?

The greatness of Britain sprang in the first instance from the development of her natural resources at home, then from the development of the natural resources of the world. The richness of the United States today can be attributed to the capital increment that resulted from the development of the coal of Pennsylvania, the iron ore of Messabi, the copper of Montana and the oil and gas and electric power of so many of the states.

A nation grows rich not on the basis of index numbers of people employed, regardless of how high the wage rates. It grows rich through the growth of capital assets in the hands of its citizens. The Spaniards consumed the capital assets of the Incas and when the supply ran out the country was doomed to mediocrity. The British became rich by developing the resources of the world and using the increment to finance ever widening investments.

In the modern world the state taxes the profits its enterprisers make, it taxes their individual income and when they die it taxes their estates. But after all the tax gathering, vast sums are left which ultimately go to build great universities, hospitals and other institutions.

If Canadian capital was developing our own resources, all these institutions would be built in Canada and Canada would be enriched from succession duties. When they are developed by foreign capital, the foreign state is enriched by the taxes gathered, and all such institutions are built abroad. It is as simple as that.

Editorial

In Canada there should be an advantage in being a Canadian

The five-fold over-subscription of the Alberta Gas Trunk Line stock raises a number of fundamental side-issues for Canadians. The first and most obvious implication, is that Canadians are now more eager than they have been previously to invest their money in the equity side of oil and gas development. Secondly, the notion that Canadians could not have financed Trans-Canada themselves is preposterous on its face. The trouble with Trans Canada was two fold — it was badly sold and was subjected to a steady barrage of often unfair criticism.

The fault with Trans-Canada lay with its original sponsors and top management. They were, and are, promoters of little faith. It was they who peddled the notion that we could not build the line without an American market outlet. It was they who failed to finance it in the U.S. It was they who failed to appreciate the magnitude of the market that would develop in Canada for gas. It was they who failed to advance the ball when it was given them. Only the stubbornness of Mr. C. D. Howe, who rescued them time after time, saved them from bankruptcy. Yet had they given this project the right leadership at the right time, if they had appealed to the imagination of the Canadian people in the right way, the money could have been raised. Alberta Grid demonstrated that fact.

It seems to us that there is a lesson in Alberta Grid for the Alberta Government as well. Albertans want to participate in the building of their province and their country. Should the Government not now take steps to re-examine its reservation and leasing laws to give Canadians the sort of advantage they deserve in obtaining access to resources to develop? With over 84,000,000 acres of Crown land under reservation and lease in Alberta, the scope for Canadian money is obviously limited.

Let's put it this way: There ought to be a definite advantage to being Canadians in Canada. It has been because Canadians have been at a disadvantage in competition with foreign tax dollars that title to so much of our natural wealth has gone to outside investors. The people of Alberta were given a definite advantage in the opportunities provided by Trunk Line. They reacted in a fashion that stunned the beholders. Now that we have enticed the public out of its pre-occupation with "security" let's go on from there. Let's encourage them to take the millions rejected by Trunk Line and use it for the development of other branches of our industry. Let both Ottawa and Edmonton give Canadians every possible encouragement to get in and stay in rather than to "get in, get a profit and get out".

Editorial

The safest and best market for Canadian crude is in Canada

As any of the reverend clergy will avow, the test of character is not how we behave when everything is going good, it is how we behave during adversity. What is true of individuals is true of nations and if the Canadian oil industry ignores that fact in connection with oil markets in the United States it must inevitably suffer a rude shock. The best place in which to find markets for the crude Canada can produce is in Canada. No market available within the United States can offer even a second grade substitute for the domestic Canadian market. Presently we are moving Alberta crude freely into the newly built refineries in the State of Washington. We naturally hope that this market will grow with the years and there are some indications that it will — provided the Americans do not discover large reservoirs of crude oil in Washington, Oregon or Idaho.

Within the past month, this nation was hit two hard blows by Washington. First of all the Eisenhower administration admitted being forced by political pressure to impose tariffs on Canadian zinc. Then it renewed an embargo on Canadian rye. Both steps are taken as a result of political pressure exerted by powerful regional groups who cannot meet the competition of Canadian products. Canadians outside the oil industry long ago learned the bitter lesson that their American market can be closed to them as a result of political pressure.

The oil industry today is being penalized a dime a barrel on crude shipped southward. Despite all the friendly gestures now being made about not putting Canada on an oil import quota, nothing is being done to remove this duty. Nothing will be done so producers whose crude feeds the American market will continue to pay a 10-cent tax to the United States to get into that market.

It is, therefore, at least a dime a barrel better to seek to widen Canadian markets for western crude. A prominent American oilman, in a recent visit to Calgary, said he did not think removal of the 10-cent duty would increase Canadian crude sales to the U.S. If 10 cents is not a big enough lever to open the flow lines to the U.S., is it a big enough counter-weight to keep our oil from flowing into Montreal? Surely much of the arithmetic used to date to talk us out of the Montreal market is unrealistic. Of greater importance than economics is refinery process decision. A refinery set up to handle one crude will not shift to another except for reason more compelling than 10-cents a barrel.

Once western crude serves the Montreal market, it will continue to serve it for the same reasons the Venezulan crude is now being used — the refineries are all set up to handle it. It follows that the Montreal market is eminently worth having for that reason alone. No refiner is going to shut off his steady flow of western crude through a pipeline because a cargo or two of distress crude kicks around the eastern seaboard. The big question is how and when can we get to Montreal?

This is the problem that should concern us. The day after a nearby native source of crude is discovered, pressure will develop in the United States to back out Canadian crude. That is inevitable. When it could happen to zinc, when it could happen to so many other Canadian products, it can happen to oil. So let us not make the mistake of assuming that the Puget Sound is a natural and permanent outlet for Canadian crude. Let us only hope that it is, and get on with the job of organizing the pressures that are needed to capture the Montreal market for western crude.

Western Oil Examiner Editorials
What's wrong with hiring local engineering consultants?

For at least 30 or 40 years, a favorite topic of the viewers-with-alarm has been our inability to keep so many of our best trained and ablest scientists at home. The explanation is simple enough. There are greater opportunities and greater rewards for such gifted people in the United States. So we have all wondered, from time to time, how we could reorganize things so as to create opportunities in Canada. We have a suggestion. It is to give engineers and geologists the same rights in their chosen areas of endeavor as we give to lawyers, doctors and even chiropractors.

The idea occurred to us at a recent pipeline hearing before the Alberta Conservation Board. Before the board, to testify as to factual material being presented, paraded a clutch of imported experts. The cost of bringing these learned gentlemen all the way from New York, Houston and California was substantial.

We were struck by two questions: Are there no resident engineers capable of doing this work? If there are not, how can we encourage the establishment of consulting engineering firms?

We are informed that there is available in Calgary engineering skill equal to any of that of the foreign engineers, and there would be more and better engineers available to the industry at home if the business of bringing in outsiders from force of habit were stopped. Then let's stop it. Let's have our Conservation Boards all adopt the policy of listening to testimony only from resident experts. We do not permit outside lawyers to come in and take cases before our courts. The medical profession is given positive protection for its monopoly. So are all the other professions. Why should the engineers and geologists have to face competition from fly-by-nighters who come in, skim off large gobs of cream and flit to other fields?

One reason why the big American firms get so much work is because the New York brokers who finance pipelines with other people's money, demand reports from engineers in whom they have confidence. To butter up the brokers, Canadian companies naturally employ the big name outfits because it gets them around one hurdle. But to the extent that this practice militates against the establishment of a thoroughly competent reservoir of engineering consultants in Canada, it is against the best interests of Canada and the oil industry. That it is bad public relations is demonstrated by the way in which opponents of gas export used the appearence of American experts to try to undermine the case for export.

Of this there can be no argument—the more use that is made of foreign firms, the less work there will be for our local engineers, the less chance there is for them to grow into large and prosperous consulting practices. If these firms wish to do business in Canada they should establish permanent offices here. They should then actively recruit for employment as many Canadian engineers as possible. Some large firms have already done so, and all power to them. But in permitting imported experts to appear before our boards to discuss matters that could be well handled by local people, we are actively discouraging other American engineering firms from following that example.

The oil and gas industry has already supplied job opportunities for thousands of Canadians and has encouraged hundreds of young Canadians to proceed with their education through college degrees. In the beginning, when there was a real shortage of skilled engineers and geologists, it was both right and necessary that large numbers of them be brought in from outside. Now that we have created pools of engineering skill our next step must be to enlarge those reservoirs by creating the maximum possible opportunity for local people in the consulting branches of the industry. We do that for lawyers. We can and should do it for engineers and geologists.

The good in the Levy report

On balance, we believe that the sponsors got their money's worth from the Levy report. At the very least, it is the basis for discussion which will spread out from it in all directions like ripples in a pond. True, it shows signs of hasty preparation. True, also, the writing is often pedantic and repetitive. The great virtue of the report, however, is that it opens up many new topics for discussion in the oil industry and constructively points a way to the solution of some problems.

For the Western Oil Examiner there is much comfort in the report. It completely vindicates our position, that there were more than price factors involved in the choice of crudes. For many months we have
(Continued on Page 4

Western Oil Examiner Editorials

(CONTINUED)

There seemed to be a tendency on the part [of t]he industry spokesman to regard the hearings [as] a sort of police court at which they were on [trial] for something. After the rude way in which [Ea]stcoast witnesses were handled perhaps this [rest]raint is understandable. Nevertheless, Mr. [Bor]den himself and several of his colleagues [lean]ed over backwards to encourage witnesses [to] expatiation on original themes. But ideas [cam]e out like impacted teeth.

[T]he commission was serious, obviously, in its [sear]ch for a formula on which a national gas [rese]rves policy could be based. It does no good [to di]scard the notion that proven reserves suf-[ficie]nt for 30 years are needed if no alternative [rule] is devised. The 30 year rule itself was [ado]pted largely by default. The near and long-

term national interest of Canada must not only be protected—it must be done in a way which will be acceptable to the Canadian people. The commission wants the help of the industry in finding a formula. Indeed, in view of the tremendous task it has before it, it needs all the help it can get from anybody.

It is on this score that we are convinced that its no-cross-examination rule makes no sense. Many good ideas might well be brought out and expanded under the guidance of knowledgeable lawyers. Lack of cross-examination had a stupifying influence upon the hearings. If the commission is completely wedded to this procedure it is unfortunate. But if it is, then its own legal staff should be expanded for it was under-gunned at the Calgary hearings.

Mr. White is entitled to talk through his hat

The contribution which Imperial Oil has [mad]e toward growth and the general welfare of [the] Canadian oil industry has been substantial. [It h]as provided the leadership the industry needed [whe]n it needed it. Without its splendid record [of fi]nding markets for our crude oil, we'd have [no i]ndustry today. So on its record, Imperial Oil [is en]titled to nod occasionally, to be wrong once [in a] while, to exercise a little poetic license now [and] then. Even so we don't think that Mr. [Whi]te's criticism of the proposal to pipe western [crud]e to Montreal was worthy of himself or his [com]pany.

[Su]ch a proposal would involve penalties both [to p]roducers and consumers, he said. He sug-[geste]d that the price gap of today might widen in [the f]uture and warned of the intense east coast [com]petition.

No one denies that, within certain limits, [there] is intense competition for markets by own-[ers o]f foreign crude. We have all heard cases of [Vene]zuelan crude being offered for 50 cents a [barre]l below posted prices. But the Montreal [refin]eries do not buy distress crude at give-away [price]s. Mr. White's own refinery depends entire-[ly fo]r its Montreal supplies upon its associated [comp]any, Creole Petroleum Corporation. His [comp]any is more than willing to sacrifice a fancy [imm]ediate profit from distress crude in favor of [long] term continuity of supplies. It buys its [crud]e by the year, not by the tanker load.

Well, if Imperial is prepared to sign long [term] contracts with Creole at posted prices, and

import it in long-term chartered tankers, why not the same for western crude? We all know, of course, that Imperial now has to find markets for two barrels of its feet-dragging competitors for every barrel of its own Canadian crude it uses. This, of course, works to the disadvantage of Jersey and to the advantage of its competitors. So it is natural for the parent company to use as much of its own crude as possible in Imperial refineries.

Placed in this perspective, most Canadians would have been sympathetic with Mr. White's position. We have pointed to the unfairness of our current pro-ration to market rules in this regard many times. If certain mid-West American majors would lift even one finger to find a use for their Canadian crude, our problem would be eased. Imperial has found markets for its discoveries. They have not.

Obviously, the case Mr. White did not make was much stronger than the one he made. In raising the bogey of price competition in Montreal Mr. White was talking through his hat. There has been a revolutionary change in the whole world oil supply and demand picture since the big discoveries in Kuwait and Venezuela. These discoveries caused all the major oil companies to develop their own crude supplies and to use them in their own refineries. This development was what led to the U.S. curtailment of imports. It explains why Imperial uses Creole crude in Montreal. But it also makes the opening of Montreal to Canadian crude a comparatively simple accomplishment for any Canadian government.

Index

About the author

Since the 1950s, when he abandoned journalism in favour of a career as an author, James Gray has been writing books on Western Canadian history that have won critical acclaim, awards, and a large following of readers who know that Gray's history is entertaining as well as interesting. As one eastern critic explained to his readers in a review of this book, Gray has done for Western Canada's past what Pierre Berton has done for the East.

Born in Whitemouth, Manitoba, Gray grew up in Winnipeg in the Twenties — a story he tells in his first autobiographical book, *The Boy from Winnipeg*. He began writing in 1931, and sold his first article in 1933. As he explains in the opening pages of this book, he finally managed to break into journalism with a job at the *Winnipeg Free Press* in early 1935.

Gray writes about the early years of the Depression in his second autobiographical memoir, *The Winter Years*. In *Troublemaker!*, he takes the story through the next twenty years from 1935 to 1955 — "the most exciting, most elevating, most critical and most illuminating two decades in Prairie history," he says in this book.

Gray is an unusual journalist. He came to know the intricacies of the political and business stories he covered intimately — and he had a committed personal view on many subjects. As a result, he clashed with his bosses at the *Free Press* over grain policy, and percipitated a cutback in advertising to his oil and gas magazine by U.S. companies when he campaigned for greater Canadian independence in this key industry. As one reviewer noted, Gray literally kept writing himself out of jobs during his twenty-year career as a journalist.

Gray has published eight books, including *Booze*, *Red Lights on the Prairies* and *Bacchanalia Revisited*.

Other Canadian Lives you'll enjoy reading

Canadian Lives is a paperback reprint series which presents the best in Canadian biography chosen from the lists of Canada's many publishing houses. Here is a selection of titles in the series. Watch for more Canadian Lives every season, from Goodread Biographies. Ask for them at your local bookstore.

Something Hidden: A Biography of Wilder Penfield
Jefferson Lewis

The life story of a world-famous Canadian surgeon and scientist — written by his journalist grandson who has portrayed both the public and the private sides of Penfield's extraordinary life of achievement.

"One of the most valuable and fascinating biographies I have read in many years." — Hugh MacLennan

Canadian Lives 1   0-88780-101-3

Within the Barbed Wire Fence
Takeo Nakano

The moving story of a young Japanese man, torn from his family in 1942 and sent with hundreds of others to a labour camp in the B.C. interior.

"A poet's story of a man trapped by history and events far beyond his control." — *Canadian Press*

Canadian Lives 2   0-88780-102-1

The Patricks: Hockey's Royal Family
Eric Whitehead

A first-rate chronicle of the four-generation family of lively Irish-Canadians who have played a key role in the history of hockey for more than 70 years.

"A damn good story." — Jack Dulmage, *The Windsor Star*

Canadian Lives 3   0-88780-103-X

Hugh MacLennan: A Writer's Life
Elspeth Cameron

The prize-winning bestseller that chronicles the life of one of Canada's most successful novelists.

"This impressive biography does justice to the man and his work." — Margaret Laurence

Canadian Lives 4   0-88780-104-8

Canadian Nurse in China
Jean Ewen

The story of a remarkable young adventurer who went to war-torn China in the 1930s, met all the heroes of the Chinese Revolution, and survived the terrors and dangers she encountered with her ironic sense of humour intact.

"A remarkably candid book by a no-nonsense nurse." — Pierre Berton

Canadian Lives 5   0-88780-105-6

An Arctic Man
Ernie Lyall

Sixty-five years in Canada's North — the story of a man who chose the Inuit way of life.

"The main reason I decided to do a book about my life in the north is that I finally got fed up with all the baloney in so many books written about the north." — Ernie Lyall, in the preface.

Canadian Lives 6   0-88780-106-4

Boys, Bombs and Brussels Sprouts
J. Douglas Harvey

One man's irreverent, racy, sometimes heart-breaking, account of flying for Canada with Bomber Command in the Second World War.

"Tells more about what it was like 'over there' than all of the military histories ever written." — *Canadian Press*

Canadian Lives 7   0-88780-107-2

Nathan Cohen: The Making of a Critic
Wayne Edmonstone

A giant of a man, a legend, Cohen had a vision of what Canadians could achieve in the arts and entertainment — and he convinced both audiences and artists that Canadian work should and could equal the world's best.

"A man of vision, prophecy and insight." — *Ottawa Revue*

Canadian Lives 8   0-88780-108-0

The Wheel of Things:
A Biography of L.M. Montgomery
Mollie Gillen

The remarkable double life of the woman who created Canada's best-loved heroine, Anne of Green Gables.

"A perceptive and sympathetic portrait of a complex personality." — Ottawa *Journal*

Canadian Lives 9   0-88780-109-9

Walter Gordon: A Political Memoir
Walter Gordon

The gentle, passionate patriot who became an Ottawa insider and fought for his principles in a cabinet of politicians all too ready to abandon theirs.

"Valuable insight into our political history and a revealing portrait of the man himself."

— CBC newsman Norman Depoe

Canadian Lives 10   0-88780-110-2

Troublemaker!
James Gray

The memoirs of a witty, warm-hearted, irreverent newspaperman who witnessed the golden age of Western Canada, 1935-1955.

"A book of great immediacy and appeal — wise and extraordinarily revealing about ourselves." — Jamie Portman, Southam News Services

Canadian Lives 11   0-88780-111-0

When I Was Young
Raymond Massey

One of Canada's most distinguished actors tells the story of his aristocratic youth as the offspring of the most Establishment family of Toronto. The first of his two-volume memoirs.

"An urbane, humour-inflected and sensitive recollection."
— *Victoria Times-Colonist*

Canadian Lives 12   0-88780-112-9

Having trouble finding a copy of a book in this series?

If you're having difficulty finding a copy of a book in Goodread Biographies' Canadian Lives series, send us a stamped, self-addressed envelope and we'll put you in touch with a bookstore that stocks all titles in the series.

Write to:

Goodread Biographies
333 - 1657 Barrington Street
Halifax, Nova Scotia
B3J 2A1

Be sure to enclose a stamped, self-addressed envelope with your letter.

Printed in Canada

g